AF693653

The Legal Basis of Corporate Governance in Publicly Held Corporations

A Comparative Approach

STUDIES IN COMPARATIVE CORPORATE AND FINANCIAL LAW

Volume 1

Series Editor

Barry Rider
Institute of Advanced Legal Studies
University of London
Charles Core House
17 Russell Square
London WC1B 5DR

The Legal Basis of Corporate Governance in Publicly Held Corporations

A Comparative Approach

Edited by
Arthur R. Pinto and Gustavo Visentini

INSTITUTE OF ADVANCED LEGAL STUDIES

KLUWER LAW INTERNATIONAL
THE HAGUE – LONDON – BOSTON

Published by
Kluwer Law International Ltd
Sterling House
66 Wilton Road
London SW1V 1DE
United Kingdom

Sold and distributed
in the USA and Canada by
Kluwer Law International
675 Massachusetts Avenue
Cambridge MA 02139
USA

Kluwer Law International incorporates the
publishing programmes of
Graham & Trotman Ltd,
Kluwer Law & Taxation Publishers
and Martinus Nijhoff Publishers

In all other countries sold and distributed by
Kluwer Law International
P.O. Box 322
3300 AH Dordrecht
The Netherlands

ISBN 90-411-9663-3
Series ISBN 90-411-9670-6
© Kluwer Law International 1998
First published 1998

British Library Cataloguing in Publication Data
A catalogue record for this book is available from the British Library

This publication is protected by international copyright law. All rights reserved. No part of this publication may be reproduced, stored in a retrieval system or transmitted in any form or by any means, electronic, mechanical, photocopying, recording or otherwise, without the prior permission of the publishers.

Typeset in Times 10/11pt by On Screen, West Hanney, Oxfordshire
Printed and bound in Great Britain by Anthony Rowe Ltd, Reading, Berkshire

Contents

Editors' Preface

I. THE PROJECT

This book is the result of a project, sponsored by Ceradi-Luiss Guido Carli and by the Brooklyn Law School Center for the Study of International Business Law. The project was partially funded by the Consiglio Nazionale delle Ricerche, the Italian National Council for Research.*

The idea behind this project was to collect papers on corporate governance by academics in the field of corporate law from different countries.

The theme of the papers was a discussion of the legal basis of corporate governance rules of publicly held corporations in those countries. Initially a group of professors were invited to Rome, in March 1993, to discuss the overall framework of the project. From that meeting an outline was developed to guide the participants in the preparation of their papers. Draft papers were then submitted to the co-sponsors and the other participants. The participants then met in Rome in November 1995 to further refine the project.

The papers and the meetings were intended to explain the system in each country and discuss their similarities and differences. The project was not seeking to harmonize or unify the different approaches but to allow individual reflection of each system resulting from the meetings and exposure to the other systems.

In observing the universal "publicly held corporations" in the various countries, one finds similarities and differences in ownership structures, allocation of power within the corporation and in the role of the financial markets. The papers were intended to point out those similarities and differences and how they are influenced by legal systems or other factors.

We asked each author to discuss the different legal monitoring mechanisms in their country. These mechanisms include shareholders' rights, the role of the annual meeting, structure of the board of directors, rights of disclosure, role of auditors, voting systems, role of fiduciary duty and various enforcement mechanisms.

We decided to publish the papers for wider circulation in the hope that they will be useful and stimulate further discussion and reflection.

* The authors wish to acknowledge the help of Craig Abruzzo, class of 1997, Brooklyn Law School, for his assistance in editing.

II. THE SCOPE OF THE PROJECT

The scope of this project was to examine several different legal corporate systems with a primary focus on the corporate governance rules that apply to publicly held corporations.

For this purpose, the term "publicly held corporation" means any corporation which has shares held by the public at large and publicly traded in a market. This term could also apply to corporations which may have one or more controlling shareholder, so long as there is some public ownership.

The traditional paradigm of corporate law is that directors manage the corporation and the shareholders own it. Whenever public ownership occurs, there may be a failure by the directors in protecting the public shareholders. Different systems have a variety of rules to deal with this issue. The legal analysis of the phenomenon, then, has to take into account all such factors and influences. This approach is not at all new to legal scholars, since it may be traced back to the well-known work of Berle and Means.[1] In recent times, however, it has assumed greater impulse under the name of "corporate governance". The term "corporate governance", when applied in this context, can be used to bring together different kinds of rules which determine how power is exercised within the corporation. Corporate governance deals with the issue of accountability and focuses on the relationships among the participants. The rules become relevant to corporate governance when they have a significant impact on those who participate in the institution. These rules have a variety of sources, such as corporate law, banking law, securities law, labour law, bankruptcy law, etc.

In reviewing the papers, we found two significant characteristics that differentiate the way particular countries developed their corporate governance rules. These differences are the financial system of the country and how corporate interest is determined (i.e. the determination of which groups participate in corporate governance).

III. THE FINANCIAL SYSTEM[2]

An important issue that should be taken into account when analyzing the corporate governance rules is the effect of the country's overall financial system on the financing of the corporation.

The corporation can be viewed in financial terms as a mechanism for collecting capital from investors in the expectation of a return. The way a particular country organizes its financial activity determines where and how this capital is allocated and it ultimately determines the corporation's financial structure. The resulting financial structure establishes who are the significant participants in the corporation. Since corporate governance focuses on how the power is exercised in a corporation, the rules develop from the reality of the financial structure.

[1] A. Berle and G. Means, *The Modern Corporation and Private Property* (1932).

[2] In this context, the term "circuit", rather than "system", would be technically more correct: "system" looks at the overall aggregate mechanisms, whereas "circuit" better gives the idea of the routing of the financial resources from the ultimate surplus savers (households) to the ultimate deficit savers (firms), whether such routing takes place through intermediaries or through direct contract.

In looking at several systems, we see two principal models:[3] a market-oriented model represented by the US, and a bank-oriented model represented by Germany and continental Europe.

In the market-oriented model, the corporations collect capital directly from the public, and the public investors directly bear the business risk of their investment. Securities are spread out among the public at large, and the financial markets are very competitive. In the market-oriented model there is often no significant shareholder involved in the corporation. In the bank-oriented model corporations collect capital primarily through banks who serve as intermediaries with the public. The banks play an important role in the corporations as primary suppliers of capital. They act as both creditors and in some cases significant owners of stock. This bank-oriented model is often characterized by the presence of major shareholders.

The description above of the two models, however, needs further elaboration in order to understand the development of corporate governance rules. If one looks more closely at the different systems, it can be observed that in the market-oriented model corporations have a wider choice of financing alternatives and greater competition among suppliers of capital. In terms of debt, a corporation can choose to sell in to the public directly or privately to banks or a variety of other financial institutions such as insurance companies or pension funds. In terms of equity, corporations can choose to raise capital in the public markets or privately through sales to institutions or large investors. This competition creates a less centralized system of financing, with a greater number of sources of funds, and a more diffuse control of the corporation.

In the bank-oriented model, there is competition among banks to provide capital but often a single bank group will dominate the financing of the corporation. While there may be an active securities market to provide funds from the public, it can be found that the banks also dominate these markets. Banks tend to become "universal" in the services they offer (either as a single company or as a group of companies). Thus, for example, in Italy (and even in France and more so in Germany), the Council of the Stock Exchange has a strong bank representation. In addition, most mutual funds and broker/dealer firms (and surely the most important) are bank affiliates. The bank domination is further evidenced by the fact that the development of the securities markets in most of these countries (e.g. France, Japan and Germany) involves stock rather than debt. This allows banks to maintain their dominance as the fundamental providers of credit.

With the market-oriented model resulting in a diffusion of power among the numerous suppliers of capital, the corporate governance rules reflect this reality. For instance, in the United States, a major focus of its rules has been to protect the individual investors as shareholders or creditors. This protection has been enforced in a variety of mechanisms many of which are based upon concepts of consumer protection. Thus, rules have encouraged the development of securities exchanges that ensure prompt liquidity to investments, and have provided disclosure and enforcement mechanisms that create direct accountability.

[3] A model is a schematic representation of reality. Although any model representation may not be completely accurate and precise, since it does not take into account all possible peculiarities of the system, it helps analyze and compare different systems without having to deal with details. Such details, in fact, although important are eliminated in the model description since they do not really change the overall framework of description.

With the bank-oriented model which results in a greater concentration of power, the corporate governance rules take into account the predominant presence of large investors and stakeholders. In this context, corporate governance rules implement legal devices that assume the existence of an active shareholder, without the need to protect individual shareholders. For instance, there is the use of shareholders' agreements, wider use of shareholders' meetings to make significant decisions (e.g. in Italy the shareholders approve the balance sheet, decide upon the distribution of dividends and upon the raising of new capital).[4] But even within the bank-oriented model, which is characterized by strong concentration of ownership, there can also be the development of a securities market which serves a useful function. The securities market in fact helps to increase the corporations' own funds, but without causing any significant change in the banks' role in the internal power structure. The securities markets are usually focused on the trading of stock, rather than debt. As a result of this strong concentration of ownership, the rules that govern markets tend to be less consumer oriented than the market-oriented model, with less disclosure and less effective enforcement mechanisms for public investors towards the corporation.

There are numerous reasons why a particular country developed its system. In looking at the US and Europe, the role of the State historically in the economy is different. An additional reason is the effect on the European economy from World War II, which devastated European and Japanese industry and personal savings. This crisis required a strong intervention by the State which needed to supply and direct investment in industry. Often this was accomplished through State ownership of banks (e.g. France) and by encouraging private investments through the banks by both insuring these savings and by not allowing bank failures. Through banks the State could influence, directly and indirectly, industrial development. Banks were viewed as a stable form of investment. In addition, the State would protect its local financial markets from competition, which further solidified the banks' power.

In the US the economy after World War II was the strongest in the world and thus State intervention was not required. But even when there was a crisis such as the Great Depression of 1929, the role of the State was to strengthen the public markets (federal securities laws) and further limit the role of banks in financing of corporations (the Glass-Steagall Act of 1933). This decision reflects both an economic and political decision to decentralize power.[5]

IV. CORPORATE INTEREST

The issue of corporate interest concerns the determination of which groups participate in corporate governance. There appears to be two different approaches to this issue.

A shareholder model views the primary responsibility of corporate directors to its shareholders. While other interests are relevant to decision making, the primary focus remains the shareholders.

A constituency model expands the responsibility of the directors to not just the shareholders, but to other interests as well, and more particularly labour. This model

[4] In these instances where the shareholders' meetings have such powers, the single shareholder has the right to go to court and claim that the decision taken at the meeting is invalid.

[5] M. Roe, *Strong managers, weak owners* (Princeton, 1994).

views the corporation as a firm comprising several components which include capital, labour, creditors, consumers and the community.

In determining whether a particular system fits into a model, the relevant issue is the power expressed in the corporate governance rules. For example, in Germany labour is given power through its membership on the Supervisory Board which appoints corporate managers. In the Netherlands labour, through the Works Council, may oppose the appointment of managers, and has a right to give advice in management matters. In Japan, the interest of labour appears to be protected by the custom which keeps the membership of the Board consisting of former employees. In contrast, the US has some fairly recent statutory enactments in some states which appear to expand the fiduciary duty to interests other than the shareholders. However, these provisions are of little consequence because there appears to be no enforcement mechanism and in any case they do not seem to have increased the role of these constituencies in corporate governance.

It appears from the country chapters that the shareholders in those countries which adopt a constituency model have not been adversely affected. However, one finds a constituency model where a bank-oriented system is prevalent, as opposed to a market-oriented one. The fear that, if one considers labour (or other constituencies) within corporate interest, the managers will not pursue the shareholders' interest is less likely when there are dominant shareholders. It is worth noting that, in those countries adopting the constituency model, the concern for labour's interest is not just a peculiarity of the corporate legal system, but it reflects the general attitude towards the creation of an economic framework that attempts to institutionalize cooperation between labour and capital (co-determination).

In those countries that adopt the shareholder model, it appears that labour and other constituencies rely on other mechanisms outside of corporate governance rules to protect their interests. For example, labour uses collective bargaining and labour laws to further their interests, while creditors use contract and bankruptcy law.

V. THE ALLOCATION OF MANAGERIAL AND EXECUTIVE POWER

In terms of the board of directors, there are different approaches to its structure. In some countries (e.g. Germany, the Netherlands), we see a two-tier board where one serves in a supervisory function and the other a managerial function. While this two-tier structure may facilitate co-determination it also serves a different purpose through the separation of these two functions (in the Netherlands employees do not serve on the supervisory board although they have a veto power on appointments). In the one-tier system, one often finds both internal executive directors and external non-executive directors, each of which can take on similar functions (i.e the inside directors manage and the outside directors supervise). But with the two-tier system there are significant formalities and rules that govern the relationship between the two boards, while the one-tier system is more informal. It is unclear whether this formality ultimately makes a difference in the functioning of the board.

Despite such different structures, a significant common feature is that the allocation of managerial and executive power is quite homogenous and very concentrated. Generally, there is a defined set of individuals who ultimately run the corporation. For this reason, management tends to be a professional elite who are specialists and who are often responsible for their own replacement. For instance, in the United

States the officers are appointed by the directors, although in fact the officers choose the directors that the shareholders' meetings approve of, since they manage the voting system mainly through the use of proxies. In the Netherlands, instead, the appointment mechanism of members of the supervisory board in the *structuur* regime works through co-optation, i.e. it is the directors themselves that have the legal power to appoint their successors.

VI. THE FUTURE

All the chapters point out that in every country there is discussion and debate urging for changes of the corporate governance rules. Such proposed changes are primarily aimed at adapting corporate reality to the changing environment, without affecting, however, the fundamental institution of the corporation as a legal instrument for the promotion of economic development.

Most of the discussion centres upon issues of greater accountability of corporate directors to their constituencies (e.g. the Cadbury and Greenbury Reports in the UK, the Viénot Report in France and the American Law Institute Principles of Corporate Governance in the US). However these debates are a natural development resulting from the rapid evolution and progress of the markets and technologies. In some cases such reforms constitute the legislative response to specific crises and problems resulting from inadequacies in the rules.

In Europe it can be observed that there is a movement towards greater development of the open markets, especially for stocks. At this point in time these developments do not appear to be changing the banking orientation of the systems. However, the development of securities markets is encouraging greater efficiency in the financial world.[6] Corporations will profit from a greater variety of sources of funds which will allow them to better adjust their financial structure to their needs.

The crisis of the public pension systems and the diminishing presence of the State in the economy (for EC reasons and for budget reasons) has led to channelling savings through institutional investors (pension funds, mutual funds, investment companies, etc.). This phenomenon, the so-called "institutionalization of savings", is already quite developed in the US and in the UK where, so far, it does not appear to have caused substantial change in the corporate governance rules. The main question is, however, whether any changes in corporate governance rules will occur in the future as a consequence of the institutionalization of the markets.

A change to be observed in the US is a slow erosion of the barriers set up by the Glass-Steagall Act between banks and industry. Commercial banks are in fact starting to be able to operate with securities, although still in very specific fields, but this development may not be as significant because of the competitive environment in the US for access to capital.

One phenomenon that is concerning all countries is the growing globalization of the markets, both for goods and for capital. In general, however, this has not led to any major change in corporate governance rules. Countries have reacted to the urge towards greater competition and uniformity coming from the globalization process

[6] The EC-driven liberalization of the capital markets, while allowing capital resources to freely flow towards the most profitable assets, is forcing greater competition among financial intermediaries and it is thus forcing banks to develop their activities in new operative segments, further differentiating their services to corporations.

with an effort to maintain their national identity as to their traditional corporate governance system. Indeed, any changes that have taken place seem to respond to a logic of protection of local markets, rather than to a logic of greater aperture (e.g. the takeover statutes and regulations in most European countries; the holding of a "golden share" by the State when privatizing State-owned companies).

A different phenomenon is the European integration process. This process, however, is political rather than just economic (as instead globalization is): as it goes on, especially once the single European currency is realized, it will constitute a very powerful push towards greater competition and, thus, greater uniformity in the corporate governance rules, even without any European company statute.

Arthur R. Pinto
Professor of Law and
Co-Director of Brooklyn Law School Center
for the Study of International Business Law
Brooklyn, NY, USA

Gustavo Visentini
Professor of Law and
Director CERADI-LUISS
Guido Carli University
Rome, Italy

1

France

*James A. Fanto**

I. INTRODUCTION

This chapter evaluates how well French corporate law facilitates a corporate governance favourable to capital market investors.[1] French corporate governance is a timely subject. From the perspective of one who tries, from the other side of the Atlantic, to follow developments in French business and finance,[2] corporate governance has the attention of the French legal, business and financial communities.[3] French legal thinkers are increasingly examining corporate governance in their country and in other countries to understand solutions to corporate governance problems and to reflect on the French corporate governance situation.[4] Several assumptions are made in this chapter. First, economists, finance theorists and management scholars of large public corporations all recognize a central characteristic of corporations that arises from the legal and practical nature of the corporate

* Associate Professor, Brooklyn Law School. I thank Dean Joan Wexler of Brooklyn Law School for a summer stipend that enabled me to do research for this chapter. I also thank Alice Pezard of the Groupe Caisse des Dépôts, Professor Arthur Pinto and Professor Norman Poser for their suggestions, and Jeffrey L. Kochian of Cornell Law School for his research assistance. The chapter develops positions presented in my book, James A. Fanto, *Corporate Governance in American and French Law* (1997) and was previously printed as "The Role of Corporate Law in French Corporate Governance", 31 *Cornell International Law Journal* 1 (1998).

1 French corporate law and securities law are not separate areas, but are part of the same legal code. All references to French corporate law herein are from Dalloz, *Code des Sociétés* (Paul Le Cannu éd., 1996).

2 See James A. Fanto, "The Transformation of French Corporate Governance and United States Institutional Investors", 21 Brook. J. Int'l L., p. 1 (1995).

3 One thinks of recent reform proposals for French corporate governance. See *Commission des Opérations de Bourse, 27ème Rapport au Président de la République*, pp. 85-89 (1994); *the Conseil National Du Patronat Français, Association Française des Entreprises Privées, The Board of Directors of Listed Companies in France* (10 July 1995) (hereinafter, the "Viénot Report," named after Marc Viénot, the chief executive of Société Général, who presided over the committee that prepared the report); Philippe Marini, *Rapport au Premier Ministre sur la Modernisation du Droit des Sociétés* (13 July 1996) (reform proposal on French corporate law) (hereinafter, the "Marini Report"). See infra Section VIII.

4 Good examples appear in a special issue (no. 31, hiver 1994) of the *Revue d"Économie Financière*. See, e.g. Olivier Pastré, "Le gouvernement d'entreprise: questions de méthodes et enjeux théoriques", 31 R. Écon. Fin., p. 15 (1994); Jean-Marie Thiveaud, "De la gouvernance des grandes sociétés: un incessant différand dans l'espace et le temps", 31 R. Écon. Fin., p. 243 (1994).

© Cornell University 1998

"personality": the separation between management that operates an enterprise and shareholders who own it. Corporate governance addresses this separation by designing, or altering, a firm's governing structure to ensure that managers, who are after all shareholders' "agents," operate the firm for shareholders/owners, not for other purposes.[5]

From the agency perspective, since corporate law creates the corporate personality and establishes legal relationships between shareholders and managers, the efficacity of this law can be judged by how well it facilitates the alignment of managers' interests with those of shareholder/owners and addresses any abuses in the relationship. Yet law is only one part of corporate governance. Because a corporation exists in so many domains, such as in product, service and capital markets, other forces pressure managers to respond to shareholders. Corporate governance from an agency perspective thus implicates many social activities and gains from study by numerous disciplines.[6] This chapter focuses only on the law's contribution to the alignment of shareholder and manager interests.

The second assumption is that there has been so far no one economically superior answer to the agency problem. At any time, in different developed and developing countries, and even in the same country, there have been, and are, numerous solutions, or attempted solutions, to the problem of ensuring that managers operate firms for the shareholders' benefit. That corporations in different countries have functioned successfully and profitably in national and world markets suggests that, at the very least, several approaches to aligning management and shareholder interests work or have worked.[7] According to a metaphor used in legal and economic reflections on corporate governance, companies, like biological organisms, have "adapted" different corporate governance practices to their circumstances.[8]

If different corporate governance practices exist, and have existed, in corporations and countries throughout the world and if firms function successfully in their markets despite these differences, corporate governance must be a cultural product. An understanding of corporate governance in any country thus demands an identification of the forces that shape, at a given time, relationships between shareholders and managers.[9] These forces include legal doctrines influencing shareholder/manager relationships, pressures from social groups that have a stake in a particular governance solution or structure and a country's traditions of firm ownership.

This chapter's presentation of the role of law in French corporate governance acknowledges the cultural background of this phenomenon. Yet economic destiny

[5] For a classic statement of this position, see Oliver E. Williamson, *The Economic Institutions of Capitalism*, pp. 298-325 (1985).

[6] See, e.g. Michael C. Jensen, "The Modern Industrial Revolution, Exit, and the Failure of Internal Control Systems", 68 J. Fin., p. 830 (1993) (discussion from finance perspective); John Pound, "The Rise of the Political Model of Corporate Governance and Corporate Control", 68 N.Y.U. L. Rev., p. 1003 (1993) (discussion from public policy perspective).

[7] See, e.g. Andrei Shleifer & Robert W. Vishny, *A Survey of Corporate Governance*, 52 J.Fin., pp. 737, 769–773 (1997) (discussing success of different corporate governance systems).

[8] See generally Ronald J. Gilson, "Corporate Governance and Economic Efficiency: When do Institutions Matter?", 74 Wash. U. L. Q., p. 327 (1996); Mark J. Roe, "Chaos and Evolution in Law and Economics", 109 Harv. L. Rev., p. 641 (1996).

[9] See James A. Fanto, "The Absence of Cross-Cultural Communication: SEC Mandatory Disclosure and Foreign Corporate Governance", 17 NW. J. Int"l L. & Bus., pp. 119, 134-37 (1996).

and corporate governance are no longer entirely under the control of any nation state. Corporate law scholars debate whether cultural factors in corporate governance, at least in the developed world, are being undermined and corporate governance is "converging" chiefly because of a transformation in the world business environment. To use Michael Jensen's characterization,[10] the industrial world is in the middle of a massive restructuring that began around the middle of the 1970s. Developments in technology (particularly in communications technology) permit lower-cost completion of certain economic tasks and links between previously separate work, all of which produces overcapacity that makes some enterprises, and indeed industries, obsolete. The technology also leads to different enterprise organization, which replaces elaborate hierarchies of decision-making with more flexible, flatter work environments that facilitate rapid responses to given tasks.[11] This different economic environment implies rapid product changes and response to customer needs. Because of other events (i.e. breakdown of the Socialist block, lessening of trade barriers), product market competition, already exacerbated by technological and organizational changes, is heightened as companies *globally* compete against one another. Businesses that use technology and human resources efficiently stand a better chance of prevailing in their product markets.

Technological changes also enable different investment behaviour and capital-raising. Investors, whether individually or through financial intermediaries, have increased access to investments throughout the world, and companies can raise capital in different markets and from other than domestic investors. The companies best able to take advantage of new capital-raising opportunities and financial technology to address various kinds of company risks gain an advantage over their competitors by having a lower cost of capital and a more efficient use of this capital.[12] For maximum financing flexibility, a company must find ways of bringing in capital market investors.[13] This competition for capital often subjects companies to new, or at least increased, pressures as they cannot remain complacent with their investors (who are often foreign) nor feel that they have a captive, passive group of investors with few investment alternatives.

No one has yet identified the corporate governance that will best aid companies (and thus countries) to survive in these circumstances.[14] As a third and final assumption, this chapter assumes that the above forces are pushing corporate governance throughout the developed world towards a capital market shareholder-based system similar to what has existed for a long time in the U.S. It argues that, for at least the past two decades, French legal policy-makers have attempted to create a legal environment conducive to, and enabling of, market capitalism and the corporate

[10] See Jensen, supra note 6, pp. 835-847.

[11] See "A fortress against change, A Survey of Business in Europe", *Economist*, 23 November 1996, pp. 3-5.

[12] See, e.g. J. Mark Ramseyer, "Columbian Cartel Launches Bid for Japanese Firms", 102 Yale L. J., pp. 2005, 2006 (1993).

[13] Cf., Shleifer & Vishny, supra note 7, at p. 769. Of course, not every company must use domestic or global capital markets; one might well expect, however, competitive world-class companies to do so. Cf., Marco Pagano, et al., *Why Do Companies Go Public? An Empirical Analysis,* p. 39 (Centre for Economic Policy Research Discussion Paper No. 1332, 1996).

[14] See Rafael La Porta, Florencio Lopez-de-Silanes, Andrei Shleifer & Robert W. Vishny, *Law and Finance*, pp. 40-42 (National Bureau of Economic Research Working Paper No. 5661, 1996) (considering what legal system best promotes shareholder capitalism).

governance that accompanies it. Since an appropriate legal environment would enhance shareholder rights and address the kind or kinds of agency problems that surface in the new context, and since Anglo-American laws developed for this "Berle-Means" situation[15] best produces this legal environment (because Anglo-American corporate finance has generally involved raising money from capital market investors), French legal policy-makers have borrowed legal techniques characteristic of this "strong manager, weak owners" context. It thus makes sense to review how successfully they have done their work.[16]

After setting forth in Section II an account of the cultural and historical background of French corporate governance and an overview of the structure of ownership of large French firms, the chapter discusses how well French policy-makers created legal solutions to the kind of agency problems that arise in a shareholder-based corporate governance. Section III describes the basic legally-mandated methods whereby dispersed shareholders address their lack of control over an enterprise: the right to information about the firm and its governance and the related right to vote, generally through a proxy. Section IV considers the elected representatives of shareholders in the corporation, the directors, and the manner in which French law aligns their interests with those of shareholders.

Section V examines the obligations of directors and others in the special, but important, case of treatment of minority shareholders, generally in a change of control or restructuring. This leads to Section VI, which studies the role of law in a central phenomenon of market capitalism: the takeover, whether friendly or hostile. Section VII explores shareholder suits. Finally, Section VIII concludes with a look at proposals for legal and other reform to French corporate governance.

II. THE CULTURAL BACKGROUND TO FRENCH CORPORATE GOVERNANCE

Corporate governance practices are cultural and historical products. Culture means here the conceptual framework whereby individuals, generally of the same country, understand, and mediate the pressures of, the world and motivate and explain their actions. That corporate governance practices are cultural is clear from the fact that the corporation is a meaningful and purposeful human response to economic and social pressures. The relationship between owners of capital and the managers who use it – the heart of corporate governance – is part of the response. The law, for example, gives shareholders certain rights and responsibilities as to the corporation, their fellow owners and sometimes non-shareholder citizens, and members of the culture understand in these terms what it means to be a shareholder. This under-

[15] See Adolf A. Berle & Gardiner C. Means, *The Modern Corporation and Private Property* (Transaction Publishers, Murray L. Weidenbaum & Mark Jensen, int., reprinted 1991) (classic statement on U.S. corporate governance or market capitalism, with its dispersed shareholders and strong managers).

[16] I make a theoretical argument about the efforts of French legal policy-makers to design a corporate law that promotes market capitalism and that thus helps French enterprises adapt to current economic circumstances in James A. Fanto, *The Role of Corporate Law in the Adaptation of French Enterprises* 1998 Colum. Bus. L. Rev., p. 97. This work evaluates in detail what these policy-makers have done.

standing motivates the actions of shareholders, as well as of shareholders' agents. To say that something is cultural thus implies an understanding of its social and ideological origins.

These observations are not new to anthropologists and historians of culture.[17] Under the influence of a biological evolutionary model,[18] some economists and legal scholars also suggest that the existence and endurance of such phenomena as the corporation require an historical explanation.[19] An economic discussion should take precedence in any analysis of corporations and corporate governance practices because of the centrality of these human creations and activities in a country's economic life. That discussion, however, can be complemented by cultural and historical explanations of corporate governance practices that account for the endurance of certain features (whether economically "rational" or not) in these practices.

A standard account of Western corporate governance describes the emergence of the corporation as a dominant form of business organization in the nineteenth century.[20] According to this account, technological developments in that century made possible the accomplishment of large, complex economic tasks, such as the construction and operation of national railroads. Firms needed to grow significantly to attain the size necessary to use these technologies and to accomplish the tasks efficiently in national, as opposed to local, markets. Since the technologies and related business practices worked successfully in many areas of economic life, small businesses increasingly ceded the field to the large.

These developments brought specialization to the large corporation. The increased size of enterprises demanded more capital than local financing and even retained earnings could generally provide. Firms often had to turn to outside investors, who were dispersed nationally and internationally, and who would not necessarily commit all their funds to any one investment.[21] Since any investor generally provided little of the total capital of an enterprise, he or she did not have the same involvement in the business and incentive to monitor its employees as had an owner of a smaller business. The new technologies, moreover, demanded a specialized management training and expertise to ensure the efficient operation of a complex enterprise. A new professional management class appeared, with all of the features that characterized professional expertise, for example, professional schools and organizations.[22] The new large firm thus separated ownership from control, a situation differing from the traditional overlap between the two functions in smaller firms.

[17] See, e.g. Clifford Geertz, *After the Fact: Two Countries, Four Decades, One Anthropologist,* p. 43 (1995).

[18] See, e.g. Stephen Jay Gould, *The Panda's Thumb: More Reflections in Natural History* (1980).

[19] See, e.g. Douglass C. North, "Economic Performance Through Time", 84 Am. Econ. Rev., p. 359 (1994); Gilson, supra note 8, pp. 331-334; Roe, supra note 8, pp. 643-646.

[20] See, e.g. Alfred D. Chandler, *The Visible Hand: The Managerial Revolution in American Business* (1977).

[21] The story is a complex one. Dispersed investors could invest in large enterprises only if a capital market infrastructure and/or financial intermediaries existed to move their funds efficiently to the firms. This infrastructure also permitted investors, to use Professor Gilson's words, to "specialize in risk bearing", i.e. to diversify their investments over numerous large enterprises to reduce the firm-specific risks of their portfolio. See Gilson, supra note 8, p. 331.

[22] For work on the professionalization of engineers and business managers, see Burton J. Bledstein, *The Culture of Professionalism: The Middle Class and the Development of Higher Education in America* (1978); Magali Sarfatti Larson, *The Rise of Professionalism: A Sociologic Analysis* (1977).

In the U.S., the separation was acute and had certain consequences. As Adolf A. Berle and Gardiner C. Means observed some 60 years ago, because of the separation, it was no longer clear that, as had generally been the case previously in U.S. businesses, the large corporation was governed for its owners.[23] In many cases management could operate large corporations for significant periods of time for its own benefit and without particular concern about dispersed shareholders, who could rarely mobilize to challenge and change management.[24] The story of the rise of the corporation and the separation of ownership and control in large firms is also true of businesses in Western European countries, including France, even if the smaller size of these countries' markets initially limited the impact of the scientific and management technologies on creating large enterprises there.[25] While specialization in investment and management functions occurred outside the U.S., it did not necessarily lead to the opposition between powerful managers and powerless shareholders characteristic of the U.S.

In his authoritative account of U.S. corporate governance, Professor Mark Roe explains that U.S. cultural forces helped maintain the separation between corporate ownership and control.[26] In his view, as the examples of corporate governance in other countries demonstrate, financial institutions could address this separation. A financial institution could make a large equity investment in a corporation, given its resources as a financial intermediary for smaller investors. Its significant stake in an enterprise would give it the incentive to monitor management closely, and it could thus act as a counterweight to management's power.[27] By shaping U.S. law, however, the U.S. cultural forces of populism and federalism kept U.S. financial institutions from assuming a corporate governance role.[28]

23 See Berle & Means, supra note 15, pp. 78-82.

24 In their view, a serious corporate governance problem, the disenfranchisement of the owner, developed:

> "In examining the break up of the old concept that was property and the old unity that was private enterprise, it is therefore evident that we are dealing not only with distinct but often with opposing groups, ownership on the one side, control on the other – a control which tends to move further and further away from ownership and ultimately to lie in the hands of the management itself, a management capable of perpetuating its own position. The concentration of economic power separate from ownership has, in fact, created economic empires, and has delivered these empires into the hands of a new form of absolutism, relegating 'owners' to the position of those who supply the means whereby the new princes may exercise their power."

See ibid., p. 116.

25 See Chandler, supra note 20, at p. 499 ("Smaller and slower growing domestic markets in Western Europe and Japan lessened the interest of manufacturers in adopting new mass production techniques and also reduced the incentive to build large marketing and purchasing organizations.").

26 Mark J. Roe, *Strong Managers, Weak Owners: The Political Roots of American Corporate Finance*, pp. 26-49 (1994).

27 Not all scholars share the view that financial institutions are beneficial monitors of firms for other shareholders. See, e.g. Jonathan R. Macey & Geoffrey P. Miller, "Corporate Governance and Commercial Banking: A Comparative Examination of Germany, Japan, and the United States", 48 Stan. L. Rev., pp. 73, 90-99 (1996).

28 See Roe, supra note 26, pp. 53-145. To take only one example, from an early date U.S. commercial banks (i.e. those that make loans and take deposits) were not allowed to own shares in industrial companies, were prohibited from expanding nationally, could not join together in expansive holding company systems and were separated from investment banks.

France

A similar cultural-economic story explains French corporate governance.[29] A brief outline, based upon accounts by economists, historians and legal scholars of French business and business law,[30] might go as follows. Separation of ownership from control arising from the growth of the modern large firm and the specialization of management appeared in the French economy. Yet, for a number of reasons, this enterprise structure did not produce a firm "type" similar to those of other developed economies (i.e. large vertically integrated firm with mass produced, consumer-oriented or technologically sophisticated goods, with numerous diversified product lines, and a coordination among operating divisions) until following World War II, and, even then, that kind of U.S.-style firm did not dominate the French economy.[31] Firms operated originally in a small, primarily rural market and only gradually gained a size that could efficiently use management expertise. The weakness of French capital markets and the small size of banks also hindered the growth of large firms that in other countries occurred through mergers and funding of large projects to develop new technology.[32] French business growth came not within hierarchically-organized firms but through projects funded and owned by different groups of industrial firms with financing capabilities.[33] Family ownership in France also did not give way to manager-dominated firms, and the development of projects and expansion of firms often resulted from family relationships.[34] In fact, technologically competent managers (who in other countries took control of companies) often worked in France under the supervision of family owners. As they were generally trained in the State system, they often relied upon State contracts and aid and thus did not develop marketing skills that would lead them to create large consumer-oriented firms.[35]

When the large firm emerged, one distinguishing feature of French corporate governance's solution to its management agency problems has been the role of the French State. Since the seventeenth century, the State has been involved in, and has directly or indirectly owned, large economic undertakings. Although there have been periods of classically liberal markets with private ownership of major enterprises in France,[36] the State's influence has usually been felt in these firms. The *économie mixte* of the post-war years, which the 1981 nationalizations furthered,

[29] Professor Roe discusses non-U.S. corporate governance systems, as have other U.S. legal scholars. See, e.g. Roe, supra note 26, pp. 169-186; Macey & Miller, supra note 27. Like most U.S. scholars, however, they focus on German and Japanese corporate governance. See Fanto, supra note 9, p. 120, n. 4 (listing citations); Edward B. Rock, "America's Shifting Fascination with Comparative Corporate Governance", 74 Wash. U.L. Q. 367, p. 367, n. 1 (1996) (same). The amount of non-U.S. work on non-U.S. corporate governance is starting to grow. See, e.g. Theodor Baums, et al., *Institutional Investors and Corporate Governance* (1994) (surveying corporate governance in numerous countries).

[30] For an excellent brief cultural history of French corporate law, see Claude Ducouloux-Favard, "L'histoire des grandes sociétés en Allemagne, en France et en Italie", 44 R. I. D. C. 847 (1992).

[31] See Maurice Lévy-Leboyer, "The Large Corporation in Modern France", in *Managerial Hierarchies: Comparative Perspectives on the Rise of the Modern Industrial Enterprise*, p. 117 (Alfred D. Chandler, Jr. & Herman Daems, eds., 1980).

[32] See ibid., pp. 124, 146.

[33] See ibid., pp. 139-145.

[34] See Alain Alcouffe & Christiane Alcouffe, "Control and Executive Compensation in Large French Companies", 24 J. L. & Soc'y, pp. 85, 88 (March 1997); Alfred D. Chandler, Jr. & Herman Daems, "Introduction", in *Managerial Hierarchies: Comparative Perspectives on the Rise of the Modern Industrial Enterprise*, pp. 1, 7 (Alfred D. Chandler, Jr. & Herman Daems, eds., 1980).

[35] See ibid., pp. 132-37.

[36] See William N. Goetzmann & Philippe Jorion, *A Century of Global Stock Markets*, p. 19 (unpublished paper, Dec. 1996 draft) (showing data on French stock market goes back at least until 1921).

with its State ownership and control, either direct or through financial institutions, most recently exemplified the State's traditional corporate governance role.[37]

From the agency perspective, in State-oriented corporate governance management was subject to the oversight of a powerful, dominant shareholder. Using methods available to a controlling shareholder, as well as special ownership rights arising under nationalization laws, the French State kept management in check for much of the post-war period. Because of its direct or indirect controlling interest in a company, it appointed managers and directors and replaced them by decree.[38] State representatives also had the legal right to oversee and inspect the operations of a firm. The State's influence also arose from the identity of its agents, because managers and directors were usually former State bureaucrats who, by background and training, shared the State's goals and were inclined to favour State purposes.[39]

State ownership and control evolved during the post-war period from its dominance of companies to "relational" investing:[40] the State opened the capital of nationalized companies to private investors, and gave management more freedom to pursue business strategies, with the State agreeing upon long-term goals and being ready to intervene when additional capital was needed or when problems developed. The French "Statist" corporate governance was highly successful, as the economic results of the three decades following World War II (*Les Trente Années Glorieuses*) demonstrated. In collaboration with the State, managers exercised their business expertise to produce "national champions" that, in many cases, competed successfully in the world markets.

In all but several "sensitive" economic sectors, however, the State's ownership and control of private companies are diminishing due to several reasons. There has been in France, as elsewhere in Europe and around the world, a loss of confidence in the State's competence to manage enterprises in the new global market competition. The State often operated a profit-making business for purposes (e.g. to address unemployment, distribution of credit and public services) unrelated to the specific financial well-being of the firm. This approach worked when France was reconstructing and modernizing its war-torn economy and when its markets were highly regulated and closed. It can be argued that the approach does not work well when private companies must compete in international markets and rapidly adapt to new technologies.[41] With its market liberalism and goal of lessening European trade barriers, State subsidies of industry and budget deficits, the European Union has also pressured the State to sell off its participations in enterprises. Beginning for two

[37] See Jean-François Eck, *Histoire de l'Économie Française Depuis 1945* (1994); Fanto, supra note 2, pp. 28-40; Fanto, supra note 16, pp. 100–109.

[38] See generally Jean Kerninon, *Les Cadres Juridiques de l'Économie Mixte* (1992). In some cases, a business enterprise would simply become part of a French State department or ministry.

[39] See Michel Bauer, *Les 200: Comment Devient-On Un Grand Patron?*, pp. 123-97 (1987) (describing State path to executive success).

[40] See Jill E. Fisch, "Relationship Investing: Will It Happen? Will It Work?", 55 Ohio St. L. J., pp. 1009, 1010 (1994) ("Relationship investing may be described as a large long-term financial commitment by an investor to a portfolio company in exchange for a say as to how it is run.") (footnote omitted).

[41] This statement oversimplifies a complex matter. A firm's success depends upon the goals that are set for it, the definition of such goals and the monitoring of those entrusted with achieving the goals. Under such a definition, State-owned firms could be said to have achieved success – it all depends upon their goals; in certain situations they might be the best appropriate for achieving specific goals. See Saul Estrin & Virginie Pérotin, "Does ownership always matter?", 9 Int'l J. Indus. Org. 55, pp. 58-64 (1991).

years in 1986 and then resuming in 1993, privatization of State-owned companies has been going forward and shows no sign of ending (despite occasional delays).[42]

What will be corporate governance in large French companies once the State's influence declines? It is useful here to mention the importance of these companies in the French economy, and current information about their capital and ownership structure. Since a listing on a stock exchange is a sign of a company's size,[43] stock market capitalization of French companies, which is approximately 32 per cent of France's gross domestic product,[44] shows that large companies are significant in the French economy. Although it is not possible to obtain an exact idea of the capital structure of listed companies, available data suggests that, over the last ten years, nonfinancial industrial companies, have decreased their debt financing and increased their funding from equity capital and retained earnings. (Financial companies, such as banks, generally have a highly leveraged financial structure.) Like U.S. companies, French companies have approximately 30-40 per cent of equity and retained earnings.[45] Numerous factors, including high interest rates (which discourage continued debt financing), privatization and improvement in French stock markets, have influenced this increase in equity capital.[46]

Stock ownership in these large firms is concentrated, but not in the hands of financial institutions. Of the 120 listed non-financial companies in an index of the Société des Bourses Françaises, the weighted average percentage holding of the five largest shareholders for 1995 was 48.2 per cent (in comparison to comparable U.S. figures of 25.4 per cent).[47] Other data suggest that, out of the 416 largest French firms in 1995/1996, 24 per cent of the identifiable stockholders in these firms had holdings of more than 50 per cent in a given firm, with 16.5 per cent of the stock-

[42] See Fanto, supra note 2, pp. 49-56. At the time of completion of this chapter, a Socialist government has just again taken power in France and stated that it might well bring the French privatization programme to a halt. See "Bad for business?", *The Economist*, 7 June 1997, p. 51. I suggest that the government will not be able to have it both ways: to use State and even private enterprises for purposes other than profit-making and to promote the economically liberal goals of the European Union. Privatization in some form is likely to continue, as it did under earlier Socialist governments. Whether reform of French corporate law will go forward is more uncertain.

[43] Listing on France's "first market" (La Cote officielle) requires that at least 25 per cent of the company's share capital be in the hands of the public and that the company have three years of published financial accounts (the last two audited). See Règlement CMF, arts. 3-1-11, 3-1-14. French market authorities demand that the share capital of a listed company be substantial. See Hubert de Vauplane & Jean-Pierre Bornet, *Droit de la Bourse*, p. 350 (1994).

[44] This is out of a GDP of FF 7,681 billion. See OECD Economic Surveys: France 1997 166 (1997) (hereinafter, OECD France). This represents a significant shift from the 20 per cent figure of approximately ten years ago (1986). See Raghuram G. Rajan & Luigi Zingales, "What Do We Know about Capital Structure? Some Evidence from International Data", 50 J. Fin., pp. 1421, 1448 (1995).

[45] See OECD France, supra note 44, pp. 123-125 (French non-financial companies have 36.2 per cent of their capital structure in equity (share capital and retained earnings) in comparison to 33.3 per cent for U.S. companies). Looking at data primarily from 1987-1991 and attempting to be more restrictive in their definition of debt, Rajan and Zingales find that companies in the G-7 countries have similar leverage (with the exception of companies in Germany and the U.K. that have lower leverage). See Rajan & Zingales, supra note 44, p.1438. This result cautions against a ready characterization of countries with relatively small capital markets as necessarily having more leveraged companies. Rajan and Zingales do find that, from 1982 to 1991, French companies decreased their leverage and that, from 1984-1991, the external financing of French companies, although low as a fraction of total financing, was primarily equity. See ibid., pp. 1432, 1439.

[46] See OECD France, supra note 44, pp. 124-125.

[47] See ibid., p. 113.

holders having holdings larger than 75 per cent.[48] Depending on the data source, financial institutions (banks, insurance companies, mutual funds) own approximately 20-37 per cent of the equity capital in listed companies, but these holdings are generally not controlling positions.[49] Another significant shareholder source is French non-financial companies, which also own approximately 20 per cent of the listed companies and whose shareholdings are more concentrated than those of financial institutions.[50] Households own 34 per cent of listed companies, and of these wealthy individuals and families have significant stakes in companies.[51] Foreigners own approximately 20 per cent of listed French firms.[52]

Since large French companies are seeking equity capital, French investors (and, to a degree, non-French investors) are critical to them as capital providers. The statistics show that the State is no longer mediating (and, given the trend to liberalized markets, cannot mediate) this investment. The question is whether the State, which is accustomed to a corporate governance role, will really abandon this arena with its declining ownership. As the recent French parliamentary elections show, many French citizens continue to turn to the State as a problem solver, and the French history of a centralized State and of social acceptance of concentrated financial and other power is different, for example, from the U.S. populist preference for local centres of power and fear of centralized financial institutions. The State, moreover, retains the possibility of influence in some

[48] See Paul Windolf, *The Governance Structure of Large French Corporations: A Comparative Perspective*, pp. 17-19 (manuscript on file with author). Professor Windolf's data suggest that 63 per cent of the large French firms in his sample (i.e. 262 firms) have a majority shareholder, and 87 per cent (373 firms) have one shareholder with a holding greater than 25 per cent (in the U.S., this figure is approximately 4 per cent (9 firms)).

[49] For the general breakdown, see Andrea Goldstein, "Privatizations and Corporate Governance in France", BNL Q. Rev., pp. 455, 475 (No. 199, December 1996) (chart based upon 1994 data prepared by OECD, for which Mr. Goldstein works). See also OECD France, supra note 44, p. 111. Professor Windolf's data produces slightly different results: banks own 20.2 per cent of the 416 largest French firms, insurance companies own 12.1 per cent, and funds 5.2 per cent. His database may be more restricted than that of the OECD. These institutions do not generally have controlling positions: together, they are controlling shareholders in only 48 out of 416 companies in his database. See Windolf, supra note 48, p. 19. The limited control position of French financial institutions is related to legal obstacles that generally keep their holdings at the non-controlling level (e.g. banks are generally limited to holding 10 per cent of any non-financial company, insurance companies and mutual funds to 5 per cent). See Goldstein, supra note 49, p. 477.

[50] See Goldstein, supra note 49, p. 475; OECD France, supra note 44, p. 111. For example of the 262 companies in his database with a majority shareholder, approximately 59 have a French industrial company as such shareholder. See Windolf, supra note 48, p. 19.

[51] Goldstein's data indicate that households (including ownership through financial intermediaries) own 34 per cent of listed company stock. See Goldstein, supra note 49, at p. 475. See also OECD France, supra note 44, at p. 111. In Professor Windolf's database, direct individual and family ownership (which does not include ownership through financial intermediaries) is 12.8 per cent: moreover, individuals and families have controlling (greater than 50 per cent stakes) in 29 companies, and significant stakes (between 10 per cent and 49 per cent) in 56 others. See Windolf, supra note 48, at p. 19. Professor Windolf feels that his database in fact understates family ownership, since many families own additional shares through nonfinancial companies. See ibid., at p. 18, n. 25.

[52] See Goldstein, supra note 49, p. 475; OECD France, supra note 44, p. 111. Professor Windolf's data show that some foreign shareholdings are concentrated (e.g. of the 180 firms with a 75 per cent shareholder, 40 per cent (72) had a non-financial foreign firm in this position, which suggests that the firm is a subsidiary of a foreign firm). See Windolf, supra note 48, p. 19. See also Alcouffe & Alcouffe, supra note 34, p. 89 (giving a similar breakdown of ownership of the largest French companies).

privatized firms.[53] In firms where it no longer has, or never had, direct or indirect ownership, its influence may be exercised through other means (e.g. awarding of contracts) and through managers, who still largely originate from the State bureaucracy.[54] It is hard to imagine France without a State influencing the policies of major French enterprises.

Yet with the State abandoning, or at least reducing, its corporate governance role, will other institutions fill the State's place as a strong counterparty to French management? As Professor Windolf and Michel Bauer explain and as noted above, an account of French corporate governance should not ignore the importance of family ownership of large French enterprises.[55] They argue that family ownership has been an enduring and dynamic kind of capitalism in France, rather than only a stage on the road to an inevitable capitalism of dispersed shareholders and strong managers. Some of the most profitable large French companies in recent years have been family-owned and controlled, often through complex pyramids of ownership structure.[56] Families could replace throughout French large firms the State's ownership role, because their ownership has always existed side-by-side with that of the State. Since families also cultivate within themselves talented members as managers, as well as recruit managers from the State career path, they are not passive owners and present yet another solution to agency problems in the corporation.

As the French economist Olivier Pastré observes, financial institutions may also assume a new corporate governance role.[57] Banks and insurance companies can act as investment vehicles for small investors, either by investing proceeds of deposits in enterprises or by managing funds placed with them specifically for equity investment. Many French observers of their corporate governance feel that, despite the withdrawal of the State from companies' capital, there are characteristics of French corporate governance that distinguish it from a classic Anglo-American market capitalism.[58] Those hostile to market capitalism favour the emergence of a capitalism of strong financial intermediaries.[59]

[53] See Alice Pezard, "The Golden Share of Privatized Companies", 21 Brook. J. Int'l L., p. 85 (1995) (describing the "golden share" used, for example, in the privatization of the Société Nationale d'Elf Acquitaine that gives the State a veto on major transactions involving Elf). The actual State shareholding of listed firms is not significant (2 per cent of listed firms), but such figures do not necessarily elicit indirect State ownership and influence. See Goldstein, supra note 49, p. 475; OECD France, supra note 44, pp. 111, 118-22. Professor Windolf's data suggest that the State still controls (greater than 50 per cent shareholding) 32 of the 416 largest French firms. See Windolf, supra note 48, p. 19.

[54] See Bauer, supra note 39. See also Goldstein, supra note 48, p. 479.

[55] See Bauer, supra note 39, pp. 51-120; Windolf, supra note 48, pp. 15-16. See also Morton Keller, "Regulation of Large Enterprise: The United States Experience in Comparative Perspective", in *Managerial Hierarchies: Comparative Perspectives on the Rise of the Modern Industrial Enterprise*, pp. 161, 164 (Alfred D. Chandler, Jr. & Herman Daems, eds., 1980).

[56] See OECD France, supra note 44, p. 127 (pointing out the good results of family-owned companies, such as LVMH, l'Oréal, Carrefour, Castorama). See also Alcouffe & Alcouffe, supra note 34, p. 90 (pointing out that French groups have proved to be dynamically efficient because, with centralized control, they can respond rapidly to changes in markets and technology; yet such control is often incompatible with rights of minority shareholders).

[57] See Olivier Pastré, *Les Nouveaux Piliers de la Finance*, pp. 101-131 (1992).

[58] See, e.g. Olivier Pastré, "Les dix commandments du gouvernement d'entreprise", in *Rapport Moral sur l'Argent dans le Monde 1996*, pp. 201, 203 (1996) ("Quatrième commandment: tu assumeras la spécificité du capitalisme à la française.").

[59] See, e.g. Michel Albert, *Capitalisme contre capitalisme*, pp. 1171-1192 (1991).

Yet financial institution monitoring is not without practical and theoretical difficulties, as well as problems specific to France. Although bank-centred corporate governance looked good in comparison to U.S. governance during the early 1990s (a time of U.S. recession),[60] the main models of bank-centred corporate governance, German and Japanese corporate governance, are now revealing problems. They are suited to economic circumstances that are passing (e.g. reconstruction, closed national markets, preference for debt financing), but may not be well adapted to present economic conditions.[61]

In France, there is also no tradition or experience of financial institution capitalism. As explained above, for legal reasons their shareholding percentage has been insignificant, and they have generally served as a financier and advisor to a strong shareholder (e.g. a family or the State).[62] The possible involvement of financial institutions in corporate governance also has a "dark" side, at least from the perspective of control over managers.[63] François Morin has drawn attention to the creation of the *noyaux durs* or cross-shareholdings among companies at the time of privatization, which structures are "centred" around a financial institution (or group of such institutions). While financial institutions provide companies with financial and restructuring advice, the cross-shareholding protects management of each company in a network from capital market pressures: for no financial or industrial shareholder controls another company in the network.[64] This "*capitalism à la française*" produces and maintains a management oligarchy, for managers are subject to no countervailing power. It may also allow the State to influence industrial policy covertly through the managers and indirectly to protect national industries against foreign "invaders." Yet if financial institution monitoring takes this form, where institutions favour, rather than check, management control, shareholders drawn into companies' capital by privatization will suffer from a dominant management and French companies with such ownership structures will feel too late product market discipline.[65]

60 For a recent summary of this scholarly trend, see Roberta Romano, "Corporate Law and Corporate Governance", 5 Indus. & Corp. Change, pp. 277, 297-313 (1996). See also Rock, supra note 29, pp. 375-386.

61 And market capitalism is making inroads, albeit slowly, in both countries. See, e.g. "Making Companies Efficient: The year downsizing grew up", *The Economist*, 21 December 1996, pp. 97-99.

62 See OECD France, supra note 44, pp. 111, 125; Windolf, supra note 48, at p. 16. Crédit Lyonnais was the one French example of a bank with significant equity stakes, but its spectacular failure has cast doubt in France on the wisdom of this form of corporate governance. See Goldstein, supra note 49, pp. 475-476.

63 For the term, see Edward B. Rock, "Controlling the Dark Side of Relational Investing", 15 Cardozo L. Rev., pp. 987 (1994).

64 See François Morin & Claude Dupuy, *Le Coeur Financier Européen*, pp. 47-54 (1993). See also François Morin, "Le règle capitaliste entre laxisme et détournement", in *Rapport Moral sur l'Argent dans le Monde 1996*, pp. 207, 210-211 (1996). The Viénot Report offers a view of cross-shareholdings often heard in business circles in France, i.e. that it is a temporary phenomenon that will disappear when French companies can raise capital from other French sources (pension funds, once they are created, and other financial institutions that have not traditionally invested in equity). See supra note 3, p. 14 ("In this respect, the existence of cross-shareholders may be viewed as a transitional phenomenon in French capitalism, and one whose elimination as quickly as possible would appear highly desirable.").

65 See generally François Morin, "Privatisation et dévolution des pouvoirs: Le modèle français du gouvernement d'entreprise", Rév. Écon., pp. 1253, 1263-1266 (No. 6, November 1996). As Jensen observes, product market discipline is inevitable, but when it strikes, it may destroy an enterprise, with much human costs. It is thus useful to have other management control systems that would permit

Yet another French corporate governance outcome may be possible, a market capitalism, which also has French cultural origins.[66] As noted above,[67] for maximum financing in global competition French worldclass companies need to attract capital market investors, whose investment presumes a liquid and well-regulated stock market. Non-French investors, who are making significant investments in these companies, also favour market capitalism.[68] Since, moreover, the State can no longer fulfill the retirement demands for an aging population and still meet EU budget restrictions, there is a need for private pension funds, which must turn to equity investments to maximize their returns.[69] On the basis of an Anglo-Saxon model, these funds prefer a shareholder- and market-based corporate governance and, because of their mobility, they will penalize countries and companies producing less than adequate returns. French persons and organizations, particularly the Commission des Opérations de Bourse,[70] are also pushing for a market capitalism solution and emphasizing the development of French capital markets and an openness to foreign investors.

French corporate law will play a role in determining the French corporate governance "outcome".[71] For example, corporate law of the post-war years had a "Statist" character that both reflected and promoted the State's control of enterprises. The concept of the *intérêt social*, which permeates the French corporate code, permits directors to consider the interests of all constituencies in deciding upon corporate strategy[72] and thus allowed the State-owner to use controlled corporations for purposes other than profit-making. For the past two decades, however, French legal policy makers have changed corporate law to make it more hospitable to capital market investors. How well have they achieved their goals?

III. INFORMATION AND VOTING

If market capitalism separates shareholder ownership from management control, a central purpose of corporate law in this context is to enable shareholders to monitor and discipline managers. A main monitoring method is shareholder voting, whereby shareholders elect, or reelect, the agents under whose direction a corporation is operated and approve decisions by these agents on major corporate actions. For this form

cont.
a more rational and productive transformation of an enterprise. See Jensen, supra note 6, pp. 850-851. In fact, French privatized companies have recently been the least profitable of large French firms. See OECD France, supra note 44, pp. 125-126.

66 See William James Adams, *Restructuring the French Economy: Government and the Rise of Market Competition Since World War II*, pp. 249-254 (1989) (describing the historical strength of economic liberalism in France). See also Keller, supra note 55, p. 164.

67 See supra Section I.

68 See generally Fanto, supra note 2, pp. 22-28; Jean-Paul Valuet, "Fonds de pension américains: incidences de leur politique d'actionnariat sur les sociétés françaises", *Bourse et Produits Financiers* (January-February 1996).

69 See Centre For European Policy Studies, "Corporate Governance in Europe", pp. 29-30 (CEPS Working Party Report No. 12, 1995).

70 See Comm'n des Opérations de Bourse, 27ème Rapport au Président de la République, pp. 85-89 (1994).

71 These ideas are explained more fully in Fanto, supra note 16, pp. 109-112.

72 See Viénot Report, supra note 3, p. 5.

of monitoring to be meaningful, shareholders must have information. Management control, in fact, is based upon management's access to, and its expertise in understanding, corporate information. As Robert Clark explains in his classic hornbook on corporate law, "[t]he basic reason for a shareholder inspection right is to insure managerial accountability to shareholders."[73]

A. French Shareholders' Legal Rights to Information

Professor Conard once observed that U.S. state corporate law rules on the provision of information to shareholders were "rudimentary" compared to those of many other industrialized countries.[74] This remark is true for French corporate law, for under the laws governing the French corporate form most used for public companies, the *société anonyme*, the shareholder has the right to see a significant amount of information. A shareholder can inspect, at the company's main place of business, documents prepared prior to the company's annual shareholder meeting for the last three years (among other things, its financial statements, a list of directors, any reports by the directors or by the statutory auditors (*les commissaires aux comptes*), any explanation of resolutions submitted at the meeting, together with background information on the candidates for board membership, total compensation to directors), minutes of these shareholder meetings and a list of those present.[75] At all times a shareholder can also obtain the company's certificate of incorporation (*les statuts*) and a list of directors and statutory auditors.[76] Directors who prevent this disclosure are subject to criminal sanctions.[77]

It appears that a shareholder of a French company has the absolute right to undertake, without justification, an inspection of records and to have the information ready for his or her perusal. It is unclear, however, how effectively a shareholder can use the inspection right to gather information about other shareholders in order to contact them and thus collectively to contest management. In his report, Senator Marini suggests that French corporate law should be amended to compel a company to give a requesting shareholder all the information it has about shareholders' identities (not just the few names actually registered on the company's books), a suggestion indicating that there are problems with the existing law on information disclosure.[78] Shareholder information rights under French corporate law are thus likely to be more useful to shareholders in a closely held corporation or to large shareholders in a large public corporation (e.g. family owner), than for capital market investors. This limited utility perhaps explains their origin. While a shareholder in a closely held corporation or a large shareholder may use the rights to safeguard its ownership stake and to contest management, it is difficult to imagine that a

[73] Robert C. Clark, *Corporate Law*, p. 103 (1986).

[74] See Alfred F. Conard, *Corporations in Perspective*, pp. 325-327 (1976).

[75] See Loi No. 66-537 du 24 juillet 1966, arts. 168-170. See also Michel Jeantin, *Droit des Sociétés*, p. 104 (2nd ed. 1992). See infra Section IV.C.

[76] See Décret No. 67-236 du 23 mars 1967, art. 153.

[77] See Loi No. 66-537 du 24 juillet 1966, art. 445.

[78] See Marini Report, supra note 3, at pp. 89-90. See also Philippe Merle, "Les contrôles internes", in *La Modernisation du Droit des Sociétés: Premières réflexions sur le Rapport Marini*, pp. 41, 42 (Jean-Jacques Daigre, ed., 1996) (agreeing that there are problems with access to shareholder lists).

capital market investor, with little invested in a company, would have the necessary economic incentive to exercise these informational rights.[79]

The most important legal means whereby capital market investors acquire information about publicly traded firms is through mandatory disclosure. Such disclosure under French securities laws, fairly recent and not as extensive as that required of companies under, say, U.S. law and regulation, has gradually become more developed, which suggests that French legal policy-makers are attempting to create a legal climate favourable to capital market investing. That before 1967 securities regulation was not really an identifiable area of French law and no specialized government regulator existed to ensure the flow of accurate information to capital market investors underscores the historical unimportance of such investors in France, and thus in French corporate governance, in comparison to other shareholders (e.g. the State, financial institutions, controlling families). The major government market regulator, the Commission des Opérations de Bourse (the "COB") has gradually grown in power (and size) since that time, particularly from laws passed in 1988 and 1989.[80] Two other market authorities, successors to earlier self-regulatory organizations and regulators of market participants in the stock exchanges (e.g. brokers and listed companies), the Conseil des Bourses de Valeurs (now renamed the Conseil des Marchés Financiers ("CMF"), by Loi No. 96-597 du 2 juillet 1996) and the Société des Bourses Françaises ("SBF"), were also established in 1988 and saw their powers extended over the years in matters such as broker regulation, listing procedures and tender offers.[81] Disclosure to investors has improved with the increased power of these French market authorities.

The initial public sale of securities in France requires the disclosure of information in a prospectus (the *note d'information*) that, pursuant to COB regulations, includes detailed business, financial and offering information. Without COB approval, the prospectus cannot be used, nor can the summary prospectus that is disseminated to the public to generate interest in the securities. The listing of securities, which generally accompanies (or precedes) their issuance, also involves considerable disclosure. Under the direction of the CMF, the SBF prepares a *dossier* whereby the company supplies it with historical financial and business information, and the listing is subject to COB veto. French listings also require the company to continue to provide exchange authorities with information about corporate events that substantially affect the company and its shareholders and with interim financial results.

Yet French mandatory disclosure, while increasingly comprehensive, may not fully promote capital market financing. From the COB's perspective, more progress is needed with what in the U.S. would be called continuous reporting. The COB has

[79] In France, small shareholders can act collectively through shareholder associations, but this is a recent legal possibility under French corporate law. See Loi No. 66-537 du 24 juillet 1996 (as amended by Loi No. 94-679 du 8 août 1994).

[80] Two major legal reforms, the Loi No. 88-70 du 22 janvier 1988 and the Loi No. 89-531 du 2 août 1989, significantly increased the oversight, investigatory and enforcement powers of the COB with respect to disclosure and market manipulation. See generally Thierry Schoen, *The French Stock Exchange: A Practical Guide for Investors and Advisors*, pp. 4-10 (1995); Michel Germain, "Les sociétés qui font appel public à l'épargne", in *La Modernisation du Droit des Sociétés: Premières réflexions sur le Rapport Marini,*, pp. 31, 32 (Jean-Jacques Daigre, ed., 1996) (pointing out that the COB's regulations constitute another corporate law for listed companies); Leslie Goldman, "The Modernisation of the French Securities Markets: Making the EEC Connection", 60 Fordham L. Rev. S227, S237-S245 (1992).

[81] See generally CMF Règlement Général.

observed that, while information flows to investors from several sources in French companies, it is not well-organized. The investor (or the market professional)[82] has no one document to look at to understand the overall business, financial situation and governance of a company.[83] The COB thus encourages companies to file with it a *document de référence* that would serve this purpose and to develop as a basis for this *document* the annual report customarily prepared for shareholders at the annual meeting.[84] The COB's efforts suggest that it recognizes the capital market investor as an important figure in French corporate finance, which is not entirely surprising since, without such investors, the COB would have little *raison d'être*.

B. Shareholder Voting

The most significant corporate governance aspect of voting concerns the subjects on which a shareholder of a large corporation can vote, for voting is one of the few legal methods whereby the shareholder can directly influence the policies of this separate legal personality that is the corporation. Since the corporate form takes advantage of centralized and specialized management, which should be free to operate the business (otherwise, what is the purpose of a corporate form?), these subjects are limited. From a governance perspective, the most important subject is the shareholders' election of directors, under whose supervision the corporation is operated, at the annual shareholders' meeting. French corporate law is generally in line with the laws of other countries in allowing shareholders to vote on only a few subjects. At meetings, whether ordinary or extraordinary, French shareholders vote on major decisions affecting an enterprise (e.g. election of directors, changes to its certificate of incorporation, mergers).[85]

French voting procedures are highly regulated by law and ensure that shareholder voting is not an empty formality.[86] Some aspects of the French law on shareholder voting, however, suggest that, from a corporate governance perspective, it was until recently designed to regulate not so much the relations between management and numerous shareholders as between management and a smaller group of concentrated owners. These aspects have led some scholars to conclude that the French legal tradition is not favourable to capital market investors.[87] In the U.S., for example, capital market shareholders are protected through the practice of "one

82 If the French securities markets are efficient (and evidence suggests that they are), investors rely upon market price, which is established by the activity of market professionals (e.g. doing fundamental analysis about companies and trading on their research). See generally Ronald J. Gilson & Reinier H. Kraakman, "The Mechanisms of Market Efficiency", 70 Va. L. Rev., pp. 549, 557 (1984).

83 See Comm'n des Opérations de Bourse, 26ème Rapport Au Président, p. 44 (1994): "[f]orce est de reconnaître qu'il n'existe pas, aujourd'hui dans notre pays, un instrument d'information qui réunisse l'ensemble de ces caractéristiques [bases d'information, fiables, complètes, actualisées et aisément accessibles non seulement sur son activité, sa stratégie, ses résultats, mais aussi sur les décisions de ses assemblées ou sur les modifications de ses statuts]."

("It is necessary to recognize that there does not exist, today in our country, an information document that combines all of these characteristics [trustworthy, complete, recent and easily accessible sources of information, not only on its activities, strategy, financial results, but also on the decisions of its shareholders or on admendments to its certificate of incorporation"] (all translations are the authors)).

84 See Comm'n des Opérations de Bourse, supra note 70, p. 23.

85 See Loi No. 66-537 du 24 juillet 1966, arts. 153-157.

86 Ibid., arts. 160 to 177-1.

87 See La Porta, supra note 14, pp. 18-20.

share, one vote", i.e. that all common or "ordinary" shares have equal voting rights.[88] By contrast, French corporate law allows a company to give a shareholder double voting rights if he or she holds shares in registered (as opposed to bearer) form for at least two years (this shows that France does not literally have the "one share, one vote" rule). This legal possibility does not seem particularly well-suited for, and may even harm, capital market investors who buy and sell shares frequently and who are more likely to hold shares through financial intermediaries than directly with the company.[89]

The weakness of capital market shareholders arises from their number, geographical dispersion and small shareholdings. It follows from these characteristics that shareholders are unlikely to act as a cohesive group at shareholders' meetings. There is little economic incentive for them to attend meetings at all, or even to vote, so long as they can easily sell their shares. To facilitate shareholder participation in the corporate enterprise, corporate law should allow a shareholder to vote by proxy, that is, to instruct another individual to cast his or her votes on particular resolutions or for the election of directors. Yet French regulation akin to full proxy voting in France is of relatively recent origin. Under French law, a shareholder could always give his or her vote to a spouse or another shareholder, or simply provide a "blank" power to management.[90] Only in 1983 did French corporate law allow a shareholder to vote by mail (*par correspondance*), and it was not until 1988 that detailed rules were instituted regulating the manner of, and management's conduct regarding, this kind of voting.[91]

The relative recent origin of this French proxy regulation and the lack of use of the French proxy process again suggest that capital market investors are only gradually becoming significant in French corporate finance. If major French companies increasingly seek equity capital from these investors (whether French or non-French), more French legal and regulatory attention has to be given to this process. The recent use of proxy solicitation by shareholder activists in the Eurotunnel context demonstrates that French shareholders are discovering the advantages of organizing themselves through the proxy.[92] Capital market investors may also become more assertive and begin to oppose some current French corporate voting restrictions, such as the double voting privilege and the ability of a company to limit the

[88] State corporate law enables a corporation to be structured with different classes of shares with differing voting and economic rights. See, e.g. Del. Gen. Corp. L. §151(a). However, the SEC and the major U.S. stock exchange, the New York Stock Exchange (the latter through its rules), traditionally opposed the use of "dual-class" common stock, where some shareholders have no or fewer voting rights, in large publicly owned companies. The dual-class issue surfaced in U.S. corporate governance in the 1980s when management sought in some cases to recapitalize their companies' capital structure with dual-class stock so as to maintain control in the face of the threat of hostile takeovers. See, e.g. *Williams v Geier*, 671 A.2d 1368 (Del. 1996). While the story of the SEC's opposition to dual-class stock is an interesting one, see Richard W. Jennings, et al., *Securities Regulation: Cases and Materials*, pp. 714-716 (1992) (summarizing the story), it suffices to say that, while not absolutely prohibited, shares with unequal voting rights, whether arising from dual-class stock or some other attribute (such as the length of shareholding), are the exception, rather than the rule, in the U.S.

[89] See Loi No. 66-537 du 24 juillet 1966, art. 175. See also infra Section VIA, n. 204 and accompanying text (describing principle of "one share, one vote" in France).

[90] See Loi No. 66-537 du 24 juillet 1966, art. 161; Maurice Cozian & Alain Viandier, *Droit des Sociétés* 310 (9th ed., 1996). A single shareholder could thus obtain the proxies of many fellow shareholders.

[91] See Loi No. 83-1 du 3 janvier 1983, art. 161-1; Décret No. 67-236 du 23 mars 1967, art. 131-1 et seq. (as amended by Décret No. 86-584 du 14 mars 1986 and Décret No. 88-55 du 19 janvier 1988).

[92] See Joel Chernoff, "Shareholder power grows: France's first proxy solicitations are big step forward", Pens. & Inv., 19 (10 June 1996) (this technique was designed by the U.S.-trained shareholder activist, Sophie l'Hélias).

number of votes a shareholder can cast at a shareholders' meeting to a ceiling amount, a limitation that, in the circumstances of market capitalism, helps protect management from collective shareholder action.[93]

Senator Marini recommends making the French proxy process more responsive to and more protective of capital market shareholders, and thus more favourable to market capitalism. He suggests that one reform, based on a Swiss model, would involve appointing for shareholders' meetings an independent official (a *mandataire indépendant*) to whom small shareholders could send their "blank" powers and who would be more inclined than management to act on their behalf.[94] He would also enhance the ability of small shareholders to act collectively in their shareholder and investor organizations by facilitating the formation of these associations.[95] In addition, borrowing from U.S. law Senator Marini recommends that French institutional investors, such as mutual funds and private pension funds, be under a legal obligation to vote and to explain to their clients their voting policies.[96]

IV. DIRECTORS AND OTHER SUPERVISORS OF MANAGEMENT BEHAVIOUR

Corporate directors are of critical importance in the corporate governance of publicly owned firms. Elected by shareholders, they are expected to represent shareholder interests, even if their primary obligation runs to the legal "personality" of the corporation. Although they do not manage the corporation's operations, directors are supposed to "direct," or to supervise, its business. A corporate director thus occupies the ideal middle position between management and shareholders. He or she can generally supervise the former on behalf of the shareholders and can pay, if not the same

[93] See Loi No. 78-741 du 13 juillet 1978, art. 177. In effect, the legal ability to put a ceiling on voting by any one shareholder suggests both that French corporate governance is changing (i.e. that there may no longer be a controlling shareholder, like the State, in a company's capital, for, if there were such a shareholder, no protective ceiling would be necessary) and that French company managers are afraid of the outcome of this transformation (they want the protection that the ceiling gives them when there is no dominant shareholder).

In addition, French law allows a company to require that shares other than those registered on a company's books be "immobilized" for five days up to the date of the meeting, if a shareholder holding such shares wants to vote. See Décret No. 67-236 du 23 mars 1967, art. 136. This process could well deter market capitalism, since capital market investors may be reluctant to immobilize their shares for even a short period. See La Porta, supra note 14, p. 19.

[94] See Marini Report, supra note 3, p. 92.

[95] See ibid., pp. 94-95 (e.g. recommending that these organizations include bearer, as well as registered, shareholders).

[96] See ibid., p. 99. See also Jean-Paul Valuet, "L'identification des actionnaires des sociétés cotées", *Rév. Sociétés*, pp. 707, 725-728 (October-December 1996) (discussing legal problems that may hinder voting in French companies by non-resident shareholders and that need to be solved since these shareholders are likely increasingly to exercise their voting rights, and proposing that financial intermediaries be allowed to transmit the vote of shareholders, if these intermediaries receive the permission of shareholders and disclose their intermediary status to the issuer). In commenting upon the Marini Report, Professor Merle suggests that more emphasis should be placed on the better use of voting par correspondence, rather than on new methods of shareholder voting. He also cautions against pushing French institutional investors to vote before installing safeguards to prevent their abuse of the vote. See Merle, supra note 78, pp. 45-47.

A law authorizing the creation of private pension plans in France has been passed. See generally "Plan épargne retraite: Mode d'emploi", *Le Point*, 15 March 1997, pp. 81-86.

amount of attention as management to the business, at least more attention than can the owners themselves. That directors often have considerable business experience also makes them well-suited to this role. As a corporate structural matter, therefore, the director could address the agency problems presented by market capitalism.

In practice, however, the director has often been a corporate governance disappointment. Not only does a typical director have interests not necessarily identical to those of shareholders (they are, after all, different persons, although, under French law, directors must be shareholders), nor is he or she directly answerable to them (again, the primary responsibility is to the corporation), but the director is much more likely to be a representative of management than of shareholders. Managers, not shareholders (except shareholders contesting management), have the main say in nominating directors, and thus directors are beholden to management for their position. Directors frequently come from management ranks (the chief executive of a French company is also its chairman of the board), or former management, are business executives of other companies, who, on account of their own positions, would be sympathetic to management's desire to run a company without any interference, or are in occupations (e.g. investment banking, law, business consultants) that provide services to a corporation and whose business success may depend upon management's good graces.[97]

Even if directors were single-mindedly focused upon protecting shareholder interests against management overreaching, they are at a disadvantage for simple logistical reasons. Since a corporate board acts only at meetings and since, except in a "crisis," its meetings occur infrequently, directors (who generally have other full-time positions) do not have much time to supervise management. It is also questionable whether this meeting time, as well as the necessarily limited pre-meeting preparation, is adequate to enable them to comprehend the complex business of a large public company. Directors have a right to information about the corporation. The information, however, generally comes not from an independent directorial staff, but from management, which can thus control its content and presentation.[98]

Much corporate legal (and other) scholarship in the last three decades suggests ways of addressing the passivity of boards of directors functioning in market capitalism and of making boards more responsive to shareholder interests. One reform, which has now become something of a reality in Anglo-American jurisdictions, is to have the majority of directors be "outside" directors, i.e. not from management.[99] This reform has not proved to be a panacea, because it does not deal with the indirect

97 General research on boards of directors suggests that this background of directors, as well as other social factors (e.g. group behaviour and loyalty), conspires to ensure that boards are deferential to management and passive in protecting shareholder rights. See generally Ada Demb & F.-Friedrich Neubauer, *The Corporate Board: Confronting the Paradoxes* (1992); Jay W. Lorsch & Elizabeth McIver, *Pawns and Potentates: The Reality of America's Corporate Boards* (1989). The French situation is more acute since chief executives in large French companies are considered to have almost dictatorial powers. See infra Section IV.A.

98 The Viénot Report recognizes these problems with board operation, although it does not consider that they require change in French corporate law. For example, it observes that boards of French companies "meet three to four times a year, and in practice meetings last around two hours." Supra note 3, p. 16. It also recognizes that directors receive information about the company only from management. See ibid., p. 17.

99 See generally American Law Institute, 1 *Principles of Corporate Governance: Analysis and Recommendations*, pp. 110-114 (1994) (discussing recommendation from group of legal practitioners and scholars that corporate boards in large public companies should consist of a majority of outside directors).

influence of managers on directors, nor does it resolve the issues of lack of director time and expertise. More recent suggestions have been to have "professional" directors, who would make a full-time job of being a director in several companies and who could develop expertise in monitoring company management[100] and to have a chairman of the "supervisory board" not be an "insider" (i.e. company employee), which would help insulate outside board directors from management influence.[101] Current research identifies the importance of tying board compensation to company share performance, which links the interests of board members and shareholders more closely.[102] While legal and non-legal efforts to make corporate directors more effective monitors for shareholders continue,[103] basic corporate law addresses the agency problem by imposing upon directors specific duties and by establishing guidelines on ways in which directors can satisfy these obligations.

A. The General Obligations of a Director

French corporate law attempts to ensure that directors take their positions seriously and thus monitor management for the benefit of shareholders by setting a standard for director conduct. As a preliminary matter, it is useful to say a few words on French board structure. Although there are two legally possible board structures,[104] the following summary concerns only the one that is widely used. Under French law, a board of directors or *conseil d'administration,* whose members shareholders elect, "administers" the affairs of the French *société anonyme*.[105] The law gives the *conseil* broad powers to act on the company's behalf.[106] It elects from its members a president, who assume "sous sa responsibilité, la direction générale de la société," who "représente la société avec les tiers" and who essentially has all powers not reserved to the shareholders and to the board.[107] The actual direction and operation of a com-

[100] See Ronald J. Gilson & Reinier Kraakman, "Reinventing the Outside Director: An Agenda for Institutional Shareholders", 43 Stan. L. Rev., pp. 863 (1991). See also Laura Lin, "The Effectiveness of Outside Directors as a Corporate Governance Mechanism: Theories and Evidence", 90 NW. U. L. Rev., pp. 898 (1996).

[101] See 1 *Principles of Corporate Governance*, supra note 99, at pp. 115-133 (discussing function and composition of audit, nominating and compensation committees). See also William A. Klein & John C. Coffee, Jr., *Business Organization and Finance: Legal and Economic Principles*, pp. 151-152 (1996).

[102] See Charles M. Elson, "Shareholding Directors Create Better Corporate Performance", 11 *Issue Alert*, p. 3 (May 1996) (describing report of the National Association of Corporate Directors' Commission on Director Compensation). See generally Romano, supra note 60.

[103] For a discussion of the impact of this research on reforming French boards, see Section VIII, infra.

[104] French law provides for two forms of board structure: a board of directors (*conseil d'administration*) that selects one of its members as the chairman and chief executive (*président directeur général* or "PDG"), see Loi No. 66-257 du 24 juillet 1964, art. 89, et seq., and a supervisory board (*conseil de surveillance*), which names an executive board (*le directoire*) and selects a president thereof, art. 118, et seq. The second structure, which is rarely used in France, is modelled on the German system. See Claude Ducouloux-Favard, *Société Anonyme, Aktien Gesellschaft, Società Per Azioni,* pp. 120-129 (1992).

[105] Loi No. 66-537 du 24 juillet 1966, art. 89.

[106] Loi No. 66-537 du 24 juillet 1966, art. 98 (from Loi No. 67-559 du 12 juillet 1967 and Ordinance No. 69-1176 du 20 décembre 1969) ("Le conseil d'administration est investi des pouvoirs les plus étendus pour agir en toute circonstance au nom de la société; il les exerce dans la limité de l'objet social et sous réserve de ceux expressément attribués par la loi aux assemblées d'actionnaires."). ("The board of directors is granted the most extensive powers to act in every circumstance in the name of the corporation; it employs these for the corporate purpose and subject to those powers that the law expressly grants to shareholders meetings.")

[107] Loi No. 66-537 du 24 juillet 1966, art. 113 (from Loi No. 67-559 du 12 juillet 1967).

pany thus lie in the president's hands, subject to the board's supervision. The board can also give the president the ability to appoint one or more individuals, known as *directeurs généraux,* to assist him (it is generally a "him") in company management.[108] These "directors" are in addition to non-*directeur* executives and to the president, who is himself a *directeur général* and goes by the title of *président directeur général* or the "PDG." The PDG thus has considerable statutory powers and is perceived to be all powerful in his company.[109]

A director's (*administrateur*'s) responsibility to the corporation (and thus to the shareholders) is stated in the French corporate code and explained in the related jurisprudence. As the late Professor Jeantin remarked, "[l]es dirigeants sociaux (gérants ou conseil d'administration (ou directoire) dans la société anonyme) ont l'obligation positive d'agir, en toutes circonstances, dans l'intérêt de la société. A défaut, leur responsibilité est engagée."[110] In particular, the code provides that

> "Les administrateurs sont responsables, individuellement ou solidairement, selon le cas, envers la société ou envers les tiers, [1] soit des infractions aux dispositions législatives ou réglementaires applicables aux sociétés anonymes, [2] soit des violations des statuts, [3] soit des fautes commises dans leur gestion."[111]

Shareholders cannot relieve directors of this responsibility by ratifying an action or decision of the directors alleged to be in violation of their duties.[112]

The closest of the above three "duties" to a basic "duty of care" is the obligation of directors to avoid any "fautes commises dans leur gestion."[113] The French corporate code, however, fails to define this concept. French jurisprudence suggests that the concept sets a high standard for director behaviour. In his treatise on the subject, Professor Gibirila explains that a director is expected to act as a prudent, diligent and active person under the circumstances of this position in the corporation, and that he or she cannot use lack of experience or knowledge as an excuse.[114] He admits that this *faute* is difficult to establish with precision, particularly for *administrateurs*, as opposed to the misconduct of *directeurs* (i.e. management) who are actively engaged in business

108 Loi No. 66-537 du 24 juillet 1966, art. 115.

109 See Ducouloux-Favard, supra note 30, p. 872 (describing how the PDG structure appeared during the Vichy regime and was modelled upon a German corporate governance structure). As Senator Marini has observed, French corporate law gives the PDG power almost equal to that of the board, and some cases managers of large French companies are now using this power unchecked by the former means of internal control (i.e. State oversight). See Marini Report, supra note 3, pp. 8-9, 39-40.

110 See Jeantin, supra note 75, pp. 134-135. (Author's translation: "The members of the board of directors are responsible, individually and jointly, as the case may be, to the company or to third parties, [1] for violations of laws or regulations applicable to corporations, [2] violations of the certificate of incorporation, [3] errors of management.")

111 Loi No. 66-537 du 24 juillet 1966 (from Loi No. 67-559 du 12 juillet 1967), art. 244. (Author's translation: "Company management (managers on the board of directors (or the supervisory board) in the corporation) have a positive obligation to act, in all circumstances, in the interests of the company. Failing that, this responsibility is engaged.")

112 See Loi No. 66-537 du 24 juillet 1966, art. 246 ("aucune décision de l'assemblée générale ne peut avoir pour effet d'éteindre une action en responsabilité contre les administrateurs pour faute commise dans l'accomplissement de leur mandat.").

113 Professor Gibirila admits that the obligation of a director to avoid the "faute de gestion" sometimes overlaps with his or her other duties, i.e. to avoid breaking the law and committing a "violation des statuts". See Deen Gibirila, *Le Dirigeant de Société: Statut Juridique, Social et Fiscal*, p. 439 (1995).

114 See ibid., pp. 430, 439.

operations, and that the doctrine is applied on a case-by-case basis.[115] Directors must take an active interest in the enterprise and scrutinize the actions of the PDG and the other *directeurs généraux*. An important part of their *gestion* is to ensure that they have adequate information about the business and the PDG's conduct thereof.[116]

An example of the seriousness with which French law treats a director's obligation to supervise company management is the director's liability if the company becomes bankrupt. Under French bankruptcy law, a director is personally liable if there are not enough assets to cover creditors' claims, if he or she committed a *faute* de gestion and if the *faute* "contributed" to the deficiency.[117] In this context, too, the law fails to define what constitutes a *faute de gestion*. The legislative history of the section suggests that a director may be liable even on the basis of simple negligence.[118] Although it is difficult to prove a director error and many reported cases deal with gross nonfeasance or malfeasance,[119] this legal obligation and penalty reinforce the supervisory responsibilities of a French company director.[120]

At first glance, the French legal "duty of care" is puzzling from a corporate governance perspective. One might expect not to find it in French corporate law, because the duty would seem to go hand in hand with protection of capital market investors, who have not historically been numerous in France. Yet the opposite is true: the duty to avoid *fautes de gestion* is as severe as, if not more severe than, any "duty of care" in the Anglo-American legal context.[121] A duty of care, however, does not *necessarily* indicate a corporate governance of capital market investors. A legal obligation like the duty of care is useful in every corporate situation, since by definition the corporate form involves a delegation of responsibility to those who do not own the property that they are to manage. After all, the foundation of the duty of care, as other corporate duties, lies in basic agency law. One should thus expect to see the duty wherever the corporate form exists: in economic terms, a general "open-ended" obligation imposed upon directors is the most cost-efficient manner of monitoring their behaviour for long periods of time in unforeseeable circumstances.[122]

The important fact is not the existence of the duty, but its *use*. In a country like the U.S. where market capitalism has a long history, the duty has been refined to protect capital market investors in different events that occur in public companies (e.g. proxy contests, mergers, the hostile takeover) without deterring management from making business decisions. In France, the duty has not received similar

115 See ibid., pp. 439-440.

116 See ibid., p. 441.

117 See Loi No. 85-98 du 25 janvier 1985, art. 180.

118 See Gibirila, supra note 113, p. 479.

119 See ibid., p. 480.

120 Directors are also subject to criminal penalties for abuse of their functions. See ibid., pp. 540-564.

121 Under Delaware law, for example, the duty of care requires that a director not be grossly negligent and that he or she act reasonably under the circumstances of the director's position (e.g. size of the corporation). See, e.g. *Smith v Van Gorkom*, 488 A.2d 858 (Del. 1985). A director's compliance with the duty of care often turns on whether, in taking any action (which generally means deliberating upon and voting for a resolution proposed by management), the director has adequately informed himself or herself, and debated with his or her peers, about the action in question. The American Law Institute's definition of the duty of care specifically states the further qualification that it "includes the obligation to make, or cause to be made, an inquiry when, but only when, the circumstances would alert a reasonable director or officer to the need therefor." 1 *Principles of Corporate Governance*, supra note 99, pp. 138-139 (§4.01(a)(1)).

122 See Frank H. Easterbrook & Daniel R. Fischel, *The Economic Structure of Corporate Law*, p. 91 (1991).

development because controlling shareholders, like the State and families, had other means to police, and direct, management. The French duty of care will become an important protection for French (and non-French) capital market investors as these investors become more numerous in the capital of French companies.[123] In fact, the Viénot Report and the Marini Report both urge French directors to take their basic "duty of care" more seriously.[124] That this duty is attracting more attention from French legal policy-makers suggests that it may soon assume a more important role in French corporate governance.

B. A French Director's Duty of Loyalty

Since the corporate form uses agents and this use raises the possibility of conflicts of interest between agents and principals, an expected obligation imposed on directors is a duty of loyalty to or a duty to deal fairly with the corporation.[125] Officers and directors of large public corporations with capital market investors should particularly have this obligation because they control the property of shareholders who cannot each monitor their agents' behaviour, and because these managers thus have the opportunity to engage in opportunistic behaviour at shareholders' expense.[126] For example, a director (or officer) may directly or indirectly do business with the corporation on terms favourable to him or her, but not to the corporation; he or she may cause the corporation to give him or her extraordinarily high compensation; and he or she might use corporate property or information for his or her benefit.[127] Since disclosure discourages self-seeking management actions, disclosure obligations also help to prevent these abuses in large public companies.

French corporate law imposes upon managers and directors a duty of loyalty and regulates their conflicts of interest. As a general matter, it limits the comparable positions that an officer or director may occupy, although the limitations are not particularly restrictive. No individual can be a member of more than eight boards of directors of *sociétés anonymes* in France,[128] nor can he occupy the position of PDG in more than two companies.[129]

[123] In both the U.S. and France, directors are under an obligation to obey the law and the corporate articles of incorporation. These obligations, while important, are at the outer bounds of corporate governance, i.e. they address serious management abuse.

[124] See Marini Report, supra note 3, pp. 42-43; Viénot Report, supra note 3, pp. 20-21.

[125] The ALI uses the term "duty of fair dealing" to emphasize the obligation of officers, directors and control persons to avoid conflicts of pecuniary interest with the corporation. See 1 *Principles of Corporate Governance*, supra note 99, pp. 199-200.

[126] Some academic literature criticizes the importance of imposing this duty upon managers. The reasoning is that, if managers divert wealth from shareholders through conflict of interest transactions, shareholders can simply reduce management compensation accordingly. Other scholars believe that management wealth diversion to itself hurts shareholders. See, e.g. Lucian Ayre BebChuk & Christine Jolls, *Managerial Value Diversion and Shareholder Wealth*, pp. 1-3 (Harvard Law School John M. Olin Center for Law, Economics, and Business Discussion Paper No. 179, 1996) (summarizing debate).

[127] These categories are taken from Clark, supra note 73, pp. 141-146.

[128] See Loi No. 66-537 du 24 juillet 1966, art. 92. This restriction does not include board positions that a natural person occupies as a representative of a legal person (i.e. a company), nor up to five additional positions in companies that are at least 20 per cent-owned by a company in which one is already a board member.

[129] See Loi No. 66-537 du 24 juillet 1966, art. 111. Senator Marini proposes restricting this *cumul des mandats* so that the eight-board membership restriction would include board positions now exempted from it and that a PDG would be restricted to four board positions (not counting his board

French conflict-of-interest rules also reach management and director self-interested transactions. Under French law and subject to certain exceptions, a director or an executive (or any of their relatives) is prohibited from borrowing money, or receiving a guaranty, from his or her corporation.[130] This rule not only protects shareholders and creditors from an improper use of corporate funds, but it also has a "moral" purpose of preventing improper management and director behaviour that may injure a corporation's reputation and thus its ability to raise capital.[131] In the event of a violation, the company can either have the contract declared void or seek damages from the offending officer or director. In addition, this misfeasance subjects a director or manager to criminal sanctions for improper use of corporate property, i.e. *abus de biens sociaux*.[132]

French law does not prohibit all transactions between a director or officer and a corporation; it simply subjects them to a strict prior approval process. Other than contracts in the ordinary course of a corporation's business (i.e. "conventions portant sur des opérations courantes et conclues à des conditions normales"),[133] any contract between a director or executive and his or her corporation, between the corporation and another corporation or business in which he or she is an owner, director or executive, and between the corporation and someone with whom the director or executive is otherwise linked must be preapproved by a specific procedure.[134] This rule applies to any special compensation, other than the *jetons de présence*, for members of the board of directors,[135] but does not apply to the board's determination of compensation for the PDG (see below). French law broadly defines the kinds of contracts subject to this preapproval procedure so that it covers any agreement (whether written or not) that might allow directors or executives to benefit at the company's expense.[136]

Under the approval procedure,[137] the "interested" director or officer must inform the board of directors about the conflict of interest (i.e. transaction and/or contract in which he or she has, directly or indirectly, an interest). The entire board (not a board

cont.

seat in the company and membership on boards of its subsidiaries). See Marini Report, supra note 3, p. 45. His reason for this recommendation, however, is not to address conflict-of-interest as to "upgrade" the quality of French board members and executives.

[130] See Loi No. 66-537 du 24 juillet 1966, art. 106. A bank in corporate form may lend money to its directors or officers on the same commercial terms as it treats regular clients.

[131] See Gibirila, supra note 113, p. 382.

[132] See Loi No. 66-537 du 24 juillet 1966, art. 437 ("Le président, les administrateurs ou les directeurs généraux d'une société anonyme qui, de mauvaise foi, auront fait, des biens ou du crédit de la société, un usage qu'ils savaient contraire à l'intérêt de celle-ci, à des fins personnelles ou pour favoriser une autre société ou entreprise dans laquelle ils étaient intéressés directement ou indirectement" will be punished by imprisonment from 1-5 years and/or receive a fine of FF 2000 to 2,500,000).
("The president, members of the board of directors or managing directors of a corporation who, in bad faith, will have made a use of the company's goods or credit that they knew was contrary to its interests, for personal ends or to favour another company or business in which they have a direct or indirect interest".)

[133] Loi No. 66-537 du 24 juillet 1966, art. 102.

[134] Article 101 of the Loi No. 66-537 du 24 juillet 1966.

[135] See Loi No. 66-537 du 24 juillet 1966, art. 109. The jetons are simply compensation paid to directors for their attendance at board meetings.

[136] See generally Gibirila, supra note 113, pp. 389-390.

[137] The procedure is set out in the Loi No. 66-537 du 24 juillet 1966, art. 103.

committee, and acting without the voting participation of the interested director or directors, who cannot even count toward the board quorum or cast a vote) must authorize the transaction by a specific decision after receiving adequate information about the transaction and deliberating formally on its merits. Once the board approves the transaction, the affair can proceed.[138] The PDG must inform the company's statutory auditors (*les commissaires aux comptes*) about the transaction. Prior to the next annual shareholders' meeting, the auditors must prepare for the shareholders a report on this transaction, as well as on any other similar transactions, including those that the statutory auditors may have discovered and that did not in fact receive the board pre-authorization. At the annual meeting, shareholders are asked to approve the transaction (without counting votes of the interested party). Failure to obtain shareholder approval, however, does not render the contract void, but may lead to liability of the interested director, and possibly the board, for any damages suffered by the corporation because of this non-approval (e.g. if the contract or transaction were contingent upon shareholder approval).[139]

Fraud nullifies an "interested" contract. In the absence of fraud, the contract is void if the board of directors did not pre-approve it, provided that the corporation suffered damages as a result.[140] A shareholder vote at a general meeting can remove the voidability of the contract if shareholders approve it after receiving a special report of the statutory auditors on the reasons why the board did not follow the proper pre-approval procedures. As noted above, moreover, a violation of the duty of loyalty by a director or officer can give rise to criminal liability. Fraudulent use or taking of corporate assets can lead to this penalty, as can the intentional use of goods or the credit of a corporation for a director or executive's personal ends or for his or her other business to the detriment of the corporation (the classic *abus de biens sociaux*).[141] Similarly, criminal liability attaches when directors or executives abuse their powers or positions for other self-interested purposes.[142]

Having entrusted their funds to corporate managers, French shareholders receive the legal protection that this "duty of loyalty" provides. Managers realize that, if they do not follow the pre-approval process and their self-dealing is detected and proves to be unfair to the corporation, it will be voided and that they shall suffer any losses arising from unwinding the transaction, as well as criminal liability. From a capital markets perspective, these laws ensure that shareholder funds are not diverted to management's personal uses and that shareholders need not impose a significant discount on a corporation's share price as compensation for the risk of management self-dealing.[143]

A potentially troubling kind of self-dealing arises in management compensation. By law, the French board of directors alone determines the compensation of its president and general director;[144] it cannot delegate this matter to a compensation committee, nor does this determination come within the above approval procedure for

[138] In certain cases, pre-approval by shareholders can substitute for board approval. See Gibirila, supra note 113, p. 403.

[139] See Loi No. 66-537 du 24 juillet 1966, art. 104.

[140] See Loi No. 66-537 du 24 juillet 1966, art. 105.

[141] See Loi No. 66-537 du 24 juillet 1966, art. 437.

[142] See ibid.

[143] The duty may thus be the most efficient (i.e. least costly) way for shareholders to monitor corporate agents. See Easterbrook & Fischel, supra note 122, pp. 90-108.

[144] See Loi No. 66-537 du 24 juillet 1966, art. 110.

contracts or transactions involving a conflict of interest. Individual compensation of executives (as opposed to the customary disclosure of global compensation figures for all executives) has generally been kept secret in French companies, and French securities laws require no detailed disclosure of it (even though complete disclosure might deter serious compensation abuses). Given the considerable power of the PDG over other directors (and the likelihood that other directors, themselves often PDGs or former executives, would be generous with the PDG's compensation package) and the secrecy of compensation arrangements, the possibility for abuse exists in French management compensation.

Yet in France there has been no significant debate over executive compensation, which has not generally been viewed as a corporate governance problem.[145] Since the State and family ownership have for some time offered a strong counterweight to company management, they may well have kept compensation within reasonable bounds. This lack of attention to executive compensation may change, however. As the State recedes from its influence in some large companies, the opportunity for management opportunism in compensation increases. Capital market investors (whether French or non-French) may thus begin to pay more attention on how French management compensation is determined and demand more information about individual executive compensation. Market forces alone may effect change in this area.[146] Yet the board's legal obligation in setting compensation will likely come under increased scrutiny and French jurisprudence in this area will be developed.

French corporate law thus addresses management and director self-dealing in a detailed manner. Again, this is not surprising, because the French corporate form rests upon a basic agency relationship and there is a need in any such relationship to find an economical way of guarding against overreaching by the agent. If anything, French corporate law may be too strict in discouraging management/corporation contracts that might arguably be beneficial to both parties and in penalizing management under criminal law for minor violations of the duty.[147] In fact, in his proposed reform to the French corporate code Senator Marini suggests softening or eliminating criminal penalties on directors and managers of French companies for conflict-of-interest transactions when these managers do not personally benefit from a particular transaction.[148]

In the conflicts-of-interest area, French law is well-suited for a closely held corporation. Yet in a public company where capital market shareholders predominate

145 See Pastré, supra note 4, p. 32.

146 Because of pressure from non-French shareholders, some French executives are "voluntarily" disclosing their compensation. In economic terms, this could be seen as an effort by agents to "bond" with their principals (and which reduces the discount that investors would assign to a company's shares for the risk of management opportunism on compensation). See "France's Boardroom Revolution", Wall St. J., 17 Oct. 1995, at A20 (discussing executive compensation disclosure by management at Lyonnaise des Eaux).

147 Indeed, the prevalence of criminal sanctions for violations of a duty of loyalty goes hand in hand with the State's involvement in companies, for a violation of corporate law or a company's *statuts* (certificate of incorporation) implicates State interests. See infra Section VII.D.

148 See Marini Report, supra note 3, at pp. 112-121. The French Court de Cassation has recently held that criminal sanctions for an abus de biens sociaux may not lie when a director or manager does not personally benefit from the transaction. Judgment of 6 Feb. 1997, Cass. Crim., 1997 Bull. Crim. (Fr.) (LEXIS, Intlaw library, Frprcs file), at 20–21 (holding that bribe paid indirectly by company president to government official seeking reduction of amount company owed government did not constitute, without any more showing, a payment for president's personal interest).

there is the need for disclosure about management and directors, and their dealings with the company, that discourages self-dealing. Here, as exemplified by executive compensation, French law is not completely developed.[149] To further capital market financing in France, more disclosure on management and its potential conflicts is needed, disclosure that would deter self-dealing and act as a useful "signal" of management's loyalty to shareholders. If this disclosure is improved (and if other internal controls on management are instituted), it makes sense to eliminate the criminal penalties for minor duty of loyalty violations.

C. Monitoring Through Accounting

Shareholders rely on other parties inside, or working for, the corporation to ensure that the corporation is being operated on their behalf.[150] One check on management behaviour comes from an auditor or accountant, who may be either a corporate agent or independent professional, depending upon the circumstances of his or her employment. Since a business operates for profit, and since this profit depends not only on the product or services offered, but also upon information about and control of expenses and revenues (among other things), individuals who design company financial control systems and produce financial information are critical to business success. Since neither executives nor directors have the time, nor often the expertise, to do this work, since they need financial information in making business decisions and since such information may disclose their misbehaviour, the establishment of financial controls and the preparation of financial statements are significant in corporate governance, as are the accountants performing this work.[151]

For any French company of a significant size, French corporate law gives an official corporate governance role to accounting professionals: it designates as part of the *contrôle des sociétés anonymes, les commissaires aux comptes.*[152] These *commissaires* are similar to a U.S. external auditor. Elaborate rules, which govern eligibility for the position, ensure that *commissaires* cannot have, either directly or indirectly, any relations with management, owners or affiliates of the company (or their relations) and that they cannot take positions in the company following the conclusion of their mandate. Other regulations require that *commissaires* be independent accounting professionals who are under the jurisdiction of regional and national commissions, as well as under the *Cours d'Appel.* Only a French court can remove the *commissaires* for cause.

149 Since potential conflicts of interest are the subject of a report by the statutory auditors to shareholders and require a shareholder vote of approval at the annual meeting, the financial press may publicize them, which will have the requisite deterrent effect.

150 There are also forces outside the corporation that monitor agent behaviour. These forces, such as product and capital market pressures, are not properly the subject of an analysis of legal corporate governance. See Jensen, supra note 6, p. 850.

151 For a recent reaffirmation of the importance of accounting in corporate governance, see Louis Lowenstein, "Financial Transparent and Corporate Governance: You Manage What You Measure", 96 Colum. L. Rev., p. 1335 (1996).

152 See Loi No. 84-148 du 1er mars 1984, arts. 218-235. See generally Jeantin, supra note 75, pp. 144-156.

The basic role of the *commissaires* is to audit a company's accounts. This is not a one-time effort for the end-of-fiscal-year accounts, but work that extends throughout the year and involves a review of any other prepared accounts as well as continuous checks on a company's internal financial control systems.[153] Whether or not they "certify" a company's accounts, the *commissaires* must report on them to both the board of directors and to the shareholders, and the latter must vote to ratify the accounts and can do so only after receiving the report.[154] The *commissaires* must also verify any other company accounts, as well as any management reports on a company's financial situation. In accomplishing these tasks, the *commissaires* cannot participate in company management and must guard their independence from it. The requirements that the *commissaires* notify the board and shareholders of any irregularities that they discover in the company's accounts and that they alert the French public prosecutor to any serious problems therein exemplify this independence.[155] Under French law, the accountants are liable to the company and to third parties for damages arising from their negligence.[156]

The duties of the *commissaires aux comptes* are related to French law's requirements on publication of financial statements. At the end of each fiscal year, the board or managers of large French public companies must establish, among other things, an inventory, financial statements and a written report on the management of the enterprise, as well as other information on current assets and liabilities, the value of shares held in the company's investment portfolio, financial results and plans pertaining to financing.[157] Management makes this information available to the *commissaires* for verification prior to the shareholders' annual meeting.[158] At mid-fiscal year, a company's board or management gives a preliminary review of balance sheet information and pre-tax revenues, again to be reviewed and certified by the *commissaires*.[159] Similarly, every four months a company must prepare a statement of its net revenue, separated into categories of activity and compared with that in preceding periods.[160] The end-of-the-year information is published in an official legal journal, as is the semi- and tri-annual information.[161]

The corporate governance conclusions that can be drawn from French legal requirements on financial statement certification are similar to those discussed with respect to directors' duties. Verification of accounts by the *commissaires* as a way of detecting management abuse has been present in France for a long time, as one would expect given the importance of accounting in any evaluation of business

[153] See Loi No. 83-353 du 30 avril 1983; Loi No. 85-11 du 3 janvier 1985; Loi No. 66-537 du 24 juillet 1966, art. 228.

[154] Loi No. 66-537 du 24 juillet 1966, arts. 230, 233.

[155] See ibid. For example, Art. 233 provides that "ils [les commissaires] révèlent au procureur de la République les faits délictueux dont ils ont eu connaissance, sans que leur responsabilité puisse être engagée par cette révélation."

[156] See Loi No. 66-537 du 24 juillet 1966, art. 234. The commissaires also have a duty to notify the board, and ultimately the shareholders, of any information coming to their attention indicating that the company is in financial difficulty. See Loi No. 84-148 du 1er mars 1984, art. 29. The commissaires are criminally liable for any serious dereliction of their duties.

[157] See Loi No. 66-537 du 24 juillet 1966, arts. 340, 340-1, 341-1 (from Loi No. 83-353 du 30 avril 1983 and Loi No. 84-148 du 1er mars 1984).

[158] See Décret No. 67-236 du 23 mars 1967, arts. 243, 244 (from Décret No. 85-295 du 1er mars 1985).

[159] See Décret No. 67-236 du 23 mars 1967, art. 244-1, 297-1 (from Décret No. 85-295 du 1er mars 1985).

[160] See Décret No. 67-236 du 23 mars 1967, art. 297 (from Décret No. 85-295 du 1er mars 1985).

[161] See Décret No. 67-236 du 23 mars 1967, arts. 295, 296 (from Décret No. 83-1020 du 29 novembre 1983).

results. Yet in recent years the *commissaires* have become more important as greater financial reporting obligations (subject to *commissaire* review) have been imposed upon large French companies; the enhanced position of the *commissaires* basically came from 1984 amendments to French corporate law. These developments point to French legal policy-makers' recognition of the increased importance in France of capital market investors, who, together with the market professionals acting on their behalf, need reliable information about companies "certified" by outsiders. That the *commissaires* are given such broad powers of continuous review and reporting (even to parties outside the corporation) represents an attempt by French law to equalize the balance of power (if only in the information area) between management and shareholders and to push the board to take its oversight duties more seriously.[162] To improve further the internal controls on management of French companies, Senator Marini recommends increasing the responsibility of the *commissaires.*[163]

While this corporate governance role of the *commissaires* is important, as is their responsibility to detect serious management errors, it is ultimately limited, precisely because of the restrictions on their participation in management. They simply cannot provide *all* of what dispersed capital market shareholders often need: adequate representation in the supervision of a corporation that would provide a source of strategic advice to, and a strong check on, executives *before* serious problems develop. As their role is now defined, the *commissaires* cannot fully address difficulties arising from a separation of ownership and control in a public corporation, if such difficulties become acute in France with the increase in capital market investors. It is important to understand the unique role of the *commissaires* and their corporate governance contribution through accounting. Yet they should not be seen as a substitute for an effective board of directors.[164]

V. GOVERNANCE ISSUES RELATED TO THE ELIMINATION OF MINORITIES

An important event for a corporation and its shareholders is a major transformation of the corporation's business. Investors who have elected to fund a particular kind of venture may not want to be equity holders in a different enterprise. Several central legal corporate governance issues in such cases can be stated as follows: do corporate directors conduct themselves appropriately in deciding upon the transformation and do the shareholders have any input into the decision? Can shareholders who disapprove of the transformation exit the corporation's capital without incurring

162 In addition to the *commissaires,* French law allows shareholders representing 10 per cent of the capital of a corporation to petition a court to appoint an expert to review the management of specific business operations. See Loi No. 66-537 du 24 juillet 1966, art. 226 (from Loi No. 84-148 du 1er mars 1984). And, under French law, representatives of employees (the *comité d'entreprise*) can demand considerable information from management. See Jeantin, supra note 75, pp. 156-157. Associations of shareholders also have considerable power to address management abuses.

163 See Marini Report, supra note 3, pp. 99-104 (recommending, among other things, to improve the *commissaires'* audit of an enterprise and to give them more powers to address problems in financial accounts).

164 Senator Marini thus misses this point when he worries that the use of independent directors in France may create a conflict with the *commissaires.* See Marini Report, supra note 3, p. 42. There can be no such conflict, since the *commissaires* are not legally responsible for the direction of an enterprise.

"unfair" losses? These issues are important in a market-based system of corporate governance where dispersed capital market investors cannot easily oppose transformations proposed by management for collective action reasons. The following discussion first briefly explains the legal decision-making structure of the major forms of corporate transformations and its corporate governance import. It then discusses the availability of exit for a French shareholder objecting to a transaction and the absence of special obligations placed upon directors in the elimination of minorities from a corporation's capital.

A. Decision-Making in Corporate Transformations

A corporate transformation may involve a combination of a corporation with another (a "merger") or a sale of all, or substantially all, of the corporation's assets to such other corporation. Generally in either event, the resulting business may look different, either because it combines previously separated enterprises or significantly expands (or decreases) current operations.

Under French law, the legally mandated decision-making structure for some major corporate transformations is straightforward and helps correct the shareholders' informational disadvantage, which is likely to be critical when shareholders must decide whether to approve a major transaction and/or exit a corporation's capital. In a classical merger (where both companies, rather than their subsidiaries, are involved in the transaction), the board of each French company must establish a *projet* that describes, among other things, the transaction, the reasons therefore, and the exchange ratio, and the substance of this *projet* must be published in an official legal publication.[165] A corporation must make available to its shareholders at its corporate headquarters additional information on the transaction, which includes recent financial statements of both companies as well as a report by special *commissaires à la fusion*, appointed by a commercial court, who examine whether, among other things, "le rapport d'échange est équitable."[166] Shareholders of each company must approve the transaction by a two-thirds vote of shareholders present at a special shareholders' meeting.[167] A sale of a major part of a corporation's assets may follow a similar procedure, although, in practice, only shareholders of a company purchasing assets for shares are guaranteed the right to review the decision.[168]

Under French law, shareholders do not have a say in all corporate decisions regarding major transactions. An acquisition may be structured in such a way, for example, to avoid the legal requirement of shareholder approval, e.g. if a corporation conducts an acquisition or merger through a subsidiary organized for that purpose

[165] See Loi No. 66-537 du 24 juillet 1966, art. 374 (Loi No. 88-17 du 5 janvier 1988); Décret No. 67-236 du 23 mars 1967, 254-255. The COB supervises the disclosure to shareholders in this merger context. See Marie-Claude Robert, "The Internationalization of the Markets and the Experience of the French COB with Mergers and Acquisitions", in *European Takeovers: Law and Practice*, pp. 403, 404 (Klaus J. Hopt & Eddy Wymeersch, eds., 1992).

[166] See Décret No. 67-236 du 23 mars 1967, 258; Loi No. 66-537 du 24 juillet 1966, art. 377.

[167] See Loi No. 66-537 du 24 juillet 1966, art. 376.

[168] See ibid., art. 387. For shareholders of the selling company, a sale of all of the assets might amount to a liquidation under French law, which would trigger a shareholder vote. See Cozian & Viandier, supra note 90, p. 573. The Viénot Report recommends that a board should conduct a major sale or divestiture of a company's assets only after receiving shareholder approval, although such is not now required under French law. See Viénot Report, supra note 3, p. 6.

(known as a "triangular" merger or asset sale). A board of a large corporation may use such a structure so that it can conduct an acquisition or sale without having to present it to the shareholders for their approval. The structure of a corporate group thus permits the group to conduct significant mergers and acquisitions at the subsidiary level without the approval of the parent corporation's shareholders. Finally, if, as is often the case, a controlling group or family dominates a public company, a shareholder vote to approve a merger is not particularly significant, even when shareholders receive the vote, because the dominant shareholder controls the outcome.

B. The Shareholders' Right of Exit

In some countries, such as the U.S., corporate law grants shareholders the right, in certain major transactions, to demand that the corporation repurchase their shares at "fair value" if they disagree with the transaction. This right, known as the appraisal or dissenters' remedy, owes its origin to a former feature of corporate law mandating a unanimous shareholder approval of any major transaction. This unanimity made little sense as the number of shareholders increased, for it allowed one shareholder to stand in the way of an economically favourable or necessary transaction, with the alternative being an unwieldy and unexpected corporate dissolution. Historians of the corporate form suggest that, in exchange for the loss of their historical veto right, shareholders received the right to walk away from an enterprise with the fair value of their share.[169]

The appraisal remedy has a corporate governance purpose. With the loss of a veto over transactions and the accompanying rise of majority rule, minority shareholders become subject to potential abuse by a control group or person. If, moreover, corporate managers can plan a major transaction and, because of the apathy of dispersed shareholders, acquire the necessary majority support for it, capital market investors opposed to the transaction are at the mercy of management, even where no control group exists. A right of dissenting shareholders to force a corporation to cash them out may thus check majoritarian and management overreaching and constitutes another legal method of addressing the positional weakness of capital market investors.[170] The effectiveness of the appraisal remedy for corporate governance purposes depends, however, upon its availability and facility of use. In the U.S., for example, the remedy is not available in every transaction and its costs make it prohibitive to small shareholders.[171]

[169] 2 *Principles of Corporate Governance*, supra note 99, pp. 291-314, presents the origins of the U.S. appraisal remedy and a summary of scholarly work on it.

[170] See ibid., pp. 292-293.

[171] Under a typical U.S. state corporate law, a shareholder does not receive the appraisal right in every major transaction: nearly every state corporate law grants a shareholder an appraisal right where his or her corporation is merging into another (but not necessarily where another corporation is merging into his or her own); in certain states, shareholders receive this right when their corporation is selling all, or substantially all, of its assets. See ibid., pp. 358-379 (summarizing in a chart, as of 1994, state corporate laws on appraisal). Delaware corporate law, for example, does not give a shareholder an appraisal right upon a sale of all or substantially all of a corporation's assets. The right also does not attach when a corporation conducts a major transaction through a subsidiary. In some cases, as under Delaware corporate law, a shareholder of a publicly traded corporation (or a corporation with a certain number of shareholders) does not have an appraisal right, even in a "classic" merger, provided that, as a result of the transaction, he or she ends up holding shares of a publicly traded corporation, whether his or her own or another. See Del. Gen. Corp. L. §262(b)(2).

This kind of appraisal remedy (i.e. a judicial determination of fair value) does not generally exist under French corporate law. A shareholder of a French corporation involved in a merger cannot request that the company purchase his or her shares at fair value. The absence of this right is serious in French corporate governance where controlling shareholders can decide upon a merger and the terms of the transaction.[172] In certain cases, however, shareholders in French publicly owned companies have the rough equivalent of appraisal through CMF regulations. If a person or group of persons acquires more than one-third of the shares of the surviving company in a non-merger context (i.e. by purchasing a control block from a controlling shareholder), such person or group is required to make a buyout offer for all of the outstanding shares (this provision will be discussed in more detail below and in the next Section).[173]

In a merger where minority shareholders are offered cash or other non-share consideration in return for their shares (i.e. they are "frozen out" of the enterprise), they also have no immediate right to approach a court to ask for a determination of the "fair value" of the consideration offered for their shares. Yet the above CMF rule may have already come into play to ensure that minority shareholders have some exit strategy: i.e. if a party had become a dominant shareholder (greater than one-third shareholder) through a prior share acquisition. In this acquisition situation, the CMF demands that the offer include a justification for the price offered in exchange for the shares and can hold up the offer if it finds that price unacceptable.[174] An independent French agency, if not immediately a court, thus examines the substance of an offer in a transaction that may eventually lead to a merger.[175]

There are several additional possibilities of exit for minority shareholders when a supermajority shareholder exists (having 95 per cent of the votes), a situation that might follow a tender offer or another significant transaction (e.g. where a few shareholders declined, or neglected to, tender their shares in the original offer). Either the minority can request the CMF to order the majority holder to make them an offer to purchase their shares, or the majority on its own initiative can propose the offer.[176] In either case, the CMF reviews the "fairness" of the offering price. Pursuant to a recent change in French law and similar to a situation common in the

cont.

Appraisal is a potentially cumbersome and expensive process: as a typical statutory procedure indicates, a shareholder must elect the remedy prior to the shareholder vote on the transaction; he or she must file a petition requesting a court to determine the "fair value" of the shares as of the date before the transaction; and this determination demands a trial with all its pre-trial proceedings and costs, particularly on valuation issues. For an example of the procedural complexity of appraisal, see Del. Gen. Corp. L. §262(d)-(k). See also 2 *Principles of Corporate Governance*, supra note 99, p. 293 (giving the standard criticisms of the appraisal remedy). During the appraisal proceeding (unless the shareholder withdraws from it), the shareholder receives no dividends nor has any other rights (e.g. voting) as to the shares. This procedural difficulty, which requires the involvement of lawyers, guarantees that the only shareholders electing appraisal are those with a significant stake in the enterprise, not small capital market investors.

172 See Eddy Wymeersch, "Problems of the Regulation of Takeover Bids in Western Europe: A Comparative Survey", in *European Takeovers: Law and Practice*, pp. 95, 104 (Klaus J. Hopt & Eddy Wymeersch, eds., 1992).

173 See CMF Règlement Général, art. 5-4-1.

174 See ibid., arts. 5-2-5, 5-2-7.

175 French shareholders can challenge CMF determinations in the French Cour d'Appel, a procedure that thus involves French courts in valuation disputes. See Décret No. 88-603 du 7 mai 1988, art. 3.

176 See ibid., arts. 5-5-1 to 5-5-6.

U.S.[177] The 95 per cent supermajority shareholder can now compel the minority to take the offer and exit the corporation's capital (i.e. effect a "squeeze-out").[178] In this case, the law provides that the CMF evaluate the minority's shares using valuation methods accepted in the financial community.

Shareholders in a French public company also receive an official exit in certain cases involving a sale of all or substantially all of a company's assets (and in other major corporate events).[179] Under CMF regulations, if a controlling shareholder decides upon the sale, it must alert the CMF and begin a procedure to repurchase shares of the minority shareholders (a procedure that again involves CMF review of the offering price).[180] Under French law, a shareholder is presumed to control a corporation if he or she holds 40 per cent of the votes (and no other shareholder holds more) or if facts suggests that, with a smaller holding, he or she controls shareholder decisions.[181] And French shareholders of public companies can always "exit" by selling their shares into the market, albeit sometimes at a discount.

Are capital market shareholders in France really worse off than their counterparts in countries whose laws provide for a judicial evaluation of a "fair" exit price as a result of a proposed major transaction, such as an appraisal remedy or an appraisal equivalent? French law does not offer shareholders an exit in every situation (e.g. merger) where, for example, corporate law of a typical U.S. state would provide this relief. Where French law offers shareholders an exit, it has an independent market agency, not a court, first review the terms of the offer, so that minority shareholders do not have to bear the expense of arguing with the company over the proper valuation of their shares (although dissatisfied minority shareholders can proceed to the French *Cour d'Appel* to challenge a CMF determination, generally on the basis of its approval of a company's valuation methods).[182] If the CMF and the COB take seriously their substantive review of offering price in these situations, as a practical matter in the cases where minority shareholders are given an exit, the French exit alternatives may be more useful for minority shareholders than a solely court-based appraisal remedy with all its litigation expenses.[183] This independent review of price is critical for capital market shareholders in France where, because market capitalization is smaller and market liquidity is less than in, say, the U.S., the option of selling shares into the market may not always be the best way of realizing their "fair" value.

C. Additional Protection for Shareholders in Freeze-Outs

Because capital market shareholders are in a vulnerable position in a freeze-out (i.e. in a situation where they are being "cashed out" of a company's capital by a controlling shareholder electing to merge the corporation with a special acquisition vehicle), they may well need special legal protection. Generally weak in relation to

[177] See Del. Gen. Corp. L. §253(a) (allowing a 90 per cent shareholder to merge its subsidiary into it without any vote of subsidiary's shareholders).

[178] See Cozian & Viandier, supra note 90, p. 409. See CMF Règlement Général, arts. 5-6-1 to 5-6-2.

[179] For a list of these events, see Marini Report, supra note 3, pp. 71-72.

[180] See CMF Règlement Général, art. 5-5-5.

[181] See Loi No. 66-537 du 24 juillet 1966, art. 355-1.

[182] See Marie-Noëlle Dompé, "Offres publiques: Réglementation et contestation", *Petites Affiches*, pp. 27, 28-30 (No. 7 12 juin 1994).

[183] The evidence suggests that these market authorities do take their review seriously. See Robert, supra note 165, pp. 414-416 (also noting that the COB reviews disclosure relating to such transactions).

management, they are even weaker against a management and board representing a major shareholder who pursues his or her own interests and who may thus desire to eliminate them from a corporation's capital – a situation not uncommon in France, given the extent of family and controlling group capitalism. In this situation, managers and the board of directors could be inclined to offer a price to the minority shareholders that favours the dominant shareholder. At an informational disadvantage, the minority shareholders cannot be sure that they are receiving a "fair" price, and the market itself may impose a "discount" on their shares because of their minority position and because of its own lack of information about the controlling shareholder's plans for the corporation.[184] Given the controlling shareholder's dominance, the minority shareholders have few options but to take the price offered in the merger.[185] To protect shareholders in these circumstances, U.S. corporate law enhances directors' duties of good faith, care and loyalty and U.S. federal securities laws impose specific disclosure requirements upon the merging corporations and controlling shareholders.[186]

Under French corporate law, there has not been comparable development in the enhancement of the duties of directors in the freeze-out. Oversight by market authorities may be dealing adequately with abuses by controlling shareholders in certain situations, e.g. by mandating a buy-out offer to the minority shareholders under the CMF's supervision and ultimately court review. If the CMF is providing adequate supervision of such offers and their offering price, it is questionable whether any additional check on the majority shareholder and its "controlled" directors is needed in these cases. Since, moreover, French directors are by law held to high standards of behaviour and required to avoid conflicts of interest, and their misbehaviour subjects them to civil and criminal penalties, a shareholder in a French company appears now to have the legal basis for bringing a civil suit in a freeze-out situation against a director who, in approving a merger involving a corporation's controlling party on the other side of the transaction, failed adequately to analyze the transaction from the perspective of *all* the shareholders and followed without question the controlling shareholder's demands.[187]

Whether more jurisprudence on directors' duties and more disclosure will develop in France in this kind of transaction depends upon future restructuring of French companies and any perception that current French law inadequately protects

184 See Clark, supra note 73, pp. 508-509 (describing how majority shareholder may depress market price of stock to take advantage of minority shareholders).

185 Of course, there are often valid reasons to eliminate minority shareholders from a business, e.g. to take a company private and save the cost and trouble of a public company.

186 See, e.g. *Weinberger v UOP, Inc.*, 457 a.2d 701 (Del. 1983) (Delaware cause of action for unfair treatment of shareholders in a freeze-out); 17 C.F.R. §240.13e-3(d) (1995) (requiring any company, or affiliate (which includes a controlling shareholder thereof), that, among other things, effects a "freeze-out" of minority shareholders with the result that the company becomes privately held (a "going private transaction") to file with the SEC, and to disclose to minority shareholders, the information listed on Schedule 13E-3 (requiring information about the transaction and its procedure)). Small shareholders can easily find attorneys willing to take cases based on a violation of either of these laws on a contingency basis since there is an economic incentive to such counsel, i.e. numerous minority shareholders can be joined in a "class action", which means the potential recovery for the lawyer, who generally takes one-third of the damages awarded, is increased. For small shareholders, the suits thus offer a more practical form of redress than appraisal.

187 Of course, the difficulty of bringing and financing such a suit may undercut its usefulness. See infra Section VII.

minorities. U.S. legal developments on treatment of minorities can be traced to a period of restructuring in U.S. public companies that often resulted in the "going private" of formerly public companies and the elimination of minority shareholders. Since present French market policy is to encourage more public shareholders, not to eliminate those who exist, French finance circumstances may not now lead to similar legal developments. Yet because of the likely continued existence of dominant shareholders in French public companies and their control over major transactions, it may become important to enhance the duties of directors towards all shareholders in such transactions, such as mergers, so as better to attract public investors into French capital markets.

VI. FRENCH LEGAL CORPORATE GOVERNANCE AND THE MARKET FOR CORPORATE CONTROL

The market for corporate control (i.e. the takeover market) characterizes market capitalism. For some Europeans, this kind of restructuring is hostile and wasteful.[188] If managers do not produce immediate results or, even sometimes if they do (if a financier wants to take advantage of their success), a potential buyer is always in the wings, and investors, eager for quick profits, are ready either to sell to this buyer (or to some other bidder drawn into the contest by the lure of easy gains) or to professional traders (*arbitrageurs*) who make a living by purchasing shares in these circumstances and by thus putting companies into "play". Managers have no choice but to focus upon short-term results and defensive measures, at the expense of long-term projects and research and development. The restructuring generates enormous transaction costs and ultimately benefits only the financiers, investment bankers and lawyers. It invariably destroys companies, which must be broken up and sold to pay off the debt that buyers incur to finance their purchases, and injures creditors and employees to the benefit of shareholders and these parties, who principally capture the wealth gains.[189]

Some scholars agree with this portrayal of the market for corporate control and others, even if they do not absolutely condemn the hostile tender offer, which characterizes this market, find it a blunt instrument for restructuring.[190] The generally accepted view of economists, finance theorists and many business law professors, however, is that the market for corporate control addresses the basic agency problem of disciplining management in a market capital situation and that its nefarious effects have been greatly exaggerated.[191] For them, the threat of a tender offer keeps in check powerful managers, who are always tempted to take advantage of shareholders by engaging in negative net present value investments, and forces them to make the restructuring called for by economic circumstances.[192] The most vilified

[188] See Albert, supra note 59, pp. 75-98.

[189] See generally Margaret M. Blair, *Ownership and Control: Rethinking Corporate Governance for the Twenty-First Century*, pp. 61-68 (1995).

[190] For a useful summary of positions both critical and supportive of takeovers, see Victor Brudney & William W. Bratton, *Cases and Materials on Corporate Finance*, pp. 939-956 (4th ed., 1993).

[191] See, e.g. Michael Jensen, "The Takeover Controversy: Analysis and Evidence", reprinted in, Donald H. Chew, Jr., Ed., *The New Corporate Finance: Where Theory Meets Practice*, pp. 465-491 (1993).

[192] See, e.g. Jensen, supra note 6, pp. 850-852.

form of a tender offer, a leveraged buy-out or "LBO", which is a purchase of a company by funds borrowed on the security of the assets of the company itself, often followed by a bust-up sale of the company, makes perfect sense from a finance perspective, as shareholders cash out and the excessive leverage keeps management within tight fiscal constraints. Many scholars, therefore, regret the lessening of the popularity of the hostile offer in the U.S., which they attribute to laws passed at the urging of managers and other interest groups (e.g. labour unions) unwilling to accept the needed restructuring, which threatens their positions.[193]

The takeover has been, and continues to be, an important aspect of business restructuring in any market capitalism situation,[194] and it is necessary to review how French law regulates this phenomenon. In some countries, such as Germany, there is little to say about the market for corporate control because of the relative absence of tender offers in them. France is not such a case. There have been many tender offers in France, but few have been hostile.[195] According to Professor Wymeersch, French tender offer regulation, like that in most other continental countries, has been used to eliminate public shareholders after a control block of shares has been transferred between parties, such as groups or families; it generally does not effect control changes.[196] French corporate law regulates tender offers in detail, although the law, and related court decisions, are relatively recent, i.e. the product of the 1980s and 1990s. A complete explanation of this law and of its corporate governance effects is beyond the scope of this chapter.[197] The following only summarizes some striking features of the French regulation of tender offers from a market capital perspective and suggests that French regulation limits, but does not eliminate, the French market for corporate control.

A. French Legal Impediments to the Market for Corporate Control

Numerous provisions in French law give management (with the board's acquiescence) time to prepare its defences and power to make a company an unfavourable candidate for a takeover. Management of French companies have an "early warning" system, for French corporate law requires shareholders (alone or *agissant de concert* – a complicated term of art) passing certain defined thresholds (5 per cent, 10 per cent, 20 per cent, 33 1/3 per cent, 50 per cent, 66 2/3 per cent) of the company's capital or voting rights to declare their existence (within five business days to the CMF and within 15 calendar days to the company) or to lose for two years (or such longer period that the CMF imposes) voting rights on the shares in excess of the thresholds.[198] Companies can also lower the thresholds to .5 per cent and increments thereof. Since companies know the identity of shareholders having shares in registered form (i.e. *titre nominatif*

[193] See Roe, supra note 26, pp. 226-230.

[194] See Jensen, supra note 6, pp. 831-835. See also Pound, supra note 6, pp. 1011-1017.

[195] See OECD France, supra note 44, p. 118 (observing that, although merger and acquisition activity in France is far below that of the U.K., it leads other European countries).

[196] See Wymeersch, supra note 172, pp. 101-103.

[197] An excellent discussion of French tender offer regulation and its background (to which the following discussion owes a great deal) is found in Schoen, supra note 80, at pp. 79-145. See also Cozian & Viandier, supra note 90,pp. 600-615; André Tunc, "Les Prises de contrôle par l'intermédiare du marché", in *Corporate Takeovers Through the Public Markets*, p. 157 (Phaedon John Kozyris ed., 1996).

[198] See Loi No. 66-537 du 24 juillet 1966, arts. 356, 356-1, 356-4.

or on the company's books), this law is useful where shareholders hold them in bearer form (*au porteur*) and where parties are acting *de concert.*[199]

These declarations of share ownership alert the management of a target company to the identity of new significant shareholders. COB regulation supplements this disclosure by requiring an acquiror of more than 20 per cent of a company's voting rights to declare whether, in the next 12 months, it intends to continue to acquire shares, take control of the company or request a seat on the board.[200] Supporting this regulation, as well as the early warning law, is the rule regarding acting *de concert*, which is broadly defined to refer to agreements to acquire or sell voting rights.[201] This term, which has a detailed jurisprudence, covers an agreement by several persons to act jointly to take control of a company. Moreover, any agreement among shareholders dealing with a preferential purchase and sale of shares (e.g. right of first refusal) must be disclosed to the CMF, which makes it public.[202]

Under French law, management can also take defensive measures to ward off hostile bidders and avoid market discipline. A peculiar feature of French corporate law is that its charter (or a special shareholder meeting) may grant double voting rights to shares held in registered form for at least two years.[203] From one corporate governance perspective, which is often heard in France, this provision rewards "patient" capital and thus promotes long-term relationships between shareholders and management. From a market capital perspective, however, the device allows management to create a "friendly" shareholder group whose influence in the company grows, while that of capital market investors (who likely hold securities in bearer form, thus making them ineligible for double voting rights) declines. In addition, under French corporate law, a company's charter may permit it to limit the total number of voting rights of any shareholder to a set percentage (the rule must apply to all shareholders), which places serious obstacles to a change of control.[204] The

[199] Since all French shares are "dematerialized", this shareholding distinction has no physical meaning. Shares of French companies are "held" in the official French depositary, SICOVAM: registered shares are in a company account (or in the account of a bank acting as the company's agent) with this depositary, and bearer shares are held through financial intermediaries that also have SICOVAM accounts. French law permits a company's certificate of incorporation to provide that the company can ask SICOVAM to require the intermediaries to identify the beneficial shareholders (the company's bearer shares are then known as *titres porteurs identifiables*). See Loi No. 66-537 du 24 juillet 1966, art. 263-1 (added by Loi No. 87-416 du 17 juin 1987). This cumbersome procedure does not always produce accurate information. In fact, with the growth of international, particularly Anglo-Saxon, investors in the capital of their companies, French managers are concerned that the law does not adequately permit them to identify non-resident shareholders. See generally Valuet, supra note 96, p. 708 (noting problem and proposing solution whereby financial intermediaries identify their non-French shareholders). The need for the "early warning" system thus remains.

[200] See Règlement COB No. 88-02.

[201] Article 356-1-3 of the Loi No. 66-537 du 24 juillet 1966 provides that "[s]ont considérées comme agissant de concert les personnes qui ont conclu un accord en vue d'acquérir ou de céder des droits de vote ou en vue d'exercer des droits de vote pour mettre en oeuvre une politique commune vis-à-vis de la société."

[202] See Loi No. 66-537 du 24 juillet 1966, art. 356-1-4 ("Toute convention conclue entre des actionnaires d'une société cotée sur l'un des marchés réglementés français comportant des conditions préférentielles de cession ou d'acquisition d'actions doit être transmise au conseil des bourses de valeurs qui en assure la publicité.").

[203] See ibid. art. 175. These double voting rights can be limited to French or EU shareholders.

[204] See ibid. art. 177. Although, apart from double voting rights, French corporate law does not permit the issuance of shares having supervoting rights (see art. 174 for the "one share, one vote" principle),

COB disapproves of these limitations when they are not coupled with "outs", i.e. that the limitation disappears once a party acquires a majority of the voting rights,[205] and Senator Marini recommends a change to French law to this effect.[206]

The characteristic "closeness" of the French business world reinforces the effect of these limitations on voting rights. Although blatant abuses (e.g. secret agreements among companies and shareholders, secret holdings of shares) are now illegal, as noted earlier,[207] managers can create a friendly shareholder group (a *noyau dur*) of other companies, often bound together in elaborate cross-shareholdings with one another. The group's shareholders agree to hold their shares for a specified period of time, to limit the number of shares of the target any of them can acquire and to give the others a right of first refusal if they dispose of their shares. They may also hold warrants exercisable for shares of the target in certain events. While the corporate governance implication of this arrangement is subject to debate, it is clearly a defensive device for company management in privatized companies that no longer have the State as a major shareholder.[208]

As French takeover history has shown, these defences are not impregnable, although French tender offers generally occur as consensual, rather than hostile, transactions. French shareholders can remove board members without cause at a shareholders' meeting.[209] French law strictly limits a company's repurchase of its shares to a reduction of capital,[210] and it removed much of the defensive benefit of

cont.
which could have an anti-takeover effect, a French company can issue non-voting shares with dividend priority, see art. 177-1.

205 See Schoen, supra note 80, p. 111.

206 See Marini Report, supra note 3, pp. 93-94 (recommending that French corporate law should require that these limitations become void once a shareholder has acquired over 50 per cent of the voting rights so that they do not seriously impede changes in control). This recommendation, however, does not address the situation where a significant shareholder (or shareholders) does not want control of a company, but wishes to express its displeasure with management through its vote.

207 See supra Section II.

208 See Fanto, supra note 2, pp. 59-67. See generally Morin & Dupuy, supra note 44; Tunc, supra note 197, p. 162. On the legality of these agreements, see generally Jean-Jacques Daigre & Monique Sentilles-Dupont, *Pactes d'actionnaires* (1995). While recognizing the pro-management effect of the *noyaux*, Senator Marini does not believe that legislation can address this phenomenon, because he attributes it to the small size of the French capital markets that pushes companies to look to other companies for their capital. See Marini Report, supra note 3, p. 44. He does recommend that the French State not establish new cross-shareholdings in future privatizations, see ibid., p. 50, and that existing ones be adequately disclosed to investors, see ibid., at p. 69. In some privatizations, moreover, the French government retains an absolute veto right (*l'action spécifique*) on major transactions, such as a change of control, which removes the company completely from the corporate control market. See generally Pezard, supra note 53.

209 See Loi No. 66-537 du 24 juillet 1966, art. 160.

210 See ibid. art. 217. Unlike the case for U.S. companies, French companies cannot repurchase their shares as an alternative way of returning cash to shareholders (instead of through dividends) or as a way of changing their capital structure when debt financing is cheaper than equity financing. See Richard A. Brealey & Stewart C. Myers, *Principles of Corporate Finance*, pp. 373-374 (4th ed., 1991) (discussing finance reasons for share repurchase). If the shareholders agree, a French company can repurchase its shares to "stabilize" its share price, see art. 217-2, but it cannot hold more than 10 per cent of its own capital and such "treasury" shares have no voting or dividend rights, see art. 217-3. Senator Marini recommends expanding the ability of French companies to repurchase shares, as does an organization of French company management. See Marini Report, supra note 3, p. 62; Conseil National du Patronat Français, Propositions de Modifications du Cadre Législatif et Réglementaire du Rachat Par Une Société de Ses Propres Actions (fiche No. 1, Sept. 25, 1996). Yet neither

having subsidiaries hold a company's shares (*auto-contrôle*) for defensive purposes,[211] although shares can be sold to employees, who are generally favourable to management and hostile to outsiders threatening a restructuring. A company cannot grant defensive "lock-up" options on its assets, generally either directly or indirectly.[212] While warrants and other special preferred shares may be placed in the hands of friendly parties, it is questionable whether the kinds of poison pills permitting a bargain purchase of a target or an acquiror's shares would be permitted under French corporate law.[213]

B. French Procedural Regulation of a Tender Offer

French tender offer procedures demonstrate both the restrictions and flexibility of French law. If a person (or persons acting in concert) acquires (directly or indirectly) more than 30 per cent of the votes of a listed company, he or she must make a public offer for the remaining shares (with some exceptions).[214] The rule (designed to comply with an earlier version of the EU's proposed Thirteenth Directive) protects minority shareholders if a person assumes control gradually through market purchases or all at once by a purchase of a control block.[215] From the perspective of protecting capital market shareholders, the rule makes particular sense in a capitalism (such as that of France) where these investors co-exist with, and are usually at the mercy of, controlling shareholders or organized groups of shareholders, for it gives capital market investors an exit upon a change in control. In a similar vein, the CMF may authorize a person (or persons) who has obtained more than 50 per cent of the voting rights or shares to purchase the remaining shares by holding itself ready for a set period of time to acquire any shares tendered on the market.[216] Both these procedures, however, discourage control changes, and the monitoring of management such changes promote, by making them more expensive to bidders than, say, a tender offer simply for majority control of a company.[217]

cont.

Senator Marini nor the CNPF addresses the anti-takeover implications (e.g. defensive use of the repurchase by company management to reduce number of outstanding shares) of their proposals.

211 See Schoen, supra note 80, p. 118.

212 See ibid., p. 122.

213 See ibid., pp. 131-133. If a French board has already received from the shareholders the delegated authority to issue new shares, it may undertake such issuances (to a friendly party) as a takeover defense. See Tunc, supra note 197, p. 181.

214 CMF Règlement Général, Article 5-4-1. Under Article 5-4-3, an acquiror taking control of a company that holds more than one-third of the capital or votes of a listed company must make a bid for the listed company, provided that this holding represents "une part essentielle" of the assets of the acquired company. The mandatory bid procedure also applies to a greater than one-third shareholder that increases its holding by an additional 2 per cent in a period less than a year.

215 Before 1992, a bidder passing this threshold had to make an offer for only two-thirds of the shares. See Schoen, supra note 80, pp. 81-83.

216 See ibid., pp. 99-103.

217 Cf., John C. Coffee, Jr., "Liquidity versus Control: The Institutional Investor as Corporate Monitor", 91 Colum. L. Rev., pp. 1277, 1316 (1991). Professor Wymeersch argues that such "mandatory bid" procedures are not as capital market shareholder friendly as they seem. See Eddy Wymeersch, "The Mandatory Bid: A Critical View", in *European Takeovers: Law and Practice*, p. 351 (Klaus J. Hopt & Eddy Wymeersch, eds., 1992). According to him, since they make a change of control potentially expensive to the bidder (which must acquire all the shares if it triggers the procedure), they actually encourage bidders to negotiate control transactions first with the existing controlling shareholder

Under another French tender offer procedure, a party may launch a "voluntary" tender offer for the shares of a company, but, again, the offer must be for all of the shares.[218] Subject to the CMF's approval, the bidder can condition the offer upon receiving at least a set percentage of shares (e.g. enough to give it the majority of the votes). Since a tender offer for less than all of the shares of a company is often viewed by the French market, and by market authorities, as coercive of capital market shareholders, as a practical matter it may not matter from the offeror's perspective that it must bid for all the shares, even if it does not expect to acquire all of them.[219]

French regulation also affects tender offer price and may thereby benefit capital market shareholders because, when coupled with the rule regarding an all-shares offer, it deters low-priced, coercive bids. It is difficult, however, to see the need for an "official" substantive review of price, so long as the all-shares requirement exists, for a successful tender offer usually involves giving shareholders a premium to market price. The review may make sense where a public tender offer follows a transfer of a controlling block because it ensures that, in this potentially coercive "freeze-out" situation, some independent body reviews whether capital market investors obtain the "fair price" for their shares.[220] The CMF conducts the price review and examines obvious evaluative measures (premium to market price, asset price, p/e ratio, etc.).[221] Whether this price review in fact hinders tender offers in France depends upon how restrictively the CMF applies the regulation.

Aside from price review, French tender offer regulation ensures that the capital market investor receive information about the bid and the bidder and time to consider the offer. Through a bank or banks acting on its behalf, a bidder presents a *dossier* to the CMF that describes, among other things, its purpose in making the offer, its existing shareholding in the target, any share minimum that must be tendered and the price offered and a justification thereof.[222] The CMF reviews the offer for five business days and can require modifications to it or refuse it altogether. At the same time that the CMF is conducting its review, a bank acting on behalf of the bidder must file a draft prospectus (*note d'information*) with the COB that includes such information as the bidder's identity, its intentions as to the company's future operation and listing for the next 12 months, the price offered, financing for the offer, any agreements between the bidder and others regarding the acquisition, and financial information.[223] The COB may demand supplemental information, disapprove of the prospectus altogether (which it rarely does) or even give its own views on the offer, which must be included in

cont.

(which is generally present in French public companies), and the bidder and such shareholder may structure the transaction in a way that eliminates the need for a mandatory bid or that benefits them at the expense of minority shareholders in the target. In other words, the mandatory bid requirement discourages hostile changes of control that occur through the market. See ibid., pp. 360-364.

218 See CMF Règlement Général, Art. 5-2-2.

219 French regulation also requires that a voluntary tender offer be for all "titres donnant accès au capital ou au droits de vote" and thus include preferred and convertible shares.

220 In the "garantie de cours" (i.e. where a majority shareholder stands ready to purchase all shares tendered on the market), the bidder must generally offer the same price to public shareholders as it paid in purchasing a control block. See Schoen, supra note 80, p. 101.

221 See CMF Règlement Général, Art. 5-2-7. See also Schoen, supra note 80, pp. 83-84.

222 See CMF Règlement Général, Art. 5-2-5.

223 See COB Règlement No. 89-03, Art. 7.

the prospectus.[224] Once the prospectus is approved, the bidder sends it to the target company and publishes it in a financial paper (unless, in this latter case, all the company's shareholders hold shares in registered form, in which case the prospectus is simply sent to all of them).[225] Upon receiving the bidder's prospectus, the target must file its own prospectus with the COB describing, among other things, the shareholding structure of the company both at the time of filing and a year earlier, any agreements it has with respect to the offer and the board's views on the offer (as well as minority views of the board, if any), and financial statements.[226] This prospectus must be made public in the same manner as the bidder's. Both the bidder and the company must update their prospectuses if the information presented therein becomes materially inaccurate.

Shareholders have 20 business days in which to decide whether to accept an offer (they can withdraw their tenders at any time before the end of the offering period). If a competing bidder wants to make a tender offer, it must do so at least five business days before the close of the first offer.[227] Upon this new bid, any tenders to the original offer become void, and shareholders have until the end of the second bid to decide whether to accept either offer, or none. In fact, in response to a competing offer, the original bidder must announce its intention either to maintain its bid, withdraw or increase its offer.[228] More importantly, a competing bid must be at least 2 per cent over the initial bid; and any response to it must involve an additional 2 per cent increase over its bid (and so on).[229]

French market authorities generally take the view that bidders must have equal chances to compete and disfavour extreme management efforts either to favour one at the expense of its shareholders or to block a tender offer altogether.[230] French law strictly regulates purchases of securities by a target or bidder outside the bid and requires disclosure of any such purchases or special defensive measures or agreements.[231] It appears that lock-up options on key assets or special share option arrangements would not be acceptable under French law.[232] Management of a French company can resist a tender offer and, as noted above, it has many ways of doing so. Once a bidder appears, however, management does not have the freedom to take a "scorched earth" approach.

C. Summary

The best sign that French regulation is not a significant impediment to tender offers is that they occur with some frequency in France, although they again do not necessarily have the same change-in-control effect as would be the case for U.S. tender

[224] COB decisions are subject to the judicial review of the Paris Cour d'Appel. Décret No. 90-263 du 23 mars 1990, art. 6.
[225] See ibid., Arts. 10, 12.
[226] See ibid., Art. 11. If the transaction is a friendly one, the bidder and the target can file a joint prospectus.
[227] See CMF Règlement Général, Art. 5-2-14.
[228] See ibid., Art. 5-2-15.
[229] See ibid., Art. 5-2-24. However, a new bidder need not increase the original offer price if it meets that price while suppressing any minimum share acceptance condition.
[230] See Schoen, supra note 80, p. 131.
[231] See ibid., pp. 89-90.
[232] See ibid., pp. 128, 131-33.

offers.[233] In fact, if French companies draw in more capital market shareholders and if the networks of company cross-shareholdings diminish in importance, there could be a rise in this form of restructuring and its accompanying disciplining of management. In such an event, shareholders are adequately protected by current French law, and, if abuses develop, the CMF and the COB have the power to increase their review of the transactions.

If, however, hostile tender offers increase in France, management may begin to oppose them. In fact, management in companies without a dominant shareholder may take such action if its other defences, such as the *noyaux durs* and continued State ownership, diminish. Recently, for example, the Conseil National du Patronat Français has proposed changes to French corporate law specifically designed to enhance management's ability to resist unwanted tender offers: to request the CMF to prolong a tender offer up to 40 days to give managers the time to call an extraordinary shareholders' meeting, where shareholders could approve management strategy contrary to the offer (e.g. an asset sale, a merger with a "white knight"), and to lower the French company law declaration of share ownership and future intentions from the present 20 per cent threshold to 10 per cent.[234] It will be interesting to see whether, with such legal efforts to resist the transactions, there will be increased development in areas of French law (e.g. directors' duties in a tender offer) that have so far not received much attention and that might protect shareholders against opportunistic management resistance.

VII. CORPORATE GOVERNANCE AND SHAREHOLDER SUITS

Although imposing duties upon company directors has by itself a corporate governance impact, punishing those who fail to fulfill their duties helps ensure that directors take them seriously. Similarly, mandatory disclosure has the corporate governance effect of correcting the informational disadvantage of dispersed investors if it is enforced. Shareholder legal action against the board and managers constitutes an enforcement mechanism for board duties and company disclosure. In the eyes of many Europeans, this monitoring characterizes market capitalism: litigation against companies and their agents has become so prevalent in the Anglo-Saxon world that board members and managers cannot take any business action, or make any statement about company prospects, without running the risk of incurring numerous suits that are costly and time-consuming to defend and that make company management overly cautious in the future. Yet shareholder suits against management are possible under French law.

[233] See ibid., pp. 3-16 (describing the recent history of French securities markets, which in effect centres around tender offers).

[234] See, e.g. Conseil National du Patronat Français, Déroulement des Offres Publiques (le 10 octobre 1996; fiche No. 2, sept. 25, 1996; fiche No. 3, sept. 25, 1996) (discussing these proposals). See als Valuet, supra note 96, at p. 708 (discussing proposal to allow French companies to identify non-French shareholders as partly justified by takeover concerns). Another form of politically-motivated resistance to tender offers in France is the promulgation of laws, such as the privatization law allowing for the "golden share", that make it difficult for non-EU members to acquire "sensitive" French companies. Since many potential bidders for French companies may come from outside France, management may play upon nationalist feelings to push for the enactment of other laws impeding or preventing tender offers by foreigners.

A. The French "Derivative" Lawsuit

Directors owe duties to the corporation, which is a separate legal personality, and only indirectly to shareholders. Any violation of these duties harms the corporation, and thus, again indirectly, the shareholders. In enforcing the director obligations, therefore, shareholders are really acting on the corporation's behalf against *its* agents. Their lawsuit is thus derivative, i.e. it derives from the corporation's right to sue.[235]

From this basic concept of a derivative shareholder right of action arises the potential procedural complexity of the lawsuit, which also raises difficult substantive issues that have corporate governance implications.[236] Although the lawsuit "belongs" to the corporation, it often makes sense for shareholders to bring it. Since the corporation acts through its directors and managers, they are unlikely to want to sue themselves or one of their number. Some outside party is needed, and who best to pursue the directors than the residual owners of the corporation? By contrast, because the suit *is* the corporation's, the corporation through its agents should have the right, as in all litigation, to decide whether the costs of a lawsuit justify its benefits, whether, if a suit is begun, it should be pursued, and how far, and whether other corrective action is more appropriate. As in other "problem" situations, corporate solutions less costly than litigation could address any conflict of interest in the board's decision on a derivative lawsuit. Since any recovery from a lawsuit accrues to the corporation, moreover, and since any individual shareholder generally receives (again indirectly) only a small part of such recovery, he or she has little economic incentive to bring the suit.[237] Outsiders to the corporation, such as lawyers specializing in such actions, may thus be the driving force behind many of these suits.

The French "derivative" lawsuit exists without much of (or any debate concerning) procedural complexities. The duties of French directors and officers are owed to the corporation as such, and, since any violation directly harms the corporation, its representatives (i.e. the directors) should bring the lawsuit. And, in fact, the lawsuit belongs to the directors under French law.[238] Yet French law allows a shareholder or group of shareholders to bring a lawsuit in the company's name (*l'action sociale* ut singuli).[239] Only current shareholders can bring the lawsuit, which will not be dismissed if the requisite group of shareholders loses the statutory minimum before the end of the litigation.[240] There are restrictions on this collective shareholder lawsuit, however, some of which restrict its effectiveness for capital market shareholders. In general, for share-

[235] When directors harm shareholders "directly" (e.g. by abusing minority shareholders), shareholders have a direct, not a derivative, lawsuit. The distinction is not always easy to draw. See 2 *Principles of Corporate Governance*, supra note 99, pp. 18-20 (discussing distinction with examples of each). The following discussion focuses on the derivative suit, but direct lawsuits clearly have a corporate governance impact as well (see Section VIIB, infra).

[236] For a general discussion of these issues, see Klein & Coffee, supra note 101, at pp. 195-201; 2 *Principles of Corporate Governance*, supra note 99, pp. 4-9.

[237] A large shareholder would have more incentive because he or she would capture more of the gains. An argument can also be made that, if the derivative suit improves corporate governance in general because it puts directors in other firms on notice that the threat of a lawsuit is real, gains to shareholders cannot be limited to the recovery of damages for a specific violation in a firm, but extend to the improvement in corporate governance in all firms. See, e.g. Klein & Coffee, supra note 101, p. 200.

[238] See Cozian & Viandier, supra note 90, p. 283.

[239] See Loi No. 66-537 du 24 juillet 1966, art. 245.

[240] See ibid.

holders to act, they must represent at least 5 per cent of the company's share capital, a percentage that is gradually reduced as the company's capital increases over FF 5 million.[241] It is not clear that a successful prosecution or settlement allows recovery of legal expenses by the prosecuting shareholder or shareholders.

French law does not give directors much control of the derivative suit nor entitle their views to any special status before the court hearing the lawsuit. Shareholders must join the corporation as a necessary prosecuting party in the suit, but it is not clear that directors can refuse a shareholder request that the company be a plaintiff.[242] Directors cannot dismiss a derivative suit, once it has begun. French law, in fact, declares invalid any clause in a company's articles of association requiring a prior resolution of the shareholders to bring a derivative action (or completely renouncing their right ever to bring this kind of action) and also states that the shareholders cannot vote to extinguish a lawsuit.[243]

Under French law, moreover, there are no legal features as "demand" and "demand excused," which in the U.S. give directors considerable power to dismiss derivative complaints that they disfavour.[244] This may simply show that the derivative lawsuit has not so far been widely used against French directors or officers. If, however, shareholders begin to use this instrument more vigorously to punish management, managers and directors might lobby for statutory or judicial relief against the suits, which could take the form of giving them more control over the actions through such devices as the "demand" requirement.

B. The French "Direct" Shareholder Lawsuit

A French shareholder also has the right to bring a direct lawsuit, and shareholders can act together in prosecuting this suit.[245] In the direct action,[246] a shareholder could make a complaint that he or she was individually harmed by the failure of board members (and others in the company) to provide the accurate disclosure of a company's financial position mandated by French company law (a cause of action not unlike a securities suit under U.S. section 10(b) of the Exchange Act).[247] If numerous shareholders were similarly harmed, they could delegate to one or more of them, the right (*mandat*) to act on their behalf before the courts, provided that the "main plaintiff" receive an authorization from each shareholder in writing that identified the mandating shareholder and the number of shares that he or she possessed.[248] Again, the costly nature of such suits undermines their effectiveness.

241 See Décret No. 67-236 du 23 mars 1967, art. 200 (amended by Décret No. 88-56 du 19 janvier 1988).
242 See Décret No. 67-236 du 23 mars 1967, art. 201.
243 See Loi No. 66-537 du 24 juillet 1966, art. 246.
244 Generally, under U.S. corporate law, a shareholder must make "demand" on the board to see if it wants to proceed with the lawsuit, unless the demand can be "excused" (e.g. when the board is involved in the challenged transaction). In the latter case, if demand is excused and the shareholder proceeds with the suit, the board still may make a recommendation to the court concerning the suit, which, if the recommendation is done properly (through a committee of independent directors), is generally entitled to considerable deference. See 2 *Principles of Corporate Governance*, supra note 99, p. 55 (for discussion of complexity of the demand requirements and jurisprudence thereunder).
245 They can also act collectively in prosecuting the French "derivative" suit.
246 See Loi No. 66-537 du 24 juillet 1966, art. 245.
247 See Schoen, supra note 80, at p. 187.
248 See Décret No. 67-236 du 23 mars 1967, art. 199 (added by Décret No. 88-56 du 19 janvier 1988).

C. Protection Against Lawsuits For Directors

The above picture is not complete without a consideration of who pays any monetary award assessed against an offending manager or director. If directors and managers do not bear the financial burden of monetary penalties, the corporate governance impact of the legal duties imposed upon them is somewhat undermined (yet a successful lawsuit against a director may, for example, carry a "reputational" penalty even if he or she suffers no financial loss). The issue involves balancing different corporate governance goals. If financial penalties against management are too draconian, capable persons may decline to accept director or officer's positions, to take necessary risks, or to make useful disclosure, all of which could hurt the operation and market evaluation of a business and would thus produce *negative* corporate governance effects.

One possible outcome is for corporate law to allow a corporation to indemnify, and/or to purchase insurance for, its directors and officers, when these individuals have made honest mistakes of judgment, but not when they have engaged in intentional misbehaviour and self-serving transactions. Persons would not want to occupy corporate positions unless individual directors or officers were protected in situations where they had not gained personally and had simply committed errors of judgment, even if somewhat egregious ones. A judgment or large settlement could seriously impair or wipe out the assets of even a wealthy individual. With insurance, moreover, a corporation, and indirectly its shareholders, do not have to bear all the costs of its officers and directors' negligence, because the risk of misfeasance is spread among all corporations as a cost of doing business.

Directors and officers in France can obtain insurance policies for most civil penalties assessed against them, except for those arising from fraudulent conduct or from intentional misbehaviour.[249] Yet there seem to be no provisions under French law that allow a company to indemnify directors for adverse judgments, expenses of lawsuits or settlements. This result is not surprising. If there have been relatively few lawsuits in France from capital market shareholders, because there were few such shareholders and large controlling shareholders had other ways of disciplining management, there would not have been much need for protection of management and directors against lawsuits and large judgment awards.

D. Summary

The existence of collective direct shareholder suits, the constraints on the board's ability to dismiss derivative suits and the limited protection of directors from significant monetary penalties suggest that at least the letter of French law gives complaining shareholders some power to prosecute lawsuits against directors and management in France. Yet these lawsuits are infrequent and thus have not had much corporate governance effect, whether positive or negative. This lack of use may be partly due to the shareholder group number restriction and the uncertainty as to recovery of plaintiffs' expenses. No group of French lawyers, moreover, appears to exist who specializes in such lawsuits and who would thus have an economic incentive to bring them *and* to lobby for legal developments that would make them easier

[249] See Gibirila, supra note 113, p. 433.

(i.e. less costly) to pursue. It is not entirely clear what explains this social phenomenon, although the "closed" nature of the French financial community and business lawyers and the accompanying fear of social exclusion and ostracism from undertaking an activity not favoured by the "group" may offer some justification.[250] Where group shareholder action has emerged in France, it has been in associations of small shareholders that act on their own behalf and that have not developed a large "plaintiff's bar" to support them.[251]

The situation may be changing, however. There are a few lawyers in the French financial and legal community, generally with foreign training, who are beginning to experiment more with the legal possibilities of French corporate law for collective action purposes.[252] While creating an "industry" that benefits themselves (much the same way that U.S. plaintiffs lawyers do), they appear so far to limit their representation to large minority shareholders and not to stray from the accepted norms of appropriate behaviour in the French business and business legal community. It remains to be seen whether with success and with the entry of more non-French investors (whom these new lawyers/businessmen(women) also represent) in the capital of French companies, these individuals will further develop lawsuits, and related legal techniques, as an important corporate governance device.[253]

If, moreover, French corporate law is reformed in accordance with the suggestions of Senator Marini, there may well be more shareholder suits. In one respect, his reform proposal is hostile to collective shareholder legal action because he recommends against adoption in France of the "class action" mechanism where an attorney can receive a contingency fee for representing a large group of similarly situated shareholders, if the lawsuit is successful.[254] He believes, however, that the monitoring of directors and management by criminal sanctions (one of the main forms of oversight in France) must give way to direct shareholder action, including through shareholder lawsuits.[255] He even recommends that judges receive more training in economics and finance because of the likelihood that (if the reform occurs) they will hear more cases involving shareholder/management disputes.[256] One could criticize Senator Marini's lack of receptivity to collective shareholder action in lawsuits (he

250 In the U.S., it is probably fair to say that the plaintiffs' bar that specialized in such suits and many of the legislators and judges who favoured their legal development came at first from ethnic groups (e.g. Jews, Italians) that were traditionally excluded from other financial work. Cf., Ronen Shamir, *Managing Legal Uncertainty: Elite Lawyers in the New Deal* (1995). The lack of a similar bar in France may owe something to the absence of a clearly defined "outcast" group among the business bar that needs to find a source of livelihood.

251 One thinks here of the *Association nationale des actionnaires français* and the *Association de défense des intérêts des actionnaires minoritaires.*

252 The most well-known of this small group would be Sophie l'Hélias of Franklin Global Investments, a bilingual lawyer with both French and U.S. legal and business school training. See "Fair shares", *The Economist*, 15 Feb. 1997, p. 65 (discussing her activity). There is also Déminor (a Belgian investment house) with which she was previously associated.

253 See generally Fanto, supra note 2, pp. 22-28.

254 See Marini Report, supra note 3, p. 96 . He declines to recommend adoption of the contingency fee arrangement in France because of the problems that have appeared with it in the U.S.

255 See ibid., p. 87.

256 See ibid., p. 124. This chapter has mentioned only in passing the French court system and its availability to hear commercial law disputes. Suffice it to say that basic shareholder disputes are heard by a *Tribunal de Commerce*, with the possibility of appeal to the Cour d'Appel and ultimately to the Cour de cassation. See generally Christian Dadomo & Susan Farran, *The French Legal System*, pp. 60-63, 82-89 (2nd ed., 1996).

is favourable to such collective action in other contexts, such as voting) because capital market shareholders must join together in these actions for economic reasons. Yet the overall thrust of his proposal is to facilitate shareholder suits.

It is important to mention here the role of French criminal law in monitoring corporate agents. As Senator Marini has observed, French corporate law is extremely criminalized: a director's violations of duties may well subject him or her to criminal penalties.[257] This made sense with State ownership and control of enterprises, for violation of almost any corporate law could conceivably implicate State interests and justify a criminal penalty.[258] And criminal penalities are one of the major ways in which the State punished violations by its agents who directed and managed its corporations. Yet, with privatization and the increase of capital market shareholders in France, it is necessary to distinguish those obligations that a civil action by interested parties could appropriately enforce and the few that implicate societal interests in such a way as to demand criminal sanctions. This is a delicate reform in France because numerous management abuses in French companies might suggest a continuing need for criminal actions[259] and – what might in fact explain these abuses – because new means of controlling corporate agents have not yet been fully put in place. The Marini Report recommends limiting the scope of criminal sanctions to serious intentional and fraudulent violations of corporate law (e.g. those involving misstating company accounts, abuses in issuing stock, serious hindrance of shareholders' information and voting rights, self-interested transactions) and developing civil actions for the parties harmed by other management and director failures to fulfill legal obligations.[260] If the reform becomes law, a new era may begin for French shareholder lawsuits.

VIII. CONCLUSION

This chapter has considered how well French legal policy-makers have adapted French corporate law to promote market capitalism, i.e. whether it addresses the "weak" position of capital market shareholders. Its general conclusion is that, in many cases, French law provides protection for these shareholders, but that the law is often of recent origin or is not yet adequately developed and is rarely used. This state of affairs makes sense, for market capitalism, while not new in France, has only recently become more important as the State abandons its position in the capital of major corporations. The growing corporate governance role of French law is most

[257] For a brief summary of financial and corporate crimes, see Claude Ducouloux-Favard, *Délits financiers et boursiers, Dictionnaire Permanent Epargne et Produits Financiers*, feuillets 53 (15 mars 1995).

[258] See Bernard Bouloc, "Le droit pénal des sociétés", in *La Modernisation du Droit des Sociétés: Premières réflexions sur le Rapport Marini*, pp. 69, 69-73 (Jean-Jacques Daigre, éd., 1996) (describing the evolution of the criminalization of French corporate law, which owed much to the State's responses to scandals concerning public companies).

[259] See "France: Who's next?", *The Economist*, 13 July 1996, p. 48 (discussing French company executives and politicians subject to criminal proceedings).

[260] See Marini Report, supra note 3, pp. 106-110. Professor Bouloc cautions that the Marini Report's effort to decriminalize corporate law will be difficult since, even if statutory criminal violations are eliminated, there remain violations under criminal law based upon common law. See Bouloc, supra note 260, pp. 73-78.

visible in the area of securities laws where, for the past two decades, French legal policy-makers have been trying to provide French capital market investors with the kinds of protection to which investors in traditional capital market systems are accustomed. As French capital-raising places more emphasis on stock market funding and as French corporate governance no longer involves State monitoring of managers, French corporate and securities law will play a more critical role in French corporate governance than it has done previously. Even if family ownership, in the absence of the State, assumes a larger role in France, family firms still need to turn to capital market investors for additional financing and thus have to ensure that the corporate governance system in place protects these investors.

One could hardly talk about legal reform to French corporate governance without discussing the Viénot Report, which has occasionally been cited in this chapter. The Report shows that, in the minds of some important French business and legal practitioners, French corporate law must be used more to counter the weakness of capital market shareholders in the face of management power. Nearly all of the report's recommendations, which others have discussed and evaluated,[261] have this purpose. Although not suggesting any concrete legal reforms to French law, the Report attempts to reinvigorate the board of directors through informal recommendations by making its members take their duties more seriously, an orientation that makes sense in a new finance situation where capital market investors must rely upon the board to protect their interests. The Report thus recommends that all boards have at least two independent members (who, since they have no company ties or other links with the company, would not be under management's influence), that there be special board committees dealing with such critical subjects as audit, remuneration, and board nomination (all that go to the heart of supervision of management and its conduct of a company and that should thus have some independent director membership), and that board members not only take seriously their legal duties (to be informed about company matters and to avoid conflicts of interest), but they also be in a better position to fulfill them (e.g. have enhanced rights of access to company information). The Report urges boards to provide more information about their activity and the company's operations to shareholders and to involve shareholders more in critical company decisions – recommendations designed to improve the monitoring ability of capital market investors themselves.

Yet the Report is somewhat schizophrenic. From the perspective of market capitalism, improvements to board structure and behaviour are designed to enhance the monitoring of managers by the primary agents working for the shareholders – the directors – and thus to curb management power and prevent its inevitable domination of the board. Nowhere, however, does the Report specifically acknowledge this purpose and logic or explain that its reforms are based upon this agency framework. Rather, the Report emphasizes that French company law is founded upon a different theoretical basis, i.e. that the board serves company, not shareholder, interests.[262]

[261] See, e.g. Daniel Hurstel & Thomas Bieder, "Est-il urgent et indispensable de réformer le droit des sociétés au nom de la 'corporate governance'?", Rev. Soc., p. 633 (oct.-déc. 1995); Alice Pezard, "À propos du Rapport Viénot sur le gouvernement d'entreprise", in *Rapport Moral sur l'Argent dans le Monde 1996*, p. 197 (1996).

[262] See Viénot Report, supra note 3, p. 2 ("This framework is rooted in a principle which the Committee considers essential, namely that whatever a board's membership and procedures may be, its members collectively represent all shareholders and it must at all times put the company's interests first.")

From an agency perspective of countering management power, this justification for decision-making simply invites managers to "divide and conquer": rather than serving company interests (whatever they are), executives can play various company constituents (e.g. creditors, employees, shareholders) off against one another to maintain their own primacy. One is left wondering, therefore, about the purpose behind the "voluntary" reforms proposed by the Report, if, as it appears, the reforms do not have this agency justification.

In the Report the recommendations are presented as "clarifying" the flexibility of French company law and board structure for investors unfamiliar with them and as improving board behaviour in a minor way.[263] From a cynical perspective, the Report could be seen as acknowledging the power of international, primarily Anglo-Saxon institutional investors (it was released in French and in *English*) without recommending any fundamental changes to the French system.[264] If, moreover, the State continues to influence significantly large firms or if many firms fall under family control, recommendations to enhance capital market investor power are likely to be muted. A more charitable view of the Report's approach is that it advocates informal corporate governance reforms because its drafters realized that change in this area (which may lead to serious restructuring of French industry) is likely to be a highly charged political subject. And, from an agency perspective, a complete U.S.-style system of corporate governance is not needed where counterweights to management (e.g. families and continued State influence) exist.

Any French legal reform promoting a corporate governance protective of capital market investors requires a serious reconsideration of the foundations of French corporate and securities law and of French corporate governance in general. This is not to say that French law is now inflexible, or that it requires major changes to accommodate market capitalism, whose growth in France it is clearly facilitating. Like the drafters of the Viénot Report, for example, French corporate law scholars have shown that this law can embrace with little difficulty many of the reforms (e.g. use of independent directors, specialized board committees) proposed in Anglo-Saxon countries to improve the monitoring ability of direc-

cont.

(emphasis in original). Professor Alain Couret explains well this intellectual foundation of French company law. See Alain Couret, "Chronique: Le gouvernement d'entreprise: la corporate governance", 22 *Recueil Dalloz Sirey*, pp. 163, 165 (1995).

263 See Viénot Report, supra note 3, p. 1 ("Privatization and the growing presence of non-resident investors on the Paris stock market has led to the rapid emergence of a new type of shareholder with little knowledge of the rules and practices applied by the boards of directors of listed companies in France. Such shareholders have naturally sought clarification.").

264 A cynic might also suggest that, since U.S. scholars and practitioners produced their "Principles of Corporate Governance" and their U.K. counterparts their "Cadbury report," the French felt obligated to do the same, without acknowledging that they were simply following an Anglo-Saxon model (thus, the briefness of the Viénot Report). Olivier Pastré observes that the drafters of the Viénot Report were responding to the concerns of non-French institutional investors. See Pastré, supra note 58, p. 203.

The Commission des Opérations de Bourse has done much to publicize in France U.S. and U.K. corporate governance developments. See, e.g. Marie-Noëlle Dompé & Alain Dorison, "Entretiens de la COB", Jeudi Novembre 1994: "Les Pouvoirs dans l'Entreprise" (1994); Bulletin COB, octobre, décembre (1994) (discussing ALI Principles and Cadbury report). See also André Tunc, "Le governement des sociétés anonymes: le mouvement de réforme aux États-Unis et au Royaume-Uni", R. I. D. C., p. 59 (No. 1, 1994).

tors.[265] Yet without a reconsideration, and possibly a reformulation, of the basis of the law, any reforms will work at cross-purposes with other sections of the corporate code. If more French corporate governance disputes come to court, judges will also have considerable difficulty in developing a jurisprudence out of statutory provisions that have no unified intellectual perspective.[266]

This chapter has referred to Senator Marini's proposal on the reform of French corporate law.[267] More important than the specific proposals in the Report is the overall spirit of the proposed reform that clearly supports market capitalism. The Report observes that Anglo-Saxon and German legal traditions, respectively, have historically influenced French corporate law (perhaps, as France turned to one or the other as a political ally).[268] The German influence prevailed in the major 1966 reform of French corporate law, and this result adversely affected the usefulness of French corporate law for business in current economic circumstances.[269] That influence supported the "institutional" nature of the corporation (particularly the large corporation), which in turn promoted the State ownership and control of large enterprises that typified the postwar years and which privileged social purposes and other constituencies in an enterprise over its shareholders. According to the Report, this view of the corporation as an institution is an example of the "Statist" character of, and thus rigidity in, legal obligations and relationships arising under French corporate law: it observes that this law "demeure contraignant, très fortement imprégné d'ordre public."[270]

The Report argues that French corporate law must move away from this Statist approach to return to an approach compatible with the Anglo-Saxon perspective. It explains that enterprise adaptability to current economic circumstances demands this transformation. The institutional or Statist approach to corporate law no longer works well (i.e. does not contribute to such adaptability) as the State recedes from its commanding position in the economy and the capital of large corporations. Not only, because of the rigidity of Statist corporate law, can enterprises not adapt readily to changing economic circumstances, but managerial agents, no longer checked by State controls and increasingly operating in market capitalism, can now use the "*intérêt social*" strategically to pursue their own interests, generally at the shareholders' expense.[271] These adverse effects of the Statist approach have serious consequences because business competition in France is part of the global product and capital market competition, because French companies must compete for investors and because law

265 See, e.g. Paul Le Cannu, "Légitimité du pouvoir et efficacité du contrôle dans les sociétés par actions", Bulletin Joly 637 (juillet 1995); Nathalie Dion, "Corporate governance et sociétés françaises", *Édit. du Juris-Classeur, Dr. des Sociétés* 8 (juillet-août 1995).

266 See Pastré, supra note 58, p. 205 (noting the increased power of judges in French corporate governance and their need for a more sustained economic formation).

267 See Marini Report, supra note 3. Many of the reforms proposed by Senator Marini have been suggested by other commissions or groups studying French corporate law. See ibid., p. 6 (listing previous reform suggestions). See also Conseil National du Patronat Français, *Pour Une Réforme en Profondeur du Droit des Sociétés* (juillet 1996 No. 3) (proposing many corporate law reforms that the Marini Report adopted). Such reforms are unlikely to proceed quickly, however, now that a Socialist majority has taken control of the French parliament.

268 This is a common observation in French business and legal circles. See, e.g. Albert, supra note 59, pp. 263-287 (discussing France as something of a battleground between the German and Anglo-Saxon approaches to company management).

269 See Marini Report, supra note 3, p. 5.

270 See ibid., p. 18.

271 See ibid., pp. 8-9.

plays a role in this competition, particularly by encouraging capital market investing. If, therefore, corporate law handicaps French enterprises, especially in their capital raising, they, and France, will suffer in the global competition.[272]

The main purposes of the Report are, therefore, to simplify French corporate law (i.e. to eliminate its numerous rigidities and formalities that are costly to enterprises and that owe their origin to the Statist approach), to give businesses more choice in their use of the corporate form and to enhance shareholder rights. In other words, the turn towards an Anglo-Saxon model means making French corporate law contractual, flexible and friendly to capital market investors.[273] Parties should find in corporate law possibilities of legal relationships that they can adjust to their circumstances, which will in turn enable them to adapt their business relations (e.g. shareholder-manager relations) better to the economic situation facing them. This approach, which is well-known to U.S. business law scholars,[274] is to consider corporate law as enabling, that is, as providing default rules for a contract, i.e. that between shareholders and their agents, and as occasionally mandatory where it needs to resolve certain structural abuses in contractual relationships.[275] In its approach, the Report looks to laws in other countries (particularly Anglo-Saxon ones), especially on basic shareholder/management relations (i.e. corporate governance). The French use of the contractual approach makes sense because Anglo-Saxon investors are increasingly present in the capital of French companies (holding approximately one-third of the capital) and are familiar with it.[276]

[272] See ibid., p. 17 (emphasis in original):

> "Par ailleurs, on ne peut méconnaître que la compétition économique met également en concurrence les systèmes juridiques. De ce point de vue, la lourdeur et les rigidités du droit français des sociétés constituent un handicap. Parmi les éléments pris en considération dans le choix du pays d'accueil d'une société commerciale, nul doute que la faculté d'adaptation de l'instrument juridique aux besoins spécifiques de l'entreprise et aux modifications de l'environnement économique et social soit un facteur important."
>
> "Moreover, one should not fail to recognize that economic competition also places into competition legal systems. From this perspective, the heaviness and rigidity of French law constitutes a handicap. Among the elements taken into account in the choice of a country of location for a business, there is no doubt that the ability of adaptation of its legal system to the specific needs of the business and to changes in the economic and social environment would be an important factor."

[273] See ibid., p. 17 ("Ces considérations militent en faveur de sa simplification et, plus encore, de sa contractualisation. Mais ce qui justifie fondamentalement cette démarche, c'est le constat de la très grande diversité des projets des créateurs d'entreprise et de leurs besoins.") (emphasis in original) ("these considerations argue in favour of its simplification and, even more, of its contractualization. But what fundamentally justifies this approach is the realization of the very great diversity of projects of entrepreneurs and of their interests.").

[274] See generally Easterbrook & Fischel, supra note 122, pp. 1-39.

[275] See Marini Report, supra note 3, p. 9 ("En effet, la société est d'abord une technique d'organisation juridique des entreprises. Celles-ci doivent pouvoir trouver dans le droit non pas des entraves, mais les outils nécessaires à leur développement. La loi doit donc mettre à leur disposition des formes sociales aussi souples que possible tout en garantissant la sécurité juridique des salariés, des créanciers et des clients. Son rôle est moins d'interdire que de permettre.")

("In effect, the corporation is first a technique of legal organization of businesses. They must be able to find in the law, not road blocks, but the tools necessary for their development. The law must therefore put at their disposition business forms as flexible as possible while all the time protecting the legal status of employees, creditors and clients. Its role is less to prohibit than to permit.").

[276] See ibid., p. 6.

Much more than the Viénot Report, therefore, Senator Marini offers a reconceptualization of French corporate law that is sensitive to, and explicitly acknowledges, changing corporate governance in France and the changing nature of agency problems in that country's large enterprises. Yet any reformulation of French corporate law may, and will likely, not result in a wholesale adoption of an Anglo-American style market capitalism. For a reformulation, which involves a reconsideration, of the foundations and function of French corporate law and corporate governance may reveal the historical "weight" of some current French corporate governance practices that prevents them from being easily changed. As some have observed,[277] strong management in French companies has historically served purposes, such as providing a necessary alternative to an ineffectual board or to one dominated by conflicting interests. That a corporate board primarily focuses on company interests has not only a powerful intellectual foundation in the institutional theory of a corporation, but, since it also allows the board to consider interests other than those of shareholders, it could be (and has been) used in particular economic circumstances to promote social harmony. As noted earlier,[278] the State has been involved in large enterprises, and the *noyaux durs* organized around financial institutions may simply be an indirect continuation of this phenomena. And family capitalism, including on a large scale, has been and remains important (a phenomenon that Senator Marini does not directly address). A reaffirmation of "other" capitalisms than market capitalism and their continued existence in French economic life may undermine, or limit, legal reforms useful for capital market shareholders.

Legal reform relating to French corporate governance is therefore daunting, not only because French corporate governance is rapidly evolving, but also because few studies exist on the nature of this system and its evolution. In such circumstances, Olivier Pastré's admonition that a thorough *national* analysis of French corporate governance is needed and that this analysis must involve different disciplines and approaches rings true.[279] Only this kind of reflection can intelligently guide legal reform. The analysis will not be easy, not only because of its complexity, but also because it will bring to the forefront competing groups, which stand to gain by the triumph of one or another form of corporate governance.[280] As in all human endeavours, whatever emerges from the analysis will be the result of compromise and the power, intellectual or other, French or non-French, of those involved in the debate. Yet without a sustained *French* public analysis and discussion, French corporate governance will still be shaped, although largely away from the public's eyes, and valuable alternatives and solutions, which might have surfaced in an open debate and might have prevailed, may well never come to light.

277 See Pastré, supra note 58, p. 204; Tunc, supra note 264, p. 72.

278 See supra Section II.

279 See Pastré, supra note 58, pp. 201-203. This is not to suggest that none of this work has been done. One has only to think of the writings (many of which have been cited herein) by Bauer, Le Cannu, Morin, Pastré, Thiveaud, Tunc, to name just a few. There is simply more work needed. See also Gérard Charreaux, éd., *Le Gouvernement des Entreprises: Corporate Governance Théories et Faits* (1997).

280 See Yves Dezalay, *Marchands de Droit: La Restructuration de l'Ordre Juridique International par les Multinationales du Droit* (1992).

2

Germany

*Rolf Birk**

I. DESCRIPTION OF THE PUBLICLY HELD PHENOMENON

A. Spread of the Publicly Held Corporation and its Economical Significance

In German corporate law, the stock corporation (*Aktiengesellschaft*, AG) and the *Gesellschaft mit beschränkter Haftung* (GmbH), which is comparable to the American close corporation, are the predominant types of business organizations. All other forms of corporations therefore can be neglected in our context. The phenomenon of corporate governance has been discussed extensively in all its aspects in recent years with respect to the stock corporation, with an emphasis on theoretical questions, i.e. mainly problems of interpretation of the existing law.

Before discussing some of the issues related to corporate governance in German law, the historical background of the law of corporations shall be described. The traditional purpose of the AG is the transformation of the savings of private households into permanently committed investment capital to secure the financing of capital intensive projects in the hands of private entrepreneurs.[1] In that respect, the AG serves to concentrate and tie capital.

The number of AGs decreased continuously between 1950 and 1985 from 2,550 to 2,141, and increased slightly between 1986 and 1990 to 2,682.[2] The number of GmbHs, the German version of a close corporation, however, is significantly higher. The GmbH was conceived as the form of organization for small to mid-sized companies where the need of capital is not so great. Further, the GmbH usually has a limited number of shareholders.[3] The significance of the GmbH is reflected by the numbers: between 1974 and 1992 it increased fourfold from 112,063 to 509,949,

* Professor of Law and Director of the Institute for Labor Law and Industrial Relations in the European Community – Universität Trier.

[1] Assmann, in: *Großkommentar zum Aktienrecht*, p. 292 (1992, Einleitung Randnr. 292).

[2] Cf. Assmann, supra note 1, pp. 294-297, 306.

[3] In 1974 the AktG was amended and has introduced the "kleine AG" (small AG) as a closed corporation. For the details see Lutter, "Das neue 'Gesetz für kleine Aktiengesellschaften und zur Deregulierung des Aktienrechts'" in: *Die Aktiengesellschaft 1994*, pp. 429 et seq.; Planck, "Kleine AG als Rechtsform – Alternative zur GmbH", in: *GmbH Rundschau 1994*, pp. 501 et seq.

© Kluwer Law International 1998

with the share capital increasing from 58,753 million DM to 231,600 million DM. The proportion AG: GmbH is 1:200. The reasons for their growth are many, and to discuss them in detail would go beyond the scope of this chapter. Therefore, I shall leave this discussion for another day.

In 1990, there were a total of 2,682 AGs with a total capital of 194,109 million DM. Of those 501, AGs with a capital stock of 69,262 million DM were listed on the stock exchange (*börsennotierte* AG). The capital stock (*Grundkapital* or *gezeichnetes Kapital*) represents the minimum of assets of a corporation as specified in the by-laws. Its purpose is to provide creditors of the corporation with a basis for credits and stock to satisfy liabilities; § 7 of the AktG provides that the capital stock of a corporation has to amount to a minimum of 100,000 DM. Only a limited number of the AGs listed on the stock exchange are so-called *Publikumsgesellschaften*, i.e. publicly held corporations. At the beginning of 1987, there were only 19 so-called *Publikums*-AGs with at least 100,000 shareholders, while 29 AGs with at least 50,000, 78 AGs with at least 10,000, 102 AGs with at least 5,000, 117 with at least 2,000 and approximately 400 AGs with at least 1,000 shareholders. At the end of 1987, shares were held as follows: approximately 20 per cent by private households, 30 per cent by companies, 14 per cent by foreigners, 11 per cent by banks, 10 per cent by insurance companies and 6 per cent by the State or public entities.

Today, the AG is the typical form of organization for large companies. A company is considered large, when its turnover amounts to billions, the workforce is over 10,000 employees and the capital stock and equity capital sums up to several million DM. In 1988, of the 100 largest German companies, 67 were organized as an AG. Among the 20 largest companies, 17 were AGs. In only 28 of the 100 largest companies, the majority of shares were owned by a large number of different shareholders (*Streubesitz*). The 100 largest companies were linked by 187 joint undertakings.

In 1988, there were personal links in 76 controlling bodies of the 100 largest companies, there were representatives of the management of other corporations belonging to this group.

From those data, one can get some understanding about the significance and structure of the AG.

B. Formation of a Publicly Held Corporation

Publicly held corporations are listed on the Stock Exchange. The formation of such a corporation is complicated and costly. It is regulated extensively in §§ 23-53 of the AktG. The act of formation of the corporation takes place in a series of steps. The incorporators are required to subscribe all the shares to pay an initial capital. When a publicly held corporation is formed, a bank has to participate in the act of formation in so far as the bank takes over the shares and sells them exclusively. It is not lawful to offer the shares directly at the time of the formation for subscription by the public.

The different steps of the procedure of formation will only be described here, but not analyzed in detail. The steps are as follows: the adoption of the by-laws, the subscription of the shares by the incorporators, the appointment of the supervisory board and auditors for the first accounting period, as well as the appointment of the board of management by the supervisory board, the making of the formation report by the incorporators, the making of the financial and non-financial contributions, the application for registration of the AG in the commercial register filed by the incorporators, the board of management and the supervisory board, the checking of the application by the competent court, and the actual registration by that court. When registered, the corporate existence of the AG begins. Once the formation process is completed, the procedure for issuing the shares and their admission to quotation follows. These procedures are regulated in detail by the *BörsenG* and the *Börsenzulassungsverordnung*.

In the case of a publicly held corporation, the shares are generally taken over by a consortium of different banks in order to then sell them through the stock exchange to the public looking for investment opportunities. The condition for those shares being admitted to trade on the stock exchange is the admission by a special commission. The admission is only granted after a prospectus which sets forth the essential facts and data necessary to assess the share is issued to inform the potential investors. The legal obligation to issue such a prospectus is imposed by § 36 of the *BörsenG* which holds the issuing corporation and banks liable for false representations made willfully or recklessly, the so-called *Prospekthaftung*.

C. Restrictions of the Transferability of Publicly Traded Shares

In exceptional cases, the transfer of shares is subject to restrictions. In general, shares are bearer shares (*Inhaberaktien*) and therefore transferable to anybody without the consent of the corporation. The transfer takes place according to the general rules for the transfer of movable property (§§ 929 et seq. of the BGB).

The transferability of shares can be conditioned in the by-laws, to be subject to the consent of the corporation: those shares are called *vinkulierte Namensaktien* (§ 68 of the AktG). If a corporation wants to place restrictions on transferability, it must be stated in the by-laws. There are no limits imposed on the kind of possible reasons to grant or to refuse the consent, but the restrictions cannot go as far as making a transfer practically impossible.

An indirect restriction of the transferability of shares can be achieved by not granting voting rights or by denying pre-emptive rights when there is an increase in stock.

D. Public Securities Market

Today the stock market is part of the capital market. Historically, the capital market was a role model for the former, but goes much beyond the securities market and therefore will not be dealt with.[4] The public securities market does not only include the trade of stock and other securities at the stock exchange but also sales outside of the stock exchange, for instance sale of securities directly from banks to their clients (over-the-counter market).

The trading of stock can take place either on the Stock Exchange or outside of it. There is no obligation to use the stock exchange to sell or buy securities. The stock exchange, however, guarantees a bigger transparency and trustworthiness. From an economic point of view, the stock exchange is still the most important market for securities. From a legal point of view, the protection of investors is clearly and unequivocally regulated by German law. There is, however, a growing influence by the directives of the European Community.

[4] Cf. Assmann, in: Assmann/ Schütze, *Handbuch des Kapitalanlagerechts*, 1990, § 1 Randnr. 1 et seq. (pp. 1 et seq.).

The majority of shares of German corporations are not traded publicly on the stock exchange. Only about one-fifth of the AGs are listed at the stock exchange. At the same time, however, with regard to the number of shares, the publicly held corporations are dominant with a volume of 4,900 million DM as compared to 2,700 million DM for non-publicly held corporations.[5]

With regard to trading on the stock exchange, one differentiates between three market segments: the official trade market (*amtlicher Handel*), the regulated market (*geregelter Markt*) and the over-the-counter market (*Freiverkehr*).[6] The official trade market where the stock exchange price is determined by stock brokers, only encompasses shares that have been specially admitted for the trade by the stock exchange. This is the case for most corporations traded on the stock exchange.

The regulated market created in 1987 is meant to be the place to trade shares and profit participating certificates known as *Genußscheine* of smaller and mid-sized companies. There are fewer requirements for admission to the regulated market than for the official trade. The prices are determined by freelance stock brokers.

In the over-the-counter market shares and option bonds (*Optionsschuldverschreibungen*) of corporations with a low capital stock, as well as foreign shares are traded.[7] The corporations whose shares are listed at the stock exchange can be divided into the following the market segments:

	1989	1990
official trade	386	386
regulated market	100	115
over-the-counter market	93	94

The volume of stock trading on the exchange is considerable. In 1984 the turnover at the German stock exchanges amounted to 85,000 million DM in shares and 110,000 million DM[8] in securities with a fixed rate of interest.

The possibilities to invest in shares are relatively limited because of the small number of publicly held corporations. Private households are of limited importance as investors.[9] Whereas in the mid-Sixties approximately 26 per cent of the shares were still owned by private households, at the end of 1987, this number had decreased to only 20. On the other hand, the number of institutional investors in publicly held corporations grew, which also influenced the organization of the AG.

Private households only play a secondary role as investors. Other groups play a more dominant role with respect to the publicly held corporations. In 1988, the distribution of shares of AGs among the various groups of investors was as follows: private households (29.5 per cent), companies (30.5 per cent), State or Public entities (5.7 per cent), institutional investors (12.2 per cent) and foreigners (22.1 per cent).[10]

The economic reconstruction of Germany after World War II was realized without a significant use of an organized capital market (stock market). Self-financing or financing with outside capital was predominant among the corporations. Private

[5] Von Rosen, in: Assmann/ Schütze, supra note 4 ,§ 2 Randnr. 224, p. 66.

[6] The english term "over-the-counter-market" is much broader than the term "Freiverkehr" which means only the "free market" in the stock exchange.

[7] Franke, in: Assmann/ Schütze, supra note 4, § 2 Randnr., 87-93, p. 44.

[8] Obst/ Hintner, *Geld-, Bank- und Börsenwesen* (38th ed., 1988), p. 1015.

[9] Assmann, supra note 1., Einleitung Randnr., 307 et seq.

[10] Ibid at 311.

savers had little confidence in the securities market. They were more concerned with acquiring long-term consumer goods and therefore the forming of capital was less important for them. A lot of capital that could have been used for investments in the Seventies and Eighties flew into the "grey market" which offered a significantly larger amount of investment opportunities than the organized capital market.[11] The "grey market" is the market for all investments that are not publicly traded at the organized market, such as the stock exchange and includes investment opportunities such as commodity future transactions and shares in large partnerships.

E. The Structure of the Securities Market

The securities market is divided into two sections: organized trade at the stock exchange, which is regulated by statute; and the market outside of the stock exchange known as the grey market, which is not subject to particular legal rules. While the regulated securities market has a more or less clear legal structure, this is not the case for the free or grey securities market to which only the general rules law apply. The main source of law for the regulated securities market is the Börsengesetz of 1896 (last amended in 1989); it is complemented by a number of special statutes and regulations. In addition to the Börsengesetz, there are regulations set up by the stock exchanges themselves. The power to promulgate and to enforce these regulations is based upon their autonomy as self-governing bodies. The "Conditions for Deals at the Frankfurt Stock Exchange" (*Bedingungen für Geschäfte an der Frankfurter Wertpapierbörse*) are an example of such regulations.

The BörsenG does not influence directly the organization and the internal relationships of the AGs. This is the function of the corporate law.[12]

In the securities market outside of the regulated stock exchange the following securities and investment possibilities are traded: shares listed at the stock exchange before the opening and after the closing of the floor by telephone between banks; Euro-bonds not listed at German stock exchanges; shares in open mutual funds; shares of smaller corporations; equity interests in closed corporations and limited partnerships.

F. Government Presence in the Regulation of the Market

The influence of the government on the regulated securities market is twofold. First as the legislature, the State has passed a number of legal rules – in part based upon legislative acts from the EU – to regulate the securities market. Secondly it has to supervise the stock exchange permanently, as in the German legal understanding a stock exchange has an official function. Stock exchanges are non-independent statutory bodies even though the legal entity in charge of the stock exchange either is a private association or the local chamber of commerce.

This legislative and administrative presence of the State may influence investments by private persons both in a positive and in a negative way. For instance, the rules on the listing of securities at the stock exchange were enacted, inter alia, to protect the public from fraud by requiring the submission of a prospectus. Its goal is to put the investors in a position to ascertain and judge the person issuing the share

[11] Assmann, in: Assmann/ Schütze, supra note 4,§ 1 Randnr. 8-15, pp. 5-8.

[12] But the Wertpapierhandelsgesetz 1994 is regulating now the insider problem in §§ 12-10.

and the share itself, and it therefore has to inform the investor about the essential facts and legal relations, for instance about the status of the assets, the financial position and the profits (see § 38 of the *BörsenG*, §§ 13-42 of the *Börsenzulassungsverordnung*). When the legislation sets standards that are too high, this can have a negative impact on particular kinds of securities, as the public will then look for other investment opportunities and that particular kind of security will lose its importance as an instrument to finance a corporation.

The State supervisory body or the agents of the stock exchange cannot directly interfere with particular transactions. In that respect, the State supervisory body does not hinder trade in securities.

A different question is, to what extent is a change of the existing regulation of the stock exchange or a total deregulation deemed to be necessary? The opening of the markets within the EU puts pressure on the legislators of the Member States to check the necessity of existing limits and to possibly abolish them, as they might otherwise discriminate against the domestic market participants.

II. THE CORPORATE STRUCTURE

A. The Distribution of Power Within the Corporation

The AktG contains relatively comprehensive regulations concerning the powers and competencies of the different agents of the AG. However, important questions arise as to whether this regulation and the statutory model of the AG on which it is based satisfy the practical needs of the corporations. The AktG provides for three agents within one AG: the shareholders' meeting, the supervisory board as the agent supervising the management and the board of management as the agent managing the AG and representing it legally.

Contrary to American or English law, the AG in Germany is not organized according to a single-board system. Rather, German law is characterized by a two-tier-system, in which the board of management and the supervisory board share the control of the corporation. Further, under the AktG, the shareholders' meeting as the agent of the shareholders is placed above the board of management and the supervisory board. The statutory distribution of powers in the AG is modelled for the publicly held corporation. Whenever a particular corporation does not correspond with this statutory model, there are a number of frictions between the different classes of agents. Such a friction can appear, when the reciprocal relationship between the supervisory board is inverted. Normally, the role of the supervisory board is that of a supervisory organ, while the board of management is supposed to manage the corporation. Depending on the actual structure of a corporation, the distribution of powers may vary from the statutory model. For instance new tasks, that could not be foreseen by the legislator, are assumed by the supervisory board. Frictions can also appear in corporations that are part of a group of companies. For instance, a group of corporations is set up in different divisions that reach beyond a single corporation; in those instances the corporation has a different sphere of responsibilities from the model corporation contemplated by the legislator of the AktG.

The nature of the decisions made within an AG differentiates between those that are considered fundamental decisions and those which are of minor importance. The fundamental or structural decisions are in principle, within the power of the shareholders' meeting. The shareholders' meeting for instance has the power to define the object of the corporation and the goal of the corporation, to elect the representatives of the shareholders in the supervisory board, and to decide changes in the legal structure of the corporation. The day-to-day management and the administration are left to the board of management (§§ 76-78 of the AktG) that is controlled by the supervisory board (§ 111of the AktG).

While it is not possible to be a member both of the board of management and of the supervisory board, the line between the respective duties of each body is not very clear. The management, as such, is in the hands of the board of management, which is controlled by the supervisory board. Before its five-year term is over, the supervisory board can only dismiss the board of management for a good cause. This guarantees an independent management to the board of management for this period of time. Beyond that the extent to which the supervisory board participates in the management of the corporation cannot be generally stated. The statute provides for a participation of the supervisory board in the setting up of the annual statement of accounts (§ 172 of the AktG) and in the making of singular and fundamental management decisions (§ 111(4) of the AktG). Provisions in the by-laws may identify certain types of decisions that can only be made with the previous consent of the supervisory board. But the influence of the supervisory board can be much more important than that, and even go as far as bringing about a change of the members of the supervisory board and the board of management.[13] In those cases, the supervisory board takes over the power to determine the long-term policy of the corporation.

The relations and the distribution of power between the agents are in principle regulated by statute which only leaves limited possibilities of private autonomy (see § 23(5) of the AktG), i.e. to the by-laws of the corporation. Section 111(4) of the AktG however permits it or the by-laws to develop the supervisory board to some extent into an agent involved in the administration of the corporation.

B. Employee Participation

The constitution of the supervisory board is regulated specifically in the AktG (§ 96), the Betriebsverfassungsgesetz 1952 (§§ 76 et seq.), the Montan- und Mitbestimmungsgesetz (including the amendments to it by the Mitbestimmungs-Ergänzungsgesetz 1956) and the Mitbestimmungsgesetz 1976. All corporations irrespective of the size of their workforce are in principle subject to employee's participation through employee representatives in the supervisory board under § 16 of the Betriebsverfassungsgesetz; the employee representatives are entitled to one-third of the seats on the supervisory board. The employee participation requirement does not apply to enterprises serving certain ideological purposes (*Tendenzunternehmen* such as newspapers) nor to family-owned companies with less than 500 employees. If a corporation is not subject to the employee's participation requirement, the supervisory board consists of members elected by the shareholders' meeting. In corporations with 2,000 employees or more, the employee representatives are entitled to half of the seats in the supervisory board both under the Mitbestimmungsgesetz 1976 and the Montanmitbestimmungsgesetz 1951. Thus there are the representatives of the shareholders and there are members of the supervisory board that are elected

[13] Wiedemann, *Gesellschaftsrecht*, vol. I, 1980, p. 342.

by the employees as their representatives or that are sent to the supervisory board by trade unions. The relevant statutes stipulate that the different groups of employees such as blue collar workers, white collar and managerial employees have their own representatives. When the Montan- Mitbestimmungsgesetz 1951 is applicable, § 4(1)(c) provides for the election of an additional member by the shareholders' meeting at the proposal of the supervisory board to serve as neutral person, to avoid a deadlock in the supervisory board.

In corporations in which half of the supervisory board consists of the representatives of the employees, the Montan- Mitbestimmungsgesetz 1951 (§ 13) and the Mitbestimmungsgesetz 1976 (§ 33) also regulate the composition of the board of management. They stipulate that one member of the board of management always has to be a managing director representing the employees (*Arbeitsdirektor*); this implies that the board has to consist of more than one person. Under the Montan- Mitbestimmungsgesetz 1951 (including the amendments to it by the Mitbestimmungs- Ergänzungsgesetz 1956) the managing director representing the employees cannot be appointed against the will of the employees' representatives.

C. The Functioning of the System

In view of the different types of corporations that exist and which have entered the legislation since 1994, there is no uniform model of function. The "big" AG is still shaped according to the statutory model of the publicly held corporation, but there are different types that have developed over the years. This is why the distribution of powers and competences is one of the most important subjects of this field of law. It cannot be described briefly how the respective competencies of the three agents of the ERG have varied.

Two types of AGs with totally different decision-making structures can however be distinguished.[14] One type is the corporation that is controlled by the shareholders and where the supervisory board and the board of management are instruments of the shareholders' meetings. About 90 per cent of the existing AGs belong to his group: small family companies, corporations with a single shareholder, subsidiary corporations in a group of corporations, but also publicly held corporations with a single majority shareholder or several major shareholders acting together. All important decisions are taken by the majority shareholder or the majority of shareholders. Not only do they determine the composition of the supervisory board and the board of management, but they are also consulted in significant business decisions by the members of the supervisory board and the board of management.

The central problem is the protection of minority shareholders. The AktG does not contain comprehensive guidelines for the protection of minorities. The dominant position of a corporation within a group of corporations is the only aspect of majority oppression that has been regulated by statute in more detail.

The second type of AG is the publicly held corporation, in which none of the numerous shareholders is in a position to actually influence the supervisory board or ordinary business decisions. This form deviates from the statutory model in so far as

[14] Kübler, *Gesellschaftsrecht* (4th ed., 1994), pp. 164 et seq.

the shareholders are excluded from the development of the objectives and decision-making process in the corporation. This is the quintessential "split between ownership and control" that Berle/Means described in 1932.[15]

The decision-making structure in publicly held corporations is of a very complex nature. The voting rights of the overwhelming majority of small shareholders in the shareholders' meeting are exercised by the depository bank. This so-called voting right of nominee shareholders (*Depotstimmrecht*, §§ 125-128, 135 of the AktG) can be exercised by banks that keep shares in custody for their owners. They are mostly small shareholders that have given a proxy in writing allowing the banks to exercise their voting rights at the shareholders' meeting. The bank representatives have a substantial power to exercise their influence as they are not bound by any instructions from the shareholders. However, as long as the corporation is successful, the banks do not use their influence. The corporation therefore enjoys a considerable degree of autonomy.

The supervisory board appears in this case as the instrument of the board of management. This is especially true when some of its members are also members of the board of management of other corporations. This affects its function as the agent controlling the board of management. The supervisory board becomes an advisor of the board of management and more and more loses its capacity to control it. The strong interlocking relationships between large corporations and banks are a typical characteristic of the German economic system.

The fundamental problem in regulating the publicly held corporation lies in the protection of the shareholders from a self-interested and an incompetent management.

D. Basic Rights of Shareholders, Managing Directors and Members of the Supervisory Board

1. Shareholders Rights

(a) The Rights of the Shareholders' Meeting

The shareholders' meeting is the agent of the corporation in which the shareholders exercise their rights by voting (§ 118(1) of the AktG). In general, the shareholders' meeting has the power to make fundamental and structural decisions. For instance the amendment of the by-laws (§§ 119, 179 of the AktG), measures capital increase as well as of capital reduction, the dissolution of the corporation, the transformation (§ 362 et seq. of the AktG), mergers and consolidations (§§ 353 et seq. of the AktG), the consent to so-called agreements between corporations. Such decisions, in order to be valid under the statute, must be made with a qualified majority of at least three-fourths of the capital represented at the vote. The decisions have to be registered in the commercial register. In addition the shareholders' meeting has the capacity to make other fundamental decisions, that are not mentioned in the statute, such as the acquisition of substantial equity interests in other corporations or whether to spin off a division of the corporation into a sub-

[15] Berle and Means, *The Modern Corporation and Private Property* (1932).

sidiary. These powers have been developed by the Bundesgerichtshof in its jurisprudence and are not specially granted by statute (*ungeschriebene Hauptversammlungszuständigkeiten*).

According to § 119(1) of the AktG, the shareholders' meeting also decides the following continuous matters: the election of the members of the supervisory board (§ 119(1)(1) of the AktG) unless they are elected in accordance with § 101(2) of the AktG; the use of the accumulated earnings (§ 119(1)(2) of the AktG); the acceptance of the reports of the members of the supervisory board and the board of management (§ 119(1)(3) of the AktG); the election of the auditors (§ 199(1)(4) of the AktG).

Additionally, there are a number of other statutory powers of minor importance mentioned by §§ 103, 142 of the AktG.

(b) The Legal Position of the Individual Shareholder

A shareholder is member of the AG. The status gives to the individual shareholder administrative, financial and controlling rights that are regulated by the statute in detail. As long as they are not based upon mandatory law, they can be modified by a decision of the shareholders' meeting. Section 53a of the AktG forbids the discrimination of any shareholder (principle of non-discrimination of the shareholders, *Prinzip der Gleichbehandlung der Aktionäre*).

The administrative rights include the right to participate in the shareholders' meeting (§§ 139, 140 of the AktG) as well as the right to vote, that enables the shareholder to participate in the decision-making process of the corporation. The voting right cannot be excluded or limited. The shareholder can in principle only exercise his administrative rights at the shareholders' meeting.

The financial rights secure his participation in the paid dividends and the use of the common assets. This includes the right to his share of the profit (§ 58(5) of the AktG). The distribution of the accumulated earnings can however be limited or excluded by the by-laws or by a decision of the shareholders' meeting.

The rights of control confer to the shareholder a right of access to information that he needs to exercise his administrative and financial rights. The main right of control is the right of disclosure under § 131 of the AktG.

By bringing an action under § 243 ff. of the AktG, a shareholder can challenge the validity of decisions of the shareholders' meeting. In addition to that, the jurisprudence of the Bundesgerichtshof has given the shareholder the power to challenge the validity of any decision or action that affects him.

2. *Managing Directors* (Vorstand)

(a) The Rights of the Board of Management

The board of management is the agent in charge of the management and the legal representation of the AG (§§ 76(1), 78(1) of the AktG). The board of management manages the corporation independently of the shareholders' meeting and the supervisory board. Hence it is the actual agent who is in charge of the day-to-day operations of the corporation. The other agents have only very limited participatory rights in this regard. Actions of the managing board cannot be subject to the approval of the shareholders' meeting. Under § 111(4) of the AktG the supervisory board can only ask the board of management to seek its prior approval for specific kinds of decisions. The scope of those decisions cannot be defined in such an extensive manner that the supervisory board actually participates in the management. A strong influence over the management is however possible when the AG is part of a group of corporations (see § 308 of the AktG for the group of corporations set up by contract, *Vertragskonzern*).

The board of management is bound by the corporate purpose as defined in the by-laws. But this does not have any impact on the legal validity of the decisions made and the contracts entered into by it as the agent legally representing the corporation. The board of management can only be made liable internally to the corporation for deals made in violation of the defined purpose (i.e. ultra vires).

When there is more than one member of the board of management, the management is divided into different areas of operation (production, sale, finances, personnel, etc.). This structure is mandatory for corporations which are subject to the participation requirement under the Montan- Mitbestimmungsgesetz 1951 and the Mitbestimmungsgesetz 1976. Both statutes require the appointment of a managing director representing the employees (*Arbeits-direkor*), who has certain competencies for questions regarding the personnel. Moreover § 76(2)(2) stipulates that the board of management of a corporation with a capital stock of more than 3 million DM must consist of at least two persons, unless otherwise stated by the by-laws. When a board of management has more than one member, the supervisory board can elect one of them as the president of the board of management. The genuine management functions of the planning, coordination and control of the corporation as well as the main entrepreneurial decisions are in the hands of the entire board of management.

(b) The Legal Position of the Individual Member of the Board of Management

The members of the board of management frequently are persons who are not shareholders of the corporation (so-called foreign agency, *Fremdorganschaft*). When this is the case a separate contract for services is the basis of their legal relationship with the corporation. They have a right to be compensated for their work. A member of the board of management is not considered an employee.

The hiring of a member of the board of management has to be distinguished from his appointment, which is an act of corporate law. The supervisory board can appoint a member for a maximum term of five years which may be renewed as many times as wished.

When the board of management consists of more than one member, the management and the legal representation of the AG are performed by all the members of the board acting together, even if each of them is responsible for a particular area of operation. The by-laws can, however, provide for a different solution.

3. Supervisory Board

(a) The Rights of the Supervisory Board

The supervisory board has a duty to supervise the management (§ 111(1) of the AktG). This responsibility does not only encompass the formal duties of the board of management, but includes the entire area of business operations and their consequences. Therefore ongoing dialogue and counselling with the board of management are vital. If the supervisory board has a concrete reason to disapprove of the conduct of the board of management, it can tighten its control by making certain operations subject to its approval. The supervisory board may also dismiss those members of the board of management (§ 84(3) of the AktG).

In order to guarantee an effective control, the statute grants the right to audit the books, the correspondence, the cash balance and other forms of assets. In addition, the board of management has to inform the supervisory board in a comprehensive manner about the business policy, the state of affairs, the turnover and the profitability of the AG.

In addition to the above-mentioned functions, the supervisory board represents the AG legally vis-à-vis individual members of the board of management, calls in the shareholders' meeting, controls the annual report and the proposal by the board of management to use the profits (§ 171 of the AktG).

(b) The Legal Position of the Individual Member of the Supervisory Board

Similar to the board of management, members of the supervisory board enter into a legal relationship with the corporation to provide services within its duties. In general, a member of the supervisory board is entitled to a compensation, which is either fixed by the by-laws or granted by the shareholders' meeting. All the members of the supervisory board have the same rights and duties. An individual member of the board can challenge the validity of decisions of the supervisory board by analogy with §§ 241 et seq. of the AktG.[16]

E. Distribution of Powers Between the Different Agents

Under German law, the board of management and the supervisory board have an obligation towards the shareholders to protect their interests. They also have a duty to act primarily in the "interest of the corporation". In doing this they must take into consideration the competing interests involved (shareholders, employees, trade unions, banks, business partners). The obligation to guarantee the existence of the corporation comes first. This duty may lead to the exclusion of those interested in merely making profits. The board of management and the supervisory board have a fiduciary position vis-à-vis the corporation and those participating in it. Corporations that are subject to the employee participation requirement have a duty to take into account the interest of the employees which is stipulated explicitly by statute. The relation between the agents of the AG and thereby the distribution of power between them is regulated in detail by statute and is mandatory. Therefore it may seem that there are no significant possibilities for flexible arrangements by the involved parties. But this impression is misleading. In reality, the influence of a particular agent can vary considerably. The supervisory board may limit itself to an *ex post* management control without getting involved in its business initiatives. Or it may exercise its powers to participate in personnel and business decisions. It can become the agent in charge of the corporation. Hence there are weak and strong

[16] Cf. Raiser, *Recht der Kapitalgesellschaften* (2nd ed., 1994), p. 155.

supervisory boards. Which of them is to be found in a particular corporation depends partly on the personalities involved, but mainly upon the composition of the shareholders and the regulation of the participation in management. Let us illustrate this by two examples.

If all the shares are in the hands of a single shareholder (i.e. natural person, State or public entity or a dominant corporation), he can appoint persons of his choice to the supervisory board. In such a case, the board of management depends to such a high degree on the sole shareholder that there is not much room left for management's discretion. The board of management is merely the executive agent for the supervisory board.

If the ownership of a corporation is held by a large number of shareholders as in true-type publicly held corporations, the shareholders' meeting generally does not participate in personnel or business decisions. The board of management presents to the shareholders' meeting nominees that are close to him, and that will not create any trouble for him. Because of a lack of alternatives, they are elected. The general meeting in making these decisions, only confirms the proposals submitted by the board of management. It only sustains the board of management. Even when the business results are poor, the shareholders' meeting may criticize the board of management, but it will not be in a position to take significant action.

F. The Fiduciary Duty

Fiduciary duty is a recent development in German corporate law and is an important feature of corporate governance and has different functions.[17] It refers not only to managers, but also to shareholders. This fiduciary duty exists for every shareholder in relation to the corporation and in relation to the other shareholders. In this respect German law goes much beyond the American regulation. It is therefore not only limited to majority shareholders. Conflicts between the majority and the minority of the shareholders or between large shareholders and the board of management are resolved with reference to fiduciary duty only when no other explicit legal rule applies.

This relatively comprehensive fiduciary duty has been developed by jurisprudence over the course of time. The specific contents of the fiduciary duty depends on the aspects of the particular case, and especially on the structure of the involved corporation. The fiduciary duty is principally a code of conduct for large shareholders and groups of shareholders that are in a position to influence the management of the corporation significantly and who have the power to take advantage of the other shareholders. It can also apply to a minority shareholder who must refrain from obstructive behaviour under their the fiduciary duty. Sanctions for breach of the fiduciary duty can be the obligation to act or to refrain from an act, the compensation of damages caused by the breach as well as setting aside decisions of the shareholders' meeting.

1. The Fiduciary Duty of the Board of Management

This does not have the same function as in American corporate law. The conduct of the board of management vis-à-vis the corporation and the shareholders is

[17] Wiedemann, supra note 13, pp. 431 et seq.

essentially regulated by statute and therefore a need to complement this by the fiduciary duty only exists in exceptional situations. This is particularly the case in the area of proper management of the corporation. The duty to manage the corporation carefully, regulated by § 93 of the AktG is similar to the duty of care in American law. Section 93 is a general clause that encompasses numerous rules of behaviour which are broadly defined. Any kind of negligent or superficial performance of the duties is a breach of § 93. The exact kind of behaviour deemed to be a breach depends on the concrete circumstances such as the size of the corporation, its objectives, its management organization, the actual state of business and the financial structure. The standard of care is objective and is to be determined according to typical criteria.[18]

Within the framework of the interest of the corporation, the board of management makes decisions at its discretion. It has a high degree of latitude to determine the function, the business policy, the organization of the corporation and the concrete principles of management. In this respect German law takes a comparable stand to that of the American business judgment rule, which states that courts do not get involved in the management of a corporation but for major transgressions of their discretion.

Another aspect of the fiduciary duty of the board of management is its duty of loyalty to the corporation and the shareholders. It is based on the fiduciary position that is linked to the membership on the various boards. The duty requires that the members of the board of management put their own private interests behind those of the corporation and the shareholders. It also prohibits members from abusing their position to their own advantage. An example of this codified duty of loyalty is § 88 of the AktG which contains a prohibition of competition for the members of the board of management. In general, the duty of loyalty encompasses a duty not to use opportunities for the corporation for their own benefit. It is unlawful to accept or ask for a commission or bribes for deals on behalf of the corporation.[19] An opportunity can be based upon the knowledge that a member of the board of management has gained because of his corporate position or to make an advantageous deal that falls within the field of operation of the corporation. The deal must be made in favour of the corporation, or at least, the corporation has to be put in a position to determine whether or not it wants to make the deal.

2. *The Fiduciary Duty of the Shareholder*

This relates to a different set of problems and mainly is concerned with restrictions on the exercise of his rights as a shareholder out of loyalty to the corporation and other shareholders. Such a duty of loyalty falls primarily on a majority shareholder vis-à-vis his duty to the minority of shareholders. The requirements of the shareholder therefore depend on the structure of the corporation. While the concept of the fiduciary duty is at the centre of the protection of minorities it also deals with conflicts between groups of corporations as well as issues dealing with the participation

[18] *Bundesgerichtshof Wertpapier-Mitteilungen 1971*, p. 1548; *Neue Juristische Wochenschrift 1983*, p. 1556.

[19] *Entscheidungen des Reichsgerichts in Zivilsachen*, vol. 96, p. 53; *Bundesgerichtshof Wertpapier-Mitteilungen 1983*, p. 498.

in management by the employees that are not adequately regulated by statute. The fiduciary duty therefore has an important function of supplementing the statute.

III. CORPORATE GOVERNANCE

There is no expression in German law corresponding to the one of "corporate governance". As seen from the American perspective corporate governance deals with the role of the different interests relevant in a corporation and their representatives and ultimately the question of how the law regulates or should regulate these roles. German law, including employees among the agents of the AG who participate in management has already made an important step into that direction. The corporation does not only serve the interests of the shareholders.

Taking into account other interests as opposed to only those of the shareholders is visibly reflected in the notion of the "interest of the corporation" as a formula to harmonize the different powers and groups acting in a corporation. One of the questions raised in this context is, which particular interests are to be considered as relevant for the AG in certain situations. Another question to be answered is according to which criteria conflicts between them are to be decided.

But it is certain that the legislature, by institutionalizing the employee participation on both the supervisory board and the board of management, has decided that the interests of the employees are to be taken into account in the decisions of the agents of the corporation. However, it cannot be directly deduced from this concept to what extent the employee's interests are to be taken into account.

Which interests and how should those interests weigh in the decision-making process of the corporation? The answer to this question goes beyond the problems that in both the German and the American discussions are dealt with under the notion of "social responsibility". The 1937 version of the AktG contained a public interest clause (*Gemeinwohlklausel*) for the board of management in § 70(1). This section was repealed in 1965, because the legislature held that corporations would act with social conscience even without regulation. This does not only concern the responsibility of the corporation and its agents towards the public, but the relevance of particular interests of constituencies other than the shareholders such as employees, trade unions, investors, creditors and consumers.

The interest of the corporation is the guiding rule for the actions of the agents of the corporation, but at the same time its material content is rather vague. It is aimed at securing the existence, the inner stability and the success of the corporation in the market. The following actions are examples of a conduct contrary to the interest of the corporation:[20] undercapitalization, exaggerated dividends or pay ments to shareholders and employees, poor management, risky deals, risky financial transactions and their use for objectives that are not in accordance with the corporate purpose.

The interest of the corporation continues to be a variable and dynamic notion. It is defined in the course of the decision-making process between the agents of the corporation. The interest of the corporation does not set forth an order of priority of the interests to be taken into account, but rather fixes rules of conduct related to the

[20] Raiser, supra note 16, pp. 153 et seq.

corporation such as rational discussion of conflicts and a cooperative managerial behaviour. Hence, the interest of the corporation can be understood in a "procedural" rather than in a substantive sense.[21]

IV. RIGHTS OF THE SHAREHOLDERS

A. Protection of the Shareholders' Interests

As already discussed above, the rights of the shareholders can be divided into three main categories: administrative rights, financial rights and the right to control. In addition to those, there is the right to withdraw from the corporation and some special privileges for specific shareholders. Every single right belonging to the different categories protects separate distinct interests of the shareholder. Therefore, the enforcement of these different rights varies considerably from one another. The remedy available to the shareholder depends on the kind of violation.

Among the administrative rights of the shareholder, the voting right in the shareholders' meeting is the most important one. Voting rights will be discussed below at pp. 71–73.

Among the financial rights, the right to participate in the distribution of the profit (§§ 58(4), 60 of the AktG), i.e. the right to a dividend, is of central importance. In addition, there are a number of other rights including: the pre-emptive rights when there is an increase in the capital stock (§§ 186(1), 212 of the AktG), a right to be refunded when there is a capital reduction (§ 225(2) of the AktG), the right to participate in the remaining assets after liquidation (§ 271 of the AktG) as well as rights to compensation, conversion and indemnification in the cases of mergers, consolidations, transformations and provided by the law regulating groups of companies.

A corporation may impose limits on financial rights in its by-laws more easily than it may deny administrative right. These restrictions have to be explicitly allowed by statute. The right to a dividend therefore can only be excluded when the conditions of § 58(4) of the AktG are met. The exclusion of pre-emptive rights must meet the requirement of § 186(4) of the AktG.

The shareholders' rights are not transferable independently from the share, and therefore they cannot be split from the membership (so-called prohibition to split, *Abspaltungsverbot*). The right to participate in the distribution of the profit however becomes transferable once the shareholder can be split from the membership; it turns into an independent right to payment after the shareholders' meeting's decision upon the use of the profit for such payments.

The rights in the category of control include: the right of disclosure, the right to have access to certain documents of the corporation, the right to demand a special audit (§§ 142 et seq., 258 of the AktG), the right to challenge the validity of decisions by the shareholders' meeting in court as well as the right to bring a shareholder's derivative action (*Aktionärsklage*). The right of disclosure and the right to have access to certain documents will be discussed below at pp. 71–73. The shareholder may seek judicial review which determines with binding force whether the

[21] In this sense Teubner, "Corporate Fiduciary Duties and their Beneficiaries: A Functional Approach to the Legal Institutionalization of Corporate Responsibility", in: Hopt/ Teubner (ed.), *Corporate Governance and Directors Liabilities* 1985, pp. 149 et seq.

agents of the corporations have violated the statute or the by-laws. The relief granted by the courts can be through direct actions to set aside specific decisions or acts, actions for a declaratory judgment, as well as actions for declaration of nullity, or it can be a side issue in an action to recover damages.

The agents of the corporation are not controlled by the shareholder's derivative action. The other rights are limited to very specific sets of facts. German law however does not know such a derivative action by a shareholder. The shareholders can participate in the shareholders' meeting and challenge the decisions made at that meeting in court. But they do not have the right to bring a derivative action for damages against members of the corporation or particular shareholders when they have acted in breach of their duty to the corporation. The reason for this is that shareholders only have a legal relationship with the corporation itself and that they cannot exercise their rights individually outside the shareholders' meeting. The supervisory board has the power to enforce the rights of the corporation against the members of the board of management, and vice versa. A minority of 10 per cent of the shareholders can request the corporation to bring an action for damages against members of the supervisory board and the board of management because of their breach of duty to the corporation. In this case it may be necessary for the court to appoint an agent for the corporation (§ 147 of the AktG). This provision, however, has not been very significant in practice. Its purpose is to ensure that the corporation is capable of acting, when it is enforcing rights against its organs.

This legal situation has significant consequences for the distribution of powers and the inner structure of the AG. It hinders the shareholders from controlling the supervisory board and the board of management effectively. Experience has shown that claims for damages are only rarely made by one agent against the members of another agent of a corporation. For that reason, the members of management are subject to a much lower degree of legal control than comparable fiduciaries over third-party property.[22]

The more recent jurisdiction of the Bundesgerichtshof,[23] however, has significantly improved the shareholders' right to seek judicial review. Under this jurisprudence, every shareholder can seek an injunction or start an action for removal against the corporation, when the agents of the corporation have violated his membership rights "in a way that exceeds what is allowed by statute or the by-laws". This is the case, for example, when the parent corporation as controlling shareholder defeats the rights of the other shareholders. Actions for a declaratory judgment are allowed when the plaintiff has a legal interest in obtaining such a judgment. The shareholder can therefore start an action for a declaratory judgment claiming that there is a legal relationship between the defendant corporation and the subsidiary, while at the same time there is a relevant legal relationship between the shareholder and the AG. The action may be maintained if the AktG does not regulate the matter in a comprehensive manner.

Special privileges of particular shareholders or groups of shareholders such as non-voting preferred stock (§ 12(1) of the AktG) and multiple voting shares can be conferred upon them by the by-laws (§ 26(1) of the AktG). These rights may include the right to send members of the supervisory board (§ 101(2) of the AktG), and the right to use the equipment of the corporation. In one decision the Bundes-

22 Raiser, supra note 16, p. 61.

23 *Entscheidungen des Bundesgerichtshofs in Zivilsachen*, vol. 83, p. 122; vol. 103, p. 184.

gerichthof[24] has held, that an amendment to the by-laws may affect either the right to profits or the voting rights of the shareholder in order to protect the corporation from foreign control. The by-laws may also strengthen the independence of the board of management in order to protect small shareholders from large shareholders and thereby safeguarding the nature of the corporation as "publicly held". Special privileges are however not a characteristic of publicly held corporations but rather of family-owned companies.

B. The Influence of The Majority on the Shareholders' Powers

In discussing the relationship between majority and minority shareholders the fundamental question that must be addressed is whether decisions made by a majority shareholder, are bound by a duty of loyalty that limits the scope and the subject-matter of the decisions that he can make? Further, should the minority protection become part of the law of corporations? The tension between majority and minority is obvious in the AG, as the decision-making is not done per capita but according to the level of capital participation, i.e. the amount of capital participation alone is decisive, irrespective of the number of its owners. When the majority of shares and therefore votes is in the hands of one person or group, the voting process becomes moot. When this happens, the idea that a vote by the majority will reconcile competing interests no longer has validity. That there is a decision by voting is merely a unilateral act. Consequently the fundamental personnel and business decisions are made by the majority shareholder. He is in a position to dispose of the entire corporation including the capital brought in by the minority. Compared to its capital contribution, the majority's influence is out of proportion.

The law on minority protection is split. On the one hand, in 1965, the AktG sought to protect minority interests under §§ 291 et seq. This provision is only applicable to corporations that become controlled by another corporation under the terms of a control agreement or that commit themselves to transfer their entire profits to another company. In this case the minority protection consists of a guarantee of a dividend, the right to indemnification and the rights of the shareholders to bring a derivative action and the guarantee of the neutrality of the auditors; on the other hand, there is no comparable regulation by statute of the protection of the minority for the AGs that are not contractually controlled.

Regarding the limitations imposed upon the competencies of the majority, one has to distinguish between formal minority rights that, in order to be invoked, require a particular number of votes or capital such as the calling and the organization of the shareholders' meeting, the enforcement of claims for damages against members of an agent or the appointment of auditors. Other minority rights that can be exercised by every shareholder regardless of the number of shares owned consist of either the guaranteed participation in decisions or votes, or in the judicial review of actions taken by the majority through the shareholder's meeting. A greater degree of minority protection is afforded in these types of decisions.

The conflict between the majority and the minority in a non-controlled AG is regulated only to the extent that an intentional damage of the corporation or its share-

[24] BGHZ 70, 117.

holders is prohibited under § 117 of the AktG and the obtaining of special privileges is sanctioned under § 243(2) of the AktG. However, there is no regulation for situations in which the agents of the corporation act to the detriment of the shareholders, for instance: the denial of preemptive rights in the case of an increase of the capital stock, the election of the members of the supervisory board and the board of management, the so-called disguised dividends, the withholding of the profits for reasons of self-financing, the obtaining of personal pecuniary advantages by using specific knowledge.

Despite the apparent lack of minority protection, minority shareholders may demand a judicial review of decisions of the shareholders' meeting. The action to set aside a specific decision and the action for declaration of nullity are a peculiarity of German law. Only a very limited number of substantial violations of the AktG occasion an automatic declaration of nullity. If an action is brought in court, it is aimed at declaring the nullity (the so-called action for declaration of nullity, *Nichtigkeitsklage*, § 249 of the AktG). All other decisions are only voidable (see §§ 242 et seq. of the AktG) and have the legal effect that they were intended to have, before they are set aside by an action in court within a certain period of time, if there is a ground for it (see § 243 of the AktG).

The right to bring an action to set aside a specific decision is not conditional on a minimum ownership of shares, and can therefore be brought by any shareholder who was present at the shareholders' meeting. The action must be brought within a month of the meeting and the shareholder must have his protest registered on the record. However, because of the requirement that the shareholder must be present at the meeting, as a practical matter, the overwhelming majority of public shareholders cannot bring an action to set aside a specific decision, as they do not participate in the shareholders' meeting. To make matters worse, their representatives, the depository banks, usually do not bring actions in courts. Time limits make it very difficult for a minority shareholder to investigate all the motives and the legal implications behind a decision made at the shareholder's meeting that may be contrary to the corporate interest.

C. Voting Rights

The voting power corresponds to the capital participation. The voting right of the shareholder in the shareholders' meeting is not done per capita but according to the par value of shares. Even though every share confers one vote, only the par value of the share is relevant. A shareholder who owns several shares therefore also has several votes. There are two exceptions to the one share one vote rule. Shares with a multiple voting right (§ 12(2)(2) of the AktG), that can be issued under certain circumstances and preferred stock without voting rights.

The shareholders' meeting is not the place for a general exchange of opinions. The AktG itself does not contain particular rules that determine the course of the shareholders' meeting and leaves the question to the discretion of the corporations. The topics to be dealt with in the shareholders' meeting are established by the agenda. The right to speak is restricted to the topics mentioned in the agenda. It happens frequently that shareholders may want to make political statements or other contributions that are unrelated to the concrete issues that will be voted upon. The chairman of the shareholders' meeting, usually the chairman of the supervisory board, can withdraw their right to speak at the meeting.

As mentioned above, the statute allows in some cases a disgression from the "one share one vote" principle. For instance, the voting right can be excluded for preferred shares (*Vorzugsaktien* under §§ 139 et seq., if these shares are granted the right to a preference at the distribution of the profit. A more unique example, however, are multiple voting rights conferred to particular shares. Such multiple voting shares (*Mehrstimmrechtsaktien*) are illegal in principle, but exceptions can be granted by the Minister of Finance, if necessary for the safeguard of important overall economic interests (§ 12(2) of the AktG). Nowadays, such multiple voting shares are mainly found in energy corporations to guarantee the influence of the public authorities.

With the lack of statutory protection of minority shareholders, a common way to limit the influence of majority shareholders is to include certain provisions in the by-laws which limit the voting rights of the latter. But although several corporations have limited the voting rights in their by-laws, this has not become a common practice of publicly held corporations. The limits on voting rights are inflicted without regard to the level of share ownership (see § 134(1) of the AktG). But this measure increases the independence of the board of management at the expense of the shareholders' meeting. Most major publicly held corporations have limited voting rights in order to protect them from "hostile" takeovers. For instance, Bayer, Mannesmann and the Deutsche Bank have limited the voting right of a shareholder to 5 per cent of the capital stock; BASF has limited it to about 3 per cent of its capital stock.

In some cases the voting rights are excluded by statute. For instance, the corporation cannot own its own shares (§ 56 of the AktG). In the presence of cross-share holdings, the voting rights can only be exercised for a maximum of a fourth of the capital stock (§ 328(1) of the AktG). Shareholders are not precluded from voting in their own personal interest even though it might be contrary to the corporate interest. Section 136(1) of the AktG only excludes the voting right in three situations:

(1) shareholders are not allowed to exercise their voting right when the vote is on the formal approval of their own actions (for instance as a member of the supervisory board of the board of management);
(2) when the vote is upon the discharge of their obligation;
(3) when a claim of the corporation is to be enforced against the shareholder.

Because of the prohibition of splitting the voting right from membership, voting rights cannot be transferred independently from the membership or rather the share ownership and cannot be exercised by a third party in his own name. But it is possible without a problem to transfer the shares to a fiduciary, and the fiduciary can exercise the right to vote. Whether the vote by proxy, as often occurs in the U.S., is legal under the AktG, cannot be answered unequivocally. Furthermore, as a practical matter, it does not play a significant role in Germany. In Germany, the voting rights of the small shareholders are largely exercised by the banks in which the shares are deposited: they have been empowered to vote (voting right of nominee shareholder, *Banken- oder Depotstimmrecht*). Section 135 of the AktG stipulates a number of conditions under which the banks may exercise voting rights on behalf of the shareholder in order to protect their interests. However, this does not solve the problem of possible conflicts of interests between the interests of the banks and those of the shareholders.

Another way of influencing the exercise of the voting right is the obligation of a shareholder to another shareholder or a third party to exercise his voting right in a particular way. Such agreements (*Stimmbindungsverträge*) are lawful. It is a means for shareholders to join their forces and to add to their voting powers. Although agreements to exercise voting rights in a particular way are of major importance in family-owned corporations or when shares are subject to a fiduciary relationship, they are generally not common in publicly held corporations. An exception is the situation in which a voting pool is formed to gain a controlling influence on the corporation. While the "purchase of votes" (*Stimmenkauf*) is unlawful, in practice, such agreements to exercise the voting right in a particular manner are quite significant.

D. Disclosure

The right of disclosure in the shareholders' meeting is part of the control rights of the shareholder (§ 131 of the AktG). The corporation is obliged to disclose its financial, and in part its social situation. This gives the shareholder additional possibilities of disclosure. However, there is no individual right of the single shareholder to demand the rendering of accounts. It is rather an affirmative statutory duty of the corporation. There is, contrary to the situation in a closed corporation, no specific right of the shareholder to examine the books of the corporation.

The purpose of the right of disclosure is to put the shareholder in a position to make informed decisions in the shareholders' meeting. The necessary information is given to him by the management of the corporation. The shareholder can ask for disclosure of all matters of the corporation that are necessary to accurately assess an item mentioned in the agenda.

The disclosure can be refused if, according to reasonable commercial judgment, it could inflict a significant prejudice to the corporation (§ 131(3), No. 1 of the AktG) or when the requirements of § 131(3), No. 2-5 of the AktG are met. But, when is information necessary to assess an item mentioned on the agenda in an appropriate way? There is no convincing general answer to this question. The determination of relevant aspects depends on the concrete subject-matter, on a case-by-case method. Examples can only be given of the necessary information to be disclosed. The election of new members of the supervisory board depends on their personal capabilities. Therefore their personal histories have to be disclosed. Also, when formally approving the actions of the supervisory board and the board of management, the details of management are crucial. Lastly, the financial situation of a corporation is of major importance for an increase in capital stock and therefore all the relevant information has to be disclosed.

If the shareholder does not agree with the information that has been disclosed to him or if his demand has been refused, his objections along with the reasons for the company's action have to be registered in the record of the shareholders' meeting (§ 131(5) of the AktG). Afterwards he may seek judicial review of that refusal according to § 132 of the AktG. If the shareholder also has suffered damages as a consequence of the inadequate information, for instance by selling his shares under value, he has a claim for damages against the corporation.

Accounting (*Rechnungslegung*) by the corporation (§ 238 et seq. of the *Handelsgesetzbuch*) has a number of other purposes besides supplying information to the shareholders. The information distributed by the corporation can influence the investment decisions by the investors and thereby increase the yield of the available capital. It can intensify the control of the management of the corporation by the shareholders and the public and thereby increase their efficiency. Those effects, besides helping the parties involved in the corporation, are also advantageous for the general public.

At the same time, the statutory regulations have the effect of reducing the imbalance of information in favour of small investors. With regard to publicly held corporations, potential as well as existing shareholders are interested in having the most accurate information possible. Investors, as potential shareholders, understand that this information has a significant impact upon the market value of the corporation and thereby also upon the value of the shares. This is particularly true for the AG, since the stock exchange price sets the price for newly issued shares. In addition to informing potential investors, the disclosure of reliable information is necessary for the protection of the capital market and the confidence in its fairness.

The *Publizitätsgesetz* enacted in 1969, mandates big companies and hence mainly publicly held corporations to inform the general public about their economic situation. The rationale behind this statute is to improve the basis for politico-economic decisions made by State government. It is also addressed to associations and trade unions.

The provisions of commercial law with regard to the annual report (statements of accounts, annex and statement of affairs) only refer to the financial and economic situation of the company. Contrary to France, there is no duty for the AG to publish a social statement (*Sozialbilanz*) or to report on the company's relationship to the environment. A growing number of corporations, however, publish social statements on a voluntary basis or include data about the societal benefits granted by the corporation in the statement of affairs. While there are no generally recognized rules about the contents of the social statement, they normally include data about personnel, about vocational training and further education, safety at the workplace, pension schemes, social facilities, as well as about research and development facilities, pollution and measures to protect the environment.

V. CONFLICT OF INTEREST: THE PROBLEM OF THE CONTROL GROUP

Some of the issues arising out of conflicts of interests within the corporation have already been addressed earlier in this chapter. Now the conflict of interest that arises in the case of a sale of a majority participation has to be dealt with. A comprehensive discussion is however neither possible nor necessary in this context.

A. Sale of Control

If the shareholder has a majority participation in an AG and intends to sell it to a third party, this transaction will mainly affect the interests of the minority shareholders and sometimes also of the general public. When a group of companies is created by a takeover, which increases the concentration of companies in that industry it is possible that there could be a negative impact on competition. In the light of these possible effects, can a majority shareholder sell his shares without any limits? If so, does he have to transfer the excess proceeds (the so-called additional block of shares, *Paketzuschlag*), that he gets for his dominant position, to the corporation or does he have to share it with the other shareholders? Furthermore, is he subject to specific legal obligations to disclose or to register? If not, should he be?

Under German law, the dominant shareholder is under no obligation to inform other shareholders about impending transactions. Consequently they cannot assess the value of their shares correctly under the present conditions. One cannot approve of such an obligation of disclosure or information in a general way, but only under specific circumstances.[25] The excess proceeds received for the sale of the control can presumably be kept by the former majority shareholder.

B. Disclosure

After 1 January 1995, anyone who owns 5 per cent or more of the votes has to notify the corporation and the public authority controlling the securities' trade (*Bundesaufsichtsamt für den Wertpapierhandel*) in writing at the latest on the first day of the shareholders' meeting of the corporation that takes place after 1 April 1995 of the amount of his share in the voting capital (§ 41(2) of the *Wertpapierhandelsgesetz* of 26 July 1994). A person who acquires the majority interest is under the same obligation (§ 21(2) of this statute). The acquisition of the majority interest in another corporation can be made by publicly placing bids for the shares of this corporation at a price above the actual quotation of the day. Such takeover bids or tender offers are "hostile" only if they are made against the will of the corporation's management. In Germany, tender offers have only been made in a few cases, no hostile tender offers at all have been noted. As discussed earlier, in order to protect themselves against such tactics, some corporations have provided for a limitation of the voting rights.

C. Tender Offers

Tender offers give rise to a number of problems of regulation that primarily affect the information of shareholders and their equality of treatment. So far, the legislator has not adopted any provisions regarding these problems. Only the commission of stock exchange experts (*Kommission der Börsensachverständigen*) has set up non-binding rules for tender offers in 1997.[26] The Commission of the EU has, in 1990, presented a draft directive on tender offers, however, so far it has not been adopted by the Council.

D. Corporate Groups

In 1965, a new section was added to the AktG that addresses the problems that groups of companies acting in concert create in corporate law. It is a relatively detailed section which, mainly deals with the rights of the minority shareholders (outside shareholders – *außenstehende Aktionäre*).

This statutory regulation (*Konzernrecht*, §§ 291-337 of the AktG) is aimed at limiting the rights of groups of companies created by contract (control agreement-*Beherrschungsvertrag*).[27] A control agreement is the consolidation of at least two legally independent companies under a single management (§ 18(1) of the AktG). A

[25] Cf. Wiedemann, supra note 13, p. 453.

[26] These rules are reprinted in Baumbach/ Duden/ Hopt, *Handelsgesetzbuch* (26th ed., 1985), pp. 1139 et seq.

[27] For further details cf. Emmerich/ Sonnenschein, *Konzernrecht* (4th ed., 1992), pp. 135 et seq.

de facto group based upon majority participation is not dealt with in the statute. The administrative and financial rights of the minority shareholders of the controlled corporation are affected in different ways by the control agreement. For instance, the profits can be hidden entirely because they are transferred to the controlling corporation thereby denying shareholder's dividends. The AktG guarantees those shareholders either a dividend (§ 304), or it grants them a right to an indemnification if they withdraw from the corporation (§ 305).

In the de facto group of companies – most groups are de facto groups, and most publicly held corporations also belong to groups – the controlled corporation does not only have a right against the controlling corporation to compensation for damages that result from actions taken by the controlling corporation (§ 311 of the AktG), but also to compensation for damages suffered (§ 317(1), first sentence AktG).[28] If in addition, the shareholders themselves suffer damages by such actions, they also have a right to be compensated for the losses caused by the controlling corporation (§ 317(1), second sentence of the AktG). This statutory regulation is important because contrary to a control agreement there would be no contractual right to recover damages. Its significance in practice is not very important.

VI. FINAL REMARKS

In all States with free market economies, the corporation is an important form of business organization. It should not be a surprise that a certain number of principles applying to the corporation can be found everywhere. But the general approach of the legislature in regulating corporations seems to be particularly important. The American and the European models differ in so far as the former does not have such a rigid and detailed legislation as the law of corporations. Rather, the centre of the protective provisions is part of the law regulating the securities market e.g. the Securities Exchange Commission. In German law, the problem has been solved the other way round.

The question remains whether either solution is adequate to meet the issues and problems raised by the present conditions. This seems very doubtful, especially with regard to the expansion of the capital markets and the fact that the securities trading can be done by electronic means.

Both in Germany and in the United States of America, a discussion about the appropriate management and control of enterprises has been under way lately.[29] But the legislature has not yet taken any concrete action.

A new balance between the control by the capital market and the law of corporations will play an important role in a possible reform of the existing law. As far as the adequate organization as such of a company is concerned, the shareholders' value is not the predominant issue in Germany. The background for the present discussion are questions like: the proper performance of its duties by the board of management and its control in the view of the collapse of a number of companies; the resolving of conflicts of interest of members of the supervisory board, when they

[28] Ibid., pp. 330 et seq.

[29] Cf. the very recent and extensive reports in Feddersen/Hommelhoff/ Schneider (ed.), *Corporate Governance – Optimierung der Unternehmensführung und der Unternehmenskontrolle im deutschen und amerikanischen Aktienrecht,* 1996.

also have functions in other, competing companies; the abuse of the shareholders' meeting for political purposes; the position of the large commercial banks; the influence and expectations of institutional investors such as instance banks,[30] insurance companies or mutual funds and the replacement of the individual investor by the institutional investor is taking place quite slowly given the absence of privat pension funds in Germany.

The issues that are discussed in view of possible reform are the following: introduction of an audit committee within the supervisory board to improve the control of the management; decrease of the number of positions that a member of a supervisory board can hold; introduction of a shareholders' derivative action; voting rights of nominee shareholders (banks); and cross-shareholdings between companies.

For Germany as well as for the other Member States of the European Union, there is the additional problem of the harmonization of corporate law: which issues should be regulated by the EU and which should be left to the Member States? Above all, how complete should the regulation be? Which material aspects should be regulated at all?

Furthermore, it seems to be important to see the publicly held corporation is not only affected by corporate and capital market law. The concentration by external growth, i.e. by connection and interaction with other companies, has to be dealt with by anti-trust and competition laws.

Each country has areas in which it is less developed. A comparison of the different legal systems shows that there is an overall need for the legislature to address the relevant issues. It seems very likely that the problems will be dealt with. It remains to be seen whether this will lead to far-reaching reforms.

30 Cf. Baums/ Buxbaum/ Hopt (ed.), *Institutional Investors and Corporate Governance*, 1994.

3

Italy

*Eugenio Ruggiero**

I. INTRODUCTION

The corporation is the legal device at the heart of any economic system functioning according to the basic market rules associated with capitalism. The advantages such legal device offers, for example in terms of limited liability, free transferability of ownership interests, centralization of management,[1] make it the most viable device for carrying out economic initiatives, especially large-scale ones. As a matter of fact, the adoption of the corporation allows the tempering and compromise between the investors' risk aversion and the entrepreneurs' need for availability of capital resources to carry out their presumably profitable business. For such a device to work and find an equilibrium, it implies a complex system of checks and balances whereas shareholders, as owners of the invested capital, choose, and then supervise, the entrepreneurs (the directors) seeking to implement and reach the target of the investment (profit).

The crucial point is then the collection of capital resources. Understanding how such collection takes place explains the structure of the financial market and how financial resources are allocated, thus shaping the figure of the shareholder and giving greater or lesser strength, according to size, capability and professionality, to his position vis-à-vis the directors.

II. FINANCING THE COMPANY: THE STRUCTURE OF THE FINANCIAL MARKET

A financial market may be described as the meeting-point between those who have a surplus of financial resources and want to profitably invest it (typically, households), and those who have a deficit of financial resources (typically, firms) and therefore want to borrow or buy such resources from those in surplus.

* Research scholar at CERADI-LUISS Guido Carli University, Rome, Italy.

[1] W.A. Klein & J.C. Coffee, *Business organization and finance* (Westbury, NY, 1993), pp. 105-110.

© Kluwer Law International 1998

In Italy, traditionally, such meeting-point has taken place thanks to the intermediation of the banking system, which holds a central role in the allocation of financial resources (bank-centred system). The direct access of firms to the financial market through the issue of shares or debentures (market system) has always been not very significant, as opposed to what happens in other countries, for example the U.S. or England.

The central role of banks in the financial market finds its origins in a spontaneous cultural attitude of the investors favourable to banks, viewed as a "safer" place in which to put savings. However, culture would certainly not be enough to explain the phenomenon. There was also a precise political will that privileged banks, in an effort to avoid excessive fragmentation of the financing channels to the productive system.[2] A greater concentration of the financial circuits, through the banking system, allowed greater control of it in order to more effectively implement monetary, fiscal and industrial government policies.[3] Also, government action in implementing monetary and fiscal policies was rendered even more effective by the fact that most of the banking system was State owned.

The centrality of banks in the Italian financial system finds immediate evidence in the financial structure of the firms. On average, equity plus issue of debentures represents about 48 per cent of the total financial resources of companies, whereas bank loans account for 52 per cent. Indeed, equity is for the most part earned surplus, while bank loans are for the most part short-term debt, demonstrating that, on the whole, firms rely very little on their capacity to directly access the savings market to finance their business.[4]

A mirroring situation can be found with regard to the supply side of finance. Only 6 per cent of the Italian households owns stock: their financial portfolio is composed for the most part (60 per cent) of liquid assets, such as government bonds or bank and postal deposits, while 20 per cent is shares of stock (listed or non-listed).

The equity market, relinquished to the very margins of the financial circuit, turned into a highly speculative market not connected, as it should be, to the fundamentals of the real productive economy. The available data confirm the low quality of the equity market. The amount of shares publicly outstanding and regularly traded is about 25 per cent of the total outstanding shares, thus showing the thinness of the

[2] Ever since the 1930s, after the Great Depression, securities trading in the market system has always been considered a very speculative business, not fit for the public at large, but only for professionals willing to risk their assets. A systematic reconstruction of the evolution of the Italian financial market in the twentieth century can be found in G. Visentini, *L'evoluzione del sistema finanziario italiano. I problemi attuali* (Milano, 1995).

[3] Specific tax policies favoured not only the allocation of savings to bank deposits, but also the financing of companies through bank debt. The income tax reform of 1971-1973 clearly showed such favourable tax status: interest on bank deposits was taxed at a 15 per cent rate and interest on debentures issued by investment banks was taxed at a 10 per cent rate, whereas interest on corporate debentures was taxed at a 30 per cent rate. Corporate dividends, instead, concurred to forming personal income and were hence taxed progressively; indeed, until the introduction of a tax credit on dividends in 1977, dividends were subject to double taxation (corporate income tax, when earned, and, once distributed, personal income tax). In the latest years, the situation has tended to change and there is an effort to make the various tax rates on capital earnings more uniform. A new tax reform came into effect on 1 July 1998 and it generally set tax rates on capital earnings (dividends, interest, capital gains) at 12.5 per cent (27 per cent for interest on bank deposits and short-term debt).

[4] Indeed, long-term debt is there to signify a stable relationship with the company, which implies an accurate review of the economic potentials of the business engaged in by the company: such review is quite similar to the analysis needed in order to evaluate the convenience in acquiring shares in the company.

market.[5] The thinness of the market is strictly related to its liquidity and is measured by the capacity to promptly divest one's portfolio without excessive losses: in Italy, volume of trading is quite low, only 18 per cent of market capitalization, compared to 36-37 per cent in France or Great Britain, or to 50 per cent and more on the New York Stock Exchange.

The centrality of the banking system for corporate finance, and the consequent slight development of the stock market, kept the general public at a distance from investing savings into equity instruments, and favoured the safer bank deposits or government bonds. Moreover, the cost of equity, compared to the cost of debt, rises by virtue not only of the higher risk connected, but also of an unfavourable tax regime and of an excessively burdensome regulation. When adding these factors to the crowding-out effect caused by the existing huge amount of public debt, one has a fairly complete picture of the marginal role played by the stock market within the financial circuit.

This being the situation, companies have come to lack a direct confrontation with the capital market, which cannot even be said to take place through the mediation of the banking system because of the strong State presence in that industry.[6] However, such confrontation becomes even more necessary in view of the increasing internationalization and globalization of the markets, not only to help the financial stability of companies through a direct access to the equity market, but also to encourage and stimulate the development of an efficient market for corporate control where the circulation of shares becomes an indicator of the quality of the business judgment of directors.

III. THE "OWNERSHIP STRUCTURE" AND THE "BALANCE OF POWER"[7]

This section analyzes relevant data and information with regard to the main "ownership models" characterizing listed companies in Italy. The dynamics of the prevailing ownership structure in listed companies allows a better understanding of the peculiarities of the balance of power within, and among, the corporate bodies.

Actually, in the Italian case, the prevalence of the so-called "defined ownership" model[8] leads to anomalies and disorders in the balance of power, that should be carefully analyzed in order to understand the spirit and the state of the art of the Italian corporate structure.

5 The thinness (or, on the reverse, the thickness) of the market measures its capacity to absorb, with no sudden price movements, the buy and sell orders for the securities traded.

6 Examining the ownership structure of the Italian banking system, it may be noticed that most banks, and surely the largest ones, have a direct or indirect proprietary connection with the State. See G. Bisconti & L. Monaco, "Italy", in F. Schwank & F.R. Ryder (eds.), *Banks abroad*, 1986.

7 This chapter was made possible thanks to the valuable contribution of Dr. Luca Torchia and of Dr. Carlo De Gennaro. Most of the data and figures cited come from the research led by Ceradi Luiss and carried out by C. De Gennaro - M. Musolino - L. Torchia, *Struttura proprietaria e modelli di controllo con riferimento alle società italiane quotate: alcune considerazioni alla luce di una verifica empirica*, forthcoming publication, 1998. Other useful sources of information were the periodical publications issued by IRS (*Rapporto sul mercato azionario*), Centro Studi Confindustria and Consiglio di Borsa (mainly, *Fatti e cifre*).

8 See infra the table at p. 85.

The attempt in the following pages is to classify listed companies according to the "ownership model" they feature. As a background, it is necessary to examine the current listing structure of the Italian stock exchange.

The number of companies listed on the Stock Exchange is still quite low compared to the number of all "listable" companies. Data from the end of 1996 show that market capitalization accounts for only 20.6 per cent of GNP[9] (though the ratio was even lower at the end of 1994 – 17.9 per cent).

In 1996 the number of national companies listed on the Milan Stock Exchange shrank from 217 to 213 and the number of listed shares issued by national companies went from 313 at the end of 1995 to 303 in 1996. Most of the listing cancellations were due to a lack of outstanding public shares[10] or to specific company reasons (generally the opening of bankruptcy proceedings or mergers and combinations between listed companies). Market capitalization showed a steady growth, ranging from 325,568 billion lire in 1995 to 386,157 billion lire in 1996. Over the whole year, market capitalization increased by about 18 per cent. Interesting information also comes from the distribution of capitalization among listed companies: the biggest 30 companies[11] – representing 14 per cent of all listed companies – have a market capitalization of 281,472 billion lire, which accounts for 74 per cent of total capitalization. These figures confirm the tendency, already shown in previous years, towards an increase in concentration of the stock market.

So far, one first result arising from this analysis, confirming the conclusion previously reached, is that the Italian stock market cannot be said to be very significant in terms of the overall economy. This could actually be considered an anomaly when compared, for instance, to Anglo-Saxon markets. However, it is quite a typical feature for continental European economies.[12] (See the table opposite.)

One thing to notice from the table opposite is the relevance of the financial sector, which accounts for over one-third of the Stock Exchange list. A correct appreciation of this fact must consider that very often the trading in financial companies (be they banks, insurance or financial holdings) conceals the transfer of "controlling stakes" in other listed industrial or services companies. This phenomenon is usually described as the *Chinese box* phenomenon. It takes place when a holding company controls an operative company, and both the holding and the operative company are listed. The acquisition of shares in the holding company is therefore an indirect acquisition of shares in the operative subsidiary.[13] A clear understanding of the stock

[9] The ratio market capitalization to GNP, although currently showing an increasing trend (at the end of 1995 it was 18.3 per cent), reached its historical maximum in 1986, when it was 21.2 per cent.

[10] One of the reasons is that when outstanding public shares of a listed company are less than 10 per cent of the issued listed shares, the person controlling the company has an obligation to purchase all remaining shares (so-called *residual public offer*), causing the cancellation from listing. The number of listing cancellations due to this provision is also a first hint of the main peculiarity of Italian listed companies that we will later show, i.e. the high concentration of shares in the hands of few relevant shareholders.

[11] These are the so-called "MIB30 companies", the *blue chip* shares forming the Milan Stock Exchange Index (MIB30).

[12] Germany and France, for example, have very similar structures for their financial markets. See also G. Visentini, "Compatibility and competition between European and American corporate governance. Which model of capitalism?", *Brooklyn Journal of International Law*, p. 1 (1998). 1.

[13] Groups of companies are very often organized in such pyramidal structure, in order to rationalize the internal organization keeping apart the risks connected with each activity exercised, and to increase the capacity of the group to attract savings and credit. The tax credit mechanism on dividends makes such organizational structure almost completely neutral tax-wise.

Table 1 Industry Structure of the Stock Exchange List in 1996

Industry	*Number of listed shares*	*Capitalization (Billion lire)*	*Capitalization (% of total)*
Food/Agriculture	7	8,925	2.3
Automobile	13	22,207	5.8
Paper	8	1,223	0.3
Chemical	24	9,507	2.5
Construction	16	4,080	1.1
Electronics-Electromechanics	30	8,908	2.3
Plants-Machinery	9	4,532	1.2
Other industrial companies	3	363	0.1
Mining-Metal-Oil	6	64,358	16.7
Textile	23	7,844	2.0
Distribution-Retail	6	2,245	0.6
Publishing	6	11,094	2.9
Public utilities	14	106,637	27.6
Transport-Tourism	20	4,447	1.2
Insurance	22	58,138	15.1
Banking	39	57,598	14.9
Financial holdings	31	11,933	3.1
Other financial companies	4	209	0.4
Real estate	16	1,438	0.1
Financial services	6	470	0.1
Total Industrial Sector	139	131,497	34.2
Total Services Sector	46	124,423	32.2
Total Financial Sector	118	129,787	33.6

market and of the ownership structure of listed companies must take this factor into account as well.

The classification of listed companies with regard to their ownership structure requires the prior definition of the different existing patterns, according to two parameters: the number of "relevant shareholders" (i.e. the shareholders who exercise control, or, in any case, exercise influence) and the degree of identification between ownership and management.

With regard to the number of relevant shareholders, the degree of concentration of ownership, and therefore the allocation of the company in the appropriate "ownership structure" pattern, depends not only on the number of relevant shareholders but also, and mainly, on the lower or higher level of voluntary cohesion among them in the making of company decisions, that is, basically, in determining the will of the general meeting.

Where there is only one relevant shareholder, he will then be the one to exclusively determine the will of the general meeting. Where the relevant shareholders are several, they will give a common and uniform address to the management of the company when they are bound to each other through some sort of agreement, be it enforceable in law or in fact. These kinds of agreements are often formalized either by shareholders' agreements or by exchanges of share ownership (circular or cross-shareholdings). In such case, the shareholders tied by the agreement will behave as if they were a single person holding control when determining the will of the general meeting.

In either of the above forms of ownership structure, the *controlling shareholder* can always be recognized, be it the single relevant shareholder or the group of shareholders connected by a trust agreement.

Finally, when the ownership structure is characterized by a high number of shareholders, not linked by any agreement, then we have a different pattern, where the will of the general meeting is formed by the sum of the will of all shareholders acting separately from each other, without the strength or power to autonomously influence any decision.

The degree of identification between ownership and management depends upon the prevailing company structure pattern. As previously stated, when there is only one relevant shareholder, he will be the one who takes all the decisions in the running of the company. In this case a *real* overlap between ownership and management occurs.

When the *controlling shareholder* is defined by a shareholders' agreement, then the participants to the agreement itself are entrusted with the management. In this instance, as well, ownership overlaps with management. However, while the ownership constituency is formed by the members of the shareholders' agreement, the management may well be formed by persons who are part of it though they cannot be legally identified with it all. A *de facto* overlap between ownership and management occurs.

When a *controlling shareholder* cannot be found because the shareholders are atomized and fragmented, ownership is detached from management. The atomization of ownership causes disinterest in the management of the company, which is then fully delegated to the directors and officers. The shareholder views the company as a financial, and not an entrepreneurial, investment.

The existing ownership structure patterns are then the following:

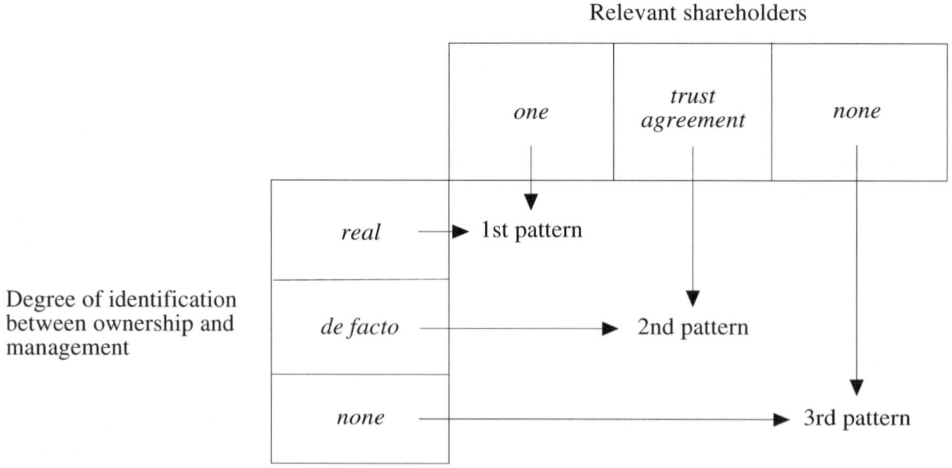

The first pattern may be called the *monodefined ownership* pattern; there is only one relevant shareholder who exclusively determines the will of the general meeting and who is entrusted with the running of the company (the main shareholder is the entrepreneur).

The second pattern may be called the *pluridefined ownership* pattern; there are several relevant shareholders who jointly determine the will of the general meeting through a shareholders' agreement, and the managers of the company are the direct expression of that agreement.

The third pattern may be called the *institutional* pattern, where there are no relevant shareholders and the will of the general meeting is *de facto* determined by the directors who somehow receive a *blank cheque* from the general meeting (the public company).

Having set the ownership structure patterns, it is now possible to classify the existing Italian listed companies according to them. MIB30 companies can be used for more accurate representation since they account for about 74 per cent of the market.[14]

The distribution of the MIB30 listed companies according to their ownership structure will then be as follows:[15]

	Companies		Market capitalization		
Ownership structure model	*Number*	*% of MIB30*	*Billion Lire*	*% of MIB30*	*% of Total*
I model (*monodefined ownership*)	23[16]	77%	256,009	88.5%	66.5%
II model (*pluridefined ownership*)	7[17]	23%	32,651	11.5%	8.5%
III model (*public ownership*)	—	—	—	—	—

The distribution of the MIB30 companies in the appropriate ownership structure patterns leads to the following conclusions.

The prevailing ownership pattern is the *monodefined* one, where the shares are in the hands of one relevant and controlling shareholder. The controlling shareholder is

[14] Using the MIB30 companies may also be helpful in neutralizing, to a certain extent, the duplications that may arise from the "Chinese box" phenomenon, since the ownership structure of the holding company, at the top of the cascade, is then reflected in all subsidiaries, be them listed or not.

[15] The table shows the situation at the end of 1996. For a clear explanation of the adopted methodology, see the research led by Ceradi Luiss and carried out by C. De Gennaro - M. Musolino - L. Torchia, *Struttura proprietaria e modelli di controllo con riferimento alle società italiane quotate: alcune considerazioni alla luce di una verifica empirica*, forthcoming publication, 1998.

[16] The listed companies included in the *monodefined ownership* pattern are: Eni, Telecom Italia, Stet, Telecom Italia Mobile, Generali, Fiat, Mediaset, San Paolo di Torino, Alleanza Ass., Edison, Rolo Banca 1473, Ras, Italgas, Pirelli, Montedison, Banca di Roma, Parmalat, Benetton, Fideuram, Saipem, Sirti, La Fondiaria, Olivetti.

[17] The listed companies included in the *pluridefined ownership* pattern are: Ina, Imi, Banca Commerciale Italiana, Mediobanca, Mediolanum, Credito Italiano, Gemina.

either another company or, more often, a single entrepreneur (the typical "family enterprise").

With the *pluridefined ownership* pattern, control of the company is in the hands of few relevant shareholders who (usually through agreements among them) exercise their authority over the management. The directors are the expression of a clearly identifiable ownership structure: the identification is not as clear as it might be in a family enterprise, though the agreement binding the relevant shareholders evidences a consolidated and lasting relationship allowing unitary guidelines for the control of the company.

Finally, no company is included in the *institutional* pattern which results in the non-existence of the pure publicly held corporation in the Italian market.

The prevalence of the *monodefined ownership* pattern is clearly a consequence of the structure of the financial circuit. Passing from a family enterprise model to a public company model would require, in the first place, the provision of effective and efficient financing sources other than the usual banking debt. This would require a much firmer policy on the government side in trying to channel public savings through the stock market as well. Efforts in this direction have been made, and are still being made, for example through the privatization of state-owned companies and the development of private pension funds. On the other hand, one thing to consider is that in other countries, the United States for instance, the "going public" phenomenon has been strongly encouraged by the entrepreneurs not only to attract greater amounts of capital to finance their businesses but also to mobilize their wealth by the increased liquidity of the publicly negotiable shares. Such needs surely constitute incentives for going public in Italy as well. However, they suffer the tension with the existing "cultural prejudice" towards public ownership of firms, on the side of both the savers and the entrepreneurs. On the side of savers, there has always been risk aversion towards firms, favoured by the existing legislative and political framework addressing savings to more reliable (and often more profitable) investments as government or bank debt. Of course, it should not be forgotten, as well, that until very recent times government debt offered very high yields, thus crowding out, for a large part, private investment. On the side of entrepreneurs, the management of firms has been dominated by the "51 per cent culture", i.e. the desire for entrepreneurs to keep firm control of their companies fearing that going public might make them lose such control.

The reasons for such situation are to be found in the evolution of Italian economic history. The productive structure of the country, as a matter of fact, has developed along the typical feature of the "prevailing owner". On one side, the "self-made" entrepreneur who runs the business centralizing all decisions, thus leading to a complete overlap of ownership and management: this feature, as we saw, is typical not only of small and medium-sized firms but also of larger firms. On the other side, in order to counterbalance the high concentration of ownership in the private sector, the "State entrepreneur" intervened in financing companies and in many cases it actually took over businesses in situation of crisis.[18] In both cases, for private ownership and for state ownership, the characteristics of a strongly centralized ownership remain and affect Italian industrial development, leaving in existence that cultural prejudice contrary to the spreading of *institutional* ownership models.

[18] State intervention in the economy through the direct ownership of businesses dates back to the beginning of the 20th century. For a detailed overview of the process, see A. Papa Malatesta, "Partecipazioni pubbliche", in *Digesto*, IV Ed., vol. X Pubblico (Torino, 1995).

The culture of 51 per cent ownership can change over time through the needs of the owners. However, such change may also be encouraged by acts of the State. As a matter of fact, in recent times the law seems to develop towards the encouragement of a greater diffusion of public shareholding, providing incentives to enlarge the basis of company control. The growing competition within the globalized markets, and within the EU in the first place, requires greater access to capital resources for companies. The traditional sources of capital, either the banking system or government investment spending, seem to be no longer sufficient to fulfill the needs of the economic system at large.[19]

Laws were passed expressly addressing the regulation of the market, supplementing the fundamental provisions of the Civil Code, concerning the internal affairs of companies, and of the Law no. 216/1974, relating to the securities markets and the solicitation of public savings. Among these laws we ought to cite, in the first place, those mainly concerned with the functioning of the financial markets: Law no. 415/1996 (regulation of investment business and of securities brokers and dealers, implementing the EU investment services directive); Law no. 157/1991 (regulation of insider trading); Law no. 149/1992 (public offers of securities and takeovers); and Law no. 385/1993 which regulates the banking system allowing banks to hold shares in industrial companies (thus accepting the EU model of the "universal bank"). However, the effort of the legislator also concentrated upon the rationalization of the financial circuits, by allowing the activity of new financial intermediaries or adapting the activity of existing intermediaries to the needs of the modern financial world. In this respect there is Law no. 77/1983, regulating open-ended investment funds, repealed in 1992 to implement the relevant EC directives; the Law no. 84/1992 regulating variable capital investment companies; the Law no. 124/1993 and no. 335/1995 regulating private pension funds; the Law no. 344/1993 regulating closed-end investment funds. Many of these laws have been recently consolidated by the Law no. 58/1998, which collects the existing regulation of financial intermediation and introduces new corporate governance provisions for listed companies. (See Section VIII below.)

A further effort is also being made to increase the supply of public shares through the sale of shares of companies owned by the State. The Law no. 474/1994, which regulates the procedures for the privatization of State-owned companies, states that one of the methods to be used in placing the shares is the public offer of securities, thus spreading public ownership. Such method has already been used in various instances, such as the sale of the shares of Credito Italiano and of Banca Commerciale, two of the biggest banks operating in Italy, of INA, the biggest Italian insurance company, of ENI, the gas and energy company, and, more lately, of Telecom Italia, the telecommunications company.

The following pages will be devoted to a closer examination of the regulatory aspects of companies, with a particular focus on the corporate governance issues for those companies that do access the public market for financing. In viewing these

[19] The situation of the Italian public debt, besides the EU prohibition on State aids, did not allow any further State financial intervention. Public debt has now reached over 125 per cent of GNP. Although figures are rapidly changing to allow Italian government spending to stay within the strict parameters set by the Maastricht Treaty, once the European Monetary Union is in place it will be hardly impossible (and in some instances even illegal) for Italian fiscal expenditure to intervene in the economy as heavily as it used in the past.

aspects, the peculiarities arising from the analyzed structure of the Italian financial market should be carefully kept in mind. In fact, the presence of a clearly identifiable owner of the company, be it a 51 per cent shareholder or a relevant shareholder (or group of connected shareholders), somehow shifts the focus of our analysis.

The traditional debate concerning corporate governance views it as a search for the balance of power between the shareholders and the management. The famous study by Berle and Means[20] evidenced a very fragmented ownership structure in the U.S. market. The public company phenomenon, due to the politics and economics of the country,[21] is still a very common one in the United States and hence the corporate governance debate reflects such ownership structure. The empirical situation is quite different in Italy, and the overview of the legal system leads to an important conclusion. In a public company context the danger that shareholders become captives of the managers implies that the regulation will then have to mainly confront this issue. Instead, in a *monodefined ownership* context, with access to the public markets as the Italian case shows, the danger is that minority shareholders become the captives of majority shareholders. The managers are the direct expression of the majority commanding shareholder (or group of shareholders) taking all fundamental decisions concerning the company. The managers' task is to implement such decisions. Therefore, the corporate governance issue that arises primarily concerns the conflict between majority and minority shareholder: in this context, the protection of shareholders from the misfeasances of directors is secondary.

One further conclusion that will be drawn from the present overview is that the main rigidities of the current Italian system lie not in the specific company regulation but in its concrete application and in the regulation and structure of the financial circuits causing the weakness of the market for shares.

IV. THE REGULATION OF COMPANIES

Italian law envisages several forms of corporate organizations for the carrying out of business activities. Such forms all differ from each other in single peculiar aspects that do not, however, prejudice the shape conferred by the general regulatory pattern concerning corporate personality for business activities.

The corporate model assumed by the legislator is the *società per azioni* (*spa*), viewed as the principal way of running business in corporate form.[22]

20 A. Berle & G. Means, *The modern corporation and private property* (New Brunswick, 1991) (original edition 1932).

21 See M. Roe, *Strong managers, weak owners* (Princeton, 1994).

22 From here on, unless otherwise specified, any reference to a company or corporation will mean reference to a "spa". There are a few other corporate entities envisaged by the legislator to carry out business. Their regulation is framed in terms of the *spa*, only pointing out the differences in operation. In the *società in accomandita per azioni* (*sapa*), the organizational structure is more or less the same as in the *spa*, with the main difference arising from the fact that directors (who are also shareholders) are severally and unlimitedly liable for corporate debts. Other minor business organizations having the corporate form are the *società a responsabilita limitata* (*srl*); this corporate form, however, has very little flexibility given the fact that its capital stock is not represented by shares, thus making it difficult to transfer ownership interests. It is also worth mentioning the existence of various types of mutual and cooperative companies. However, their peculiar organizational structure does not allow to consider them fully as an instrument of capitalistic society: distribution of earnings is limited, the capital stock is variable, participation is mainly personal and vote is granted per head. Somehow, they

The main features characterizing the *spa* are legal personality, limited liability of shareholders, free transferability of the shares, and non-liability of the persons acting on its behalf (i.e. the directors) for corporate debts. In the course of our analysis, it will be seen how these features favour the use of this model in the business community, and how they influence the balance of power within the company.

The law concerning companies is for the greatest part contained in the Italian Civil Code, issued in 1942 and subsequently amended, several times in order to implement the EU Company Directives.[23] Such legislation resembles the previous regulation of the Code of Commerce of 1882, with a few adaptations and refinements due to the experience gained in many years of application. Further relevant legislation regards mainly listed companies, their access to the public securities markets,[24] or firms operating in particular industries (banking, financial services, insurance, etc.).[25]

V. FORMATION OF THE COMPANY

The Italian Constitution establishes the right to free business undertaking, within the forms and limitations stated by the law.[26] The setting up of a company, as a method of organizing one's business undertaking, comes within such general right. The law determines fixed and uniform parameters and patterns to comply with and then leaves it to the individuals to exercise, as they think most fit, their economic freedom as it is thus defined. Hence, the formation of a company is free and only subject to a legality control to verify that the company being formed respects the parameters and pattern imposed by the law (e.g. minimum capital requirements, organizational structure).[27]

At its formative stage, the corporation is a contract and it therefore requires the presence of at least two founding members.[28]

cont.

can be considered an interesting example of "public company" in view of the widespread ownership of their shares among a large number of participants. A recent law (Law no. 59/1992) introduced a few corrections in their structure to favour greater capitalization allowing the participation of purely capitalistic members. It is also worth noticing that *banche popolari* are formed as cooperative companies, but are subject to the special banking law.

23 At the current moment, all EU company directives adopted by the Council have been implemented by the Italian legislator.

24 Main pieces of legislation in this area are the following. L. 216/1974 creates *Consob*, the Government supervisory agency for the securities market, and establishes rules directed to enhancing disclosure for listed companies. D.p.r. 136/1975 provides for the mandatory independent auditing of listed companies' accounts. D.Lg. 127/1991 implements the IV and VII EC company directives on annual and consolidated accounts. L. 149/1992 regulates takeovers of listed companies. L. 474/1994 regulates the privatization of State-owned companies. L. 157/1991 regulates insider trading.

25 In this respect it is worth mentioning the following statutes. D.Lg. 385/1993 regulates banks and other credit institutions. D.Lg. 415/1996 regulates investment and securities business.

26 Article 41 of the Italian Constitution states, in pertinent part, that "private economic undertaking is free. It cannot be carried out in contrast with social utility or so as to infringe upon human security, freedom and dignity".

27 The "concession doctrine", according to which the State granted corporate personality only for those initiatives that it deemed valuable, thus reviewing the factual merits of the initiative, was definitively abandoned since the issuance of the Code of Commerce in 1865.

28 The plurality of the members is only necessary at the formation of the company. The lack of plurality of the founding members of the company will cause the nullity of the company and, hence, its

The legality control is given to the judiciary, through the review of the articles of association and of the by-laws. This control is effected not only when the company is being set up but also, more generally, every time there is an amendment to the articles or to the by-laws. It is, however, a peculiar function exercised by the judge. He is not really exercising his typical jurisdictional powers since he is not reviewing any litigation, or contention of rights and duties: in this context the judge is actually acting as an administrative body verifying and ascertaining the fulfilment of the conditions statutorily set and, on this basis, ordering the grant of the corporate charter. During this process, although not so clear in law, the judge does maintain substantial powers to actually address the content of the articles and of the by-laws, as shown below.

As previously mentioned, the judge shall grant the corporate charter (or shall allow the amendment to the articles) once the requirements established by the law have been fulfilled. Such statutory requirements concern the existence of the prescribed items in the articles of association and in the by-laws,[29] minimum par capital,[30] the subscription of the entire share capital authorized and to be issued,[31] the actual payment into a bank of at least three-tenths of the share capital subscribed in consideration for cash and any specific government authorization required for setting up a company to be engaged in particular industries.[32]

The letter of the law seems to assign a merely passive role to the judge, were it not for the control of the clauses of the articles of association. However, judges usually do not restrain their control to check whether those clauses are actually present in the articles, but extend it to verify their substantial legitimacy. For instance, the law requires that the articles state the object of the corporation: the judge will not only see that the object is stated, but will also evaluate whether the stated object is legitimate, in terms of legality of its pursuance and in terms of its sufficient specificity. In fact, as opposed to other countries such as the U.S., a company in Italy may not be set up "for any legal purpose". Under Italian law, the object of a company, although wide, needs to be precise enough as to limit the operation of the company and, thus, clarify what sort of business risks it is going to undergo.[33]

The exercise of these scrutiny powers by the judge rarely results in official decisions since it is most commonly effected through a moral suasion process in dialogue

cont.

immediate dissolution (art. 2332 of the Civil Code). Should, however, only one shareholder remain during the course of the life of the company, there will be no effect on the company other than the unlimited liability of the single shareholder for debts taken by the company while shareholders' plurality is lacking.

A special provision of law, introduced by D.Lg. no. 88/1993 amending art. 2475 of the Civil Code (implementing the XII EC Company Directive 667/1989), allows an srl to be formed through the unilateral act of a single member. Such srl is subject to specific disclosure regulation and, in some instances, the single member may lose the benefit of limited liability.

29 Article 2328 of the Civil Code lists those items. Besides, the corporate contract must be drafted by a Notary Public in an official ("sealed") form.

30 The minimum par capital requirement is currently 200 million lire.

31 Under Italian law, the notion of authorized capital coincides with issued capital. The only, partial, derogation is at art. 2443 of the Civil Code, whereby the shareholders' meeting, through an amendment of the articles of association, may authorize the issue of new shares, delegating it to the directors for a pre-established amount, within a period of five years from the date of the resolution.

32 For example, the previous authorization by the Bank of Italy is required for setting up banking companies. See art. 14, para. 3 of the Banking Law (D. Lg. 385/1993).

33 For instance, in Trib. Lecce 19.4.1983, in *Le Società* 1984, I, 193, the registration of a company was denied because the stated object ("engaging in the construction business") was deemed to be too generic.

with the founding shareholders of the company (or with the directors of the company when the shareholders amend the articles). In practice it may condition the autonomy and self-determination of the company and its members, allowing the direct intervention of a public body in the merit of the question.[34] Such process leaves little room, if any, for debate or healthy litigation directed toward the composition of the possible contrasting interests of the parties.[35] However, it does not lead to an administrative drafting of the articles or of the by-laws: the judge cannot deny the grant of the charter on the basis of expediency. As a matter of fact, the main consequence arising from the judicial intervention is a general uniformity of the articles and of the by-laws, and this may actually represent an obstacle to innovation in the drafting of the clauses.[36]

The company formation process so described applies regardless of the number of founding shareholders or of the size of capital being subscribed, as long as there is no public solicitation for share subscription. In this latter case, the formation process is different in that it adds procedural complexities at the stage of closing the corporate contract, requiring a vote by the meeting of the share subscribers to approve it.[37] The judicial scrutiny, however, remains the same. Because of these complexities, which cause the process to be longer and hence subject to greater uncertainty, such method is hardly ever used in practice. Given the low minimum capital requirements (200 million lire), it is usually preferred to widen the shareholder basis once the company has already come into existence, through the issue of new shares.[38]

VI. THE OPERATION OF THE COMPANY: ORGANIZATION AND BALANCE OF POWER

The grant of the corporate charter gives rise to a new entity which assumes rights and duties in its own name, thus acquiring legal personality.

[34] In similar proceedings, where the judge is substantially performing administrative functions (so-called "voluntary jurisdiction"), the judge is supposed to take his decision on the basis of the facts and documents submitted to him. It is common practice, however, that the judge ask for further documents or for changes in the contents of already submitted documents. In response to this behaviour, it is altogether common that the corporate contract submitted for registration have a clause allowing the prospective director(s) of the company to amend any of the non-essential clauses of the articles in order to meet the judge's requirements. Moreover, many courts publicly issue "honorary jurisprudence", a set of guidelines, with no legal binding value, stating the attitude of the court with reference to the grant of corporate charters and to the acceptability of specific clauses for the articles of association.

If the judge refuses to grant the charter of incorporation, the only remedy available is the appeal to the Court of Appeals, with no possibility to access the Supreme Court (*Corte di Cassazione*), which only tries the law and not the facts.

[35] Clauses of the articles that usually give rise to debate as for their legitimacy concern, *inter alia*, methods of appointment of directors and limitations to the transferability of shares.

[36] A further consequence is also that any possibly controversial clause, rather than being inserted in the corporate contract, will most probably end up forming the object of a parallel shareholders' agreement, thus limiting and diminishing the transparency of the internal affairs of the company.

[37] Articles 2333 to 2341 of the Civil Code.

[38] The allotment of shares to the public is subject to the control and regulation of *Consob*. Anybody wanting to raise funds from the public needs to abide by the rules and regulations issued under the Law no. 216/1974. In particular, the law provides for the previous publication of a prospectus which gives account of the organization, the economic and financial situation and the development of the business of the person soliciting public investors.

The corporate charter implies a legally defined organizational structure for the new entity, separating, to a certain extent, the various functions needed to keep into existence and activity the new legal person created by the corporate charter. The actors operating within the corporate structure (the corporate bodies) are the shareholders, the directors and the internal supervisory board (*collegio sindacale*). As a general pattern, the shareholders constitute the property basis of the company. In view of the pursuit of their business profit, the shareholders delegate the management to the directors and, by the same token, they appoint experts to sit on the internal supervisory board, to whom they entrust the task of keeping in check the delegated management powers.

The shareholders express their will concerning the operation of the company at the general meeting. Their competence is restricted to specific issues by the law and by the articles of association.

The directors (either a single director or a board of directors) are entrusted, by the shareholders, with the management of the company. Their competence is general: they can take any action within the law and the corporate object, unless it is expressly forbidden by the articles.

The *collegio sindacale* is entrusted with the supervision of the operation of the company to ascertain compliance with the law and with the articles of association.

Finally, in listed companies the review of books and accounts and the control over the annual balance sheet must be entrusted to an independent auditing company, appointed by the shareholders' meeting and subject to the supervision of *Consob*.

A. The Shareholders

The shareholders risk their capital quotas in the company, represented by shares, and receive their remuneration in the form of dividends. Their remuneration can never be certain or fixed, since it depends on the profitability of the business carried out.

Shares issued by the company can be divided in three categories: ordinary shares, preferred shares, and savings shares. The difference between the categories regards primarily the priority scale in the distribution of dividends and/or in the reimbursement of capital when the company dissolves. In spite of the fact that the basic principle is that all shares carry equal rights, the legislator does permit the issue of categories of shares carrying different rights (art. 2348 of the Civil Code). The sacrifice of the equality principle is generally allowed if the greater priority in the distribution of dividends and/or in the reimbursement of capital trades off with limitations of the voting rights.

The standard regime is established for the ordinary shares: they carry full voting rights and may claim their dividends whenever the company shows a profit.[39]

Preferred shares enjoy a privilege in the dividend distribution and in the reimbursement of capital. The extent of the privilege is left to the shareholders to decide when drafting, or amending, the articles of association. The only legal limitation is given by the general principle, expressed by art. 2265 of the Civil Code, according to which any corporate or partnership agreement excluding one or more sharehold-

[39] However, the showing of profits in the company's annual accounts does not give rise, as of itself, to a shareholder's claim for dividends. The distribution of dividends is subject to a majority resolution of the shareholders' meeting.

ers or partners from the suffering of any losses (or the enjoyment of any profits) is void and hence carries no legal effects. As a counterbalance to the privilege, the articles of association may limit the voting rights of preferred shares to a specific competence, the so-called *extraordinary competence*.[40] Hence, preferred shares do maintain their voting right, although limited to specific important issues, and will always be able to influence the life of the corporation through that voting right.

Savings shares, instead, are a special category of shares that may only be issued by companies listed on the official Stock Exchange (*Borsa Valori*). Their regulation is at articles 14, 15 and 16 of the Law no. 216/1974. They carry neither any voting right nor the right to participate in the general meeting discussion.[41] As a balance to the complete loss of voting rights, savings shares confer on their holders the right to the distribution of minimum dividends with priority to any other class of shares.[42] This is not to say that savings shareholders become creditors of the company. Their investment is still a capital risk investment since their claim against the company arises if, and only if, the company's annual accounts show a profit. Savings shares were introduced with the express aim to spread stock ownership among the general public. In the intention of the legislator, savings shares were supposed to be an investment instrument that would better fit the needs of public investors, more interested in obtaining a continuous monetary gain from their investment, than in influencing the management through their voting. It was thought that savings shares could help stimulate the securities market in Italy allowing the entrance of many small investors: when issued, they are automatically listed on the Stock Exchange, they can be issued as bearer shares,[43] and also they carry a favourable tax regime as an incentive for the general public.[44] However, the result was not as intended.

[40] Article 2351 of the Civil Code. See infra pp. 95 et seq.

[41] Holders of savings shares, however, may appoint an agent that will participate in the general meeting to check that their rights and prerogatives are respected (without being able to vote, though). Moreover, any shareholders' resolution that directly affects the rights and prerogatives carried by the savings shares must be separately approved by an affirmative vote of the special meeting of the savings shareholders. This procedure applies to any shareholders' resolution affecting the rights and prerogatives of holders of a particular category of shares (art. 2376 of the Civil Code). For example, if the shareholders amend the corporate contract to reduce the dividend privilege in favour of the preferred shares, that resolution will only be effective after the affirmative vote of the special meeting of the preferred shareholders. The same procedure applies to bondholders and changes in the indenture.

[42] According to art. 15 of the Law no. 216/1974 the dividend yielded to a savings share must equal at least 5 per cent of the par value of the share, and must be greater than the dividend distributed to ordinary shares for at least 2 per cent of the par value. When the company shows a profit, savings shareholders can claim their dividend for that year and for the two preceding years as well (if, in either of the two preceding years, no profits accrued to the company or they were not enough to meet the minimum dividend requirements). This provision has been repealed by the recent new Law no. 58/1998, which now provides for no minimum privilege for savings shares, leaving it totally to the articles of association to determine it.

[43] Hence, they can be totally anonymous with regard to the owner, whereas all other classes of shares must be issued as registered shares (RDL no. 1148/1941 and RDL no. 239/1942).

[44] When they were introduced in 1974, savings shares were the only class of shares that, at the option of the shareholder, could be subject to a flat withholding tax (15 per cent), thus avoiding personal taxation on a progressive basis as it normally happens to dividends for all other classes of shares. However, a recent statute (art. 4 of L. 489/1994, converting DL 357/1994) introduced a similar flat withholding tax regime (12.5 per cent) for dividends of any *listed* share (be it ordinary, preferred or savings share).

Shares carrying limited voting rights (preferred shares and savings shares), on the whole, can be issued for an amount up to half the total stock capital issued by the corporation.

The voice of the shareholders within the corporation results from the collective action of the general meeting through its majority deliberations. Shareholders have no immediate contact with the outside world and every decision they adopt needs to be implemented by the directors.

The very first, and most important, decision adopted by the shareholders when they sign the corporate contract (or acquire shares in the corporation) is committing themselves to carry out a business activity. The directors' primary role is then to implement such decision. Shareholders are left with supervising, in their own interest, the behaviour of the directors. The supervision takes place with the exercise of the specific powers conferred to them by the law or by the corporate contract.

Basically, shareholders exercise their rights as *owners* of the company by appointing (and revoking) the directors, amending the articles of association,[45] and approving the company's annual accounts in order to dispose of the profits accrued to the company. No specific managerial function is thus yielded to the shareholders.[46] Thus, management discretionality of directors remains formally full and untouched, but it is quite evident that it can be influenced by the shareholders with the adoption of the decisions left to their competence. In the first place, the directors are subject to the continuous pending threat of removal if their operation does not find shareholders' approval. Also, since it is the shareholders who decide on the distribution, or the retention, of earnings, and on the raising of new capital, either through the issue of new shares or through the issue of debentures,[47] the directors will depend on these decisions before entering new business projects that require financing through stable financial capital, committed to the company for a longer term.

The shareholders must meet at least once every year, to review and approve the annual accounts (art. 2364 of the Civil Code).

The initiative to convene the general meeting of shareholders is of the directors: they must then call the meeting no later than four months after the end of each fiscal year.[48] The shareholders have no power to call a meeting by themselves.[49] The

[45] It should be noticed that the issue of new shares, increasing the equity capital of the company, requires an amendment of the articles of association.

[46] The articles of association may state – or the directors may choose – that certain transactions and operations be only effected with the approval of the general meeting of shareholders. This, however, is not there to show the attribution of a managerial function to the shareholders. Such approval, in fact, may be considered to be a previous ratification, by the shareholders, of the directors' action. However, it is not a legally binding order on the directors to take certain steps. A reservation of "managerial" powers to the shareholders quite frequent in small companies, is hardly existent for listed companies. In listed companies, a reservation of "managerial" powers to the shareholders is quite frequent in shareholders' agreements, whereby the participants agree that certain transactions be approved by them before being carried out by the directors.

[47] The issue of company debentures requires a resolution of the shareholders' meeting (arts. 2410 and 2420-bis of the Civil Code).

[48] In the by-laws, the final term may be postponed until six months after the end of the fiscal year, should there be any special reason justifying it. Usually, this is the case for holding and financial companies, which, when drafting their annual accounts, need to know whether (and to what amount) the companies they hold shares in will distribute any dividends.

[49] However, the shareholders can make a demand on the directors to call a meeting. When the demand specifies the topics to be discussed and it comes from shareholders representing at least one-fifth of the

agenda of the meeting, to be formally publicized,[50] must give clear, precise and complete information as to the whole subject-matter and proposals the shareholders will be asked to discuss and vote on.[51]

The subject-matter stated in the agenda determines which shareholders will have a right to vote on it. Ordinary shareholders will be able to vote on any subject-matter for which shareholders are competent (in the first place, for the appointment or removal of directors), whereas preferred shareholders, if the articles of association so state, will limit their vote to *extraordinary* topics (i.e. the amendment of the articles of association and the issuance of debentures).

Therefore, in their *ordinary* competence (art. 2364 of the Civil Code), the shareholders have the power to:

- approve the annual accounts of the company, and resolve upon the distribution of dividends (should profits appear);
- appoint (and remove) the directors, the members of the *collegio sindacale*, and the chairman of the *collegio sindacale*, and set their compensation;[52]
- decide upon the exercise of a liability suit against the directors and/or the members of the *collegio sindacale*;
- discuss and vote on other matters relating to the management of the company which are reserved to the jurisdiction of the ordinary meeting by the articles of association, or are submitted to its examination by the directors.

The *extraordinary meeting*, on the other hand, is called to resolve issues concerning the amendment of the articles of association, the issue of debentures, and the access to special bankruptcy proceedings (should the firm suffer a crisis).

At first sight, it might seem that the ordinary meeting, and hence the ordinary shareholders, has exclusive competence with regard to any issue which more closely concerns the actual management of the company, in the first place because it is the ordinary meeting that appoints the directors. However, the *ordinary – extraordinary* subject-matter distinction allows the formation of different majorities in the shareholders' meetings, thanks to the role played by preferred sharehold-

cont.
share capital of the company, the directors will have a duty to call the meeting, else the shareholders may obtain a court order convening the meeting. The directors, however, keep some discretionality in rejecting the shareholders' request, should they deem the topics to be discussed to be futile.

50 The calling of the general meeting needs to be published in the *Gazzetta Ufficiale* at least 15 days before the date of the meeting. For meetings of listed companies *Consob* also recommends publication in two national newspapers (*Comunicazione Consob 16.7.1990, n. SOC/RM/90004190*). The law also states that there is no need to follow any of these formalities if all the persons that have a right to participate in the general meeting (shareholders, directors and members of the *collegio sindacale*) are present: this lifting of formalities, however, is evidently addressed to small companies.

51 What is not in the agenda previously formally publicized cannot be voted upon by the shareholders. If indeed they do so, the resolution will be void and the directors will have a duty not to execute it. The only exception is when the meeting is called to approve the company's annual accounts: in such case the shareholders may also decide to bring a liability suit against the directors, even though this resolution was not in the agenda (art. 2393, para. 2). However, despite the previous publicity of the agenda, in the course of the meeting, shareholders representing one-third of the attending share capital can demand to postpone the meeting to the third following day should they not feel sufficiently informed about any particular topic being discussed.

52 The compensation of directors and internal auditors, however, might already be set out in the articles of association. In such case, in order to change it, an amendment of the articles will be needed, which is a matter for the extraordinary meeting to decide upon.

ers who can only vote on extraordinary topics. As a matter of fact, the majority group among the ordinary shareholders, the controlling shareholders, may become a minority when the subject-matter to be voted on allows preferred shareholders to vote as well. This may eventually lead to turnovers in the control group by exploiting the specific competence reserved to preferred shareholders, for instance through the decision to raise new share capital or the approval of a merger with another company.[53]

Ordinary and extraordinary meetings also differ as for the *quorums* required to adopt resolutions.[54]

Generally, shareholders must be personally present at the meeting to exercise their voting rights.[55] The possibility to grant proxies is quite limited.[56] Article 2372 of the

[53] When the company decides to raise new share capital, which requires an amendment of the articles and, therefore, an extraordinary deliberation, existing shareholders (and holders of convertible bonds) have a statutory preemptive right to subscribe the new shares issued by the company, regardless of the type of shares previously held or of the type of shares to be subscribed. The shareholders' meeting can choose to partially or totally exclude such preemptive right only if the interest of the corporation so requires, or if the consideration for the newly issued shares is to be specific goods rather than money (art. 2441 of the Civil Code).

For a specific application, see what happened in the *Mondadori* case a few years ago, where the existence of two different majorities, one for the ordinary meeting and another for the extraordinary meeting, led to litigation between the major shareholders and to a stalemate in the running of the company, which was eventually resolved by a split up of the assets of the company.

[54] Ordinary meetings are validly formed if at least half of the voting capital is present and resolutions are adopted with the affirmative vote of the absolute majority. If the first calling of the ordinary meeting is deserted, the meeting must be called for a second time (with the same agenda as in the first calling). In the second calling the meeting will be duly formed regardless of which part of capital is attending and a simple majority vote of the attending capital will be sufficient to adopt any resolution. The articles of association may set higher *quorums* for the first calling of the ordinary shareholders' meeting, but not for the second calling: courts have generally been unwilling to accept clauses prescribing higher *quorums* for the second calling because the holding of the ordinary meeting is deemed necessary for the regular running of the company. Higher *quorums* for the second meeting may easily give leeway to obstructive practices by some relevant shareholder and eventually lead to the dissolution of the company: in this respect, consider that the continued inactivity of the shareholders' meeting is an *ex lege* cause for dissolution of the company (art. 2448, para. 1, no. 3 of the Civil Code).

As for extraordinary meetings, a *quorum* is required only for the adoption of resolutions. In the first calling, resolutions will be adopted with the affirmative vote of more than 50 per cent of the voting share capital of the company (i.e. the share capital having the right to vote on the topics in the agenda). In the second calling, an affirmative vote of one-third of the share capital will be needed. However, resolutions concerning changes in the object of the company, the reorganization of the company, its early dissolution, the transfer abroad of its registered address, and the issue of preferred shares will still require a *quorum* of at least 50 per cent of the voting capital. For listed companies there is the possibility of a third calling of the extraordinary meeting, where resolutions are adopted with the affirmative vote of shares representing at least one-fifth of the voting capital, except for those resolutions previously described as requiring a special *quorum* in the second calling of extraordinary meetings (plus the ones concerning mergers, consolidations, split-ups, or the voluntary reduction of stated capital) which still require a higher *quorum* of at least one-third of the voting capital in the third calling. The articles of association may state higher *quorums* for any calling of the extraordinary meeting. The new Law no. 58/1998 changes the *quorums* for extraordinary meetings of listed companies, stating that resolutions will be approved with the affirmative vote of two-thirds of the attending capital (which, in the three possible callings, must be at least, 50 per cent, 33 per cent and 20 per cent of the voting capital).

[55] For the shareholder to attend the meeting, he must be registered as such and must deposit his shares with the company (or with a duly authorized bank) at least five days before the date of the meeting: the deposit of the shares is usually deemed sufficient, however, because it implies a duty for the company to register the shares in the name of the depositor. For listed shares there is also a centralized depository system, *Montetitoli*, that permits the transfer of share ownership without proceeding to the actual

Civil Code, as amended by the Law no. 216/1974, establishes restrictions in the proxy mechanism, with regard to how proxies are given, who can act as proxy-holder, and how many shareholders a single proxy-holder may represent. The restrictions were put in place to avoid the control of companies falling into the hands of persons not having a direct and full economic interest in the company itself.[57] The original underlying philosophy was one of economic democracy, i.e. that responsibility to run a company (via the appointment of directors) should be associated with the risk of holding shares in that company and, hence, greater power to have a saying in the management of the company should be proportional to the owned (and, hence, risked) share capital. However, such regulation went probably beyond the aimed purposes. Its strictness and rigidity actually made it more difficult, as a matter of fact, for the shareholders to participate in company activities, increasing their passivity. No effective instrument was provided to eliminate the disincentives for the "dormant" shareholder to remain such. Also, on the other side, the limited number of proxies that can be legitimately collected makes it inconvenient and practically impossible for anybody to try and take over the control of a company through a proxy fight.

In this respect, however, a dramatic change may come from the application of a new provision included in the investment services legislation.[58] In regulating the activity of portfolio management, it is in fact stated, at article 20 of D.Lg. 415/1996, that investment firms and banks, subject to the disclosure regulations set by the Minister of Treasury,[59] will be able to exercise proxies for the voting rights connected with the securities they manage on behalf of their clients. Indeed, at first glance, this provision seems to overtake the limitations imposed by the Civil Code, resulting in a further concentration of the voting power in the hands of banking institutions or of banking groups.

A special regime for the exercise of the voting rights is established with regard to companies directly or indirectly owned by the State, local authorities, or other public bodies, that are under privatization procedure.[60] For these companies, the articles of association may grant the shareholders the right to cast their vote through the mail. Actually, if the privatization has taken place through a public offer for sale of the

cont.

movement, from hand to hand, of the document. The system is regulated by the Law no. 289/1986. The share documents remain deposited at *Montetitoli*, any transfer is registered on nominees' accounts, and when a shareholders' meeting is convened, *Montetitoli* releases a receipt to the person in whose name the shares are registered.

56 For listed companies, the new law no. 58/1998 provides for an entirely new proxy regime. See infra Section VII.

57 The law states that the proxy must include the name of the proxy-holder, and can only be given for single meetings. Proxies can neither be given to subsidiaries, banks nor to the company auditing the accounts of the company holding the meeting. Moreover, the following persons may not be appointed proxies: directors, members of the *collegio sindacale*, employees of the company, of the subsidiaries, or of the auditing company. Also, the same person cannot hold proxies from more than ten shareholders or, when the company is listed on the stock exchange, from more than 50, 100 or 200 shareholders according to the share capital of the company (respectively, no more than 10 billion lire, more than 10 billion lire, or more than 50 billion lire).

58 D.Lg. 415/1996 implementing the EC Directive 93/22 of 10 May 1993. However, an even more dramatic change is the liberalization of proxies provided by the Law no. 58/1998. See Section VII. below.

59 Ministerial Decree no. 330 of 26 June 1997.

60 See art. 5 of the Law no. 474/1994, which regulates the procedures for the privatization of State-owned companies, and the regulations issued in concert by *Consob*, the Bank of Italy and *Isvap* (the supervisory agency for insurance companies).

shares, the articles must allow the vote via mail.[61] This provision is intended to favour the vote of public shareholders, to whom the privatization of State-owned companies is mainly addressed.[62]

The correct functioning of the vote via mail needs to proceed with very stringent and thorough disclosure regulations, with respect to the subject matters to be voted on and the possible alternative resolutions that the shareholders might want to adopt. The disclosure obligations concerning the agenda of the meeting must be fulfilled at least 30 days before the meeting (for all other companies, it is 15 days before) and the agenda cannot, by any means, be changed during the course of the meeting.

The shareholder can freely exercise his voting rights. The principle is well established in law, and confirmed by courts, that the shareholder does not owe any fiduciary duty either to the company or to the other shareholders.

The one important exception, although no form of fiduciary duty may be said to arise from it, is that the shareholder must abstain from voting in those resolutions where he has a conflict of interests with the company. A conflict of interests is generally deemed to be present where the pursuance of a direct personal interest of the shareholder does not allow the pursuance and realization of the company's interest. The problem arises when trying to figure out what the interest of the company is, in view of the fact that it is the shareholders themselves who are called to determine it when drafting the articles of association or addressing directors' action.[63]

The law, at least in the interpretation given by the courts, deems the exercise of the voting right to be free from any legal constraint. The shareholder should therefore cast his vote according to his own self-interest (as long as it does not conflict with the interest of the company), as he sees most fit following the meeting discussion.

On this basis, for instance, courts have always refused to enforce shareholders' voting agreements. The law prescribes – the courts' argument goes – a detailed regulation for the general meeting of shareholders to take place, requiring the directors and the members of the *collegio sindacale* to disclose the information necessary to take an informed decision. Even if the shareholder may have an idea of how he wants to vote with regard to a particular topic on the meeting agenda, at least in principle he must be able to change his mind having heard all the arguments set forth by directors, internal auditors or other shareholders during the meeting discussion. Hence, any agreement which does not allow this process to take place will be void and non-enforceable against the shareholder.[64]

[61] Such obligation will only expire when a single shareholders, or a group of shareholders tied together with a voting agreement, acquire more than 50 per cent of the voting shares in the ordinary meeting.

[62] Such provision, allowing companies to include in their articles the possibility to vote through the mail, is now extended to all listed companies by art. 127 of the Law no. 58/1998.

[63] In this respect, the courts are quite uniform in defining corporate interest as the pursuance of profit. Among commentators, the discussion centres upon the "contractual" or "institutional" nature of corporate interest.

Also to be considered is that a more flexible interpretation of the conflict of interests provision is allowing courts to deal with cases of abuse of power by the majority shareholder at the detriment of the minority (i.e. dilution of minority interests).

[64] See the cases Cass. no. 2080 of 24 July 1962, in Foro it., 1962, I, 1888; Cass. no. 1290 of 23 April 1969, in Giust. civ., 1969, I, 1695; Cass. no. 1581 of 23 April 1975, in Giur. comm., 1975, II, 575.

The existence of voting agreements among shareholders is then considered by courts a mere question of fact, which cannot affect the regular course of the meetings: the shareholder may well decide to abide by the terms of the agreement, though he cannot be legally constrained to do so.[65] The Civil Code does not mention shareholders' agreements. Other pieces of legislation do consider them without, however, giving a substantive regulation of their functioning mechanisms. Their existence is taken into account, for instance, in deciding whether a person can be said to have control over a company, hence as evidence of fact. Their legal status, however, may change with the operation of recently issued laws. For instance, the takeover statute, in an attempt to favour disclosure of the ownership structure of listed companies, orders the registration with *Consob* and the communication to the public of all shareholders' agreements (including voting agreements). As a sanction for the lack of disclosure, the statute poses the non-enforceability of such agreements:[66] it should then follow that, once the disclosure obligations have been fulfilled, the agreements should be valid and enforceable. Also, the provision allowing the exercise of voting rights via mail might be a clear indication that the legislator no more requires, as a principle underlying the functioning of companies, that resolutions be adopted as a result of the discussions within the meeting, a further step towards the full legal recognition of shareholders' agreements. Indeed, very recently even courts have started to convene that the numerous legislative references to shareholders' agreements is a clear sign of a change in the law with regard to the recognition of shareholders' agreements.[67] The final step towards the full legitimacy of shareholders' agreements comes from the Law no. 58/1998 which now gives them a substantive regulation. Article 123 of the Law, in fact, prescribes that shareholders' agreements may not have a duration exceeding three years or, should they have an undetermined duration, any party may cancel the agreement at any moment by giving a six-month previous warning. Also, article 123 states that shareholders' agreements may be cancelled at will by any party that wants to adhere to a mandatory 100 per cent takeover bid or to a voluntary 60 per cent takeover bid.

The debate in law about the validity of shareholders' agreements, however, seems not to have not affected reality. As discussed above, the Italian corporate structure is generally characterized by listed companies whose control group is tied together through voting agreements. At times such agreements are given a formal, and legally safer, guise through a variety of devices, such as the transfer of the pooled shares to a common *fiduciario* (a trustee) that will hold the shares in street name and vote in general meetings according to the instructions received following the majority

[65] Such holdings by the courts have repeatedly been seriously criticized by authors and commentators. The right to vote – they hold – is instrumental to the carrying out of the business activity the company was set up for, and it is an expression of that private autonomy which is the gist of any legal system regulating a market economy. It then follows that the right to vote can legitimately be disposed of by contract. In this line of reasoning, there are a few provisions in the Italian Civil Code confirming such thesis: for instance, when the shares are the object of a pledge, the parties can freely decide whether the voting right will accrue to the pledgor or the pledgee. Also, the assumption that the law requires that the vote follow the discussion at the meeting is said to be groundless, because the Civil Code considers as a fully functioning body the company where all shares accrue to one single shareholder (art. 2362) (though, here, they fail to consider that it is not only the shareholders who take part in the general meeting, but also the directors and the internal auditors).

[66] Law no. 149/1992, art. 10, para. 4, now repealed with similar provisions by art. 122 of Law no. 58/1998.

[67] See Cass. no. 9975 of 20 September 1995, in Giur. comm. II, 50.

decisions of the pooled shareholders. However, apart from any legal device used to ensure the enforcement of the agreements, the structure of the Italian economic system is such as to assure, *de facto*, their respect through a sort of "peer pressure" whose strength is reinforced by the restricted number of actors on stage and their numerous cross and circular ownership relationships.

The described voting mechanisms and the wide use of shareholders' agreements are the legal devices which contribute to the stability of the current corporate system, characterized by the substantial non-existence of publicly held corporations and the predominance of *monodefined* or *pluridefined* ownership structures.[68] Ownership is hardly ever totally fragmented, and the directors are, nearly in the totality of cases, the expression of some relevant shareholder or of some group of closely connected shareholders. Even where the control group is in a position of relative majority, that is it does not hold 51 per cent of the voting shares, and hence it is theoretically a possible target for takeovers, there are further elements that in practice make such turnovers in the control of companies hardly impossible. One of them, as we saw, is the existence of binding shareholders' agreements.

One further element that helps strengthen the position of relevant shareholders is the cross ownership of shares between companies. Such phenomenon is generally strictly regulated when the cross ownership takes place between a company and its controlled subsidiary: the subsidiary company, in fact, is not permitted to vote in the general meetings of the controlling company.[69] However, when no control relationship exists between two companies,[70] the restriction does not apply. A stricter rule is posed for listed companies, whereas the cross ownership of shares may not exceed, on either side, the amount of 2 per cent of the voting capital.[71]

The existence of cross and circular shareholdings allows and favours the formation of closely tied networks, whose ultimate effect is to help maintain the stability of the ownership structures, through the "freezing" of many voting rights. The effect is heightened by the limited number of big industrial and financial groups operating in the Italian financial market, whereas many times the cross ownership of shares serves as the formalization of gentlemen's agreements for collaboration or "non-belligerence".

A similar "freezing" effect is also caused by the ownership of shares held by institutional investors, i.e. mutual funds and investment companies. These investors tend to be quite conservative and passive in their behaviour towards participated companies. When they do exercise their voting rights, they usually tend to conform to current balances of power and hardly ever take any independent or

[68] As they were defined supra at p. 84.

[69] Until very recently, there was no quantitative limitation on the holding of shares of the subsidiary in the capital of the controlling company, besides the fact that such shares were to be acquired with funds coming from retained earnings of the subsidiary. In implementation of an EC directive, art. 2359-bis of the Civil Code was amended by stating that the participation of the subsidiary cannot exceed 10 per cent of the capital of the controlling company (d.lgs. n. 315/1994).

[70] According to art. 2359 of the Civil Code, a control relationship is said to exist when one company holds, directly or indirectly, the majority of the voting shares in the ordinary meeting of another company; or, when one company holds, directly or indirectly, enough voting shares to exercise a dominant influence on another company; or, when one company is able to exercise a dominant influence on another company by reason of some particular existing contractual relationship.

[71] Article 5 of the L. 216/1974. Article 121 of the Law no. 58/1998 allows the increase of such limit to 5 per cent, should the ordinary shareholders of both companies authorize it.

autonomous position. The underlying philosophy is, in fact, that the investment decision bringing the institutional investor to purchase the shares is, of itself, a declaration of agreement with the current board of directors and the current controlling shareholder.[72]

Up to now, private pension funds have played quite a marginal role in the Italian financial market, mainly because of the uncertain regulatory framework and of the high spending of the public pension system. However, a thorough regulation of private pension funds was recently issued with D.Lg. 124/1993, as amended by L. 335/1995. As a consequence of this new legislative framework,[73] there is hope that private pension funds will become important actors on the Italian financial market, thus stimulating the growth and development of the market, as it happened in other countries such as the U.S. or the U.K. In this respect, a controversial issue concerns the exercise of the voting rights connected with the shares of stock that will be held by the pension funds. The law clearly states that the vote accrues to the board of the pension fund. However, since in many instances the boards of pension funds will be made up of representations of labour as well, the attribution of voting rights to the board of the fund is raising fears that a greater direct involvement of labour in the governance of companies may diminish the overall efficiency of the system.[74] It is evident that the issue is crucial in the operation of corporate structures, especially in view of the huge amounts of financial resources that private pension funds are expected to attract.

A further element that somehow contributes to the stability of the ownership structures within the Italian public companies and that ultimately hinders the correct functioning of a proper market for corporate control is the takeover law no. 149/1992.

The takeover law was issued in order to ensure equality of treatment among all shareholders. The underlying philosophy was that when control of a company is transferred, any super price paid to gain that control should be shared by all shareholders, both the ones that sold control and the minority ones as well.[75]

This being the manifest intention of the legislator, the actual outcome of the law turned out to be, and still is, quite controversial. According to the takeover law, control of a listed company can only be acquired through a public offer for the shares of the target company. The offer must be for at least 10 per cent of the capital, and must be addressed equally to all shareholders of the same class. If control of the listed company is otherwise acquired, through private negotiations or entering a voting

[72] The situation, however, seems to be changing on the urge of institutional investors' associations (e.g. Assogestioni, the Italian mutual funds' association).

[73] At the outset, in 1993, the tax treatment connected with private pension funds was quite unfavourable when compared to similar existing investment instruments, such as life insurance. The tax treatment, and other aspects of the regulations, were then amended by L. 335/1995, which reformed the general pension system. However, no private pension fund is yet in full operation since the implementing administrative regulations have only recently been issued.

[74] The proposed alternative is to entrust the voting rights accruing to the fund to the managers of the fund (i.e. banks, insurance companies, investment companies and brokerage firms). The argument follows from the fact that it will be the fund's managers to know all about the situation of the companies in which they invested the fund's assets, hence they should be in the best position to evaluate any course of action.

[75] What used to happen was that transfers of control were always privately negotiated outside the public markets, thus conferring little significance to the prices being formed there and, hence, further depressing the prices for minority shares.

agreement, then the person who gained control must bid the public for an amount of shares equal to the one that allowed him to be in control.

The result of these regulations, characterized by great complexity and uncertainty of interpretation, has been to actually make it more difficult, and costly, for control to be transferred, plastering the market and probably not giving wholly effective protection to minority shareholders. The following case is a good example of the distortions caused by the operation of the law. Under the takeover statute, if Mr. A wants to take control of company X, of which Mr. B holds the controlling block of shares (e.g. 20 per cent), he may either privately purchase the controlling block from Mr. B, or he may try to acquire control of X through a direct offer to the public.

In the first instance, acquisition of control through private purchase of the 20 per cent of stock held by Mr. B, Mr. A would then have to launch a public offer for a further 20 per cent at the same price paid to B. The total expense for acquiring control of the company is thus doubled. At the same time, it is doubtful whether there is any corresponding benefit to the public shareholders to whom the public offer is addressed. The mandatory public offer, in fact, concerns only part of the outstanding public shares: it follows that if all public shareholders accept the offer, they will all concur *pro rata* and, hence, they will only be able to cash in only part of their original investment.

In the second instance, acquisition of control of X through a public offer, Mr. A has two alternatives. He may disregard the existence of the controlling shareholder, Mr. B, launching a hostile takeover bid and hoping that a sufficient number of public shareholders adhere to his offer. Mr. A may thus be successful in gaining control of the company, although he risks that Mr. B, with his block of shares, will be able to pose quite a powerful opposition, hindering his capacity to swiftly manage the company. Or, in the second alternative, should Mr. A want Mr. B as well to adhere to the offer, he will have to bid for a much higher price or for a much higher portion of capital. Mr. B, in fact, will concur *pro rata* with all public shareholders in the offer: he might have no convenience in adhering if he is not sure he can liquidate all of his investment (or part of it, cashing in a high amount of total revenue).[76]

The mechanisms described above show how the law helps maintain the stability of control. This makes the public markets not as relevant in terms of serving as an effective monitoring device, as instead they are in other countries such as the United States. As a consequence, the correct balance among the various stakeholders (majority shareholders, minority shareholders, directors) will then have to be found within the internal corporate mechanisms and devices.

The prevailing ownership structure shows that the actual moment of conflict and discussion within the corporation is the general meeting of shareholders. The directors may well have full powers in the management of the company, but it is a fact that they are usually backed by a clear shareholders' majority whose involvement in the company is quite a concrete and tangible one given the large stakes held. Also, the shareholders' meeting, besides appointing the directors, has the power to take many fundamental and structural decisions concerning the company, and cannot

[76] An explanation of the functioning of the takeover statute, with a more analytical description of the distortions it causes on the stock market, can be found in F. Palisi & R. Ricci, *L'obbligo di offerta pubblica di acquisto in borsa* (Roma, 1993) and R. Ricci, *L'obbligo di offerta pubblica di acquisto tra tutela degli azionisti e tutela del mercato* (Roma, 1996). In response to the critiques, the Law no. 58/1998 repealed the takeover statute, thus simplifying the regulations. See infra Section VII.

delegate such decisions to the directors. It is in fact the shareholders who decide upon any amendment of the corporate charter and, in particular, upon the raising of fresh capital,[77] the issue of bonds, the distribution of dividends after the approval of the annual accounts, and mergers or divisions of the company. As a consequence, the shareholders' meeting is a very important moment in the life of the company, and so is the shareholders' power to vote on the issues posed to their attention.[78] Also, every single shareholder, regardless of the amount of shares he holds, maintains the power to submit all the meeting's resolutions to judicial scrutiny on grounds of legality or conformity to the charter of incorporation. The resolution, should it be illegal or should it violate the charter, can then be declared invalid by the judge, as if it had never been enacted. The threat of the request for a judicial intervention is surely one of the most effective methods minority shareholders have to protect their position within the company.[79]

B. The Board of Directors

A further device to encourage the correct functioning of the company is to be found in the legal position of directors.

Directors owe the company a duty of care and a duty of loyalty. They must carry out their task with proper diligence (art. 2392 of the Civil Code) and must abstain from taking any action in which they have a conflict of interest with the company (art. 2391 of the Civil Code).[80]

77 See note 31 supra for the only case when shareholders may delegate the directors the issue of new shares.

78 This is the theory arising from the letter of the law. In practice, especially for those numerous companies where the control group is tied together by a shareholders' agreement, the actual moment when discussion takes place and decisions are taken shifts from the shareholders' meeting to the shareholders' agreement meeting. In this respect, the shareholders' meeting serves to publicly formalize previously taken decisions.

79 The law distinguishes two kinds of possible invalidity for shareholders' resolutions: voidability and absolute voidness. Voidability is the kind of invalidity striking a shareholders' resolution taken in violation of a statutory or of a charter provision set for the protection of the interests of single shareholders or groups of shareholders. Absolute voidness is instead the kind of invalidity striking a shareholders' resolution taken in violation of statutory provisions set for the protection of the general interest of the public at large, provisions that are deemed to be specifications, in the corporate area, of general principles of law (for a clear statement of this distinction, see Cass. no. 906 of 9 February 1979, in BBTC, 1980, II, 417). For instance, it has been held that a resolution deciding upon a subject-matter which was not included in the agenda of the meeting may only be declared voidable because the rules regarding the formalities for the calling and keeping of the annual meeting are designed to protect the shareholders' interest to the regular carrying out of the internal corporate activity (see Cass. no. 989 of 11 March 1977, in Foro it., 1977, I, 809). While the shareholders' resolution approving a balance sheet that does not meet the true and fair view statutory requirement (art. 2423 of the Civil Code) would be absolutely void: the interest of the general public, in fact, requires that the annual accounts be drafted so as to convey clear and precise information of the situation of the company (see Cass. no. 8048 of 3 September 1996, in Foro it., 1996, I, 2686).

The action to declare the *voidability* of a resolution can only be brought by absent or dissenting shareholders, by the board of directors and by the *collegio sindacale*. It is subject to a statute of limitations of three months from the taking of the decision. Instead, the action to declare the *absolute voidness* is not subject to any statute of limitations and can be brought by anybody, as long as they have an interest.

80 The director having a conflict of interest with the company must disclose the conflict to the board and must abstain from the decision. If he contravenes the duty of abstention, he will also be subject to criminal sanction.

The power of directors is legally independent from the majority that appointed them. Directors are not hierarchically subordinated to the majority shareholders. On the other hand, the majority shareholders, once they have appointed the directors, have no power to force them do what they would like them to do (except for replacing them). The fiduciary duty of directors is to the company and, once appointed, their powers are only subject to the law and to the articles of association. Should the shareholders want the company to be managed in a certain way, from a legal standpoint their only effective device to obtain that result is to revoke the reluctant directors and substitute them with more acquiescent persons.

The behaviour of directors is judged independently, with no possibility to find any excuse in any directive coming from the shareholders. This surely represents an incentive for directors to behave within legality, since they will enjoy no exemption from liability if they follow shareholders' resolutions. Moreover, not only do directors have a duty to the company to act diligently, but also towards the creditors of the company. Corporate creditors, in fact, may claim damages should the directors fail to respect the legal provisions posed for the protection of the integrity of the corporate capital.[81] The creditors' action may be brought only if corporate assets are not sufficient to meet corporate debts. In this case, which actually resembles a subspecies of the general duty of diligence owed by directors to the company, creditors can sue the directors to recover despite the inertia of the company.[82]

These being the liability rules,[83] however, the problem lies in their enforcement. Except for the rare case of the enforcement by the creditors, the civil liability of directors (criminal liability is obviously a different matter) is enforced by the company itself through a majority resolution of its general meeting of ordinary shareholders. The intrinsic contradiction of such system is evident. The law assigns the decision to bring an action against the directors to those same shareholders that gave them trust by appointing them. Indeed, in many cases, the director is actually one of those shareholders. The Italian corporate legal system does not envisage any form of derivative suit that single shareholders may use to force the company to recover damages from negligent directors. When the damage accrues to the company, it is the company, through a shareholders' resolution, that must action the available liability mechanisms.[84] This contradiction might be without effects were

[81] For instance, distribution of dividends arising from false and misleading annual accounts, or violations of the strict rules concerning the buy-back of shares.

[82] It is generally believed, although not so clear in law, that when creditors action such liability recovery accrues directly to the company and not to the creditors actioning the liability, as if it were some form of derivative action. However, it is quite a limited and rare hypothesis because creditors can only sue if the assets of the company are insufficient to meet corporate debts, which generally means a bankruptcy situation. Consequently, the only available case law concerns bankruptcy cases, where the distinction between a corporate suit or a creditors' suit has hardly any significance, since either suit is brought by the bankruptcy trustee (the *curatore fallimentare*).

[83] Besides being liable towards the company and towards creditors, directors may also be liable towards single shareholders or third parties for any negligent or wrongful behaviour causing direct damage to the single shareholder or third party (art. 2395 of the Civil Code). It is the case, for instance, of a director knowingly or recklessly disclosing false information about the company to a prospective acquirer of shares of the company.

[84] Article 2900 envisages a subrogatory action that allows the creditor to exercise, in substitution of the debtor, the actions and the rights that accrue to his debtor, in order to protect his own credit claims. However, this provision has generally not been viewed as sufficient to found a derivative action for the shareholder since, technically, he is not a creditor of the company.

the prevailing ownership structure of companies comprised within the previously described "institutional" pattern: in such case, in fact, the mobility of shareholders' majorities would allow a company-actioned system of enforcement to work more effectively. However, as we saw, the Italian corporate system is characterized by *monodefined* ownership structures, hence with very stable shareholders' majorities. The directors are then the direct expression of a clearly identifiable shareholder, and often the director is the shareholder himself. This being the situation, to hope that a system of checks and balances between directors and shareholders be effective is, in itself, quite unrealistic.[85] Experience clearly shows such ineffectiveness: the few cases where the company claimed damages from its directors are for the most part cases of clear fraud, or bankruptcy cases.[86]

Moreover, the ineffectiveness of the liability mechanisms is also due to the difficulty, on the litigation level, to prove directors' liability for their negligent management. The burden of proof is entirely on the plaintiff and, justly so, directors' business judgment cannot be second-guessed by courts. It then follows that the judge's review is only limited to the decision process adopted by the board and cannot extend to the merits of the actual decision or course of action.[87] The burden of proof is no lighter in conflict of interests cases either. Here as well, the plaintiff (the company), in order to hold the directors liable, must prove the conflict, the damage to the company and the proximate causation.[88]

C. The Internal Supervisory Board

The legal organizational structure of companies envisages a mechanism by which the behaviour of directors is supposed to be kept constantly under control in the interest of shareholders. The mechanism takes place through the operation of the internal supervisory board, the *collegio sindacale*.

The rationale for the existence of such body lies in the fact that the shareholders operate their control through the general meeting, a complex and articulated body that usually meets only once a year or by initiative of the directors.[89] It would then be unrealistic to think that they could effectively supervise the management of the company, and take the consequential resolutions, only by meeting once a year. For this purpose, the law provides that they appoint an internal supervisory board, composed of three (or five) persons, so called *sindaci*.

The functions that the law assigns to the *collegio sindacale* are:

[85] In theory, if the director is the controlling shareholder himself, he is not allowed to vote in resolutions deciding upon the exercise of a liability suit against him, because he clearly has a conflict of interest in the matter (art. 2373, para. 3). However, the prohibition is easily avoided if the director controls the company not directly, but by controlling or influencing the operation of a controlling company.

[86] Once the company is declared bankrupt, the liability of directors is enforced by the *curatore* (the public official encharged with the management and liquidation of the company assets), who can bring the action with no need to make any previous demand on the shareholders. He only needs authorization from the judge supervising the bankruptcy proceedings.

[87] See Cass. no. 280 of 16 January 1982, in *Giust. civ.*, 1983, I, 603.

[88] An example of how in conflict of interests cases the burden of proof may be made lighter comes from the American experience. In U.S. corporate law, in duty of loyalty cases, it is well-established case law that the plaintiff should prove the existence of the conflict, and it is then the director that must prove the fairness of the transaction in order to escape liability.

[89] We said before that a qualified minority of shareholders (20 per cent) can force the directors to call a meeting. In listed companies, however, reaching that minimum threshold is in practice very difficult, since holding that amount of shares generally means controlling the company.

- the review of the legality of the management of the company;
- the supervision on the observance of the law and of the articles of association in the general operation of the company; and
- the auditing and control of the company's accounts.[90]

The *sindaci* must attend all meetings of the board of directors and the general meetings of shareholders. Individually, they have the power to inspect and control the company, although any official resolution must be taken collectively by the board. The prerogatives of the *sindaci* find evidence in their power to formulate comments and observations to directors and shareholders in their respective meetings. They have an autonomous power (and duty) to call the general meeting of shareholders, either substituting the directors if they omit to do it, or when they are notified by shareholders holding at least 5 per cent of the shares of serious irregularities in the operation of the company that require immediate reaction. Also, at the annual shareholders' meeting called to approve the balance sheet, they must present a report that comments and makes suggestions on the results evidenced in the accounts. Moreover, the *collegio sindacale* can challenge in court any allegedly illegal resolution of the general meeting of shareholders and any resolution taken by the board of directors tainted by a conflict of interest.

The *sindaci* are liable to the company for the carrying out of their functions. Their liability is actioned by the company along the same criteria (and difficulties) seen for the directors. Also, the *sindaci* can be called liable jointly with the directors if they omitted to supervise their behaviour, and a correct supervision on their side would have avoided any harm to the company.[91]

In the end, the role of the *collegio sindacale* is quite similar to the role envisaged for outside (or non-executive) directors in the American and English corporate systems. However, one main difference lies in the fact that *sindaci*, not being directors, can only review the legality of the management decisions and can never enter the merits, unless such decisions are manifestly negligent.[92]

There are a few drawbacks, however, to the effective functioning of the system of supervision envisaged through the operation of the *collegio sindacale*.

In the first place, there seems to be a contradiction in the system since the same majority that appoints the directors also has the power to appoint the *collegio sindacale*. Hence, the *sindaci* are the expression of the same control group that expresses those persons they are supposed to supervise. The law seems to partially correct such contradiction by establishing that the *sindaci* be not related to the directors of the company and have not any continuous work relationship with the company or its subsidiaries. Also, the persons appointed as *sindaci* must meet very strict professional requirements.[93]

[90] In listed companies the auditing function must be assigned to an independent auditing company to be chosen among the ones included in a special list held by *Consob*, the supervisory agency of the securities market.

[91] Also this case shows the dramatic difficulty, in terms of required burden of proof, for the enforcement of liability of the members of the *collegio sindacale*. The plaintiff would have to prove the negligence of directors causing damage to the company, and then the inertia of the members of the *collegio sindacale*, whose action would have avoided all, or part, of the damage to the company.

[92] In such case, in fact, a manifestly negligent management decision would require the *sindaci* to intervene, since negligence is the legal limitation on directors' behaviour.

[93] Following the Eighth EC Directive, the law now requires that all the *sindaci* be selected among those included in an official list, kept by the Ministry of Justice, of professional accountants (*revisori contabili*).

A further drawback is that the office of *sindaco* is a personal office. *Sindaci* are not allowed to have any staff to help them carry out their functions. It is questionable whether three (or five) *sindaci* can exercise a truly effective function of supervision over a company having the size of those listed on the stock exchange. One first step towards the creation of an internal auditing structure came with the law implementing the Eighth EC Directive, which states that the single *sindaci* may employ, at their own expense and under their own responsibility, collaborators to help them carry out specific auditing functions. Until now, the strictly personal structure of the supervisory board has been a great limitation on the effectiveness of their, though numerous, powers.

D. The External Auditing of Listed Companies

In companies listed on the stock exchange the auditing function must be entrusted to an external independent auditing company, whose task is to verify that the books are correctly kept and that the annual balance sheet meets the requirements fixed by the law. The auditing company, appointed by the shareholders among those registered in a special list supervised by *Consob*,[94] presents its report before the annual meeting called to approve the annual accounts. This report, which is supposed to *certify* the annual accounts of the company, is a very important piece of information not only for the shareholders, but also for the investors at large. The auditing company, when performing its task, has powers comparable to the ones of the *collegio sindacale* though not being an internal body of the company.[95] It therefore fully maintains its autonomy and it is supposed to give the public complete and unbiased information regarding how the accounts of the company are drawn and presented. The *certification* by the auditing company operates as a sort of presumption of truth and fairness of the annual accounts. In fact, contravening the general principle that any shareholder can challenge in court the shareholders' resolutions (among which, the approval of the balance sheet), when the balance sheet has obtained the auditors' *certification*, it can only be challenged by shareholders holding at least 5 per cent of the capital or, if the company has a stated capital of at least 2 billion lire, by shareholders holding shares for a par value of at least 100 million lire. As a counterbalance for such limitations, however, the power to sue on the basis of the certified balance sheet is also granted to *Consob*, that must exercise it within six months from the approval.[96]

However, such external control over companies' accounts has not given the wished for results in terms of greater transparency and disclosure on the financial market, as shown by very recent facts.[97] The ineffectiveness of the role of independent auditing companies can be imputed to several factors. On the one hand, government supervision over auditing companies and the securities market, through the

[94] In order to remain in this special list, the directors and managers of the auditing company must continuously meet the honorability and professionality requirements fixed by the law.

[95] It is to be remembered, however, that the task of the auditing company is limited to the verification and control of the company's accounts, whereas the *collegio sindacale* has the power to review the legality of the overall management of the company.

[96] However, *Consob* has only seldom exercised such power.

[97] It may be sufficient to recall the recent scandals and crises concerning listed companies such as Ferruzzi, Tripcovich, Gemina, Banco di Napoli, whose accounts had all been duly certified by an auditing company.

operation of *Consob*, has not been very effective probably for a general misunderstanding and confusion as to the actual role to be played by *Consob*. When this independent agency was set up, in 1974, it was supposed to become the tutor of disclosure and information for the benefit of the securities market. Instead, it ended up being the prudential regulator and the overall tutor of the whole securities market: its powers and range of action was more and more enlarged, losing sight of its original and fundamental informational task. On the other hand, private supervision, through the actioning of the liability mechanisms, has not been effective either, because of the extreme difficulties on the side of the plaintiff in sustaining the heavy burden of proof.[98] Also, for many years there was little litigation because it was quite unclear who the auditors owed their duties to: only to the company, under contract law, or to the shareholders as well, under tort law? In these last few years, however, a few cases recognized that the auditing company is liable towards investors as well.[99]

VII. PROSPECTS FOR CHANGE

In the last couple of years, as in the rest of the world, the debate about corporate governance has become one of the hottest issues in Italian corporate and business environments. The globalization of the markets is forcing the regulators to have a closer look at corporate balances of power in order to adapt national corporate structures to the needs and challenges of a rapidly changing and ever more integrated world economy.

In 1996, one first legislative step was taken when the Italian Parliament approved a law delegating the Government to issue legislation that would enhance powers of minority shareholders and strengthen systems of control over listed companies.[100]

In response to such delegation of legislative power, the Government set up a Committee headed by the Director General of Treasury, Professor Mario Draghi, with the task of designing new corporate governance rules for Italian listed companies.

In December 1997, the Draghi Committee presented a draft bill that was definitely issued as the Law no. 58 of 24 February 1998, coming into effect on 1 July 1998.

The main issues on which the new law sets relevant changes concern proxy rules, takeovers, cross ownership of shares, shareholders' agreements, liability suits and, in general, initiative powers for minority shareholders.

With regard to proxy rules, the law liberalized the collection of proxies. As a result of the new rules, any shareholder having more than 1 per cent of the voting shares and registered for at least three months, even if it is a director or a bank, may call for proxies from any other shareholder in order to intervene and vote in a shareholders' meeting.

98 For a long time, auditors were deemed to be only liable for gross negligence. Very recent cases, however, have clarified that this is not their standard of care, thus making liability suits more effective in prospective (Trib. Milano 18.6.1992 and Trib. Torino 18.9.1993).

99 See the cases cited in note 98.

100 Article 21, para. 4, of the Law no. 52 of 6 February 1996, delegates the Government to consolidate existing legislation regarding securities intermediaries and securities markets, and to issue new rules regarding listed companies with respect to the internal supervisory board, the powers of minorities, shareholders' agreements and groups of companies, with the purpose of enhancing investors' and minority shareholders' protection.

As for takeovers, the previous takeover statute is being totally repealed by new, simpler, regulations, providing that any shareholder acquiring more than 30 per cent of the ordinary shares of a listed company must launch a takeover bid on all remaining ordinary shares. The price of the mandatory bid must be at least equal to the average between the highest price paid by the bidder in the previous 12 months and the average market price for the shares in the same 12 months.[101]

The limit to cross ownership of shares remains 2 per cent, although companies may increase it to 5 per cent if there is authorization by the shareholders' meeting.

The new rules set a time limit of three years to shareholders' agreements, to be registered with *Consob*, also establishing that the agreement is automatically cancelled should one of the participating shareholders want to adhere to a mandatory takeover bid.

Relevant changes concern the powers by minority shareholders. One important provision allows minority shareholders (5 per cent or lower, if permitted by the charter) to directly enforce liability against directors, members of the supervisory board or officers without having to make previous demand on the general meeting of shareholders (a sort of derivative suit). Also, other regulatory changes favour initiative powers by minority shareholders lowering the number of shares needed to exercise effective monitoring on management (calls for a general meeting, denouncing to the internal supervisory board or to the Court).

The proposed draft bill has been generally greeted with great appreciation, since it is deemed to favour a positive renovation of the legal framework in which listed companies are going to operate, providing greater protection to public investors.

However, at a closer look, the result of the new legislation may not really be as investor oriented as intended.[102] Indeed, the only provisions that seem to grant greater protection to public shareholders are the ones granting greater powers to minorities (i.e. derivative suit, initiative powers, etc.): however, such greater powers are altogether connected to quite relevant holdings of shares in listed companies (5 per cent or 10 per cent), amounts that very often allow shareholders to actually hold control of public companies.

It is difficult to see how the new provisions on the cross ownership of shares or on the mandatory takeover bid for all the shares of the company when having more than 30 per cent may be said to increase investors' protection. Cross ownership of shares

[101] In two instances, the shareholder acquiring more than 30 per cent of a listed company is not obliged to bid for the 100 per cent of the shares. The first instance is when the 30 per cent (or greater) shareholding is acquired as a result of a voluntary takeover bid for all the ordinary shares. The second instance, instead, is when the 30 per cent (or greater) shareholding is acquired as a result of a voluntary takeover bid for 60 per cent of the ordinary shares fulfilling the following conditions: the bidder has not acquired more than 1 per cent of the shares of the target company in the previous 12 months, and the bid is approved by a majority of non-controlling shareholders. Also, *Consob* shall regulate further instances when the mandatory bid provision does not apply even though the acquiror holds more than 30 per cent of the shares. In the first place, no mandatory takeover bid applies when the 30 per cent (or greater) stake does not give control because there is already a controlling shareholder. Besides, no mandatory takeover bid shall apply when the 30 per cent threshold is overcome as a result of bankruptcy reorganizations, intra-group transfers, temporary transactions, mergers, divisions, or events not dependent upon the will of the acquiror.

[102] For a first overall comment on the draft bill on corporate governance, see A. Nuzzo – D. Casadei – E. Ruggiero, *Testo unico delle disposizioni in materia di intermediazione finanziaria. Osservazioni e commenti in relazione al progetto di disciplina delle societa quotate*, Ceradi-Luiss research paper, 1997.

is, as of itself, a device to encourage greater stability of the controlling stakes in a company. The mandatory takeover bid, on the other hand, makes it more difficult, and more expensive, for controlling stakes to circulate, thus hindering the correct functioning of the market for corporate control. It is generally argued that the mandatory bid provision is intended to give all shareholders the possibility to exit the company when control of the company is transferred: however, it is hard to imagine somebody having the financial resources needed to face the total bid obligation for most of our listed companies. The most likely final result will be to allow enduring stability of control while having an amount of shares lower than the 30 per cent threshold.

Secondly, the new proxy rules assign a fundamental role to banks, thus granting them even more power in the ownership structures of listed companies. Any proxy solicitation, in fact, must take place through a bank (or through a securities broker/dealer) acting as a proxy company, unless it is the bank itself to collect the proxies. Also, if the liberalization of proxies is intended to be a device to allow greater participation of public investors to companies' meetings, the collection of proxies should take place in the interest of the shareholders. In this regard, however, it is hard to imagine that public shareholders will be available to bear any cost to exercise their vote through the proxy: hence, if any collection of proxies takes place, it will be the person soliciting the proxies to bear all costs, which can only be explained if that person has its own self-interest to pursue through the collection of proxies. There seems to be an intrinsic conflict of interests that the new law does not specifically address.

Lastly, the validity of shareholders' agreements finds full legal citizenship. However, shareholders' agreements are legal devices that, far from protecting or strengthening public investors, protect controlling shareholders. Even the provision affirming the immediate cancellation of the agreements when the company is the target of a takeover bid, which should favour the market for corporate control, is quite limited in its effects, since its operation is restricted to cases of mandatory (i.e. 100 per cent) takeover bids.

No effective measure was taken in order to implement and strengthen those legal devices specifically addressed at the protection of public investors. For instance, no change was proposed with regard to the role and liability of the auditing company, whose task is absolutely essential in reading and evaluating listed companies' annual accounts. Also no improvement was made as to the functioning of the internal supervisory board, or as to greater effectiveness, in terms of allocation of the burden of proof, of liability suits against company directors.

Indeed, the Law no. 58/1998 seems to go in the direction of consolidating existing ownership structures, while giving an appearance of greater attention to public investors' needs.[103]

[103] This conclusion is also reached by G. Visentini, "Osservazioni sulla recente disciplina delle società azionarie e del mercato mobiliare (Spunti di riflessione sulla sensibilità democratica nell formulazione delle scelte politiche)", in Riv. soc., 1998, 172.

4

Japan

*Hideki Kanda**

I. INTRODUCTION

The purpose of this chapter is to describe various aspects of corporate governance in Japan. The focus is on publicly held business corporations in Japan. Section II describes the legal framework. Section III sets forth factual situations. Section IV comments on recent theories about Japanese corporate governance. Section V concludes the chapter.

II. THE LEGAL FRAMEWORK

A. Organizational Form

Two of the most important aspects of business planning are decisions about organizational form and about sources of capital. Both decisions are influenced by legal rules about organizational structure as well as prevailing tax rules. In Japan, aside from sole proprietorship, businesses can be organized in one of six organizational, or legal, forms: *kumiai* (partnership), *tokumeikumiai* (limited partnership), *gomeigaisha* (incorporated partnership), *goshigaisha* (incorporated limited partnership), *yugengaisha* (limited company) and *kabushikigaisha* (stock company).[1] While a detailed description of each of these organizational forms is beyond the scope of this chapter, a brief discussion follows.

Among the six forms, only *kumiai* and *tokumeikumiai* enjoy single tiered income taxation, by which income tax is not imposed at the "entity" level and individual investors report their proportional share of the profits earned by the entity in their personal tax return. But *kumiai* does not offer limited liability to their investors, and while *tokumeikumiai* offers limited liability to investors, if the number of investors is ten or more, withholding tax will be imposed, making the *tokumeikumiai* form more costly. Consequently, *kumiai* and *tokumeikumiai* are

* Professor of Law, The University of Tokyo.

[1] Note also that a trust is sometimes used to do business in Japan. The most well-known is an arrange ment called a "land trust".

© Kluwer Law International 1998

Table 1 The Number of Corporations in Japan

Type	*Amount of Capital*	*Number*
Kabushikigaisha (stock company)	10 million yen or less	739,000
	above 10 million and less than 100 million yen	523,000
	10 million yen or more	32,000
	TOTAL	1,295,000
Gomeigaisha (incorporated partnership)		19,000
Goshigaisha (incorporated limited partnership)		78,000
Yugengaisha (limited liability company)		1,633,000
	TOTAL	3,024,000

As of June 1992
Source: Ministry of Justice

unpopular for a large business in Japan. The other four forms are all incorporated types (some of which provide investors with limited liability and others do not) and are subject to "double taxation". While *gomeigaisha*, *goshigaisha* and *yugengaisha* are given flexibility under statutes as to their internal governance structure and related matters, they are unsuitable for raising a large amount of funds in the capital markets.[2] Thus, in Japanese practice, all publicly held business firms take the *kabushikigaisha* form, which is similar to a business corporation in the U.S. and a public company in the U.K. (See Table 1 above.)

B. Company Law

Japan has a set of statutory rules for business firms, and the most important part of Japanese company law is found in the Japanese Commercial Code (Law No. 48 of 1899, as amended) ("Code"). The Code was originally modelled on the German Commercial Code of the late nineteenth century, but after World War II, a number of American rules were incorporated into the German-based rules. While provisions of the Code regarding the governance structure of *kabushikigaisha* (or stock company) are complex, their essence can be summarized as follows.[3]

The Code begins with the familiar position that shareholders are the owners of a stock company. A shareholders' meeting elects directors, and makes decisions about "fundamental changes" to the company, such as a merger, a sale of substantially all

[2] Shares in these organizations are not freely transferable. Also, issuing new shares requires approval of all the members or at the members' meeting.

[3] For a detailed description of company law in Japan see, for example, Koichi Kusano, "Corporate Law of Japan", in Haig Ochigian (ed.), *The Law of Commerce in Japan*, pp. 19-37 (Prentice-Hall, 1993).

the firm's assets, and an amendment to the firm's charter. There must be at least three directors. These directors are elected at the shareholders' meeting and form the board of directors. The board in turn elects representative directors, the Japanese counterparts of U.S. officers or executives. There must be at least one representative director. Representative directors are managers, and they run the company. The Code requires that the board of directors make important corporate decisions and supervise the management.[4] Each director, as a member of the board, owes a duty of care and loyalty to the company. The Japanese Commercial Code has a unique statutory provision that requires directors to pay damages to third parties if they act in bad faith or are grossly negligent in running the company or supervising other directors.[5] A director's liability to the company may be enforced by shareholders through a derivative law suit. Shareholders have familiar rights, such as the right to make proposals, the right to ask questions to directors and statutory auditors (although the Code calls this the director or auditor's "duty to explain"), and the right to examine the company's books and records.

A stock company must have *kansayaku*, often (somewhat misleadingly) translated as statutory auditor.[6] Statutory auditors are elected at the shareholders' meeting, and do not have to be accountants or other professionals. A "large company", defined under the statute,[7] must have at least three statutory auditors, and at least one of them must be an "outside" statutory auditor. A statutory auditor is "outside" when he has not been a director or an employee of the company or its subsidiary for at least five years preceding his appointment as auditor. In a "large company", there must be at least one full-time statutory auditor. A statutory auditor is responsible for overseeing the activities of management. This is understood to mean confirming the legality of management's activities.

In addition, a "large company" must have an accounting auditor (*kaikeikansanin*), who must be a certified public accountant or certified auditing firm. An accounting auditor is elected at the shareholders' meeting, and is responsible for auditing the company's financial statements before they are submitted to the annual shareholders' meeting, where the audit opinion is also submitted. The statute requires cooperation between accounting auditors and statutory auditors, providing complex rules, the details of which are beyond the scope of this chapter.

C. Securities Regulation

The Securities and Exchange Law in Japan (Law No. 25 of 1948 as amended) ("SEL") was modelled after the U.S. federal securities laws, specifically the Securi-

4 The board's decision-making power over "important matters" cannot be delegated to managers. Commercial Code, Art. 260.

5 Commercial Code, Art. 266-3. This provision was very often enforced where a closely held company went into bankruptcy and its creditors sued the directors for the amount of the company's debt owed to the creditors. Litigation under this provision has been unpopular for publicly held corporations. The recent popularity of shareholder's derivative suit in public corporations (which enforces the director's liability against the company), however, may suggest that litigation under this article may arise in the future for public companies.

6 The word "auditor" implies a professional, such as a certified public accountant, who engages in auditing accounting documents. A statutory auditor does not have to be a professional, and more importantly, his duty is as broad as to supervise the management.

7 A "large company" is a stock company having either capital in the amount of 500 million yen or more, or total (on balance sheet) debt in the amount of 20 billion yen or more.

ties Act of 1933 and the Securities Exchange Act of 1934. The SEL provides two basic sets of rules for investor protection: mandatory disclosure and anti-fraud rules. Thus, when a firm attempts to issue "securities", it must file a registration statement with the Ministry of Finance ("MOF"), which must include certain information specified under the rules promulgated by the MOF. Further, a company whose securities are listed on a stock exchange, traded "over the counter", or the number of whose registered shareholders is 500 or more is subject to the reporting requirements of the SEL: reporting is semi-annual, and the company's annual report must be audited by a certified public accountant. Also, a company which filed a registration statement with the MOF when it issued securities is subject to the same rules.[8]

The anti-fraud rules include prohibitions of somewhat broadly defined fraudulent activities, such as those prohibited under section 10(b) of the U.S. Securities Exchange Act of 1934, and more specific activities of securities companies, such as fraudulent solicitation of customers. Insider trading is also regulated. There has been little private litigation regarding violations of the disclosure or anti-fraud rules under the SEL.[9]

D. Other Laws

Needless to say, other laws also affect how Japanese companies are run. For instance, the Anti-Monopoly Law (Law No. 54 of 1947, as amended) prohibits a holding company.[10] It also prohibits banks and securities firms from holding more than 5 per cent of the total issued shares of any company unless they obtain special authorization from the Fair Trade Commission or fall within very narrow statutory exceptions.[11] For insurance companies this limitation is 10 per cent. Also, tax laws may have important effects on the way in which Japanese firms are organized and structured.

III. PRACTICE

A. Who Owns Japanese Public Companies?

There are over 8,000 "large" stock companies as defined above. As of 31 March 1996, there are 2,334 public companies listed on the eight stock exchanges in Japan, and the Tokyo Stock Exchange has 1,776 listed stock companies. Today, the owner-

[8] In 1996, there were 4,285 "reporting companies" that were subject to reporting requirement under the SEL.

[9] Note, however, that there is a vast amount of litigation between brokers and customers. When customers suffer losses from their investment, they often sue the broker on the ground that the broker did not explain the risk of investment in soliciting the investment.

[10] Anti-Monopoly Law, Art. 9. This provision was introduced during the U.S. occupancy with the concern about the revival of *zaibatsu* – conglomerates existing before World War II. What is per se illegal is the establishment of a "pure" holding company whose primary purpose is to hold shares of other companies. An operating company (an auto manufacturer, for instance) may have subsidiaries, and this structure (that is, subsidiaries owned by operating companies) is quite common in Japan.

In 1997, a bill for lifting the ban on pure holding companies was passed in the Diet.

[11] Anti-Monopoly Law, Art. 11.

ship structure of listed companies in the eight stock exchanges is roughly as follows. Individuals own 24 per cent of the total shares listed on the eight stock exchanges, financial institutions own 41 per cent (banks owning 27 per cent, life insurance companies 11 per cent and investment trusts 2 per cent),[12] and non-financial companies own 24 per cent. Thus, stock ownership of public companies in Japan is quite institutionalized, and the effectiveness of corporate governance forces by shareholders depends upon the behaviour of these institutions. (See Table 2 overleaf.)

Unlike in the U.S., banks may hold shares of other companies for investment purposes (under Article 65 of the SEL, the Japanese version of Glass-Steagall), but as mentioned above, they cannot own more than 5 per cent of a single company under Anti-Monopoly Law. A typical manufacturing company has ten bank shareholders, each owning 2 to 3 per cent, as well as 20 other major corporate shareholders.[13] Also, mutual stockholding by companies is common, and known as *keiretsu*. But high percentage two-way holdings are unpopular. That is, Company A's holding of Company B's shares may range from 1 per cent to 100 per cent, but Company B typically owns 1 to 2 per cent of A's shares. As mentioned above, banks and insurance companies are subject to the anti-trust limitations.[14]

B. Non-Stockholder Constituencies

In addition to shareholders, there are a number of other constituencies that influence Japanese corporate governance. Among them, employees and banks are the most important. While employees are not owners of their company under the Japanese legal system,[15] commonly observed facts may suggest that Japanese companies are run in the best interest of the employees and not the shareholders. For instance, when a firm faces financial distress, management cuts dividends before it starts firing employees. Under Japanese practice, most directors and statutory auditors are elected from former employees of the company. Life-time employment, compensation tied to seniority, and company-by-company labour unions were often pointed out as three distinctive characteristics of Japanese companies and functioned to keep employee supremacy alive in past decades.

However, even if Japanese companies are run for the benefit of employees, it does not necessarily mean that shareholders are victimized. One commentator developed a model in which Japanese firms are run on the bargain between shareholders and employees.[16] The proposition that Japanese companies are not run for the best interest of shareholders, however, lacks empirical support.[17]

[12] Note that trust banks and life insurance companies manage pensions in Japan.

[13] See Toyo Keizai Inc., *Japan Company Handbook* (quarterly publication, every year).

[14] Who owns banks and insurance companies in Japan? The ownership structure of these institutions is quite diverse. See *Japan Company Handbook*, supra note 13.

[15] Codetermination – which requires employee representation on the board – is not adopted in the Japanese law.

[16] Masahiko Aoki, "Toward an Economic Model of the Japanese Firm", 28 *Journal of Economic Literature*, p. 1 (1990).

[17] Recent empirical studies suggest that Japanese companies are run for the best interest of shareholders. See Steven Kaplan, "Top Executive Rewards and Firm Performance: A Comparison of Japan and the U.S.", *Journal of Political Economy*, p. 102 (1994); Steven Kaplan & Bernadette Minton, "Appointments of Outsiders to Japanese Boards: Determinants and Implications for Managers", 36 *Journal of Financial Economics*, p. 225 (1994). See also Erik Berglöf & Enrico Perotti, "The Governance Structure of the Japanese Financial Keiretsu", 36 *Journal of Financial Economics*, p. 259 (1994).

Table 2 Stock Ownership by Type of Investors (All Listed Companies) (%)

	Government and local government	*Financial institutions*	*Securities companies*	*Business corporations*	*Individuals and others*	*Foreigners*
1960	0.2	30.6	3.7	17.8	46.3	1.3
1965	0.2	29.0	5.8	18.4	44.8	1.8
1970	0.2	32.3	1.2	23.1	39.9	3.2
1975	0.2	36.0	1.4	26.3	33.5	2.6
1980	0.2	38.8	1.7	26.0	29.2	4.0
1985	0.8	42.2	2.0	24.1	25.2	5.7
1990	0.6	45.2	1.7	25.2	23.1	4.2
1995	0.6	41.4	1.4	23.6	23.6	9.4

Source: Ministry of Finance, The National Conference of Stock Exchanges

Banks are important players in Japan, too. Japanese companies rely more on banks than on capital markets for debt finance. The relative underdevelopment of the Japanese bond markets might be, at least in part, the result of a political victory by the banking industry.[18] Banks thus are important. But how they operate is far from clear.[19]

The bank-customer relationship in Japan has several distinct characteristics. Some of them are common in other business relationships in Japan, while others are unique to banking transactions. Banking transactions between banks and their customer firms in Japan show three unique characteristics. First, banks and their customer firms engage in a very wide range of transactions, from straightforward lending to more complicated types of transactions, such as swap transactions. It is common for a bank to hold shares in their customer firms. Secondly, a company usually establishes a long-term contractual relationship with several banks. One of these banks typically serves as the "main bank". Thirdly, banks obtain a strong legal position under a standard form contract known as the Banking Transactions Agreement, but they sometimes show behaviour that looks quite inconsistent with their strong legal position. For instance, when a firm is in a financial trouble, the traditional behaviour of the main bank (which usually has a first mortgage over the firm's property securing its loans) is to pay off other debts (debts which are legally subordinated to the bank's claim) and pay off outstanding debentures or bonds.

These three distinct characteristics are found in many situations, including daily credit transactions, rescue actions when the customer firm is in financial distress, and in the bank's stockholding in their customer firms. All of them, however, have

[18] The "eligibility standards" for bonds – a customary rule which only permits companies meeting the standards to issue bonds in Japanese public markets – were established by the banking industry for the decades after World War II. However, they were abolished recently.

[19] Opinions are split as to whether banks are influential in Japanese corporate governance. See infra Section IV.

begun to evaporate in recent years as many banks suffer bad loans and seek the source for their writeoff.[20]

C. Managers, Directors, and Statutory Auditors

Boards of directors in Japan are homogeneous. The board of directors in a typical large Japanese company consists of about 25 men, most of them being at least 50 years old. They are all former employees of the company. There are almost no executives from other firms, no women, no academics and no outsiders of any kind. These directors elect managers. Managers are the highest rank in the life of "salary man", the phrase which describes a typical university graduate under the life-time employment system in Japan.

Statutory auditors are similar. Outside auditors, introduced by the Commercial Code amendment in 1993, are mostly former employees who meet the statutory test of non-affiliatedness because they did not serve as employees for the five years immediately preceding appointment as an outside auditor.

A number of firms recently announced that they will reduce the number of directors and statutory auditors. Their explanation is that this is necessary and appropriate because they began cutting the number of employees to cope with current unfavourable economic conditions.

D. Capital Markets

In general, as capital markets grow, two implications for corporate governance are produced. First, firms favour capital markets more than banks because the former usually is a cheaper source of capital. As a result, the presence of banks in corporate governance inevitably reduced. Secondly, equity investors in the capital markets become important actors in corporate governance because the law usually treats them as owners of the issuing company. More specifically, what we observe in some (but not all) countries is the institutionalization of investors and the emergence of hostile takeovers.

1. Investor Institutionalization

Investor institutionalization produces difficult questions of how regulation should respond. It also produces the question of whether institutions play a role in corporate governance.

Today in Japan, as mentioned above, capital markets are highly institutionalized, but institutions almost never exercise their voting rights and remain "stable" shareholders.[21] While they are active traders of shares, at least until recently, they remained stable shareholders by selling and buying back the same share when they wanted to realize capital gains or losses.[22]

[20] In recent years, some (though not most) banks began selling (and not simultaneously buying) stock of their customer firm to create the source for the writeoff of bad loans. The result is the decrease in their influence over the firm.

[21] In Japan, the notion of "institutional investors" usually includes not only insurance companies and pension funds, but also banks and industrial companies.

[22] This way of the realization of capital gains or losses and the maintenance of the degree of stock ownership can be achieved under the cost-based accounting rule.

2. *Takeovers*

Under the SEL, the regulation of stock tender offers was first introduced in 1971. The regulation was somewhat restrictive, notably in its requirement that the offeror must file a registration statement ten days before it initiates an offer. This requirement of a ten-day waiting period and other restrictive rules resulted in only three tender offers prior to the amendments made in 1990.

The 1990 amendments "modernized" the rules on stock tender offers. In general, the new rules are comparable to those in the U.S. Basically, the law provides disclosure requirements in connection with, and substantive rules of, tender offers for equity securities (including convertible bonds and bonds with stock purchase warrants) of a "reporting" company, as explained above. A stock tender offer exists when the person[23] making the offer, after consummation, would be the owner of more than 5 per cent of the securities in question. The person making the offer must file a registration statement with the MOF and make a public announcement, typically in a newspaper. He may commence the offer on the day following the public announcement. The items for disclosure in the registration statement and the public announcement are specified in detail by MOF regulations. Also, as in the United States, there are detailed rules governing the tender offer process. Among others, rules on the withdrawal of an offer, changes in the condition of the original offer, the mandatory period of an offer, and the fair treatment of those who respond to an offer are of particular importance.

There are at least two differences between the U.S. and Japan in the regulation of stock tender offers. First, in Japan, an open market purchase, that is, a purchase of stock in the stock market provided at a stock exchange, is not subject to tender offer regulations. Secondly, and more importantly, while a tender offer typically means an offer to many shareholders, the Japanese regulation is applicable when the offeror acquires stock from a small number of shareholders (ten or less), if, after consummation, the acquiror would be the owner of more than one-third of the securities of the company involved.[24] The premise underlying the second rule is that even a private purchase must be disclosed when a big shareholder (or one with more than one-third ownership) would emerge. But the necessity of this rule is controversial, and indeed, an "inadvertent" tender offer may occur where, for instance, a creditor who holds securities as collateral attempts to enforce his security interest.

An ownership disclosure rule, a popular companion of tender offer regulation, was also introduced in Japan in 1990. Certain disclosure obligations are imposed on persons owning more than 5 per cent of the equity securities of a company, as under section 13(d) of the U.S. Securities Exchange Act of 1934.

In practice, only nine tender offers took place by the end of 1993, all of which were friendly. Despite the large number of mergers, consolidations and asset sales in Japan, the number of stock tender offers has been very limited. There have been no (successful) hostile takeovers in Japan. One might ask why this is. In light of the fact that hostile takeovers helped to discipline inefficient managements in the United States in the 1980s, a related question may be whether Japan lacks effective mecha-

[23] The term "person" is broad, including groups of two or more persons who are "insiders" or act together.

[24] One might characterize this as a unique form of the "mandatory bid" rule, a rule popular in some jurisdictions in Europe.

nisms to discipline management in public corporations. A somewhat more difficult question is whether the law, particularly the regulation of tender offers, has something to do with the unpopularity of tender offers, and the non-existence of hostile takeovers in Japan.

The conventional explanation for the unpopularity of hostile takeovers in Japan is that stock prices of major public companies are too high to attract potential acquirors[25] and that the existence of cross stockholding makes such takeovers difficult. This, however, does not necessarily mean that Japanese companies with less of a threat of hostile takeovers are less monitored. There probably are a variety of mechanisms, other than hostile takeovers, by which managers of public companies in Japan are monitored and disciplined.[26]

E. Litigations

While any country can be classified into one of a litigious and non-litigious country, even a non-litigious country needs some amount of litigation for legal rules to be enforced. If litigation is unpopular, another way of interpretation is that either legal rules are underenforced or they do not matter. If legal rules do not matter, other (non-legal) mechanisms must exist and operate to monitor public companies in Japan.

In Japan, litigation in the areas of company law and securities regulation has been rare. In recent years, however, the number of shareholder derivative suits in public corporations increased drastically.[27] While the plaintiff lost in most cases, the sudden growth of this litigation changed the practice and behaviour of directors in major corporations. Directors now carefully read the minutes of the board meetings before they sign them. They tend to seek lawyers' or other professionals' opinions when they make important legal decisions.

Litigation in the securities law area is still unpopular. The Securities Trading Surveillance Committee has discovered certain anti-fraud violations in recent years.[28] For the most part, there is reason to think that rules in securities law are not underenforced but complied with through an "ex ante monitoring" mechanism by which parties participate in the rule-making process.[29]

[25] There has been no good explanation of why (or even whether) stock prices of major Japanese companies are high. Despite the stock market decline in the recent years, price earning ratios of major Japanese companies suggest that their stock prices are, on average, still higher than what is predicted by the standard method in finance theory.

[26] See J. Mark Ramseyer, "Takeovers in Japan: Opportunism, Ideology and Corporate Control", 35 *UCLA Law Review*, p. 1 (1987).

[27] The best English written article about shareholder derivative suits in Japan is Mark D. West, "The Pricing of Shareholder Derivative Actions in Japan and the United States", 88 *Northwestern University Law Review,* p. 1436 (1994). Unfortunately, a number of important suits were filed after this article was written, and only Japanese written articles describe the very recent situation.

[28] On 20 July 1992, a committee called the "Securities Trading Surveillance Committee" (*Shokentorihikito Kanshiiinkai*) was established for the effective enforcement of the SEL. This was the result of the "scandal" in the securities and other areas in 1991. Securities companies were blamed for having compensated for the trading losses of their large customers. For details about the scandal and the introduction of the Committee, see Curtis J. Milhaupt, "Managing the Market: The Ministry of Finance and Securities Regulation in Japan", 30 *Stanford Journal of International Law*, p. 423 (1994).

[29] For the details of this ex ante monitoring, see Hideki Kanda, "Politics, Formalism, and the Elusive Goal of Investor Protection: Regulation of Structured Investment Funds in Japan", 12 *University of Pennsylvania Journal of International Business Law*, p. 569 (1991).

IV. THEORY

The comparative study of corporate governance in major countries is interesting.[30] What is compared, however, must be carefully identified. Such study also must identify the purpose of the research.

There is a vast amount of literature on the Japanese firm.[31] Most articles, however, fail to discuss the interaction between law and practice. They usually do not consider the existence of legal rules that appear to encourage different behaviour from what they think they observe about public companies in Japan. The interaction between law and practice is sometimes difficult to identify, but once it is properly identified, one can better tell how legal rules affect corporate behaviour in Japan and thus obtain a better understanding of how firms operate in Japan.

Take for example the main bank concept. While past research is divided as to whether the main bank is the most powerful monitor of its customer firm, such research does not show how legal rules affect the main bank's (and others') behaviour.[32] The focus has been on the main bank's behaviour when the customer firm is in financial distress. The conventionally observed behaviour of the main bank in such situation is to "rescue" the firm.

An interesting theory was presented that the main bank is a delegated monitor (of other creditors).[33] The problem is that this does not explain what we observe. Moreover, in theory, two questions must be answered. First, why do other creditors delegate monitoring to the main bank? And how can they freeride on the main bank's monitoring efforts (or otherwise contract with the main bank)? Secondly, why does the main bank do such "excessive" monitoring? And why does it agree to that? The explanation offered centres upon hypothetical (or implicit) contracting between the main bank and other creditors. It seems, however, that this *ex ante* approach is the source of a problem. The main bank's rescue behaviour is better explained when one focuses on the bank's behaviour after the customer firm gets into financial trouble. In such situations, the bank (which usually is the first mortgage holder) has a choice: to foreclose the mortgage or to rescue (often by employing a reorganization procedure). When a bank pursues the latter path, it is beneficial for the bank to take control of the whole reorganization process (given that the bank – and the debtor – will have better information than the other creditors). At least in the past, the main bank often paid off other debts (that were legally subordinated to its claim) and always paid off outstanding bonds. By doing so, the bank could get control of the restruc-

[30] The comparative study of corporate governance among major countries, including Japan, has attracted researchers in Japan and elsewhere. English language works by Japanese researchers include Mitsuhiro Fukao, *Financial Integration, Corporate Governance, and the Performance of Multinational Companies* (Brookings Institute, 1995) and Kenji Kojima, *Corporate Governance: An International Comparison* (A Discussion Paper, May 1995).

[31] Recent studies by economists about Japanese firms have been numerous. The key question is whether Japanese and Western firms are different. Compare Masahiko Aoki & Ronald Dore (eds.), *The Japanese Firm* (Oxford University Press, 1994) (trying to identify where Japanese firms are different from Western firms) with Yoshiro Miwa, *Firms and Industrial Organization in Japan* (Macmillan, 1996) (arguing that Japanese firms are not unique at all).

[32] A notable exception is J. Mark Ramseyer's work. See "Explicit Reasons for Implicit Contracts: The Legal Logic to the Japanese Main Bank System", in Masahiko Aoki & Hugh Patrick (eds.), *The Japanese Main Bank System*, p. 231 (Oxford University Press, 1994).

[33] Paul Sheard, "The Main Bank System and Corporate Monitoring and Control in Japan", 11 *Journal of Economic Behavior and Organization*, p. 399 (1989).

turing process. Other creditors could have disagreed, but the bank was armed with the threat of enforcing its first mortgage right.

At a more general level, Masahiko Aoki presents a model by which corporate decisions are made by interactions between shareholders and employees.[34] He also stresses the importance of "hierarchy" rather than "market" when decisions are made (particularly in the employees' decision-making process). One problem with this model is that in this model managers are passive mediators, and thus the model fails to consider managers as active players in corporate governance. He could develop a model for a three-party game, but appears to reject such a model in describing the Japanese firm.

Once one views corporate decisions in an evolutional framework, it is possible that there is more than one equilibria, and that things may move from one to another equilibrium, and then it is difficult for them to come back to the previous point. A recent "path dependency" view is another form of this theory developed in the historical context. [35]

If one views comparative corporate governance as a question of how public firms are, and should be, monitored, the existence of different governance systems across our planet is not puzzling. Different systems may operate differently. Firms under each jurisdiction are monitored by various mechanisms in that jurisdiction. Indeed, recent empirical studies are consistent with this observation.

Another perspective is to view the international comparison of corporate governance as an industrial organization question. Ronald Gilson and Mark Roe are the representatives of those taking this approach. For them, the key question is the comparison of a system having stability (i.e. a bank-centred system) with one having adaptability (i.e. a capital market-based system).[36]

V. CONCLUSION

In Japan and elsewhere, both law and practice change regularly. Each change may be viewed as a response to a scandal, pressure from other countries, or unfavourable economic conditions. Uniqueness in Japanese corporate governance, if there is such, may stem from law, practice, and (in the author's view most importantly) the gap between law and practice. Most notably, the development of capital markets, combined with other economic factors, has reduced banks' presence in Japanese corporate governance. In theory, this and other changes are within a predictable range, and confirm that firms operate properly under different governance systems.

[34] Masahiko Aoki, supra note 16. See also Masahiko Aoki, "The Japanese Firm As a System of Attributes: A Survey and Research Agenda", in Aoki & Dore, supra note 31, p. 11. Another theory that is popular in Japan but, unlike Aoki's, not outside Japan, is the "network" theory. This theory asserts that as an organizational form, there is something between "market" and "firm". But as a theory this is too broad a theory to explain the individual behaviour of Japanese firms.

[35] See Tetsuji Okazaki, "The Japanese Firm under the Wartime Planned Economy", in Aoki & Dore, supra note 31, p. 350.

[36] See Ronald Gilson and Mark Roe, "Understanding the Japanese Keiretsu: Overlaps Between Corporate Governance and Industrial Organization", 102 *Yale Law Journal*, p. 871 (1993); Ronald Gilson, "Corporate Governance and Economic Efficiency", in Mats Isaksson & Rolf Skog (eds.), *Aspects of Corporate Governance*, p. 131 (Juristförlaget, 1994). See also, Mark Roe, "Some Differences in Corporate Structure in Germany, Japan, and the United States", 102 *Yale Law Journal*, p. 1927 (1993).

5

The Netherlands

*Martijn van Empel**

I. INTRODUCTION

During the last two decades, Dutch law concerning corporate governance has changed dramatically.[1] Many of these changes can be attributed to the European Economic Community (EEC) (now referred to as the European Community, EC). The EC Treaty provides for the progressive harmonization of company law. As a result, Dutch company law is now more formalistic and elaborate then it used to be. Indeed, Dutch traditions were very much oriented towards flexibility, on the basis of the assumption that, as long as there was no proof of deceit at setting up a company, the shareholders should be allowed to decide for themselves what the rules were with regard to the distribution of powers within the company.

Until 1971, Holland only had one type of company, the *Naamloze Vennootschap* (the "classic NV"), which in principle can be compared to, for example, the French SA and the German AG. However, the statutory regulation of the NV was so flexible that it could also suit the purposes of the kind of companies which are, in other countries, normally served by the private companies, which are based upon a more intimate relationship between the shareholders (such as the French SARL and the German GmbH). In the traditional Dutch system, the bigger enterprises organized as NV, who held out to the public for financial contribution, were bound to publish annual accounts. The NVs which were organized for family company purposes were not obliged to publish their accounts. Then, in the framework of the harmonization of European company law, the First Directive on Company Law of 9 March 1968[2] imposed the requirement that every NV should publish its balance sheet and profit and loss accounts with explanatory notes. For many minor enterprises, such as family enterprises and one-man companies, all of which were carried on in the Netherlands in the form of a NV, this obligation to publish their

* Professor of Law – Europa Instituut University of Amsterdam. The author wishes to express his gratitude for the assistance by Pauline Vos (Rotterdam), Björn van der Klip (Amsterdam) and for the valuable comments by Professor Alexander Mohr (University of Amsterdam). The chapter is updated till November 1996.

[1] See J.M.M. Maeijer, *Vertegenwoordiging en Rechtspersoon, De Naamloze en de Besloten Vennootschap* (1994) (hereinafter: "Asser-Maeijer 2, III"), pp. 1-13.

[2] Directive 68/151/EEC, OJ 1968, L 65/8.

© Kluwer Law International 1998

annual accounts was unacceptable, because the appreciable costs involved did not serve any useful purpose for them. Therefore, Dutch law reacted by creating the form of a *Besloten Vennootschap* (BV). The escape from publication of annual accounts which this new type of company has provided for the time being, has been warmly welcomed. During the year 1972 over 40,000 NVs were converted into BVs. However, later on, the obligation to publish annual accounts was also imposed by EC law on BVS.[3]

The situation in the Netherlands became still more complex when in the same year, 1971, another law introduced special rules for the larger companies, the so-called "structuur companies" (whether in the form of a NV or a BV). In these large companies the institution of a supervisory board has been made compulsory and this board has been given wide mandatory powers, as shall be seen later.

Thus, from then on, there existed in effect four layers of "capital-companies" i.e. the small BV, the small NV, the *structuur* BV and the *structuur* NV. Hereunder, the *structuur* companies (BV or NV) will also be referred to as "large companies". Because the focus of this chapter is on the publicly held corporation, references hereunder will be essentially to the "small NV" and the "*structuur* NV". In this regard it should be noted that in the relevant legislation (the Civil Code (*Burgerlijk Wetboek*) Book 2)[4] identical provisions are to be found in parallel for BVs and NVs. In this chapter, references will be made only to the NV provisions because the focus is on listed companies.

Some insight into the position of shareholders in the Netherlands may be gained from the table opposite.[5]

II. THE STAKEHOLDERS

A. Management

The management board is the executive body and may be made up of individuals or corporations. It is responsible for the management of the corporation and its representation, i.e. the actions of the corporation towards third parties.[6] It is in charge of the daily management of the company. The Dutch management board combines the functions of inside managing directors and senior officers in an American corporation. Consequently, there is no position equivalent to that of chief executive officer. The management board may, however, consist of a sole member, in which event that person is customarily called the managing director or the general managing director (*algemeen directeur*). If the management board has more than one member, the responsibility of the members of the managing board is in essence a collective one. Each director shares responsibility for all decisions and acts of the management board and for the acts of each individual managing director. The management board is generally imputed to have knowledge of everything that each managing director knows or should know. It is possible to allot certain tasks to certain members of the

3 Directive 78/660/EEC, OJ 1978, L 222/11.
4 Hereunder references will be to BW Art. 2: (...).
5 Source: G.M.M. Gelauff, C. den Broeder, *Governance of stakeholder relationships, The German and Dutch experience*, Centraal Planbureau, Research Memorandum No. 127 (1996).
6 BW Art. 2:129.

	Germany	*Netherlands*	*UK*	*US*
Domestic listed companies, 1993				
number[a]	664.	140.	1927.	6098.
number per billion $ of GDP	0.35	0.45	2.04	0.97
capitalization, % of GDP[a]	25.1	61.5	132.4	83.5
per cent of total turnover[b]	10.6	–	30.5	–
Ownership of shares[c] *Percentage*				
households	16.6	20.0	17.7	50.2
non-financial enterprises	38.8	9.6	3.1	14.1
banks	14.2	0.7	0.6	0.0
investement funds	7.6	1.5	9.7	5.7
pension funds	1.9	7.9	34.2	20.1
insurance companies	5.2	5.5	17.2	4.6
government	3.4	0.0	1.3	0.0
foreign	12.2	54.8	16.3	5.4
Share of largest shareholder[d] *Percentage of largest firms*				
> 25%	85.	–	13.	–
> 50%	57.	22.	6.	–
> 75%	22.	–	1.	–

[a] Source: CEPS (1995: 7).

[b] Source: Germany and the United Kingdom 1986, Edwards and Fischer (1994: 86, 87).

[c] Source: Germany, 1993, Deutsche Bundesbank (1994: 68, 69) and CEPS (1995: 31, 32); the Netherlands, 1993, CPB extension of Swank *et al.* (1989); United Kingdom, 1993, CEPS (1995: 13) and OECD (1995c: 88); United States, 1990, Prowse (1994: 21).

[d] Source: Germany and the United Kingdom, Franks and Mayer (1993); the Netherlands Cantrijn *et al* (1993: 47).

management board,[7] but on the basis of the ultimate collective responsibility, every member of the management board can always demand that a certain decision be made by the board of management.

The law is not specific about the powers of the management board in undertaking "the management of the corporation". The powers implied in this general notion can be circumscribed by virtue of the Articles, but these can also extend the board's powers, except for those powers expressly attributed to the shareholders or the supervisory board by law. The corporation's business policies are determined by the management board within the confines of the corporate purposes, with due regard for the interests of the corporation, the shareholders, the employees, and, according to certain legal commentators, the corporation's business relations, as well as certain basic social interests.[8]

As previously mentioned, the management board is basically independent in the performance of its duties. Within the scope of the responsibilities allotted to it, it is not subordinated to either the shareholders or the supervisory board.[9] The Articles

[7] Ibid., Art. 2:9.

[8] See Asser-Maeijer 2, III, no. 293 and no. 18.

[9] H.R. 21 January 1955, NJ 1959, 43 ("Forum Bank").

may, however, require the management board to obtain the prior approval of the supervisory board or the shareholders with respect to decisions on matters set forth in the Articles (or determined by the supervisory board or the shareholders' meeting). To some extent, exception to the *Forum Bank* rule can also be allowed for in case of a subsidiary company, because here the management of the subsidiary should be guided substantially by the interests of the subsidiary as part of the group of companies.[10]

In case of a *structuur* company, special rules govern the powers of the management board. These rules supplement, and in case of conflict, overrule the rules generally applicable to corporations.

As a general rule, a member of the management board may be suspended from his powers and responsibilities at any time by a resolution of the shareholders' meeting. The supervisory board always has the power to suspend managing directors, unless otherwise stated in the Articles.[11]

The removal of a member of the management board requires a resolution by either the shareholders or the supervisory board, whichever has the power to elect the managing directors. In a "large" corporation, the supervisory board must first hear the shareholders meeting.[12] As shall be seen later, in the case of mismanagement, the Enterprise Chamber may also remove a managing director. If a corporation has a works council, the management board must give this council prior notice of an anticipated removal, so as to allow it to give advice.

With regard to the fiduciary duties of directors, the duty of care is expressed in terms of a duty to "properly perform" management tasks.[13] The duty of good faith is part of the reasonableness or fairness requirement that Dutch corporate law imposes on relationships between the management board, supervisory board, shareholders and the works council.[14] A breach of these duties may give rise to an action by the corporation or by the shareholders.

Good-faith principles govern situations in which a board member obtains personal benefit at the expense of the corporation, as well as those in which the management board denies shareholders, or the supervisory board, any powers, rights or benefits to which they are entitled. This category relates to the protection of minority shareholders, power struggles among managing directors and shareholders or supervisory directors, and the proper use of pre-emption rights.

B. Shareholders

In a non-*structuur* company, amongst the shareholders' primary powers is the power to elect,[15] suspend and remove[16] the managing directors and at least two-thirds of the members of the supervisory board. This does not apply in a "large" corporation, as shall be seen later. With respect to the election of managing and supervisory directors, the shareholders may be required by the Articles to "rubber-stamp" nomina-

[10] See Asser-Maeijer 2, III, no. 617.
[11] BW Art. 2:147.
[12] Ibid., Art. 2:162.
[13] Ibid., Art. 2:9.
[14] Ibid., Art. 2:8. With regard to the Works Council, see Judgment of 26 November 1987 of the Enterprise Chamber, NJ 1989, 271 [Ikon].
[15] BW Art. 2:132.
[16] Ibid., Art. 2:134.

tions proposed by the management, the supervisory board, a particular type or class of shareholders, or by any other person or institution, stated in the Articles as the case may be. This can be overruled only by a "super majority" of two-thirds of the votes cast in the General Meeting of Shareholders, representing more than one-half of the issued shares.[17]

The shareholders' meeting has the power to adopt the annual accounts[18] (in a "large" corporation they have to approve the annual accounts, adopted by the supervisory board). The management board must prepare the annual accounts and submit them, together with the auditor's opinion and the annual report, to the shareholders' meeting within five months after the end of the fiscal year. The annual accounts include a proposed allocation of profits, but the final allocation is made by the shareholders, subject, however, to provisions in the Articles concerning the formation and allocation of certain reserves and to any powers that the Articles may vest in that respect in the supervisory board or in the priority shareholders.

The shareholders have the right to approve major changes in the corporate structure, including amendments to the Articles, transformation of the company, mergers and dissolution of the corporation.[19]

A shareholder has to behave reasonably and equitably in all situations towards other shareholders and the corporation. This does not mean that the shareholders must uphold the corporation's interests, or that they have any specific obligation towards other shareholders.[20] This good-faith principle may, however, form the ground for an action to have a resolution of the shareholders meeting declared void by court order.[21]

It should be noted in this connection that it has been held that the interests of (even) the majority of shareholders cannot be equated with the interests of the corporation as such.[22]

The right to vote is concomitant with the ownership of shares. Each shareholder has at least one vote,[23] and the voting rights are, in principle, proportionate to the par value of the shares. The Articles may also provide for a ceiling on the number of votes each shareholder may cast or grant progressively reduced voting rights per share the higher the percentage of shares held (e.g. six votes for 10 per cent, seven votes for 20 per cent, etc.), thereby reducing the voting power of large shareholders.[24] A shareholder may be represented by proxy. The Articles may prohibit certain persons from being proxy holders.[25]

Shareholders may enter into agreements concerning most of the rights incident to the ownership of their shares. These agreements are, in principle, valid and enforce-

[17] Ibid., Arts. 2:133, 2:142(2).

[18] Ibid., Art. 2:101(3).

[19] Ibid., Arts. 2:121; 2:18(2); 2:19(1); 2:317(1), (3).

[20] HR 30 June 1944, NJ 19944, 405 ("Wennex".)

[21] BW Art. 2:8.

[22] HR 1 April 1949, NJ 19949, 465 m.n. Houwing ("Doetinchemse IJzergieterij").

[23] BW Art. 2:118.

[24] Due to reliance on more effective "oligarchic" clauses (see infra p. 139), provisions in the Articles to this effect have become rather exceptional.

[25] It should be noted that the development of large scale proxy-solicitation has been hindered by the fact that most shares in the larger corporations are bearer shares (see Asser-Maeijer 2, III, no. 288; see also P. Sanders and W. Westbroek/F.K. Buyn and P.M: Storm, *BV and NV* (1994) (hereinafter: "P. Sanders e.a."), no. 4.12. (See however below in Section VI.)

able, but they bind only the parties thereto.[26] In this case, one or more shareholders oblige themselves to vote in a certain way on a certain object. The Supreme Court ruled in *Wennex*[27] that these agreements are allowed and not in violation of the law or general principles, because the right to vote is a right of the shareholder, and he can do whatever he wants with this right to serve his own interests. On the other hand, a shareholder cannot bind himself to vote according to instructions from the management board or the supervisory board.

Every corporation must keep books and records. The shareholders are not entitled to inspect these books and records, with the exception of the shareholders' register. Shareholders representing either 10 per cent of the issued shares or a par value of NLG 500,000 (or any lower percentage or amount as provided in the Articles) may, under certain circumstances, request the "Enterprise Chamber" of the Amsterdam Court of Appeal to appoint one or more experts to investigate the conduct of the business. These court-appointed experts have full access to the books and records. This investigation (*enquête*) will be discussed later.

C. Labour

In the Netherlands a clear distinction is made between labour organized within the framework of the trade union on the one hand, and the works council (*Ondernemingsraad*), on the other. The trade union acts upon the enterprise from outside, whereas the works council acts from inside.

The period after World War II was a period of reconstruction, and there was a generally felt solidarity economically and socially, with a view to rebuilding the economy. There was also general agreement that the workforce had to play a constructive role therein, and that therefore they should be given a share in responsibility for decisions to be taken. This was generally referred to as "the harmony model" and it strongly influenced the organization of economic life in the Netherlands in the period.

The essential function of trade unions is to conclude wage agreements, or at least to see that wage agreements are concluded with individual employers. From 1945 to 1970, Holland had a so-called "guided wage policy". It was deemed crucial for industrialization that the level of wages be kept down in order to be competitive in the international world market. In essence the guideline was that there should be no wage increase beyond the increase of productivity. The mechanism in institutional terms was that the room for wage increases was agreed upon at a central level for the whole country between the two sides, i.e. organized labour and organized industry. From 1970 onwards, there was a general feeling that reconstruction had been achieved and that therefore there was now more room for individual differences of wealth created from one enterprise to another.

The historical background of the works council was in fact anti-trade union. The origins are to be found in attempts by management to have labour representatives within the company so as to make trade unions superfluous in the eyes of the employees. Accordingly, before World War II, trade unions strongly opposed the institution of works councils, because the unions claimed to be the only representa-

[26] However, it would seem that a shareholder cannot sell or otherwise dispose of his voting rights separately from his legal or beneficial ownership rights in the shares.

[27] See supra, note 15.

tives of organized labour. But also here the "harmony model" made its influence felt after World War II, and gradually accommodation was achieved.

The first Act on works councils, the WOR (*Wet op de Ondernem ingsraden*) was enacted in 1950.[28] This Act made it possible, but not obligatory, to create a works council. In 1971, a new Act made it mandatory for enterprises of a certain size to have a works council. The employer, i.e. the management, was a member as of right of the works council and was in the chair. In 1979 and 1983 there were further amendments. As from 1979, the management no longer sat on the works council as of right. In 1983 the obligation to have a works council was further extended to smaller enterprises.

As matters stand today, an enterprise with 35 employees or more must have a works council. However, it is only in enterprises of 100 or more employees that rights of the works council are really fully-fledged. With numbers between 35 to 100 employees the works council is in a somewhat intermediate position. At the other extreme, enterprises with less than 35 employees merely have the obligation to hold a meeting, twice a year, between management and personnel, so that the employees know how the enterprise is faring. It should be noted that in all this the legal form of the enterprise is irrelevant: when there is the statutory minimum number of employees in the enterprise, it must have a works council.

The members of the works council are elected by the employees of the enterprise from amongst their midst. There are special provisions to protect those who are elected against discrimination and retaliation by the employer (e.g. through protection against dismissal during their period of membership and the first period thereafter).

Under the current statute, the works council meets according to its own agenda. At least twice a year it meets with the management in a so-called "coordination meeting" in order to discuss the fortunes of the company. If there is a supervisory board, it is expected that one or more members of the supervisory board also sit in on that coordination meeting between the management and the works council, so that these members also have first hand information on what is being discussed between the management and the works council.[29]

In groups of companies, there is the possibility to have different levels of works councils.[30] The starting-point is that of the works council at the level of the enterprise of at least x employees. But if that enterprise is part of a larger organization, a "central works council" (COR) is provided for and in case of a very big group of companies, works councils are to be found at intermediate level also. The Act provides that the functions are the same at the various levels so that all issues which are decided at a particular level by the management of that level, should be discussed with the works council of that level.[31] Items which are decided at the individual enterprise level are discussed with the OR of the basic works council; decisions which are taken at the intermediate level are discussed with the "Group OR", and the very general decisions are discussed with the "Central OR". The intermediate OR and the central OR are elected by and from amongst the members of the individual works councils of the enterprises.

[28] On the subsequent stages of legislation on the subject see P. Sanders e.a., no. 13.1; Asser Maeijer 2, III, no. 453.

[29] WOR, Art. 24.

[30] Ibid., Arts. 33-35.

[31] Ibid., Art. 35.

The powers of the works council are:

(1) the right to be informed;
(2) the right to give advice on certain issues;
(3) the right to decide ("co-determination") i.e. to decide with the management.

1. The Right to be Informed[32]

The works council must be informed on a regular basis and on an ad hoc basis. Information on a regular basis relates to the annual accounts of the enterprise, the budget for the coming year, the long-term projects, and the quarterly accounts if these are published. At least twice a year, information must be provided about expectations for the near future, and the investments relating thereto. Information on an ad hoc basis refers to special situations and special events which affect the prospects and the activities of the enterprise.

2. The Right to Give Advice

The right to give advice is provided for in two different Articles, Article 25 and Article 30 of the WOR. Article 25 specifies the essential decisions affecting the life of the enterprise on which the works council should be given the opportunity to give advice: the transfer of the enterprise; the transfer of the activities of the enterprise to somebody else; the taking over and the permanent cooperation with another enterprise. With regard to the taking over and cooperation with foreign enterprises, there is an exception: the OR does not have to be consulted, unless the decision directly affects the situation in the Netherlands. The OR also has to be consulted when the enterprise ends or when there is a substantial change in the activities of the enterprise or in the organization, and when there is a change of location. Other relevant issues are the decision to hire new labour on a collective, not on an individual, basis, major investments to be made by the enterprise and major credits to be taken up from the banks. Finally, when the enterprise envisages the appointment of an outside expert to advise management on the issues mentioned above, the works council must also be consulted. They may wish to appoint their own expert who can offer counter-expertise against the experts who might be perceived as being biased in favour of the priorities of management.

The procedure is spelled out in Article 25 of the Act. The first requirement is that the information provided to the works council should be given at such a moment that there is sufficient time for a meaningful discussion by the works council, and that the advice of the works council can have a substantial influence on the decision. Moreover, there should be an explanation by the management accompanying the proposal. A mandatory coordination meeting is provided for with a view to a useful discussion on that basis. After that, the works council should be given a reasonable period of time to decide on its advice. Thereupon, the management takes its decision, under its own responsibility.

If the management decides differently from the advice, there is a delay of one month in which the decision may not be implemented and during which the works

[32] Ibid., Art. 31-31c.

council can form an appeal in law.[33] Jurisdiction for this lies with the so-called "Enterprise Chamber" of the Court of Appeal in Amsterdam.[34] It grants the appeal if the management could not reasonably have taken the decision at issue in the light of that advice. If this is the case, the decision will be declared null and void. This will also be the case when the management's decision contains no adequate statement of reasons.

The Enterprise Chamber can, when it finds that there is ground for appeal and the works council so requests, take provisional measures, while the case is pending before the Court, which may take years. It can, by way of an interim injunction, order that the decision be withdrawn or it can change the consequences of the decision.

The second issue for which the advice of the OR is required is the appointment or the dismissal of the director (Art. 30 of the WOR). The proposal, with an explanation, to appoint or to dismiss a particular person is put to the works council. Here, however, there is no appeal in law.

3. Co-determination

Article 27 of the WOR spells out the cases where approval by the OR is required. Generally, these are issues which relate to the internal organization of the enterprise. This relates for example, to regulations which govern health and safety at work, times of work and holidays, as well as regulations concerning profit sharing for employees. On all of these issues the management should have the consent of the works council. Should the works council refuse to give its consent on a certain issue, then the management can ask the court (not the Enterprise Chamber, but the *kantonrechter*, i.e. the lowest level of the judicial hierarchy) to give permission to take the decision without the consent of the works council. The court will give its permission when the decision of the works council is unreasonable or when the enterprise has to make the decision concerned for very important organizational or economic reasons.

If there is a collective wage agreement concluded between the employer and the trade unions which covers any of the issues which are listed in the Act, the wage agreement (and thus, indirectly, the trade union) prevails over the powers of the works council. In the co-determination procedure, the initiative lies with the management, not with the works council. The works council can, however, ask the management to submit a proposal.

By way of conclusion at this point it may be noted that the *Ondernemingsraad* has become an inherent element of real business life in the Netherlands. The mere fact that in the average handbook on the subject some 40 court cases brought by the *Ondernemingsraad* have been reported over the last ten years may be taken as an indication that this phenomenon is taken seriously in practice.

D. External Interests

Every corporation has an open connection with the society in which it functions. It has sometimes been argued that the corporation's institutions, especially the super-

[33] Ibid., Art. 26.

[34] See R.H. van het Kaar, "de ondernemingskamer en de ondernemingsraad", in 25 *jaar Ondernemingskamer* (1996).

visory board, should also take external interests into account. Examples of these external interests would then be the interests of the creditors, the suppliers, the consumers, and perhaps employment and other more general interests of the country or parts of the country, or more abstract interests, such as the environment, social development, etc. This could be based on the argument that, although the members of the supervisory board should, primarily serve the interests of the company, these interests are intertwined with those more general social interests. However, it would appear that such opinions have not prevailed up until now.[35]

III. DISTRIBUTION OF POWERS WITHIN THE NV

A. General

A significant characteristic of Dutch company law is the two-tier management structure consisting of the management board, which performs executive functions, and the supervisory board, which advises and supervises the management board. Each board has its own responsibilities, powers and duties, and each is legally independent from the shareholders. This two-tier system is optional for corporations that do not meet the statutory definition of "large" and for fully exempt "large" corporations. It is mandatory for corporations that have qualified as "large" corporations for more than three consecutive years. The status of a "large" corporation can be adopted voluntarily provided the corporation or a corporation controlled by it has a works council.[36]

Under the *structuur* system, the supervisory board has far-reaching powers, superseding to some extent those of the shareholders and the management board. The reduced power of shareholders is particularly noticeable when it comes to the appointment of managing directors. For corporations under the *structuur* regime, the management board is appointed by the supervisory board[37] and the supervisory board fills its own vacancies.[38] Shareholders and the works council can make recommendations and can oppose appointments that would make the supervisory board not "properly constituted".

B. The Supervisory Board[39]

Attention is paid here first to the position of the supervisory board in a "normal" company, i.e. a company which is not subject, either obligatorily or voluntarily, to the *structuur* regime. The latter will be discussed below.

The supervisory board used to be the body which supervised, in the interest of the shareholders, the board of management. The vision on the role of the supervisory board, however, has changed. The enterprise is no longer seen as a private matter for the shareholders and this changes the role of the supervisory board. The supervisory

35 See on this subject Asser Maeijer 2, III, no. 18.
36 BW Art. 2:157.
37 Ibid., Art. 2:162.
38 Ibid., Art. 2:158(2).
39 See P. Sanders e.a., Chapter 6; nos. 7.4-7.6; Asser-Maeijer 2, III, Chapter VII; nos. 366-382.

board should serve the interests, not merely of the shareholders, but rather of the company as a whole and of the enterprise which it runs.

The members of the supervisory board have collective powers and responsibilities. The supervisory directors share responsibility for all decisions and acts of the supervisory board and for the acts of each individual member of the supervisory board.[40] The supervisory board is not subordinated to the shareholders and need not accept instructions from them. Its sole concern is the interest of the corporation and the enterprise concerned. On the other hand, the management board is not subordinated to the supervisory board. Accordingly, action taken by the management in response to a decision of the supervisory board is their own responsibility.[41]

The primary responsibility of the supervisory board is to supervise the policy of the management board and the general course of corporate affairs. This includes the power and duty to intervene and to take corrective actions whenever the interests of the corporation require such action. The management board must consult the supervisory board on all important matters, including (but not limited to) any matters set forth in this regard in the Articles. The supervisory board may, on its own initiative, provide the management board with advice and request information. The management board has the statutory duty to provide the supervisory board with the information necessary to carry out its responsibilities and perform its duties within reasonable time.[42]

The Articles may require the management board to obtain prior approval from the supervisory board for actions concerning matters set forth in the Articles or in resolutions of the supervisory board.

The Articles may provide that, with respect to the appointment of managing directors, the supervisory board may make binding nominations that can only be rejected by the shareholders through a majority laid down in the Articles. By force of law a nomination can always be overruled by a "super majority" of two-thirds of the votes cast representing more than one-half of the issued capital. The supervisory board also has the power to suspend a managing director[43] (unless the Articles provide otherwise). The general meeting of shareholders can, however, lift this suspension at any time. Each supervisory director has access to all shareholders' meetings and may at any time state his opinion on matters on the agenda, even when the majority of the board has a different opinion. The supervisory board also has the power to call the general meeting of shareholders. The Articles cannot take this power away from the supervisory board.

The supervisory board consists of individuals. Accordingly, a corporation cannot be a member of the supervisory board. It may possibly consist of only one supervisory director, unless the corporation is a "large" one, in which case there must be at least three supervisory directors.[44]

The members of the supervisory board are appointed for the first time by the founders when the corporation is incorporated. Thereafter, supervisory directors are appointed by the shareholders, subject to the possibility for the Articles to provide that up to one-third of the members of the supervisory board may be elected by

40 BW Art. 2:140.
41 Ibid., Art. 2:151(2).
42 Ibid., Art. 2:141.
43 Ibid., Art. 2:147.
44 Ibid., Art. 2:158(3).

someone other than the shareholders.[45] The basic rules concerning nominations and qualifications for the election of members of the management board apply equally to members of the supervisory board. The Articles may, however, provide that holders of certain classes or types of shares, or other persons, have the power to nominate all or part of the supervisory board. The term of office is usually between three and six years, but after this period, re-election is possible, unless the Articles provide otherwise. There is a statutory overall age limit of 72.

A supervisory director is not an employee of the company. The remuneration paid to the supervisory board is determined by the shareholders unless the Articles provide otherwise.[46] Unless otherwise provided in the Articles, the shareholders may suspend or remove a supervisory director at any time without any monetary compensation.[47]

C. The *Structuur* Regime

The historical background of this regime which entered into force in 1971 is the seeking of harmony and cooperation between the various direct stakeholders in the enterprise (management, labour and capital). In the 1960s and the 1970s it was felt that a new legal arrangement should be sought for the big enterprises which form the major economic actors. More particularly, the aim was to have the workforce more involved in the management and in the overall running of the company. The introduction of the *structuur* regime was meant to reinforce the position of labour within the company. On balance, the effect was that the power of the shareholders in major companies was substantially reduced. That is, when compared to the "normal" rules as set forth in the Civil Code. In actual fact, the powers of ordinary shareholders were already largely restricted anyway through various "oligarchic" devices in the individual companies' respective Articles (see below). This explains why the introduction of the *structuur* regime met with little shareholder protest.

The political idea behind the *structuur* regime was that the bigger an enterprise becomes, the more it becomes a public institution with an impact on its environment in terms of employment, regional development, etc. It was considered that this issue relates to economic size, and is therefore relatively independent of legal form. Therefore, the specific regime applies not only to NVs but also to BVs and, more recently, to cooperatives, provided they meet the following three requirements cumulatively:

(1) the corporation's issued capital plus reserves, including its retained earnings, equal at least NLG 22,500,000;[48]
(2) the corporation or a dependent company (*afhankelijke maatschappij*) has established a works council;
(3) the corporation, together with its dependent companies, regularly employs one hundred or more persons in the Netherlands.

45 Ibid., Art. 2:143. Use of this possibility is rather exceptional and is mainly confined to appointment by public authority.
46 Ibid., Art. 2:145.
47 Ibid., Art. 2:144.
48 This amount is regulary adapted to inflation.

A "dependent company" is:

(a) a legal person in which the corporation, or any of its dependent companies, solely or jointly and for their own account, contributed at least half of the issued capital; and
(b) a partnership with a business enterprise registered in the Commercial Register in which the corporation is the fully liable general partner.

The Act also allows small enterprises which do not meet the quantitative criteria, to adopt the *structuur* regime, on a voluntary basis, provided, however, that a works council is in place. As per mid-1994, there were 577 *structuur* company registrations.[49]

The supervisory board has been made the central organ in the *structuur* regime, and every company which is subjected to the *structuur* regime, whether obligatorily or voluntarily, must have a supervisory board. At the moment of the setting up of the company or at the start of its being made subject to the *structuur* regime, the members of the supervisory board may be appointed by those setting up the company or by the shareholders, as the case may be. As soon as the *structuur* is in place and the company accordingly has a supervisory board, the members of the supervisory board are elected on the basis of co-optation, i.e. they are elected by the remaining members of the supervisory board.[50] The general meeting of shareholders, the board of management, and the works council do have, however, some influence. A vacancy must be announced by the supervisory board to the three bodies, so that they can suggest suitable candidates for possible appointment. The supervisory board is not, however, bound by these recommendations and it can appoint someone in disregard of those recommendations. It has to inform the general meeting of shareholders and the works council of the name of the person it intends to appoint. Thereupon, the general meeting and the works council can enter opposition to the candidate chosen by the supervisory board. The board of management does not have the right to oppose the appointment, because of the working relation which must exist later on between the management and the supervisory board and also because of the position of authority which the supervisory board has with regard to the board of management. When the general meeting of shareholders or the works council oppose the candidate, the matter is referred to the Enterprise Chamber of the Court of Appeal in Amsterdam.

There are three possible grounds for opposition, stated limitatively in Article 2:158(6) respectively 2:268(6) of the Civil Code:

(1) The supervisory board did not announce properly the vacancy or the name of the candidate it wished to appoint.
(2) The person as such does not have the characteristics or the personal qualities to be a good member of that supervisory board.
(3) The supervisory board would be ill-balanced, if that person would be appointed, in the sense that the supervisory board would not then have the

[49] Per P. Sanders e.a., no. 7.1

[50] BW Arts. 2:158; 2:268. It is an intensely debated issue whether – and if so to what extent – members of the supervisory board can bind themselves at forehand to secure appointment of a certain number of "representatives" of certain parties. See HR 19 March 1975, NJ 1976, 267 ("HVA-Socfin"); Asser-Maeijer 2, III, no. 371; P. Sanders e.a., no. 7.4.4.

> composition which is adequate for that particular company. It could be, for example, that the supervisory board is already dominated by persons with a financial background. Then, it may well be that the works council has a legitimate interest to propose a candidate with experience in industrial relations. The fact that the supervisory board has to serve the interests of the company as a whole does not mean that it does not matter how the supervisory board is composed. It is indeed deemed to be in the interest of the enterprise that the composition is a balanced one.

To put the issue of the "balanced composition" of the Supervisory Board in perspective, reference is made to the following table.[51]

The structure of supervisory boards in large German and Dutch companies can be shown as follows:

	Netherlands	Germany	
Year of data	1984	1986	1993
Number of companies	85.	84.	89.
Number of seats	650.	1466.	1561.
Average number of seats	7.6	17.5	17.5
Composition of supervisory board			
Non-financial companies	36.	25.	27.
Block shareholders	14.	-[a]	-[a]
Former directors	7.	-[a]	-[a]
Banks and insurance companies	13.	11.[b]	10.[b]
Employee representatives	11.	49.	49.
Politicians and civil servants	11.	5.	4.
Lawyers and professors	8.	10.	10.

a Data included in other categories: non-financial companies and banks
b Of which private banks: 8% in 1986, 6% in 1993.
Source: Netherlands: Van der Knoop (1991: 164)
Germany: Bundesverband Deutscher Banken (1995: 28)

Once the members are appointed they may be suspended only by the supervisory board itself, and they may be dismissed by the Enterprise Chamber. The grounds for dismissal, as set forth in Article 2:161(2), respectively 2:271(2), leave a large scope of appreciation as they are:

- negligence in the exercise of his duties;
- other important reasons;
- substantial change in circumstances, such as to result in a situation where the corporation cannot in fairness be expected to retain him as a member of the supervisory board.

Only the corporation itself, the general meeting of shareholders, the works council and the supervisory board can apply to the Enterprise Chamber for the dismissal of

[51] Source: G.M.M. Gelauff, C. den Broeder, supra note 5.

a member of the supervisory board. The corporation is represented by the supervisory board, the general meeting of shareholders by a representative appointed ad hoc and the works council by its chairman.

As for the powers of the supervisory board within the *structuur company* these are threefold (apart from filling the vacancies in its own ranks).

One is to elect, suspend, and dismiss the members of the board of management. It should be stressed that, accordingly, it is not the general meeting of shareholders which has these powers.[52] The general meeting is merely notified of the election. Dismissal can only take place after the general meeting of shareholders has been given the opportunity to comment, to that extent it can have some influence on the proposed dismissal. The supervisory board is, however, free to ignore the opinion of the general meeting of shareholders. Article 2:162 does not mention the works council. However, should the managing director who is about to be dismissed also be a managing director within the meaning of Article 30 of the WOR, then the works council has the right to give advice by virtue of that provision.

The second power is the decision to adopt the annual accounts of the company. Thereupon, the general meeting of shareholders has to give its approval on a "take it or leave it" basis, without the right to make any changes. Should the general meeting of shareholders refuse to approve the annual accounts, then the procedure is blocked. No approval is given to the management for the year concerned, no dividends can be paid out, until a compromise is worked out between the supervisory board and the general meeting.

The third category of powers relates to a number of important decisions relating to the life and activities of the company. These require the prior approval of the supervisory board. Article 2:164 (and 2:274) sums up the categories of decisions of the management board which require approval of the supervisory board. Examples are the ending of certain or all activities of the company, long-term cooperation with other companies, major investments, and the issue of shares and depository receipts. Approval is also needed for a proposal to amend the Articles of association (the decision itself is taken by the general meeting of shareholders) and the simultaneous termination of employment of a significant number of employees. As long as the supervisory board has not given its approval, the decision is not valid and the board of management cannot execute the decision.

All these specific arrangements make it clear that within a *structuur* company power is very much concentrated in the hands of the supervisory board. To function properly however, the supervisory board has to be trusted and supported by both the general meeting of shareholders and the works council.

There are two categories of exceptions to the basic rule of the *structuur* regime. One is a complete exemption from the regime,[53] the second is the so-called "mitigated regime", which implies a partial application of the *structuur* regime.[54]

Complete exemption applies where one corporation within a group is subject to the *structuur* regime: all the others are then exempted, because the *structuur* regime should apply at one level (and not necessarily the highest level of the company at that).[55]

[52] Ibid., Art 2:162.

[53] Ibid., Art. 2:153(3).

[54] BW Art. 2:155.

[55] See Asser-Maeijer 2, III, nos. 391-395; P. Sanders e.a., nos. 7.7.1, 7.7.2.

Complete exemption in this sense is granted to:

(a) the corporation which is dependent upon a legal person to which the special rules of the *structuur* regime apply in full or in part;
(b) the corporation which exclusively or almost exclusively restricts itself to the management and financing of group corporations and their participation in other legal persons, provided, however, that the majority of the employees of this holding or finance corporation and all other corporations of the same group are situated outside Holland;
(c) the corporation which exclusively or almost exclusively renders management, financial and other services to a corporation as set forth under (b) above and to other companies of that group;
(d) the corporation of which at least one-half of the issued capital is held as a participation under a mutual arrangement of cooperation between two or more companies which are subject to the *structuur* regime or corporations which are dependent upon these companies.

In practice, the exemptions under (b) and (c) relate only to international groups of corporations with a Dutch-based holding corporation. In order to be exempted, the holding corporation must refrain from any activity other than the holding of shares and the financing of its subsidiaries.

The *mitigated regime*[56] relates to the international dimension and it applies to:

(a) corporations in the Netherlands controlled from outside the Netherlands; and
(b) international groups with a Dutch-based holding corporation.

The following example will clarify the exceptions. At the top of the "X" group of companies there is NV "X" which is exempt from the *structuur* regime because below NV "X" there is *"X" Nederland* BV (all the shares of which are held by NV "X") which is the holding company for all activities within Holland. "X" Nederland BV, the Dutch sub-holding, is subject to the *structuur* regime. This is the reason why NV "X" is exempt from the *structuur* regime. That means that "X" Nederland BV must have a supervisory board and is subjected to the *structuur* regime. However, "X" Nederland BV in Holland is not subject to the complete *structuur* regime, but rather to the mitigated regime.

The difference between the full regime and the mitigated regime is the following. It may be recalled that there are three categories of decisions which are the privilege of the supervisory board within the *structuur* regime, i.e. the appointment of the members of the board of management, the establishment of the annual accounts and the decisions on a certain number of important items. However, these same powers normally form the basis for the control of a holding company over a subsidiary company. The power of the central board of management is normally guaranteed by the fact that the parent company holds 100 per cent or a clear majority of the shares in the subsidiary, and therefore controls the general meeting of shareholders. The *structuur* regime, however, takes away from the general meeting of shareholders those crucial powers, i.e. the appointment of the management, the annual accounts

[56] See Asser-Maeijer 2, III, no. 396, 397; P. Sanders e.a. no. 7.7.3.

and the catalogue of important decisions. This would destroy the power of parent companies over their subsidiaries, because the management of that subsidiary company has to refer to its supervisory board, not to the board of management of the holding. Due to the co-optation process for election of its members, this supervisory board may well not be composed according to the wishes of the parent company. Therefore, the cohesion of the group of companies would be put into jeopardy, which was deemed an unacceptable implication of the *structuur* regime. Accordingly, the mitigated regime has allowed for a compromise solution by retaining for the benefit of the shareholders' meeting two of the powers concerned, i.e. the power to appoint members of the board of management and the adoption of the annual accounts. The supervisory board still has the exclusive power to approve certain decisions, because it was deemed that with regard to those decisions it is important that the local setting is respected since this concerns the activities of that particular company which can indeed be distinguished from companies which are subsidiaries of the same parent company in other countries.

D. Oligarchic Constructions[57]

The notion of "oligarchic constructions" refers to those devices which make it possible for the powers of the general meeting of shareholders to be reduced to the benefit of certain specific categories of stakeholders. Different cases can be distinguished.

The first case relates to restrictions of the powers of the general meeting of shareholders as such. A very simple example would be, for instance, that members of the management board have to be Dutch, this means that the general meeting of shareholders is not allowed to appoint an Englishman. In the light of EC developments, this device has lost most of its practical relevance.

More important in practice is the device of the so-called binding proposal, i.e. a special group of persons (or even individual persons) has the exclusive right to submit a proposal on a certain issue to the general meeting of shareholders, and the general meeting of shareholders is bound by that proposal. This is allowed in Dutch corporate law, subject to the statutory limit to the effect that the proposal can be overruled by a two-thirds majority of the general meeting of shareholders, at which meeting at least 50 per cent of issued capital of the company is represented. That means that in case of a major public company with shares held by the public at large, quoted at the Stock Exchange, it will be very difficult to meet those conditions as long as that share capital is sufficiently spread. So this is a very important device allowing publicly quoted companies to take away power from the general meeting of shareholders.

The device frequently used for this purpose is that of so-called "priority shares".[58] These are generally shares to which by virtue of the Articles certain privileges are attached. The powers which the Civil Code has assigned imperatively to the general meeting of shareholders cannot be placed as such in the hands of priority shareholders. However, they can be restricted by subjecting their exercise to a proposal of, or endorsement by, the meeting of priority shareholders. Thus, Articles of

[57] See generally: Asser-Maeijer 2, III, nos. 398-414; P. Sanders e.a., no. 8.4. and Chapter 15. Voogd, *Statutaire beschermingsmiddelen bij beursvennootschappen*, 1985.

[58] See Asser-Maeijer 2, III, no. 410; P. Sanders e.a., no. 15.4.

Association regularly provide that resolutions to issue shares, to amend the Articles of association or to dissolve the company can only be taken after endorsement by, or pursuant to, a resolution of the meeting of priority shareholders. Also, in a non-*structuur* corporation, the right to present a binding nomination for the appointment of a director or member of the supervisory board may be conferred on the meeting of the priority shareholders.

Taking into account these powers, it is of course quite an issue to ensure that the priority shares are "in safe hands". This is generally attained by having them held by directors and members of the supervisory board. It is current company practice to place the priority shares in a foundation (*stichting*) the board of which consists of one or several members of the company's management (sometimes supplemented by a few "outsiders"). Under Dutch law a foundation does not have shareholders, and is completely controlled by its board, the members of which are elected by co-optation.

Appendix X to the Stock Exchange Regulations, which contains restrictions on the protective measures a company can take, provides (Article 9) that the listed company shall compile a list of the functions which the directors of the foundation hold or have held to the extent that they are relevant to the way in which they make use of the voting rights attaching to the priority shares. This list must be made available for perusal by shareholders and holders of depository receipts for shares at the company' office. Furthermore, Appendix X obliges the listed company to ensure that the management of a company does not have control of the exercise of a voting right attaching to priority shares. A maximum of half the seats on the board of the controlling foundation can be taken by members of the company's management.

Another rather simple device is the requirement of a qualified majority vote, which of course makes it more difficult for the simple majority to get their way.

A fourth category is a split in rights of shareholders. The normal classic concept of a share in a limited liability company is that it carries both economic rights (a share in the profits of the company) and legal rights (the right to attend the general meeting of shareholders, to speak there and to vote). Under Dutch law it is possible to issue depository receipts for shares. Depository receipts are issued in exchange for shares in order to separate the voting rights from the financial interest. The construction is that the shares are issued to a so-called *administratie kantoor* (administration office). This administration office is in essence a trust office. The trust office, in exchange for the shares which it owns, issues depositary receipts (*certificaten*) which evidence, on a one-to-one rate, that there is a share represented by that receipt.[59] These receipts represent the economic rights of the shares, but are not shares. They entitle the owner to payment by the trust office of an amount corresponding to the share of the dividend which is due on the "underlying" shares, but not to the right to vote. The trust office is the one who votes on the shares in the general meeting of shareholders. Most trust offices have the form of a foundation with the characteristics indicated above.

In order to be fully effective, the receipts should not be allowed to be converted back into shares again. The possibility of such conversion depends upon the conditions under which the trust office has offered the receipts at the moment of the issue of those receipts. A distinction is made between full convertibility, non-convertibility and qualified convertibility. Non-convertibility is no longer allowed by the Stock

[59] See Asser-Maeijer 2, III no. 403; P. Sanders e.a., no. 15.5.

Exchange and full-convertibility is of course of no real practical use in this regard. Again, Appendix X of the Stock Exchange Regulations imposes some restrictions, and sets forth certain conditions with regard to qualified convertibility. This will be discussed later.

The fifth category is the dilution of powers in cases of takeovers, and refers to what is referred to as anti-takeover "preference shares".[60] Generally, preference shares have a privileged position with regard to dividends. They are to be paid out of the profits a specified amount of money before the ordinary shares are paid their part of the dividend. For anti-takeover purposes, this amount is related to the market rate of interest. Where the management perceives the threat of takeover, the management may well wish to dilute the relative share position of the prospective "raider". With a view to this, the management is given the authority in advance to issue preference shares up to a certain amount. Normally this amount is the same as the capital already outstanding. Such a decision of the management board doubles the issued capital of the company, which means that the power of the opposite party is halved. Normally, these preference shares will be issued to a foundation which is congenial to the management. To complete the picture, it should be noted that Dutch law allows a company to issue shares and require payment for no more than a minimum of 25 per cent to start with. The shareholder has the obligation to pay in, if the management calls on him to pay the remaining 75 per cent, but it is allowed to start with just paying upwards of 25 per cent. So, for a limited amount of money which can be borrowed from the banks because of the "preference" entitlement, the power of the opposite party is halved.

It is essential for the issue of preference shares for this purpose that there should be no spreading out of the new shares over the existing shares. Dutch law allows a provision according to which the general meeting of shareholders (the authority for the issue of new shares) may decide, not only to grant authority to the board of management in advance to issue preference shares, but also to deviate from the normal pre-emption rights of incumbent shareholders and thus to concentrate the issue in the hands of one or more particular shareholders. The device is completed by an option agreement between the company, represented by the management board, and a foundation which is going to take the shares as soon as the board of management issues the preference shares.

Appendix X to the Stock Exchange Regulations provides in Article 2 that the foundation must be independent of the issuing company: this is the case if the majority of the board of the foundation consists of persons who are not attached to the issuing company, as would be, for example, present or former directors and members of the supervisory board. According to Appendix X, the foundation's object must be to look after the interests of the issuing company, its enterprise activities and all those involved. Appendix X also requires that the annual report and the annual accounts of the issuing company state to whom preferential shares have been issued and with whom agreements have been concluded with regard to the placing of such shares. The names of the board members of the foundation also have to be stated.

An overview of the relative importance of "oligarchic constructions" in practice is given in the following table.[61]

[60] See P. Sanders e.a., no. 15.6.
[61] Source: G.M.M. Gelauff, C. den Broeder, supra note 5.

Anti-Takeover Defences of Dutch-Listed Companies

Anti-takeover defences in 1992				
	Number of defences		*Percentage*	
Preference shares	105.		32.3	
Priority shares	79.		24.3	
Depositary receipts	70.		21.5	
Binding nomination	64.		19.7	
Voting caps	7.		2.2	
Total	325.		100.	
Number of defences	*Number of companies*		*Percentage*	
	1992	*1995*	*1992*	*1995*
Zero	16.	18.	9.1	11.1
One	52.	64.	29.4	39.5
Two	62.	67.	35.0	41.4
Three	39.	13.	22.0	8.0
Four	8.	0.	4.5	0.0
Total	177.	162.	100.	100.

Source: 1992: Cantrijn *et al.* (1993: 28-29)
1995: van Frederikslust and van Veldhuizen (1996).

E. Minority Shareholders

The Dutch Civil Code provides for a buy-out arrangement in Article 2:92 a.[62] This provision gives a shareholder who owns 95 per cent or more of the issued capital the power to require all the other shareholders to transfer their stock to him. This transfer of shares has to be required of all the other shareholders at the same time. The price is determined by the Enterprise Chamber, which may order expert valuation. An action for the mandatory sale by the minority shareholders may be refused by the Court if the sellers would suffer considerable financial damage which would not be compensated by the sales price, or if the Articles attribute special powers to the minority shares and the minority shareholder can effectively use this power in the corporation, or if the majority shareholder has renounced his right to initiate these legal proceedings against any shareholder.

Dutch law does not generally recognize the right to "force out" unwanted shareholders by means of a merger, and a merger can be used only to a very limited extent to compel certain shareholders to accept cash or notes for their shares.[63] The basic rule is that in the case of a merger, the shareholders of the disappearing company become shareholders in the acquiring company.

With regard to the rights of minority shareholders, shareholders who hold at least 10 per cent of the issued capital of the company, or such lesser percentage as the Articles prescribe, may be empowered by the President of the District Court (*recht-*

[62] See Asser-Maeijer 2, III, no. 510.
[63] BWArt. 2:311(2).

bank) to convene a general meeting of shareholders[64] provided that the petitioners have a "reasonable interest" in calling the meeting.[65]

If the annual general meeting is not held within six months after the end of the company's fiscal year, any shareholder, regardless of the number of shares he holds, may be authorized by the President of the District Court to call the annual general meeting.

The rights of shareholders described above are also vested in the holders of certificates issued with the consent of the company.

Another important right of minority shareholders is the right to petition for an investigation (*enquête*) of the management of the company. These investigations will be discussed below.

Taken as a whole, the position of the minority shareholders is a delicate one. The minority shareholder has, in principle, to accept the decisions taken by the majority of shareholders in the general meeting of shareholders. This does not mean, however, that the majority can ignore completely the interests of the minority shareholder. For example, if a majority shareholder decides not to pay out dividends for a long period of time, the minority shareholder can commence an action to have a decision of the majority shareholder declared void by court order. Such action would be based on the general provision of the Civil Code which requires a shareholder to behave reasonably and equitably in all situations towards other shareholders (and towards the management board, the supervisory board and the corporation).[66]

Of course, minority shareholders are also protected in some way by the accurate disclosure of all necessary information first of all in the form of the annual accounts.[67] Also, companies which are listed on the Stock Exchange are required to disclose any material information (i.e. information which is expected to influence quoted share prices) immediately in order to put all parties concerned in the same position and ensure that all of them possess the same information at the same time in order to limit the danger of insider trading as far as possible.

All in all, it would appear that (apart from the enquête, to be discussed below) court action on behalf of minority shareholders is exceptional.[68]

F. Disclosure of Information, the Annual Accounts

Since the enactment in 1971 of the Law on Annual Accounts, Dutch law has contained detailed provisions as to the contents of companies' accounts. This new law was introduced to implement the provisions of the EC Fourth Directive (which contains detailed requirements for the preparation of balance sheets, profit and loss statements, and the annual report)[69] and (later on) the Seventh Directive (which deals with consolidated financial statements for groups of companies).[70] Those statutory rules apply to NVs, BVs and cooperatives (*coöperaties*) and mutual insurance associations (*onderlinge waarborgmaatschappijen*).

[64] Ibid., Art. 2:110.
[65] Ibid., Art. 2:111.
[66] Ibid., Art. 2:8.
[67] Ibid., Art. 2:360-446.
[68] For two examples see HR 9-7-1990, NJ 1991, 51 (Sluis BV) and Rechtbank Zutphen, 17-1-1991, NV 1991, 107 ("Uniwest Group BV").
[69] Directive 78/660, OJ 1978, L 222/11.
[70] Directive 83/349, OJ 1983, L 193/1.

Besides the Annual Accounts, the Code also deals with the annual report by the management.[71] In addition to presenting a true and fair picture of the company's situation as of the date of the balance sheet, and of the activities of the corporation during the fiscal year, it must provide information regarding the future of the corporation, in particular regarding investments, financing, employment, and the development of sales and profit. Material events occurring subsequent to the balance sheet date must be mentioned in the annual report.

In addition, information must be supplied relating to the auditor's opinion, the statutory provisions in the company's Articles of association with regard to the appropriation of the operating results, the proposed appropriation of profits, and a list of material losses and risks that occurred since the end of the financial year.[72]

Annual Accounts must be submitted to the general meeting of shareholders for adoption. In the case of a *structuur* corporation, the Annual Accounts as prepared by the management board are first adopted by the supervisory board and then submitted to the shareholders' meeting for its approval on a "take it or leave it" basis and to the Works Council "for discussion".[73]

The responsible auditor for the auditing of the Annual Accounts, the annual report and the supplementary information, reports to the supervisory board and the management board. Shareholders have, in principle, no access to this report. The results of the audit are set out in the auditor's statement, which has to be annexed to the Annual Accounts. They can only establish whether the statement is a so-called "clean" one, stating that the Annual Accounts give a true and fair view of the company's financial situation, or contains reservations or qualifications.

Enforcement of disclosure requirements is vested in the Enterprise Chamber of the Amsterdam Court of Appeal.[74] Any interested party may bring proceedings in respect of a company's accounts. These can be shareholders, creditors, trade unions, etc., or the Attorney General acting in the public interest. They can bring an action for the rectification of the annual accounts, the annual report or the other additional information. The court order issued by the Enterprise Chamber contains precise instructions to be followed by the management board of the enterprise in drawing up the annual accounts. Non-compliance with a judicial order issued by the Enterprise Chamber is a criminal offence. There lies an appeal from the judgment of the Enterprise Chamber to the Supreme Court.

If the Annual Accounts give a misleading representation of the company's financial situation, the members of the board of management (and in certain cases the supervisory board) are jointly and severally liable to third parties for the loss they suffer as a consequence. A director who can prove that the misrepresentation cannot be imputed to him is not liable to such a third party.

Attention should also be drawn to the fact that apart from Title 9 of the Civil Code on the Annual Accounts, the Stock Exchange Manual (*Fondsenreglement*) also provides for disclosure of information to the public in certain cases. In this manual, periodic disclosure is required of publicly held companies. Articles 28, 34, 39, and 44 impose an on-going obligation on issuers as to the provision of information to investors. The issuer has to make sure every year that the public can obtain its

[71] BW Art. 2:391.
[72] Ibid., Art. 2:392.
[73] Ibid., Arts. 2:101; 2:163.
[74] Wetboek Burgerlijke Rechtsvordering (Code on Civil Procedures), Arts. 999-1002.

annual accounts and the annual report. Moreover, it must publish every fact or event that can affect the price of the issuer's securities, and it has to publish important changes in the activities or in its board of management.

Also to be mentioned in this regard is the Major Holdings Disclosure Act 1996 (*Wet melding zeggenschap 1996, Wmz '96*). This Act entered into force on 1 June 1997, replacing the earlier Major Holdings Disclosure Act by which the Disclosure of Major Holdings EEC Directive of 12 December 1988 was first implemented in the Netherlands. The Wmz '96 provides that any person who, directly or indirectly, acquires or disposes of an (potential) interest in the capital or the voting rights of a NV must give a written notice of such transaction, if as a result of such transaction the percentage of capital interest of voting rights held by such person falls within another percentage range as compared to the percentage range held by such person prior to the transaction. The percentage ranges are 0-5, 5-10, 10-25, 25-50, 50-66 2/3 and over 66 2/3. The Act only applies to NVs incorporated in the Netherlands whose shares or depository receipts are officially listed on a stock exchange located and operating in the European economic area. Before implementing of the directive, shareholders of a listed company were not obliged to disclose their shareholding other than, under certain circumstances, in a takeover situation.

The notification must be given to the corporation concerned and to the Securities Board of the Netherlands (*Stichting Toezicht Effectenverkeer, STE*) which will disclose the information as notified to the public.

If publication would be contrary to the public interest or could have serious repercussions for the corporation, on request of the corporation, the Minister of Finance can order that the disclosure to the public will not take place. No dispensation can be obtained in respect of the obligation vis à vis the STE.

Violation of the obligation to notify under the Wmz '96 constitutes a criminal offence.[75] At the request of the corporation concerned or the holder of a 5 per cent interest in the corporation's issued share capital, the competent District Court can impose several sanctions, such as suspension of voting rights, rescission of a resolution of the general meeting of shareholders in certain cases, and it can order to refrain from any further direct or indirect acquisition of shares issued by the relevant corporation during a period of five years (Article 19, Wmz '96).

G. Enquête[76]

The right to petition for an investigation into the business policy and the conduct of the affairs of a company was introduced into Dutch company law with effect as from 1 January 1971.[77] Proceedings in connection with petitions for investigations are centralized in the Enterprise Chamber of the Court of Appeal in Amsterdam.[78]

The proceedings for an investigation are initiated by the applicant filing a written petition containing a request to the Enterprise Chamber "to nominate one or more persons to investigate the business policy and the conduct of the affairs of the company, either as a whole or in part, or in respect of a particular period".

75 Wet Economische Delicten, Art. 1(2).
76 See Asser-Maeijer 2, III, nos. 515-538; P. Sanders e.a. no. 11.1.; A.F.M. Dorresteijn, "De ondernemingskamer en de ondernemingsraad", in 25 *jaar Ondernemingskamer* (1996).
77 BW Arts. 2:344-359.
78 Ibid., Art. 2:345.

A request can be filed by:

(a) the shareholders or holders of depository receipts representing the lower of either 10 per cent of the issued shares or a par value of NLG 500,000 (or any lower percentage or amount provided in the Articles);
(b) an association of employees with members employed in the company. The association must have been in existence for at least two years, and must have as its object the protection of the interests of its members as employees;
(c) others who, by virtue of the Articles or an agreement with the corporation, have been granted this right;
(d) the Attorney General of the Court of Appeals in Amsterdam for reasons of public interest.[79]

Before the filing of a petition with the Chamber is permitted, certain preliminary requirements must be met. The petitioner must first submit its complaint in writing to the management board and, where applicable, the supervisory board, and allow the company to take appropriate steps.[80] If an association of employees is the applicant, it must also consult the works council beforehand, and must give it an opportunity to express its opinion in writing. The Attorney General must mention in his petition whether or not he has given the works council the opportunity to express its opinion.

The petition is granted if the Enterprise Chamber is satisfied that there are good reasons for doubting whether the company's affairs have been conducted properly and that it is reasonable to assume that there will be a finding of mismanagement.[81] This means that there must be evidence that the elementary principles of management have been violated.

Mismanagement is generally caused by a failure of the management board to exercise proper care in managing the corporation's affairs or by failure of the supervisory board to exercise proper care in supervising the management board.

If the petition is granted, the Chamber appoints one or more persons to undertake the investigation. The scope of the investigation is defined in the order of the Chamber. All the expenses involved are initially chargeable to the company. When the results of the investigation are known, however, the company may request the court to order the petitioners to reimburse the company wholly or partly for the costs of carrying it out if it appears from the report of the investigators that there were no reasonable grounds for the petition.

The law confers powers on the investigators to obtain all necessary information from the company, its board members, and all persons employed by it.[82]

The result of the investigation is recorded in a report by the investigators and submitted to the "Enterprise Chamber" of the Court of Appeal in Amsterdam.

If the report reveals that the business of the company has been mismanaged, the investigation enters a second stage. The applicant may then, within two months after the deposit of the report, apply to the Enterprise Chamber to order appropriate remedies.[83]

[79] Ibid., Art. 2:346.
[80] Ibid., Art. 2:349.
[81] Ibid., Art. 2:350.
[82] Ibid., Art. 2:351.
[83] Ibid., Art. 2:355.

Article 2:356 sums up the possible remedies (which can be ordered also in combination):

(a) the annulment or suspension of the operation of a resolution of the board of management or of the supervisory board, or of a general meeting of shareholders, or of any other organ of the company;
(b) the suspension or dismissal of any one or more of the members of the board of management or the supervisory board;
(c) the temporary appointment of one or more persons to be members of the board of management or of the supervisory board;
(d) a temporary departure from the provisions of the Articles of Association to the extent authorized by the Enterprise Chamber;
(e) a temporary transfer of shares;
(f) the dissolution of the company.

It should be noted that even when mismanagement is indeed clearly established, the Enterprise Chamber is still free to confine itself to this finding, without ordering any remedy. From the decision of the Enterprise Chamber there lies only an appeal in cassation to the Supreme Court.[84]

One has to distinguish between the criteria for granting a petition (good reasons for doubting whether the company's affairs have been conducted properly) and the criteria "mismanagement", which comes into the picture when the Enterprise Chamber has to decide on a request for remedies. The Enterprise Chamber is free to deny an investigation, where, on balance, notwithstanding a finding of deficient management, the interests of the company in not being subjected to an "inquest" should prevail. It may be noted that the Supreme Court ruled[85] that the mismanagement of the corporation is relevant, not the mismanagement of certain persons. The mismanagement of organs of the corporation or of persons who are part of these organs has to be accounted to the corporation. This means that the Enterprise Chamber can decide that there has been mismanagement by the corporation, without perhaps being able to identify who is individually responsible for this.

It may be noted that the enquête has become a regular feature of corporate law in practice, as is evidenced by the fact that the Ondernemingskamer took 21 decisions on "enquête" issues in the year 1995 alone.

IV. TAKEOVERS

A. Protection of Shareholders

In the Netherlands, there are no government merger control regulations[86] and no legislation regulating takeovers has been enacted.

[84] Ibid., Art. 2:359.

[85] See note 82 supra.

[86] The Government has let it be known, however, that it envisages legislation with a view to national merger control procedures.

1. SER Code of Conduct

A quasi-legal Code of Conduct on Mergers has been drawn up by the Social and Economic Council (*Sociaal Economische Raad, SER*).[87] This is a permanent government advisory body within the meaning of section 79 of the Constitution which comprises 45 members: 15 nominated by employers' organizations, 15 nominated by employees' organizations and 15 independent members nominated by the Crown. This code is non-binding, it is a "code of conduct", lacking any direct legal sanction. However, the position of the SER, which supports the Code, is of such nature that it has great moral authority. The Code is supported by the national organizations representing employers' associations and trade unions and also by the Stock Exchange Association.

The Code of Conduct on Takeovers contains in Chapter I provisions designed to protect the interests of shareholders which are to be taken into account in preparing and issuing any "public offer" for shares, whilst Chapter II contains rules of conduct for the protection of the interests of employees.

The Committee on Merger Affairs (*Commissie voor Fusieaangelegenheden*) comprises 12 members: four members are designated by the trade unions, three members by employers federations, one member is designated by the Stock Exchange and four members are independent "Crown members". The chairman is always one of the independent members.

If the Committee finds that the Code has not been complied with, it can issue a public announcement or public rebuke. Moreover, if a company is found not to comply, albeit partially, with the Code of Conduct, or if it has received a public rebuke, Stock Exchange members are prohibited from providing any assistance to the company concerned in issuing or completing an offer for shares. An intended takeover by means of a public offer for shares then becomes impossible, as all stock exchange transactions have to be effectuated through a member of the Stock Exchange Association. Finally, under specific circumstances, a breach of the Rules of Conduct can be deemed unlawful in the sense of the civil law governing tortuous liability.

The provisions concerning the protection of shareholders contained in Chapter I of the Rules of Conduct apply both to the case of a public offer and, as from 1975, also to a private offer, provided such offer had been submitted to the majority of the shareholders of the target company. Chapter I aims at ensuring that the shareholders receive sufficient information about the offer and that all shareholders are given equal opportunity to accept the offer or not. It also contains provisions aimed at preventing insider dealing by management or supervisory boards.

If Chapter I applies, there is an obligatory procedure to be followed. The board of management of a company which intends to make a public offer (the offeror company) must inform the board of management of the target company (offeree company) in writing of its intention, and must invite that board to consult with the offeror about the terms of the offer. Article 4 imposes on the offeror the duty to invite the offeree to participate in consultations about the intention, the price or

[87] See Asser-Maeijer 2, III, nos. 584-595. It should be noted that on 16 February 1996, the SER proposed to review the Code both in substance and in form. As for the latter, it is proposed to have binding legislation replace the Code of Conduct.

share exchange terms of the public offer, the underlying motives for the offer, the intended policy with regard to the target NV and the attached enterprise and, in the case the offer mentions a price, about the way it will be financed. These intentions, motives and methods of financing also have to be stated in a "Notice of Offer". Should the offeror still wish to make a public offer even though the management of the target company has not accepted the invitation to consult, or discussions fail to lead to an agreement, the offeror, prior to making the public offer, must inform the management of the target company in writing of the content of and the reasons for the offer.

As noted above, it is forbidden to surprise a target company. In this regard, it has to be mentioned that if a company is going for a creeping takeover, i.e. simply buying shares as they are regularly offered to the public at the Stock Exchange, Chapter I does not apply. Obviously, however, this practice has now become largely illusory due to the transparency assured by the *Wet Melding Zeggenschap* mentioned earlier. If discussions between the two boards develop positively, the crucial moment for purposes of the Code of Conduct is the moment when "it can reasonably be expected that agreement will be reached". At that moment, although there is not yet a formal agreement, the boards have a joint obligation to inform the public and the management of the Stock Exchange in Amsterdam (Article 3).

After this first public announcement, the offeror company must, within 30 days, either make a public offer or make public its decision not to make an offer, or give some indication as to when a decision concerning the offer can be expected (with explanation as to why there is this further delay) (Article 5). A "Notice of Offer" has to be available within six weeks of the public announcement (Article 6). Each of the boards is responsible for the correctness of the information contained in this offer document. The offer must extend to all issued securities of the class to which the offer relates and to all holders of the same kind of securities.

The offer document must also state the period of time during which the offer stands, subject to unforeseen events which in good faith should allow for the withdrawal of the public offer, to be assessed upon request from the company by the Stock Exchange Board.

The offer document furthermore must state whether, during the preceding three years, securities in the target company have been acquired by the offeror or companies in the same group from:

(1) managing directors or members of the supervisory board of the target company, their spouses or minor children, or companies which any of these persons control;
(2) other natural or legal persons than those referred to above; or whether such securities will be acquired in the future under agreements entered into with those parties.

Once the offer has been published, the board of the target company must call a general meeting of shareholders in order to discuss the offer within a certain specified time. The board shall provide the shareholders beforehand with a report containing, inter alia, the reasoned position of the board whether the bid should be accepted or not. The board of the offeror company is not under any obligation to call a general meeting of shareholders except in the case when the offer relates to the exchange of shares in the target company for an issue of shares by the offeror company up to a total nominal value of more than one-quarter of the issued capital of the offeror company prior to such issue (Article 10). If a third party makes a competing offer for the shares comprised in a public offer before the end of the period accepting it, the first offeror company and the target company should immediately publish a public response (Article 3(2)(g)).

From the moment that a public announcement on the preparation or the making of a public offer has been made, the boards of management of both the offeror and the target companies must submit to the Committee on Merger Affairs reports concerning transactions and agreements in regard to shares to which the offer relates or will relate, effected from that moment. At the same time, information on existing mutual capital participations must be given (Article 3(3)).

B. The Influence of Labour[88]

In the case of mergers and takeovers, the SER Code of Conduct, Chapter II, contains rules for the protection of employees. The scope of application of Chapter II is much wider than Chapter I, discussed above. Chapter I applies only if the offeror makes a public offer or an offer to acquire a majority of the registered shares of the target company. In contrast, Chapter II applies if the target company is engaged in a merger, and a broad definition of a merger is given by Article 14(1): "the acquisition of direct or indirect control over the activities of an enterprise or part of an enterprise". The essential criteria therefore is a change in control.

The rules relating to the protection of the employees, contained in Articles 17-21 must, according to Article 15(1), be observed if either:

(a) an enterprise established in the Netherlands in which at least 100 employees are normally employed is involved; or
(b) an enterprise belonging to a group of enterprises, where normally the enterprises established in the Netherlands collectively employ at least 100 persons is involved.

The Code aims at enabling the trade unions concerned, on the basis of the information supplied to them by the enterprises involved, to reach a well founded opinion about the merits of the merger as such and its consequences. The trade unions must be given the opportunity to express this opinion at such a time when they will still be able to influence the decision relating to the merger as such. Where a public announcement is made in respect of the negotiations for a merger, the trade unions must be informed of the contents of the announcement before the announcement is made public (Article 17).

Article 18 of the Code forms the thrust of the regulation for the protection of employees. This Article distinguishes the different stages of obligatory consultations with the trade unions. Where the merger negotiations have reached such a stage as to "justify the expectation that agreement can be reached", the trade unions shall be notified thereof at once. The trade unions must be provided with an explanation of the reasons for the merger, as well the anticipated social, economic and legal consequences, to the extent that this is feasible, and the measures planned in connection therewith. Accordingly, a so-called "social plan" has to be submitted to the unions.

[88] Asser-Maeijer 2, III, nos. 596-606.

Subsequently, the trade unions must be given the opportunity for substantial discussions with a view to expressing their opinion of the merger from the point of view of the employees' interests. Consideration will be given to the measures to be taken to prevent, eliminate or reduce negative implications for the employees, including the possible grant of financial compensation, and to the basic principles of the industrial relations policy to be followed subsequently to the merger. It should be noted that consultations with the trade unions are obligatory, even where no actual losses (or other negative implications) for the employees are anticipated.

These formulas have been broadened to the effect that an explanation of the business policy in the broadest sense shall also have to be given to, and discussed with, the trade unions, enabling them to gain a reasonable insight into the proposed policy of the person who is intent on gaining control of the target enterprise.

The question of confidentiality raises delicate issues. On the one hand, breaches of confidentiality can result in a breakdown of the discussions with the trade unions, but on the other hand, the need for confidentiality may put the trade unions in a difficult position as regards the employees they represent. The termination of the confidentiality period is in practice left to the parties concerned. If they cannot agree, the ultimate decision lies (upon request) with the Committee on Merger Affairs.

It may be noted that the SER Code of Conduct focuses on the trade unions as the representatives of labour in this regard. It should therefore be stressed that, for their part, the works councils of the undertakings concerned derive a right to advise on changes in control from Article 25 of the WOR (Works Councils Act). According to this provision, the company must give the works council the opportunity to advise on its proposed decision to:

(a) transfer control of the enterprise or part thereof; or
(b) the establishment of, or the takeover or the disposal of control of another enterprise, as well as the conclusion of, the introduction of an important alteration or the termination of a long-term cooperation with another enterprise, by which is also understood concluding, significantly altering, or terminating an important financial participation on account of or on behalf of a similar enterprise.

Should the employer make a decision which is contrary to the advice of the works council, then the works council can appeal to the Enterprise Chamber in Amsterdam pursuant to Article 26 of the WOR on the ground that by not taking the interests concerned into account the company could not reasonably have come to that decision. The Enterprise Chamber can impose the obligation to withdraw the decision wholly or partly or to change the consequences of the decision. The Enterprise Chamber may also prohibit the employer from carrying out acts aimed at implementing the decision by way of a preliminary injunction.

The aspiring offeror who makes an offer for shares must seek the advice of his works council. Indeed, he aims at acquiring control of another enterprise, or at least conclude an agreement for important financial participation. This applies irrespective of whether the offer is friendly or hostile. With regard to the position of the target company, a distinction is to be made. If the target company-employer acquiesces in the offer, and positively recommends it (i.e. a friendly offer), it is a decision subject to advice within the meaning of Article 25(1)(a).

If the management of the target company resists the offer (i.e. a hostile takeover) there will, generally, be no obligation to seek advice as indicated in Article 25 of the

WOR. In practice, the "besieged employer" will certainly involve his works council in the hostile takeover, even if it is only to receive moral support from the works council for his resistance. Moreover, pursuant to Article 25, he will certainly have to seek the advice of his works council if by way of an issue of preferential shares he transfers voting control in the general meeting of shareholders to a foundation which will hold these shares.

C. Defences against Takeover

With regard to possible defences against a hostile takeover, it should be noted that such takeover bids are essentially aimed at control of the company through the acquisition of a dominant position in the General Meeting of Shareholders. Accordingly, defences for their part aim at neutralizing any such attempt by addressing shareholders' powers. This can be done by reducing the powers of the general meeting of shareholders as such, or by hindering the acquisition of a dominant position within the framework of that meeting.

Up until now, the emphasis in practice in the Netherlands has been on the former approach. Reference is made here to what has been said earlier on oligarchic constructions, and on the *structuur* regime. Experience proves that this line of defence is quite effective: no hostile takeover has ever succeeded as far as information is publicly available. By contrast – but possibly also as a consequence – rules on the voting rights of individual shareholders at the General Meeting of Shareholders have received less attention.[89]

It has been mentioned before that the Stock Exchange Association has a declared policy of reducing the scope for oligarchic constructions, as it holds the view that these reduce the attractiveness of shares quoted on the Stock Exchange and hence depress the overall price level of those shares. Discussion on this issue has been intense for some time and shows no sign of abating, as will be seen below.

At the same time, the few criticisms which are levelled at the *structuur* regime, seem to aim at enhancing the employees' position rather than that of the shareholders.[90] This barrier to hostile takeovers appears therefore to be as robust as ever. In this regard, attention must be drawn to two points. On the one hand, it should be recalled that the *structuur* regime, which is obligatory for those companies which pass the "thresholds", can also be adopted on a voluntary basis by smaller companies (provided they have instituted a Works Council). On the other hand, it is noteworthy that the *structuur* regime has received the European Commission's official blessing. Indeed, the regime has been offered as one of the options for governance structures proposed by the Commission, both in the framework of the Fifth Company Law Directive[91] and for the *Societas Europea*[92] (and its derived company forms).[93]

[89] See the overview of the "Defence measures of the 34 most actively traded companies" in P.B. Oudemans, *Dutch Defences in Legal Danger, Issues of European Integration*, 1991, p. 19.

[90] See however, A.W.A. Boot, "Naar een dynamischer structuur-regime", *Maandblad NV* 73 (1995) p. 280; A.L. Mohr, "De rol van de Ondernemingskamer in het kader van de problematiek rond beschermingsconstructies en betwiste overnames", in 25 *jaar Ondernemingskamer* (1996).

[91] See OJ EC 1983, C 240/2.

[92] See OJ EC 1989, C 263/41, 69.

[93] See OJ EC 1992, C 99/1 (see also OJ EC 1993, C 236).

D. Liability of the Management

1. Liability to the Corporation

In the Netherlands, the duty of care of the Board of Management is expressed in terms of a duty to "properly perform" management tasks.[94] What "proper performance" is, depends on the circumstances. According to the principle of collective responsibility, all duties are essentially collective. Each managing director is also responsible to the corporation for the proper performance of the specific duties assigned to him. If a matter falls within the scope of responsibility of two or more managing directors, they are jointly and severally liable, unless one can prove that the shortcoming is not attributable to him. In his defence the individual director must prove first, that he was not personally negligent, and secondly, that he did not fail in his duty to take action to avoid or prevent the consequences of the mismanagement of the collective body.

Under specific circumstances, the supervisory board may also be held liable.[95] A case in point may be that where the supervisory board acts in the place of the management board, e.g. in case of conflict of interest between the board of management and the corporation. In this case, the members of the supervisory board will be liable as members of the management board, not as members of the supervisory board. The act of approving or authorizing management decisions does not in itself constitute an act of management by the supervisory board.[96] A negligent or improper decision of the management board is not, therefore, automatically attributed to the supervisory board merely by reason of its approval.

The statutory duty to "properly perform" management tasks requires that each director discharge his duties with care, skill and diligence. A board member is not expected to guarantee the success of his actions. Each individual action must be judged on its own merits. There is no general standard similar to the "business judgment rule" in the United States. Courts are generally not inclined to second-guess actions that under similar circumstances could reasonably have been taken by other, well-informed and diligent executives in similar positions in similar types of industry or trade.

Mismanagement of corporations often arises under circumstances in which creditors of the director, including the corporation, have been defrauded, and the director's personal assets disguised. If the managing director is not able to pay damages, the claimant (including the corporation) can petition for the nullification of any transactions between the managing director and third parties that were concluded without proper consideration and with the intent to defraud the creditors or the corporation.[97]

2. Liability for Non-payment of Taxes and Premiums

If certain taxes or premiums (e.g. wage tax, social security premiums and premiums for mandatory old age pension funds) are not paid when due, the managing directors are personally liable for the full amount of taxes and premiums outstanding if non-

[94] BW Arts. 2:9, 2:149.
[95] Ibid., Art. 2:152.
[96] Ibid., Art. 2:152.
[97] Ibid., Art. 3:45; Bankruptcy Act, Art. 42

payment is caused by the "apparent negligence" of the management board over a three-year period prior to the due date. This form of liability was introduced in 1987 by the so-called Second Misuse Act (*Tweede Misbruikwet*).[98] Non-payment creates a rebuttable statutory presumption of mismanagement, unless the corporation notifies the tax collector or the social security agency within 14 days after the due date of its inability to pay. The notice must give reasons, and subsequent inquiries must be answered.

This liability can arise even though the company is not bankrupt (liability upon bankruptcy will be discussed in the next paragraph).

The notice of non-payment by the corporation is critical, since it shifts the burden of proof of the mismanagement to the tax collector or social security agency. An individual managing director can exculpate himself for the lack of proper notification only if he was unable to give the notice. Irrespective of who must prove negligence, the only available defence is that either there was no negligence or, if there was, it was not the cause of non-payment.

The law focuses on the managing directors and supervisory directors who were in office at any time during the three-year period prior to the due date, but any executives, shareholders or others who have "actually managed" (*als ware hij bestuurder*) the corporation may also be held liable.

The claim of the tax collector and the social security agency will be for the full amount of taxes and premiums due. The managing directors have the right to seek recovery from the corporation. To the extent they fail, they must share liability for the shortfall equally among themselves.

3. Liability upon Bankruptcy

In 1987, BW Articles 2:138 and 2:248 were introduced in Dutch corporate law as part of the so-called Third Misuse Act (*Derde Misbruikwet*).[99] If the corporation is declared bankrupt, the members of the management board are personally liable for the deficit in bankruptcy, if the bankruptcy is, to a significant extent, caused by "apparent negligence" by the management board over the three-year period prior to the date of bankruptcy. Either of the following constitutes a statutory presumption of apparent negligence:

(a) the corporation has not kept financial records such that all assets and liabilities can be determined at any time;[100] or
(b) the corporation has not, on a timely basis, filed with the Commercial Register the annual accounts and other financial information required.[101]

If it appears that the managing directors did not fulfil their obligations arising from Article 2:10 or Article 2:394, there exists a non-rebuttable presumption that the management board has been negligent in the performance of its tasks. This also constitutes a rebuttable presumption that the improper fulfilment of its tasks was a significant cause of the bankruptcy. In this case, each individual managing director can

[98] The "First Misuse Act" is of no relevance to this subject.
[99] See Asser-Maeijer 2, III, nos. 326-338.
[100] See BW Art. 2:10.
[101] See Ibid., Art. 2:394.

exculpate himself only by showing that he himself was not negligent and that he did not fail in his duty to take action to avoid or prevent the consequences of the mismanagement.

The law imposes liability on managing directors and supervisory directors, as well as executives, shareholders, and others who have "generally managed" the affairs of the corporation. A parent company can also be held liable for the bankruptcy of a subsidiary. Also liable are managing directors of foreign corporations that are declared bankrupt in the Netherlands and are subject to Dutch taxes. Local managers of these foreign corporations may be held liable as if they were managing directors.

The claim will be for the full amount of the shortfall in the liquidation, all to the benefit of creditors, not to that of shareholders. The court may reduce the amount of the claim, when it feels that the claim is too high compared to the seriousness of the mismanagement, or when there are also other circumstances which caused the bankruptcy of the corporation. The court can also reduce the claim for one individual member of the management board.

4. Liability for Financial Statements

If the annual accounts, including any interim figures that the corporation produces (e.g. quarterly reports), are erroneous or misleading with respect to the state of affairs of the corporation, each managing director and, where applicable, supervisory director may be liable for damages incurred by third parties.[102] A managing director can exculpate himself by showing that he was not negligent.

5. Liability for Actions During the Formation of the Company

A corporation comes into existence upon the execution before a Dutch notary of the deed of incorporation (*akte van oprichting*), which contains the Articles (*statuten*). The deed of incorporation cannot be executed prior to the receipt of a "certificate of no objection" from the Minister of Justice. Each founder must subscribe in the capital. The aggregate contribution to the issued capital is required by law to be at least one-fifth of the authorized capital.

In the absence of the required "certificate of no objection" or a valid notarial instrument at the time of formation, the court will declare that the corporation never came into existence and its pretence managing directors or those who were acting as such, or in the absence thereof the persons who acted in the name of the non-existent corporation will be bound jointly and severally with the estate to fulfil all its agreements with third parties. All other incorporation defects may result in a dissolution of the corporation by order of the court.

Article 2:180(2) provides that the managing directors are jointly and severally liable for non-compliance with the following formalities:

(a) the filing with the Commercial Register. The management board, or the notary on its behalf, must register the corporation's data in the Commercial Register of the Chamber of Commerce and deposit a certified copy of the deed of incorporation;

[102] Ibid., Arts. 2:139; 2:150.

(b) paid in capital on the date of formation is at least equal to the amount of minimum capital as prescribed by law;
(c) at least one-fourth of the issued capital has been contributed.

Until that time, the corporation does not benefit from limited liability and the managing directors remain jointly and severally liable for all obligations of the corporation.

The founders, their representatives, and others who entered into agreements with third parties are, unless specifically agreed otherwise, personally bound by pre-incorporation transactions until the date of ratification by the corporation.[103]

6. *Liability for Crimes*

Dutch law accepts the theory that a corporation can commit a crime. The individual directly responsible for the corporation's criminal behaviour may face penalties as well. There are numerous statutes that impose specific criminal sanctions on the directors of business enterprises and on those who authorize or are otherwise responsible for offences involving such matters as import and export, hazardous products, pharmaceutical and edible products, fair trade, business practices, wage and price controls, transportation, anti-trust, taxation, zoning and protection of the environment.

The civil liability for non-compliance with the statutory corporation law has been supplemented by certain criminal sanctions:

(1) intentionally publishing inaccurate financial statements;[104]
(2) involvement of a managing or supervisory director of the corporation in situations that are illegal or in conflict with the Articles, resulting in serious harm to the corporation;[105]
(3) prior to or during bankruptcy proceedings:
  - disguising profits or losses, or fraudulently disposing of assets;
  - disposing of assets at significantly less than their value;
  - giving preferential treatment to certain creditors in a manner detrimental to other creditors;[106]
(4) prior to bankruptcy proceedings:
  - failure, or gross neglect, by the corporation in keeping proper records;[107]
(5) borrowing money with the purpose of forestalling bankruptcy, knowing bankruptcy to be unavoidable.[108]

7. *Liability for Civil Wrongs or Torts*

Apart from the sources of liability mentioned above, a managing director can also be held personally liable for civil wrongs on the ground of the general provision of

[103] Ibid., Art. 2:93.
[104] Criminal Code, Art. 336.
[105] Ibid., Arts. 342, 347.
[106] Ibid., Art. 343.
[107] Ibid., Arts. 342, 343.
[108] Ibid., Art. 342.

Article 6:162 of the Civil Code, and the director's action will be judged on that basis. Under circumstances, a managing director may be held personally liable when he, on behalf of the corporation, has entered into an agreement with a third party, knowing that the corporation will not be able to comply with this obligation.

8. *Liability Within a Group of Companies*

When a company forms part of a group, the parent company controls the subsidiaries and, accordingly, it is in a position, in substance, to give instructions to the subsidiary regarding the financial, social and economic management. Frequently, economic entities and the financing of activities are centrally organized. The subsidiaries then do not borrow money from the banks themselves for their own activities, but they are financed via the parent company or via a holding especially created for that purpose. The bank, however, will only allow this type of group financing on the condition that all corporations within the concern shall be jointly and severally liable for all the debts to the bank.

When the group as a whole is confronted with economic problems, some of the subsidiaries may still function well. It may then be of great interest that those subsidiaries, are not dragged down by the bad fortunes of the group as a whole. To achieve this, it will be critical to release the profitable subsidiaries from the joint liability. This arrangement is what is referred to as a *sterfhuisconstructie* (*mortuarium construction*).[109]

There is no legal definition of this construction, so several variations are possible. Usually, the bank and the top management decide to remove the healthy subsidiaries which are doing well from the concern and to release these subsidiaries from their liability. This happens by transferring the shares of the healthy subsidiaries, which are owned by the parent company, to a new holding company. The new holding buys these shares with money borrowed from the bank. The money does not however go to the parent company, but the price of the shares will be compensated with the existing debt to the bank. The non-profitable subsidiaries stay in the concern (*het sterfhuis*, the "mortuarium"), waiting to be liquidated. The healthy subsidiaries will be able to continue on a going-concern basis.

The question has however been raised whether certain stakeholders, such as shareholders and creditors of the non-profitable companies can oppose this construction. With regard to the shareholders it is to be observed that the value of their shares was already nihil because of the bad financial situation of the company. Another question is whether the group management can make such an agreement with the bank without a decision of the general meeting of shareholders. With regard to the creditors, it can be argued that the transfer did not harm them if the shares were already pledged to the bank. Only in the situation where the shares were sold for an unreasonably small amount of money can a creditor apply to court for an annulment of the transfer.[110]

A parent company can also be held liable for the debts of the subsidiaries when it has intensively interfered in the management of the subsidiaries. There is a connection between the intensity of the influence of the parent company on the management of the

[109] See W.J. Slagter, TVVS 1983, p. 25.
[110] BW Art. 3:45 (the so-called "actio Pauliana").

subsidiary and the liability of the parent company for the debts of the subsidiary. The basis of this liability is again the general provision of Article 6:162 of the Civil Code.

An example of possible liability of a parent company on the ground of intensive interference with the management of the subsidiary, is the judgment of the Supreme Court in *Osby*.[111] In this case, a Swedish parent company was held liable by a creditor of the subsidiary, which had gone bankrupt. The parent company was blamed for the fact that it had transferred almost all the activities of the subsidiary to itself, in order to secure the money the subsidiary had borrowed from it. The Supreme Court ruled that in this situation the parent company was indeed liable in tort with regard to the creditors of the subsidiary. This was especially the case as the parent had such an influence in the management of the subsidiary that it could or should have known that the transfer of all the assets would seriously harm the interests of the creditors owing to the bad financial situation of the subsidiary.

V. THE AMSTERDAM STOCK EXCHANGE

Securities law is not a separate area of law within the Dutch legal system. It has to a large extent been shaped by more generally defined areas of law such as civil law, corporate law and administrative law. Since the beginning of the Eighties, there has been a considerable increase in securities regulations in the Netherlands. Areas which until then were unregulated or scarcely regulated have become subject to, occasionally quite strict, regulations consisting of a variety of laws, implementing regulations and policy statements. The two main reasons for this development seem to be the desire to strengthen investor protection in the securities markets and the enactment of a number of EC Directives covering almost all aspects of the issue and trade of securities.

The Securities Board of the Netherlands (*Stichting Toezicht Effectenverkeer* or STE) is the authority with principal responsibility for the enforcement and administration of several securities laws. Under the main Dutch securities statute, the Securities Transactions Supervision Act 1995 (*Wet toezicht effectenverkeer 1995*), the STE is designated as the "watchdog" of Dutch securities markets and it supervises the various securities exchanges and the off-exchange market (*buitenbeurshandel*), and grants licenses to and supervises securities firms. The STE was founded in 1988 and commenced supervising the Dutch Stock Exchange in early 1989.

The Amsterdam Stock Exchange (*Amsterdamse Effecten-beurs*) is the world's oldest regular stock market and started its operations in the early seventeenth century. The Stock Exchange Association (*Vereniging voor de Effectenhandel*) maintains and oversees the operation of the exchange. The Association is a private association of brokers-dealers which was established in 1876. It is governed by a Council comprising 17 members. The Chairman of the Council is independent, which means he is not an exchange member, and he is also the exchange's Chief Executive. Four other council members are also independent and represent the listed companies and investors, whereas the remaining 12 Council members represent member firms.

With regard to the regulation of publicly held companies, it should be noted that requirements as to the provision of information to the public are to be found in the

[111] HR 25-9-1981, NJ 1982, 443. See also Asser-Maeijer 2, III, no. 624.

Stock Exchange Manual (*Fondsenreglement*), i.e. the rules setting out the requirements for the admission of securities to listing on the Amsterdam Stock Exchange. The Stock Exchange Manual is issued by the Amsterdam Stock Exchange Association and is in itself not binding. However, an issuer who wishes to have its securities listed on the Amsterdam Stock Exchange must enter into standard form listing agreement (*noteringsovereenkomst*) with the Exchange. By signing the agreement, the issuer becomes bound by the provisions of the Stock Exchange Manual and its relevant Exhibits, such as Exhibit X, to which reference has already been made. In this way the listed company becomes contractually bound by it.

The Stock Exchange Manual grants an applicant for listing the right of appeal against rejection of the application. This appeal must be filed with and is decided upon by the STE.[112] Against the STE's decision, a further appeal lies with a special court of law, the *College van Beroep voor het Bedrijfsleven* (Trade and Industry Tribunal).

If an issuer of listed securities fails to fulfil one of its obligations under the listing agreement or the Stock Exchange manual, the Amsterdam Stock Exchange may impose certain sanctions. These sanctions include suspension of the official listing as well as cancellation of the listing.[113] Appeal is possible to the STE and after that, to the Court of Appeal from Decisions of the SER.

VI. FUTURE PERSPECTIVES

In the light of expected EC regulation, (the so-called Bangemann proposals), which allegedly penalized "regulatory takeover barriers" (such as those prevailing in the Netherlands) whilst leaving untouched "structual barriers", prevailing in other Member States,[114] the Minister of Finance announced in 1994 his intention to initiate legislation on the limits of anti-takeover measures. With a view to this, the VEUO (the Association of companies quoted on the Stock Exchange) and the VvdE (Stock Exchange Association, i.e. the association which runs the Amsterdam Stock Exchange) were given the opportunity to present their own proposals for anti-takeover regulation.

The VEUO explicitly advocated statutory regulation in which anti-takeover measures should be limited in time. The VvdE, on the other hand, was strongly in favour of regulation on a contractual basis (self-regulation).[115]

Having first reached a compromise between them, which however was rejected by the Minister as altogether too vague and complicated, VEUO and VvdE presented in September 1995 joint proposals for the second time.

Those proposals were a combination of statutory provisions and self-regulation. By way of a complete draft bill, to be included in the Civil Code, the proposed regulation and a newly to be installed "Committee on disputed takeovers" (colloquially referred to as the "Takeover Panel") would be given a statutory basis. Because of this statutory basis it would also be possible to bind the companies already quoted

[112] Fondsenreglement, Art. 65A.

[113] Ibid., Art. 65

[114] See P.B. Oudemans, *Dutch Defences in Danger, Legal Issues of European Integration*, 1991, p. 19

[115] This should be seen against the background of the Stock Exchange Association's on-going efforts to retain recognition of its self-regulatory model generally. This model is frequently criticized as being self-serving, opaque and inefficient.

on the Stock Exchange. This would not be possible with self-regulation alone, as this would not have been enough to prevail over rights acquired by virtue of the listing agreements.

According to those proposals, the Takeover Panel would base itself upon an "open norm". In forming its judgment, it should weigh all interests involved, including the interests of the target company and of the petitioner (the shareholder), and decide whether or not it is acceptable in all "reasonableness and fairness" (*redelijkheid en billijkheid*) that control is withheld from the shareholder by means of anti-takeover defence constructions.

According to the VEUO/VvdE proposals, the regulation would only be applicable to companies that have been quoted on the Stock Exchange for five years or longer. This should prevent quotation on the Stock Exchange from becoming less attractive for companies that would otherwise be ready for quotation.

Fundamental criticisms of a constitutional character have been aired by representatives of both business circles[116] and academia.[117] In essence, those criticisms relate to the crucial role allotted in the proposals to the "Takeover Panel" which has been perceived as an obligatory recourse to arbitration and a denial of due process in the courts.

At a more mundane level, an obvious criticism was that the practical effect of the arrangements proposed would still put virtually unsurmountable barriers in the way of those aspiring to an unfriendly takeover.

Both levels of criticism appear to have had their impact on the Government. In a letter of 28 February 1996 addressed to the Second Chamber of Parliament,[118] the Minister of Finance announced that finally agreement had been reached between all concerned on five basic principles, which would be further elaborated in formal legislation:

(1) The Enterprise Chamber assesses whether the projected policies of the aspiring controlling shareholder are substantially contrary to the interests of the target company and the enterprise(s) which it runs.
(2) The aspiring controlling shareholder submits his request to the Enterprise Chamber in which he explains his future policy with regard to the target company, whereupon the target company can submit its reactions thereto.
(3) A panel of experts gives its opinion to the Enterprise Chamber on those respective submissions, in the light of all relevant economic, financial and social aspects.
(4) The request of the aspiring controlling shareholder is granted by the Enterprise Chamber if his policy intentions are not essentially in conflict with the interests of the target company and the enterprise(s) which it runs.
(5) The request of the aspiring controlling shareholder is admissible only if the latter has held a share of 70 per cent of the issued capital for at least a year. In this regard "anti-takeover preference shares" are not taken into account.

It may be noted that it was emphasised by the Minister that the role of the "panel of experts" would certainly be very relevant, but would in no way be binding on the Enterprise Chamber.

[116] See M. Tabaksblat (chairman of Unilever), Maandblad NV (73) 1995, p. 242.
[117] See M.M. Mendel, Maandblad NV (73) 1995, p. 271.
[118] Document 24400, IX B, nr. 22, 1995/96.

Formal legislative proposals were announced for Spring 1996.[119]

An attempt to further the discussion was made by the publication of the Report "Corporate Governance in Nederland", eloborated by an ad hoc committee of representatives of the VEUO and of investors, together with independant experts, under the chairmanship of J.F.M. Peters.[120]

This report explicitly does not aim at new legislation but rather seeks to formulate a set of recommendations which when implemented would enhance the proper functioning of the Board of Directors, the Supervisory Board and the General Assembly of Shareholders. It is rather remarkable that in this context scant attention has been paid to employers' representatives, be it the Trade Unions or the Works Council.

Also recently, suggestions have been made publicly to address the issue discussed under a different angle, i.e. by enhancing the shareholders' position through a more active process of "proxy solicitation". It may be recalled that this phenomenon has been traditionally hampered due to the fact that virtually all shares in listed companies are bearer-shares. It has now been suggested by a representative of the VEUO that a proposal be prepared to overcome this hurdle. A mutual intermediary would be created which would have privileged access to the identity of individual shareholders through the banks where most shares are actually kept, and which would then serve as the communication channel for "proxy solicitation".[121]

The interest for this new approach is explicitly linked to the anticipated gradual demolition of "anti-takeover defences". Accordingly, management appears now more anxious to secure the support of the "average shareholder", who might prove a valuable ally against "barbarians at the gate".

On the other hand, it should be recalled, once again, that the *structuur* regime is still not fundamentally challenged in the public discussion. Even in isolation, without any further defences, this may well prove a major hurdle for "raiders" with an urgent short-run agenda. It remains to be seen, however, to what extent members of the supervisory board (with their allegiance to the enterprise as a whole) might be prepared to give unqualified support to the incumbent management against a major shareholder with a serious agenda.

Overall, it appears that, whilst the rhythm and the exact form in which changes will materialise is still far from clear, also in the Netherlands, the "management controlled firm" of Berle and Means[122] is no longer the inescapable model.

[119] At the time of writing (November 1996) no such proposals had yet been submitted.

[120] Commissie Corporate Governance, *Aanbevelingen inzake Corporate Governance*, Amsterdam (28 oktober 1996).

[121] See *Het Financiële Dagblad*, 17-19 February 1996, referring to an interview with S. Bergsma, Financieel Director Akzo Nobel.

[122] A.A. Berle and G.C. Means, *The modern corporation and private property* (1932).

6

Sweden

*Svante Johansson**

I. PUBLICLY HELD COMPANIES IN SWEDEN

A. General

In Sweden, the publicly held corporate phenomenon, as relevant to the issue of corporate governance, has been seriously discussed just recently.[1] Traditionally, Sweden has had only one form of company with limited personal liability for the owners, the *aktiebolag*.[2] Therefore, the Companies Act (1975:1385) had to operate in a manner functional for all kinds of companies, which gave little room for special rules regulating publicly held companies. Nevertheless, some rules in the Act apply only to large companies,[3] and special rules for companies whose shares are listed at the Stockholm Stock Exchange can be found in other acts, agreements and statements by self-regulating organs (SROs).

Today, Sweden is a member of the European Union, and has largely adapted, among other laws, the Companies Act to applicable EC rules.[4] One effect of the adaption process is that the Swedish limited-liability companies, in accordance with what is the case in most other European countries, since 1 January 1995, are divided into private companies and public companies. The Companies Act applies to both kinds of companies, and the significant difference between private and public companies is that only public companies are allowed to raise money by offers to the public.[5] By the changes in the act, the Second Council Directive on Company Law applies to public companies only, which must be registered as public companies and have a minimum share capital of SEK 500,000.[6]

* Associate Professor at the Faculty of Law at Stockholm University and working at the law firm Lagerlöf & Leman in Stockholm.

[1] See first G. Nord, "'Corporate governance' på Svenska", *Juridisk Tidskrift*, 1989-90, pp. 483 et seq.

[2] Furthermore, there are special rules for i.a., banks and insurance companies. These special regulations are, unless otherwise explicitly stated, disregarded in this chapter.

[3] See, e.g. chapter 8, s. 3 of the Companies Act, about the appointment of a managing director.

[4] See further about the work on adapting the Swedish Companies Act, R. Skog, "Adapting the Swedish Companies Act to the Requirements of the European Union", *International Company and Commercial Law Review*, Vol. 8, 1994, pp. 286 et seq.

[5] Chapter 1, s. 4 of the Companies Act.

[6] SEK 500,000 is approximately ECU 60,000.

© Kluwer Law International 1998

The public company, as defined in the Swedish Companies Act, must be distinguished from the publicly held company, the main topic of this chapter. Of course, most public companies will be publicly held and *vice versa*, but the Act's distinction between the two forms is formal, and there are no legal obstacles against a public company having only one shareholder or a private company having thousands of shareholders. The phrase, "publicly held companies" is in Sweden often used to describe companies with more than 200 shareholders,[7] whether private or public.

B. Statistics

Sweden has approximately 350,000 limited-liability companies.[8] The reasons for the limited-liability companies being so popular in Sweden, with only approximately 8.9 million inhabitants, are mainly found in earlier tax laws.[9] In Sweden taxes are among the highest in the world, and – particularly some years ago – it could be very profitable for a person to arrange his income in a way that reduced taxes. Since the company tax rate used to be much lower than the tax rate on income earned by physical persons, one way to substantially reduce the tax burden was to carry out a business in a limited-liability company instead of doing it as a self-employed person. Today, Swedish tax laws have been changed, and the differences between the taxation of companies and taxation of other forms of carrying out businesses have been significantly reduced.

In addition to the limited-liability companies, there are approximately 77,000 partnerships,[10] 20,000 incorporated economic associations[11] and 50,000 foundations in Sweden.[12] Sweden also has an unknown number of non-profit organizations (also called unincorporated associations), self-employed persons and a special form of cooperation called simple partnership.[13] Publicly held companies are against this background very few. Their number is probably well below 500.[14] On the other hand, publicly held companies are of great importance for the Swedish economy and business. Companies with more than 500 employees, employ 47 per cent of the workforce,[15] and the export from the 20 largest industrial companies represents approximately 50 per cent of the Swedish export of industrial goods.[16] The business carried out by publicly held companies, naturally also creates great demand for products manufactured and supplied by smaller enterprises.

[7] See, e.g. *SOU* 1989:72, part 1 pp. 463 et seq.

[8] See *Statistical Yearbook of Sweden '97,* p. 284 (Tab. 301). The figure is from the end of 1995.

[9] See, e.g. H. Nial & S. Johansson, *Bolag, föreningar och stoftelser, Norstedts Juridiska Handbok* (15th ed., Stockholm, 1994), p. 309.

[10] *Statistical Yearbook of Sweden '97,* p. 275 (Tab. 292). By its wording, this statistic deals only with unlimited partnerships. It is not clear whether limited partnerships are included or not.

[11] See, e.g. H. Nial & S. Johansson, *Svensk associationsrätt i huvuddrag* (6th ed., Stockholm, 1995), pp. 24 and 29.

[12] See *prop.* 1993/94:9, p. 40.

[13] Simple partnerships were earlier called non-trading partnerships, but since they today are allowed to trade, that term cannot be used. See C. Hemström, "Corporations and Partnerships, Sweden", *International Encyclopaedia of Law,* Suppl. 12 (Kluwer Law and Taxation, The Hague, London and Boston, 1995), p. 19.

[14] See *SOU* 1989:72, part 1 p. 461. At the end of 1995, 416 companies were registered at the Swedish Central Securities Register Depository (VPC). See *Statistical Yearbook of Sweden '97,* p. 301 (Tab. 333).

[15] *SOU* 1988:38, p. 45 and table 3:4. This figure deals with the number of employees, and not with publicly held companies, but there are no better statistics available.

[16] *SOU* 1988:38, p. 42.

C. Ownership Structure

The Swedish financial system can be described as market oriented. Due to changes in the market, the ownership structure in Swedish publicly held companies has changed over the years. In particular, the ownership has moved from physical persons to companies and other institutional investors.[17] In 1964, physical persons owned approximately 54 per cent of the shares listed at the Stockholm Stock Exchange,[18] while the corresponding figure for 1985 was only 21 per cent.[19] Today, individual shareholders account for 16 per cent of the total market value on the Stockholm Stock Exchange.[20] However, many institutional shareholders invest money on behalf of physical persons. In spring 1997, more than 51 per cent of the Swedish citizens owned shares, directly or indirectly. Large players at the Exchange are pension funds, investment companies, holding companies and insurance companies. Also, so-called mutual funds hold 9 per cent of the listed shares.[21] By purchasing shares in such funds, who diversify their investments, individuals can spread their risk in a way that is usually not possible when shares are directly owned. Swedish banks are, in principle, not allowed to own shares.

Basically, the Swedish State owns shares on an equal basis with any private investor. With some minor exceptions (none of which are of interest in the context discussed here) Swedish law does not contain any special provisions for State-owned companies. Apart from the Fourth and Fifth Boards of the Swedish National Pension Insurance Fund, who act on the market in the same manner as any other investor, the general idea is that the state shall not own shares in publicly held companies. However, for various reasons the Swedish State, including the Swedish National Pension Insurance Fund, owns approximately 8 per cent of the shares in the Swedish publicly held companies.[22]

Another group of investors, whose number is increasing in Sweden, is foreign subjects. By the end of 1983, 8 per cent of the shares in Swedish publicly held companies were owned by shareholders abroad. In September 1994, the corresponding figure was 25 per cent, and in spring 1997 30 per cent of the shares listed at the Stockholm Stock Exchange were owned by foreign shareholders. The foreign investors have mainly placed their money in larger Swedish companies, such as SKF, Ericsson and Astra, and the investments seem to be just investments and nothing more. So far, few foreign attempts of any importance to use the legal power of shareholding in order to influence the management of Swedish companies is known.

The diminishing ownership of listed shares by physical persons creates problems but can also be advantageous. Individuals who are shareholders have, of course, a strong incentive (i.e. their private economy) to supervise and question the actions taken by the companies. Private shareholders, therefore, have an important function to fill as a loud minority, that forces the directors, and sometimes the majority shareholders, to act in a fair and reasonable manner. This function is probably important

[17] See *SIND* 1980:5, pp. 29 et seq., and *SOU* 1988:38, pp. 91 and 94.

[18] See *SIND* 1980:5, p. 30.

[19] See *SOU* 1988:38, p. 91.

[20] See M. Isaksson & R. Skog, "Corporate Governance in Swedish Listed Companies", *Institutional Investors and Corporate Governance* (editors: T. Baums, R. M. Buxbaum and K. J. Hopt, Berlin and New York, 1994), p. 288.

[21] See ibid., p. 289.

[22] The figure is from 31 December 1993. The Swedish Mutual Fund Association.

not only for the development of the individual company's business, but also for the national economy.

On the other hand, private shareholders might have a limited time at their disposal for investigations of the companies. Furthermore, reasonable judgments on questions in today's complex business life often require knowledge and proficiency that cannot be expected to be found in laymen. Since the Stockholm Stock Exchange is quite an efficient Exchange,[23] minority shareholders also have the possibility of selling their shares if they are not satisfied with the way the business of the company is carried out, which in some cases might be just as influential as direct actions within the managerial field.[24] Institutional investors, on the other hand, can employ people that use the time and effort necessary to investigate the companies, and they can also hire expertise to understand the nature and impact of the issues raised. It is also more difficult for large shareholders to sell their shares on short notice, because too great a supply of shares on the market will cause prices to plummet. Institutional investors can, therefore, be forced either to accept the board's way of running the company's business or to exercise their managerial power, which might contribute to stability and planning in the long term.

Besides the factors discussed above, institutional ownership of shares suffers from two basic problems. First, the persons employed by institutional shareholders do not have the same obvious incentive as individual shareholders to watch the performance in the companies. Secondly, nothing speaks in favour of the opinion that for example insurance company employees are better suited for making managerial decisions in matters concerning, for example, mining or shipping, than the average individual shareholder.[25] However, these problems can be overcome. The employees of institutional shareholders can be given different types of incentives from their employer, and it is probably easier for a large organization to hire experts to cure a lack of expertise, than for an individual shareholder.

For many institutional shareholders, it is primarily the board that decides how to wield the power connected with the shares. However, these institutional owners too have shareholders, who can use their managerial power to order the board to use the voting power for the shares in a certain way.[26] The shareholders of the institutional shareholders are, in turn, often companies and other institutions,[27] with the same advantages and difficulties as has been described above.

A special situation occurs when a company A owns shares in a company B, which owns shares in a company C, which is a shareholder of A.[28] Since the Swedish Companies Act does not allow a company to possess its own shares, or a subsidiary to possess shares in the parent company,[29] such a relationship must permit the exis-

[23] See infra at Section II.A.

[24] Cf. K. Rydqvist, *The Pricing of Shares with Different Voting Power and the Theory of Oceanic Games* diss. (Stockholm 1986), pp. 129 et seq.

[25] Cf. H. Nial & S. Johansson, "Bolag, föreningar och stiftelser", *Norstedts Juridiska Handbok* (15th ed., Stockholm, 1994), pp. 312 et seq.

[26] See further infra at Section IV.B.

[27] Cf. M. Isaksson & R. Skog, supra note 20, pp. 289 et seq.

[28] Some practical examples of such relationships are given in *SOU* 1988:39, p. 126 and by M. Isaksson & R. Skog, supra note 20, p. 301.

[29] Chapter 7, s. 2, para. 1. See further *SOU* 1988:38, appendix 1 (R. Skog). In *SOU* 1997:22 it is proposed that companies, to some extent, should be allowed to purchase their own shares.

tence of external shareholders or involve several companies.[30] Cross ownership of the type described here was not unusual some years ago, but has today become unpopular. Instead, the same effects are to some extent achieved by using the so-called box-in-a-box construction. The possibility of cross ownership and box-in-a-box constructions creates a relatively strong defensive measure against hostile takeovers. These measures, as well as almost all other defensive measures, ought to be implemented in advance, because during a bid period the board of the target company must assume a relatively passive role.[31]

D. Becoming a Publicly Held Company

In principle, Swedish law imposes no difficulties for a company to become publicly held. The Act naturally stipulates a procedure for converting a private company to a public company,[32] but a small company can become publicly held (in the sense the term is used here) merely by an increase in the number of shareholders.

Some legal aspects arise if a company wants to list all or some of its shares on the Stockholm Stock Exchange.[33] In that case, the company must draft and issue a prospectus.[34] Furthermore, a listing on the Stock Exchange will require the company to enter into a standard contract with the Stock Exchange. However, the Exchange will refuse to accept companies that do not fulfil the demands stipulated by the Financial Supervisory Authority,[35] or by the Exchange, in accordance with Chapter 5 in the Stock Exchange and Clearing Act.

E. Transfer of Shares

As a main rule, shares in Swedish companies are freely transferable.[36] Before the adaptation of the Companies Act to the EEC rules, there was a possibility to restrict foreigners' purchase of Swedish shares. Aside from some minor exceptions, for example, the military industry, this possibility has been abolished. The Act permits a company to restrict the transferability of its shares by entering a pre-emption clause in the articles of association, by which a purchaser of shares would be obliged to offer the shares for sale to, for example, pre-existing shareholders before being registered as a shareholder, but not in any other way.[37] The Companies Act contains no special prohibitions against pre-emption clauses in the articles of association of companies with publicly traded shares, but according to regulations issued by the

[30] See further about so-called cross and circular ownership, e.g. *SOU* 1988:38, appendix 1 (R. Skog) and M. Isaksson & R. Skog, supra note 20, pp. 300 et seq.

[31] See the Swedish Industry and Commerce Stock Exchange Committee's Recommendations concerning Public Offers for the Acquisition of Shares (1988).

[32] Chapter 17, s. 1 of the Companies Act.

[33] The Stock Exchange and Clearing Act (1992:543) does not give the Stockholm Stock Exchange a monopoly on exchange activities. There are three exchanges in Sweden today, but only one – the Stockholm Stock Exchange – is a stock exchange.

[34] Chapter 5, s. 5 – 5b the Stock Exchange and Clearing Act. See also the Financial Supervisory Authority's Regulations (FFFS 1995:21) on Prospectus. The Financial Supervisory Authority is the Swedish counterpart to SEC in the USA.

[35] See the Financial Supervisory Authority's Regulations (FFFS 1995:43) on Quoting of Securities etc.

[36] Chapter 3, s. 2 of the Companies Act.

[37] Ibid., s. 3. The wording of a pre-emption clause, which is regulated in detail in the Act, is beyond the scope of this chapter.

Financial Supervisory Authority shares can be quoted at an exchange only if they are freely transferable.[38]

Another way to restrict the transferability of shares is by agreement between the shareholders. According to Swedish law, such agreements are valid and binding between the parties to the contract.[39] The company as such is not concerned by shareholders' agreements,[40] but has to accept a new shareholder even if he or she has acquired the shares in violation of such a contract. The law does not prevent shareholders in a publicly held company from entering into a shareholders' agreement, but it is in some situations required that such an agreement is disclosed.[41] The frequency of shareholders' agreements in Swedish publicly held companies is unknown, but it can be assumed that they are not too prevalent.

If a Swedish company owns more than 90 per cent of the shares, representing more than 90 per cent of the votes, in another company, the former company (the parent company) has the right to purchase the outstanding shares, and the minority shareholders have a corresponding right to require the parent company to purchase their shares.[42] Furthermore, a mandatory bid clause has been added to the articles of association of some companies.[43] Such a clause is probably not valid,[44] and no legislative measures on the issue can be foreseen.[45]

F. The Swedish Securities Market

During the 1960s and early 1970s, the transaction frequency on the Stockholm Stock Exchange was low, as was the market value of publicly traded shares during this period.[46] During the global boom of the 1980s, the picture changed completely. In 1980 approximately 13 per cent of the quoted shares were traded. In 1986 the figure had increased to approximately 38 per cent. Also, the market value of the publicly traded shares has increased significantly. During the period of 1979-1989, the gen-

38 Chapter 1, s. 1, para. 1, item a) of the Financial Supervisory Authority's Regulations on Quoting of Securities etc. In *SOU* 1997:22 the Swedish Company Law Committee proposes that it should be allowed to restrict the free transferability of shares in some other ways than by pre-emption clauses. As mentioned above, these kind of restrictions can – generally – not be used in publicly held companies.

39 See, e.g. C. M. Roos, *Avtal och rösträtt* diss. (Uppsala, 1969), pp. 287 et seq. and 302 and ibid., Comparative Notes on Shareholders' Voting Agreements, *Scandinavian Studies in Law* 1971, pp. 179 et seq. and 183.

40 See, e.g. the Swedish Supreme Court case *NJA* 1972 p. 29, J. Kansmark & C. M. Roos, *Aktieägaravtal* (2nd ed., Stockholm, 1994), p. 31; C. M. Roos, *Avtal och rösträtt* diss. (Uppsala, 1969), pp. 332 et seq. and 343 and ibid., "Comparative Notes on Shareholders' Voting Agreements", *Scandinavian Studies in Law* 1971, pp. 184 et seq.

41 See chapter 4, s. 2, para. 1, item 3 of the Act on Trading in Financial Instruments. See also, e.g. appendix 1 the Swedish Industry and Commerce Stock Exchange Committee's Recommendations for Drawing up Prospectuses. In some situations disclosure can be the result of the requirements in the Swedish Industry and Commerce Stock Exchange Committee's Recommendations Concerning the Disclosure of Substantial Acquisitions of Shares, etc. (1991), see s. II, item 2 c).

42 Chapter 14, s. 31 of the Companies Act.

43 See further R. Skog, *Does Sweden Need a Mandatory Bid Rule? A Critical Analysis* (Stockholm, 1995). Cf. art. 4, item 1 in the proposal for a thirteenth Council Directive on Company Law (COM (90) 416 - SYN 186, of 10 September 1990).

44 See *SOU* 1997:22 p. 207 and B. Svensson, *Juridisk Handbok. Bolagsrätt I* (Stockholm, 1993), p. 7:11.

45 The idea of legislation on mandatory bids is rejected in *SOU* 1997:22 pp. 300 et seq.

46 See, e.g. *SOU* 1989:72 part 1 pp. 195 et seq.

eral index (i.e. the market value of all listed shares) increased 12 times, which means an average annual increase of 30 per cent.[47]

The explanation of the fast and comprehensive development of the Swedish public securities market has been partially given above, namely the boom that lasted during several years in the 1980s. Booms did occur before that, without any similar development of the securities market. This time, however, the boom coincided with some political measures.[48] First, the Fourth Board of the Swedish National Pension Insurance Fund was in 1973 allowed to purchase shares. This measure caused a significant increase in the demand for shares. Secondly, a special tax, justified by political slogans about economic democracy, was forced on companies and some other persons carrying out business. The money raised by this tax was placed in special funds, so-called wage-earners' funds, which invested the money in shares. These funds were heavily debated and have now been abolished, but they undoubtedly contributed to the expansion of the market for shares during the 1980s. Thirdly, the slow action at the Stock Exchange, among other things, prompted the Swedish legislative authorities to create an opportunity for private persons to save money in certain forms of mutual funds, with special tax reductions.[49] These mutual funds become very popular and still exist, even though the advantageous tax rules have today been abolished. The popularity of the funds contributed – in the long run – to the supply of capital to the stock market. Finally, a long-term increase in the market values of shares is obviously in some way self-generating, in that the expectations of the players on the market are affected by the historical development of the market.

The increased significance of the public market for shares can also be observed in other fields of the Swedish economy. For example, an exchange for derivatives based on shares can operate successfully only if the market for shares is liquid and functions well. In Sweden, standardized options, futures, swaps and forward rate agreements are traded at a special exchange,[50] with a high transaction frequency and which is very successful in its business.[51]

Due to the failure of the company AB Kreuger & Toll in the early 1930s, Swedish companies are prohibited from issuing debentures, or raising other loans, on a condition that they shall be repaid by other means than a nominal cash amount or a cash amount to be determined by reference to monetary fluctuations.[52] Furthermore, the Companies Act does not allow a company to issue options to subscribe for new shares, except in connection with debt instruments.[53] Aside the exceptions mentioned, Swedish publicly held companies may, and do, raise capital in many different ways, and it does not seem possible to declare that a certain way of financing is preferred over others. New shares can be issued in the public market or privately

[47] See about the development, e.g. *SOU* 1989:72 part 1 pp. 195 et seq.

[48] See M. Isaksson & R. Skog, *op. cit.*, note 20, pp. 289 et seq.

[49] That tax rules are very important in a country such as Sweden where the taxes are high, has been pointed out supra at I.B.

[50] OM Stockholm AB.

[51] See about the derivatives exchange, e.g. *SOU* 1988:13, *SOU* 1989:72 part 1 pp. 399 et seq., *SOU* 1993:114 and *prop.* 1991/92:113 p. 86, pp. 122 et seq., appendix 10 pp. 476 et seq.

[52] Chapter 7, s. 3, para. 2 of the Companies Act.

[53] Chapter 5, s. 1 of the Companies Act. Both options to subscribe for new shares, without connection with debt instruments, and loans that shall be repaid by other means than a nominal cash amount (or a cash amount to be determined by reference to monetary fluctuations), are proposed to be allowed in Sweden in the future. See *SOU* 1997:22.

through sales to institutions or large investors. During 1995 the capital in Swedish companies increased by SEK 67,696 million by issue of new shares.[54] In terms of debt, a company can chose to sell debt instruments directly to the public or to raise capital privately by banks, insurance companies, funds or other financial institutions.

The fast and comprehensive development of the Swedish stock market has, of course, forced the Exchange to develop its structure. The Stockholm Stock Exchange is today structured as a limited-liability company, and the trade is completely computerized. The relations between the Exchange and the companies are, as indicated above, regulated by a standard contract. The actual trade is carried out by members of the Exchange, who have become members by entering into a contract with the Exchange.[55]

G. The Regulation of the Securities Market

The Swedish securities market is regulated by rules of different kinds. There are, of course, legislative acts and other regulations that apply to the market, in a broad sense. Besides the acts already mentioned, there are for example the Insider Act (1990:1324) and the Share Accounts Act (1989:827). The overall principle in all legislation concerning the securities market is to safeguard the public's confidence in the market.[56] Within the framework of that overall principle, as interpreted by the Financial Supervisory Authority, the exchanges and the players on the market are in general allowed to establish rules by self-regulation.[57]

The Financial Supervisory Authority and the Stockholm Stock Exchange have rules for membership, as well as for the trade in and quoting of shares. Under the Financial Supervisory Authority's regulations shares may be listed at an exchange only if at least 25 per cent of the shares of the class proposed to be listed is owned by the public, and the number of shareholders is at least 1,000.[58] Companies that do not comply with these demands can still have their shares listed, if the exchange determines that the market situation for the shares will be satisfying.[59] The rules issued by the Stockholm Stock Exchange are primarily aimed at guaranteeing that the securities market receives full, correct and equal information from the companies.[60]

The market is also regulated through the work of primarily two SROs. The Swedish Industry and Commerce Stock Exchange Committee issues recommendations on principle and general issues concerning companies with shares quoted on the Stock Exchange. Such companies are, according to the registration agreement

[54] *Statistical Yearbook of Sweden '97*, p. 290 (Tab. 310).

[55] At the end of 1993, the Stockholm Stock Exchange had 41 members, see *Statistical Yearbook of Sweden '97*, p. 301 (Tab. 331).

[56] See, e.g. chapter 1, s. 2 of the Act on Trading in Financial Instruments. See P.-O. Jansson, *Regelbildning på värdepappersmarknaden* (Stockholm, 1995), p. 17 passim.

[57] See, e.g. *prop.* 1990/91:142 p. 82.

[58] Chapter 1, s. 1, para. 2, item d) of the Financial Supervisory Authority's Regulations on Quoting of Securities etc. For companies with fewer shareholders, there are possibilities to have the shares noted on special lists.

[59] Chapter 1, s. 2, para. 1 of the Financial Supervisory Authority's Regulations on Quoting of Securities etc.

[60] See further infra Section II.A.

between these companies and the Stockholm Stock Exchange, required to follow four of the Committee's recommendations.[61] The Swedish Supreme Court has found an older version of this contract clause valid and possible to uphold by the use of liquidated damages.[62] In specific cases, the Securities Council[63] delivers opinions about accepted practices on the securities market. The prime task for the Securities Council is to deliver opinions on issues that cannot be tried in any other forum, but in reality the council is quite often required to take a stand on legal questions.

II. GENERAL PROVISIONS ON DISCLOSURE

A. Disclosure Requirements

The right of disclosure is regarded as very important in the Swedish law of exchanges and the securities market. The Stockholm Stock Exchange is also regarded as an efficient Exchange, in the sense that information about companies with listed shares is rapidly and widely spread.[64] Disclosure requirements are found in almost all regulations concerning the securities market. Statutory requirements include disclosure of, for example, annual and semi-annual financial reports,[65] a company's shareholder register,[66] prospectus information[67] and certain acquisitions of shares.[68] The above information is public, and accordingly serves all players on the market. After being made public, information can, of course, also be used by the authorities, and as to tax-related information (e.g. annual reports) the law generally requires that it be delivered directly to the tax authorities. The Financial Supervisory Authority has issued regulations for disclosure in certain situations, such as the issue of semi-annual reports, issue of new shares, alterations of articles of association, public offers to acquire shares and transactions with related persons.[69]

Disclosure requirements can also be found in the recommendations and opinions issued by the Swedish SROs. The Swedish Industry and Commerce Stock Exchange Committee has issued recommendations about disclosure in various situations.[70]

[61] See appendix 2 to the Registration Agreement (published in *FARs regelsamling II Börs & värdepapper.*; also available in English).

[62] *NJA* 1985 p. 343.

[63] See, about the opinions from the Securities Council, B. Kristiansson, *Aktiemarknadsnämndens praxis under tio år* (Stockholm, 1996).

[64] See K. Claesson, *Effektiviteten på Stockholms Fondbörs* diss. (Stockholm, 1987), pp. 204 et seq.

[65] Cf. chapter 8, s. 3 and chapter 9, s. 2 of the Act on Annual Reports.

[66] Ibid., chapter 3, s. 13, para. 1.

[67] Chapter 4, ss. 18-26 of the Companies Act; chapter 2 of the Act on Trading in Financial Instruments and chapter 5, s. 5-5b of the Stock Exchange and Clearing Act. The closer meaning of the information that has to be given in a prospectus is regulated by the Financial Supervisory Authority, see the Financial Supervisory Authority's Regulations on Prospectus.

[68] Chapter 4 of the Act on Trading in Financial Instruments and ss. 8-15 of the Insider Act.

[69] See chapters 2, 3 and 4 of the Financial Supervisory Authority's Regulations on Quoting of Securities etc. This regulation is, maybe, not aimed to have a direct effect on the parties on the market, but only to stipulate the requirements that must be stipulated by a stock exchange. This question is not discussed here.

[70] The Swedish Industry and Commerce Stock Exchange Committee's recommendations concern, e.g. disclosure of substantial acquisitions of shares, etc. (1994), public offers for the acquisition of shares (1988, with appendix of 1991) and disclosure of proposals for election of directors of the board (1994). Cf. chapter 2, s. 14 of the Financial Supervisory Authority's Regulations on Quoting of Securities.

Also, the Securities Council has required disclosure in certain situations.[71] Finally, the registration agreement entered into between the Stockholm Stock Exchange and the companies whose shares are listed on the Exchange, requires disclosure of information in various situations.[72] Normally, the contract requires the information to be disclosed to the Exchange, but certain clauses require disclosure to be made to the public.[73] The contract affords a company the possibility to conceal information that otherwise would be public, if publicity would cause harm to the company and the Exchange grants confidentiality in each case.[74] The Stockholm Stock Exchange has also issued some recommendations about, for example, disclosure of business activities carried out by entities related to companies with listed shares.[75]

B. Sanctions for Failure to Disclose

The sanctions for failure to disclose vary from imprisonment to a disclosure order under the penalty of a fine, depending on the obligation that has been infringed. Insider dealing is punishable by a fine or imprisonment for a maximum of four years.[76] If the directors wilfully or negligently fail to keep a correct register of the company's shareholders, they face the penalty of a fine, or imprisonment for a maximum of one year.[77] If a company during two financial years fails to file – and thereby disclose – its annual reports, the company shall be placed into compulsory winding up.[78] If the directors fail to file the company's annual report within 15 months after the fiscal year, they face personal liability for the company's debts, unless they can show that they have not been negligent.[79]

If a company whose shares are traded on a stock exchange fails to comply with its legal obligations (e.g. disclosure obligations) its shares can be deregistered from the exchange.[80] If someone fails to obey the stipulations in the Act on Trading in Financial Instruments, on the obligation to produce and file a prospectus and to disclose changes in the ownership of shares (when such disclosure is mandatory), the Financial Supervisory Authority can order him to do so under the penalty of a fine.[81] If a company that attempts to list its shares on an exchange, fails to produce a prospectus according to the rules in the Act on Exchange and Clearing Business, the shares may not be listed.

[71] See, e.g. the Securities Council's opinion 1987:11 (disclosure of agreement giving persons in managing positions right to buy options on shares in the company), 1988:3 (selected information to some shareholders), 1989:4 (disclosure of price-relevant information before issuing new shares), 1990:3 (disclosure, in a call to a general meeting, of information about an issue of options), 1990:7 (disclosure to the shareholders, of information about an issue of convertible debt instruments in an associated company), 1992:7 (disclosure, in a call to a general meeting, of information about proposed changes of terms of convertible instruments) and 1994:6 (disclosure of information about synthetic options).

[72] Sections 1-7 and appendix 1 to the Registration Agreement.

[73] Ibid., appendix 1, ss. 24 and 25.

[74] Ibid., s. 8, para. 1.

[75] 11 April 1986.

[76] Sections 21 and 22 of the Insider Act.

[77] Chapter 19, s. 1, para. 1, item 2 of the Companies Act.

[78] Ibid., chapter 13, s. 4, para. 1, item 4.

[79] Ibid., chapter 8, s. 12 of the Act on Annual Reports.

[80] Chapter 5, s. 4, para. 1 of the Stock Exchange and Clearing Act.

[81] Chapter 5, s. 3, items 1 and 3 of the Act on Trading in Financial Instruments.

Last, but not least, the registration agreement between the Stockholm Stock Exchange and the companies whose shares are listed, contains provisions that give the Exchange the power to sanction behaviour contrary to the clauses in the agreement.[82] Such sanctions include warnings, the imposition of a fine[83] and deregistration of the company's shares from the Exchange.[84] Deregistration is the ultimate sanction against listed companies but it can put the shareholders in a troublesome position. The situation becomes especially awkward when a company's shares are deregistered because of the majority's oppression of the minority. According to the Act, shares may not be deregistered if it is inappropriate from a public point of view.[85] The problems of deregistration of shares in companies with many shareholders may have caused the players on the market to believe that deregistration of shares in such companies is unthinkable. However, this has proven to be a false assumption.

III. THE RELATIONSHIP BETWEEN SHAREHOLDERS

A. General

The term "corporate governance" is in Sweden to a large extent used when the shareholders take an active part in the management of their companies.[86] An example of such corporate governance can be found in a planned cooperation agreement between the two car manufacturers Volvo and Renault. The players on the Swedish stock market were initially given the impression that the agreement gave Volvo a reasonable possibility, in the long run, to increase its share of the Volvo-Renault combined car manufacturing business. When it became apparent that this was not the case, some major shareholders in Volvo made it clear to Volvo's board that they were going to vote against the agreement at the general meeting that was supposed to decide in the matter. In this situation Volvo's board chose to cancel both the general meeting mentioned and the agreement as such.

The above example shows, together with other recent events, that shareholders at least to some extent take an active part in the running of companies in Sweden today.[87] It should also be clear that Swedish law allows shareholder intervention to almost any extent, as long as only the company's internal relations are concerned. For these reasons, issues of corporate governance in Swedish publicly held companies are, in this context, almost of a sociological nature: when, and why, do the shareholders use their power to manage their companies, instead of voting with their feet? How is the power used? However, this chapter considers mainly the *legal basis* of corporate governance, leaving aside the sociological questions.

The basic Swedish rule is that the shareholders have the power to make binding decisions in almost any matter concerning the company. The above example of shareholder governance in a Swedish publicly held company, involved no actual

[82] The clauses in appendix 2 of the agreement refers to some other sources of self-regulation. See supra at I.G.

[83] Section 10, para. 2 of the Registration Agreement. See *NJA* 1985 p. 343.

[84] Section 10, para. 1 of the Registration Agreement.

[85] Chapter 5, s. 4, para. 1, item 2 of the Stock Exchange and Clearing Act.

[86] See, e.g. Nord, supra note 1, p. 483.

[87] Some of the bigger Swedish institutional shareholders have adopted special corporate governance policies. These policies will be mentioned further infra at VI.A.

decision at a general meeting. This phenomenon can often be observed in practice,[88] but regardless of how the shareholders act to influence the management of the company's affairs, their ability to do so is normally derived from their power to vote at a general meeting.

The articles of association in a Swedish company must state the issues that shall be considered by the annual general meeting.[89] This provision, however, merely expresses the issues that *must* be considered by the meeting, and does not prevent other matters from being put on the agenda for the meeting. It is clear that the shareholders can use their voting power in almost any matter concerning the company, and thereby pass resolutions that are binding on the directors and officers of the company. It has also been assumed that the shareholders at a general meeting can express their view, in a non-binding way, on issues in which they cannot make decisions. Furthermore, each shareholder has the power to put an issue on the agenda for a general meeting, provided that he acts in writing before the meeting is called.[90] The formal rules work in a manner that creates good possibilities for the shareholders to express their opinion on different matters concerning the company. In practice, this often means that the directors of the board listen to the (majority) shareholders without a formal general meeting having to be held.

B. Theories on Voting Rights

Generally speaking, the Swedish rules about voting rights are based on one basic principle and one underlying theory. The basic principle, which is very old and has never been thoroughly analyzed, is that a person who makes an investment in shares shall have the same influence in the company as any other person who has made an equal investment. This principle speaks in favour of the rule of one share, one vote.[91] Swedish law is also based on an underlying theory which recognizes that shares can be issued and traded at different prices. Accordingly, it is pointless to attach voting rights to shares depending on their nominal value. If a company is to issue new shares, those shares are, or can be, priced on a market, where the price depends on, among other things, the voting rights of the shares.[92] Therefore, according to the underlying theory, the voting right of shares ought to follow the basic principle of freedom of contract.[93] Today's rules are a balance between the basic principle and the underlying theory, characterized by practical considerations.

C. Rules on Voting Rights

The main rule is that one share shall carry one vote at the general meeting.[94] The Act also allows companies to issue shares with different voting power, but the difference may not be greater than one to ten.[95] This limitation means that no shares without

[88] See, e.g. H. Nial & S. Johansson, *Svensk associationsrätt i huvuddrag* (6th ed., Stockholm, 1995), p. 121. See also infra at IV.B.
[89] Chapter 2, s. 4, para. 1, item 8 of the Companies Act.
[90] Chapter 9, s. 7 of the Companies Act.
[91] See *SOU* 1986:23 p. 127.
[92] See, e.g. K. Rydqvist, supra note 24, pp. 70.
[93] See *SOU* 1986:23 p. 128.
[94] Chapter 3, s. 1, para. 1 of the Companies Act.
[95] Ibid., chapter 3, s. 1, para. 3 of the Companies Act.

voting rights can be issued in Sweden.[96] According to Swedish law, shares with different voting rights constitute different classes of shares. The use of shares with different voting power is very common in Sweden.[97] The possibility to issue shares with a different voting power is regarded as useful, for example, in connection with the reconstruction of companies.[98] Another situation, where a practical need of a possibility to issue shares with different voting power may arise, is when a small company goes public. For example, an entrepreneur who has developed his company from a small firm needs more capital. The ability to issue shares with low voting power enables that entrepreneur to procure capital without having to surrender control.[99] The use of different voting power also gives an investor the possibility to choose whether he just wants to invest his money, or if he also wants to pay for control. Finally, the use of different voting power has made it possible to retain clearer ownership functions in Swedish companies than would otherwise have been the case.[100]

The shareholders preferential rights to new issued shares are, of course, very important in a system that allows shares with different voting power. If, for example, in a company where all shares carry one vote, new shares, with ten votes each, are to be issued, the minority shareholders can find themselves in an awkward position if the new shares are issued only to the majority shareholders. This risk is to some extent a reality in Swedish law today. However, a resolution to diverge from the preferential rights of the shareholders requires a supermajority,[101] and even if the required supermajority is raised, the resolution may not contradict the general clause in Chapter 9, section 16 of the Companies Act.[102]

The importance of shares having different voting power diminishes in situations where a supermajority is required. Such rules are normally constructed with consideration of both the numbers of votes cast at the general meeting and the number of shares represented at the meeting. In some situations, the requirement for a supermajority is based on the total number of shares in the company. By the use of this kind of requirement for a supermajority it is possible to allow shares with a different voting power, and still give small shareholders influence over resolutions regarded as important to them.

The use of shares with different voting power has not been accepted without debate in Sweden.[103] It is sometimes argued, for different reasons, that the rule of one share-one vote should prevail. So far, the discussions have not resulted in a change of the present rules. One major reason for the reluctance to make changes is, of course, that such an alteration would mean comprehensive changes to the picture of the con-

[96] See, e.g. H. Nial & S. Johansson, *op. cit.*, note 88, pp. 143 and 144.

[97] See, e.g. M. Isaksson & R. Skog, *op. cit.*, note 20, pp. 293 et seq.

[98] See, e.g. G. Kedner & C. M. Roos, *Aktiebolagslagen* part I (5th ed. in co-operation with R. Skog, Stockholm, 1995), 3:1.08.

[99] Cf. M. Isaksson & R. Skog, *op. cit.*, note 20, p. 288. For some legal entities, e.g. insurance companies, see chapter 7, s. 17, para. 1 of the Insurance Business Act (SFS 1982:713), there are rules stating that they may not purchase shares representing more than a certain percentage of the votes in a company. See further M. Isaksson & R. Skog, *op. cit.,* note 20, pp. 292 et seq. The use of different voting power gives such legal entities the ability to invest more money in shares, than would otherwise have been the case.

[100] See M. Isaksson & R. Skog, *op. cit.*, note 20, p. 310.

[101] Chapter 4, s. 2, para. 2 of the Companies Act.

[102] See infra at IV.E.

[103] See, e.g. *SOU* 1986:23 and *SOU* 1988:38 pp. 318 et seq.

trolling shareholders in the Swedish industry. In this context, it is questionable whether the parliament has the power to alter the voting rights connected to shares already issued, without compensation to owners of shares with strong voting power. Such legislation would typically mean that the value of shares with strong voting power would diminish, while the price of shares with low voting power would increase, which might contravene the European Convention on Human Rights.[104]

D. Conflicts of Interest of Shareholders

The Swedish rule on conflicts of interest of directors may be regarded as lenient,[105] but the rule on conflicts of interest of shareholders is even more limited. The Act prevents a shareholder only from voting on matters about the company's legal claims against himself or against a third person in which the shareholder has a substantial interest, and in matters about the shareholder's or such a related third person's discharge from tort liability or other commitments to the company.[106] The determination of the nature of a substantial interest, should supposedly be made in the same manner as the corresponding evaluation concerning directors,[107] including the valuation of the interest of directors of a company that owns shares.[108] The rules on conflicts of interest are believed to be compulsory, even in the sense that the shareholders cannot, by inserting a clause in the articles of association, expand the area of application of the rules.[109] A shareholder can, on the other hand, use his voting power in any way he wishes, and also choose to abstain from voting when he believes such a measure to be appropriate.

The rule on conflicts of interest of shareholders prevents shareholders only from voting on resolutions. Since the rule applies only to the issue of the company's claim against a shareholder, it has been regarded as appropriate that the shareholder in question is given the opportunity to state his view on the subject.[110] One effect of the rule on conflicts of interest of shareholders being more limited than the corresponding rule for directors, is that a shareholding director of the board, who cannot take part in the board's consideration on the issue of entering into a contract with him, can bring the matter to the general meeting. At the meeting, he can vote for a resolution approving the company's entry into the contract. This possibility of so-called organ-shopping is intentional, and its purpose is to create incentives to bring matters of this kind to the general meeting, whose resolutions can be submitted to the scrutiny of a court.[111]

The basic ideas underlying the limited Swedish rule on conflicts of interest are that it is impossible to determine in advance what kind of contracts and other actions

[104] See appendix 1, Art. 1, para. 1, ratified by Sweden on 17 April 1953. Cf. Title 1, Art. F, para. 2 of the Treaty on European Union.
When the present Swedish rule was issued, companies with shares with different voting power were allowed to keep their old differences, which is why there still are companies with shares with a different voting power that exceeds the present limit of one to ten. Today, the highest difference is one to a thousand.

[105] See infra at IV.K.

[106] Chapter 9, s. 3, para. 2 of the Companies Act.

[107] See infra at IV.K.

[108] See, e.g. *NJA* 1936 p. 684 and S. Johansson (Bolagsstämma, Stockholm 1990), p. 486, with further references.

[109] See H. Nial & S. Johansson, *op. cit.*, note 88, p. 164.

[110] See, e.g. *SOU* 1971:15 p. 228 and *prop.* 1975:103 p. 392.

[111] See further infra at IV.L.

that will cause the company harm, and that it is not obvious that a certain contract is disadvantageous to the company only because the other contract party is a director of the board.[112] The protection of the company and the minority shareholders is instead supposed to follow from a more substantive test, based on the concept of unfairness as stated in the two general clauses in the Companies Act.[113]

E. Other Restrictions on Voting Rights

According to Swedish law, voting rights may not under any circumstances differ depending on the identity of the shareholders.[114] On the other hand, nothing prevents a company from having shares with different voting rights depending on the issue to be voted on.[115] A company can, for example, have class A and class B shares with exactly the same rights, except when the general meeting votes on a resolution concerning replacement of directors of the board, in which case the class A shares can have ten votes per share and the class B shares one vote per share.

In Sweden, it is as a general principle not possible to separate voting rights from the economic rights of the shares.[116] The ability to use a proxy at general meetings can be regarded as a way to separate the voting power from the economic rights of the share,[117] primarily because a proxy sometimes is given in the interest of the appointed person instead of the shareholder. On the other hand, for practical reasons it seems impossible to relinquish the use of proxies. A shareholder can for various reasons be prevented from taking part in a general meeting, but still have a significant interest in influencing the meeting's decisions. Swedish law allows proxies, but regulates them quite formally.[118] A shareholder always has the right to use a proxy according to his own choice.[119] The proxy must be dated and made in writing. A proxy is valid for a maximum of one year, and can, at least as a main rule, be revoked at any time by the shareholder.

F. Corporate Governance Rules Outside the Companies Act

Rules, outside the Companies Act, related to corporate governance by the shareholders, are regarded as an important means to protect the minority shareholders in at least one situation, namely when a stock market company is to issue new shares to directors of the board or to employees of the company, to the exclusion of the shareholders preferential right to new shares.[120] According to the Act (1987:464) on Certain Directed Placements in Stock Market Companies, a stock market company may issue shares specifically designated to directors of the board or to employees of the company only after the general meeting of shareholders has passed a resolution on

112 See, e.g. *SOU* 1971:15 p. 228, *prop.* 1975:103 p. 391 and G. Kedner & C. M. Roos, supra note 98, 9:3.03.
113 Chapter 8, s. 13, para. 1 and chapter 9, s. 16; discussed further infra at IV.E.
114 See, e.g. H. Nial & S. Johansson, *op. cit.*, note 88, p. 143.
115 See, e.g. G. Kedner & C. M. Roos, supra note 98, 3:1.11.
116 See *NJA* 1915 p. 590 and 1972 p. 29.
117 Cf. S. Johansson, *op. cit.*, note 108, pp. 242 et seq.
118 Chapter 9, s. 2 of the Companies Act.
119 The company cannot regulate what person or persons that may be appointed as proxies. See, e.g. S. Johansson, *op. cit.*, note 108, p. 239.
120 Chapter 4, s. 2 of the Companies Act.

the issue, with a majority of 90 per cent of both the votes cast and the shares represented at the meeting. The Act also applies when shares are sold to persons within the restricted group and when the relevant action – whether an issue of new shares or a sale of old ones – takes place in a subsidiary to a stock market company. In the latter case the general meeting of shareholders in the stock market company, i.e. the parent company, must approve the transaction, which might be regarded as an interesting version of the judgment of the German *Bundesgerichtshof* in the so-called *Holzmüller-entscheidung*.[121] The Act also prevents the general meeting of shareholders in a stock market company from empowering the board of directors to issue new shares to persons covered by the Act. The Act on Certain Directed Placements in Stock Market Companies has formed the basis for decisions in some cases before the Swedish Securities Council,[122] but the Swedish SROs have mainly considered questions about equal treatment of players on the market and about full and correct information.

IV. THE RELATIONSHIP BETWEEN COMPANY ORGANS

A. General

The Swedish company structure is not organized exactly as the continental two-tier system, nor is it built up as a one-tier system. The legal structure of Swedish companies limited by shares, consists of at least two organs: the general meeting of shareholders and the board of directors. Companies with a share capital of at least SEK 1 million must, in addition to the board of directors, have a special managing director,[123] who may but does not have to be a director of the board. The power not reserved for the general meeting is exercised by the board, or divided between the board and the managing director.

Before considering the legal regulations that govern the distribution of power within companies, it is observed that the managerial revolution[124] can be observed in Sweden,[125] as in other countries. The primary task of the general meeting is to elect directors to the board,[126] while the business and affairs of the company as a

[121] *BGHZ* 82 p. 122 (1983). In this case, a company transferred a great part of its assets to a subsidiary. The transaction took place after a decision by the board (Vorstand), without consent by the general meeting of shareholders. The German Bundesgerichtshof found that the situation arisen contained such great dangers for the shareholders in the parent company, that the company was prohibited from taking part in any raise in the capital of the subsidiary, without prior consent from the parent company's general meeting of shareholders.

[122] See, e.g. the Securities Council's opinion 1989:1, 1990:3 and 1990:8.

[123] In companies with a share capital of less than SEK 1 million, a managing director may be appointed. In *SOU* 1995:44 it is proposed that public, but not private, companies should be required to have a managing director.

[124] See J. Burnham, *The Managerial Revolution. What is happening in the world?* (New York, 1941).

[125] See, e.g. S. Johansson, *op. cit.*, note 108, pp. 150 et seq., L. Lidén, *Makten över företaget* (Stockholm, 1973), pp. 73 et seq. passim, H. Nial & S. Johansson, *op. cit.*, note 88, pp. 120 et seq. and K. Rodhe, *Aktiebolagsrätt* (17th ed., Stockholm 1995), pp. 178, et seq.

[126] Chapter 8, s. 1, para. 2 of the Companies Act. The power of the general meeting to appoint directors is reduced by the employees right to appoint directors according to the Act (1987:1245) on Board Representation for Employees in the Private Sector. Furthermore, the articles of association can give the power to appoint one or more directors to someone else (see chapter 8, s. 1, para. 2 of the Companies Act).

main rule shall be managed by or under the direction of the board of directors.[127] Moreover, the general meeting is the only organ within a company that can pass resolutions in certain matters of great importance to the shareholders, such as a decision to liquidate the company,[128] decisions to increase or reduce the share capital,[129] appointing auditors,[130] and granting the directors discharge from liability.[131]

B. The Shareholder's Power

In general, the question of shareholder power can be approached in two different ways. In some jurisdictions, the main rule is that the general meeting cannot give orders to the board of directors in matters that are within the board's authority.[132] This solution is called the constitutional approach.[133] The second way of approaching the problem of distributing power within companies (the contractual approach) is, as indicated above, found in Sweden, for example, where the general meeting of shareholders is regarded as the supreme authority of the company. The general meeting may pass resolutions and give binding directions to the directors in all matters concerning the company,[134] with a few exceptions, some of which will be considered below. Of course, that the shareholders in a general meeting are able to pass a resolution on any matter concerning the company, is not the same thing as being able to decide whatever they want.[135] Resolutions at general meetings may not violate compulsory rules in other legislation, for example, labour laws and environmental laws. The power of the majority of the shareholders is also reduced by the provisions of the Companies Act that aim to protect minority shareholders, the company's creditors and other third parties.

With some exceptions, the shareholders' ability to protect their interests in relation to the board of directors and the managing director, is practically unlimited. The shareholders themselves can pass resolutions on managerial matters, and they can, at

[127] Chapter 8, s. 6 of the Companies Act.

[128] Ibid., chapter 13, s. 1, para. 1.

[129] Ibid., chapter 4, s. 1, para. 2 and chapter 6, s. 2, para. 1.

[130] Ibid., chapter 10, s. 1, para. 1.

[131] Ibid., chapter 9, s. 5, para. 2, item 3 and chapter 15, s. 5, para. 1.

[132] See, e.g. s. 119, para. 2 in the German Aktiengesetz.

[133] See further, e.g. S. Johansson, "The Allocation of Power Between the Management and the General Meeting of Shareholders", *Scandinavian Studies in Law* 1992, pp. 127 et seq.

[134] See, e.g. H. Nial & S. Johansson, *op. cit.*, note 88, p. 112.

An example of the power of the general meeting is found in the Swedish Supreme Court case *NJA* 1960 p. 698. The general meeting of shareholders in a Swedish company does not have the power to appoint the managing director of the company. In the case the general meeting nevertheless considered with the matter of the terms of employment for the managing director of the company. The Supreme Court found that the general meeting's inability to legally appoint the managing director, did not prevent the meeting from dealing with the managing director's terms of employment.

It is believed that it in Sweden, as in Germany (see *BGHZ* 83 p. 122 (1982); see supra in note 112), there is a limited exclusive non-statutory power for the general meeting. See, e.g. *Ds. Fi.* 1986:21 pp. 6, 66 and 69 (but cf. pp. 71 et seq.), R. Dotevall, *Skadeståndsansvar för styrelseledamot och verkställande direktör* diss. (Stockholm, 1989), p. 177; H. Nial, "Till frågan om kompetensfördelningen mellan stämma och styrelse i aktiebolag", *Festskrift till Knut Rodhe* (Stockholm, 1976), pp. 329 et seq. (see especially pp. 341 et seq.) and H. Nial & S. Johansson, *op. cit.*, note 88, p. 119.

[135] See further, e.g. S. Johansson, *op. cit.*, note 108, pp. 95 et seq.

any time, with or without proper cause, remove the directors and replace them with other persons.[136] Therefore, a view that treats the directors of the board and the shareholders as opponents with different interests, is of minor relevance in Sweden.

Even though the Swedish system for distribution of power in companies may be regarded as a bit peculiar from an international point of view, it is easy to see why the system is built up as it is. In many jurisdictions there are two kinds of companies with limited personal liability. In at least some of those jurisdictions, the owners are entitled to make decisions in all matters concerning the company, when the company is of the kind meant to be used by smaller firms. This rule makes perfect sense in a capitalistic system that acknowledges the right to private ownership. Therefore, and taking into consideration that – until 1 January 1995 – only one kind of company with limited personal liability existed in Sweden, it is easy to give an historic explanation for the Swedish system of distribution of power between company organs. Since there was only one kind of company, the same rule had to apply to all companies, from the smallest firm with one owner and (then) SEK 50,000 in share capital up to the largest company with shares listed on the Stock Exchange.

According to the Companies Act, the only forum where the shareholders may exercise their power is the general meeting, and it is as a main rule the board that calls general meetings.[137] However, aside from the annual general meeting, owners of at least 10 per cent of the shares in a company always have the right to demand that a special general meeting be called.[138] Should the board fail to comply with such a demand, a special general meeting shall be called by the County Administration Board.[139] Therefore, a company's board has no ability to prevent a special general meeting from being held, which often has the practical effect that no special general meeting has to be held. In this context, it should also be noted that the Companies Act contains certain rules that gives every shareholder the right to demand that the directors provide information about the company at a general meeting, but nowhere else.[140] This right is a right for the shareholders alone, and the board can even refuse to answer a question if it believes that an answer would lead to severe harm for the company.

C. Limitations on the Shareholder's Power

The powers of the shareholders in Swedish companies are not completely unlimited. To begin with, a resolution passed at a general meeting does not prevent a subsequent general meeting from passing a contrary resolution.[141] Furthermore, the general meeting does not possess the power to bind the company in relation to third parties. The ability of the shareholders, in their capacity of shareholders, to run the affairs of the company, has – unlike in some other countries[142] – no statutory support in Sweden. A resolution passed at a general meeting can be executed

[136] In *SOU* 1995:44 it is even proposed that clauses in the articles of association that stipulate a super-majority to pass valid resolutions to remove directors, should be forbidden in the Act.
[137] Chapter 9, s. 8 of the Companies Act.
[138] Ibid., chapter 9, s. 6.
[139] Ibid., chapter 9, s. 8.
[140] Ibid., chapter 9, s. 12.
[141] See, e.g. *NJA* 1894 p. 228, 1922 p. 122 and S. Johansson, *op. cit.*, note 108, pp. 504 et seq., with further references.
[142] See, e.g. s. 351 in Delaware General Corporation Law.

only by the board of directors.[143] The board of directors in its turn, is not allowed to execute a resolution passed at a general meeting, if the resolution is invalid because it is contrary to the Companies Act or to the articles of association.[144] The general meeting, therefore, has no ability, against the will of the board of directors, to cause the execution of a resolution that exceeds the limits set by law and the articles.[145]

The inability of the general meeting, in relation to a third party, to run the business of the company, has been extended to a rule stating that the general meeting may not take the place of the board, not even in the internal relations of the company.[146] The board's position in the company, and the directors liability in their function as a part of a company organ, are defined by compulsory law. With a few exceptions, the general meeting therefore has the power to pass resolutions on every *single* subject concerning the company, but cannot expand its power to every detail of the daily affairs of the company. The limits of the power of the general meeting in this connection are very unclear, but that uncertainty seems to be of less practical importance.

The power of the general meeting is also limited with respect to some specific decisions. First, and maybe most important, a resolution declaring dividends to the shareholders must be passed at an annual general meeting, but the meeting has not – except in situations of starvation of the minority shareholders[147] – the power to declare dividends in greater amounts than proposed or accepted by the board of directors.[148] The board may also veto a resolution on the reduction of the company's share capital, if the funds that are made available by the reduction are put at the shareholders' disposal or paid to the shareholders.[149]

However, the importance of the board's right to limit the dividends in a company should not be exaggerated. This power does not extend to an ability to prevent the minority shareholders from using their right to demand the declaration of dividends as a protection against so-called starvation or freeze-outs.[150] Furthermore, the general meeting in a Swedish company can always, with or without proper cause, remove any director that has been appointed by a general meeting.[151] Consequently, as a last resource, the shareholders may remove their directors, and instead appoint persons that share the shareholders' opinion on suitable dividends.[152] Unless all shareholders are present, the general meeting's power to remove directors is, of course, like all other matters, limited by the framework of the agenda that has been made

143 See, e.g. S. Johansson, *op. cit.*, note 108, pp. 98 et seq. The execution of a resolution passed at a general meeting can, of course, also be delegated by the board to the managing director or some other representative of the company.

144 Chapter 8, s. 13, para. 2 of the Companies Act.

145 Another matter is that the general meeting has the power to replace the directors. See chapter 8, s. 2, para. 1 of the Companies Act, and supra at IV.B.

146 See S. Johansson, *op. cit.*, note 108, pp. 151 et seq., with further references.

147 See further infra.

148 Chapter 12, s. 3, para. 1, item 2 of the Companies Act.

149 Ibid., chapter 6, s. 2, para. 2.

150 See S. Johansson, *op. cit.*, note 108, pp. 151 and 308.

151 Chapter 8, s. 2, para. 1 of the Companies Act. See *SOU* 1971:15 p. 205, *prop.* 1975:103 p. 370, S. Johansson, *op. cit.*, note 108, pp. 365 et seq., G. Kedner & C. M. Roos, supra note 98; H. Nial & S. Johansson, *op. cit.*, note 88, p. 113 and K. Rodhe, *op. cit.*, note 125, p. 201.

152 See *prop.* 1975:103 p. 237. Cf. G. Kedner, C. M. Roos & R. Skog, *Aktiebolagslagen* part II (5th ed., Stockholm, 1996) (12:3.01) and K. Rodhe, *op. cit.*, note 125, pp. 180 et seq.

known to the shareholders before the meeting,[153] but the rules leave the ultimate power to declare dividends in the hands of the shareholders.[154]

Another example of an area, where the general meeting of shareholders has no power to pass resolutions, is the appointment of the managing director.[155] The managing director is the company organ that is charged with the operation of the daily affairs of the company. He is supervised by the board of directors, whose decisions he is obliged to obey.[156] The power to appoint the managing director, therefore, rests exclusively with the board.[157]

D. Voluntary Limitations of the Power of Majority Shareholders

Since the shareholders today possess almost all of the internal power in Swedish companies, it is less interesting to discuss whether the majority shareholders can change or alter that power, beyond a few general remarks. First, the shareholders have little or no possibility to expand their power. The matters where the shareholders' power is reduced are regulated by compulsory legislation, which cannot be derogated from. The only way for Swedish shareholders formally to expand their actual power is to insert a clause in the articles of association, stating that the board may not take some actions without consent from the general meeting. Such clauses are legal only if they are restricted to some specific issues and they are hardly ever used in publicly held companies. A third party, entering into a contract with a company, do not have to pay any attention to this kind of restriction.[158] Secondly, the shareholders can reduce their power by inserting a clause in the articles of association, stating that some kinds of decisions require either approval from someone else, for example, the government, or a supermajority. Such clauses exist, but they are unusual, and are therefore left aside in this chapter.

E. Limitation of Minority Rights

Another question is whether the majority shareholders can reduce the minority's possibilities to influence the company's business and protect their interests. The answer in principle to this question is no. For decisions that demand a supermajority, for example, decisions to alter the articles of association[159] and decisions to grant the directors of the board discharge from liability,[160] the requirements can be raised, but not reduced, in the articles of association.[161] The basic protection of the minority shareholders is supposed to follow from the principle of equal treatment of the

153 See S. Johansson, *op. cit.*, note 108, pp. 299 et seq.

154 See also M. Isaksson & R. Skog, *op. cit.*, note 20, p. 298, with figures on immediate changes of management after successful takeovers.

155 Chapter 8, s. 3, para. 1 of the Companies Act states that the board shall appoint "one" managing director. The use of the word "one" means that the board in a Swedish company cannot appoint more than one managing director. See, e.g. G. Kedner & C. M. Roos, *Aktiebolagslagen* part I (5th ed. in cooperation with R. Skog, Stockholm, 1995), 8:3.01.

156 Chapter 8, s. 6, para. 1 of the Companies Act.

157 Ibid., chapter 8, s. 3, para. 1. Cf. *NJA* 1960 p. 698, ref. in note 134 supra.

158 Chapter 8, s. 14, para. 2, item 2 of the Companies Act.

159 Ibid., chapter 9, ss. 14 and 15.

160 Ibid., chapter 15, s. 5, para. 1.

161 Ibid., chapter 9, s. 13, para. 2, item 2. See, e.g. H. Nial & S. Johansson,, *op. cit.*, note 88, p. 192.

shareholders[162] and from two general clauses,[163] stating that neither the general meeting, nor the directors, may pass any resolution or take any action aimed at giving an undue advantage to a shareholder or another person to the detriment of the company or other shareholders.[164] The general clauses are compulsory and so is the principle of equal treatment of the shareholders, with the modification that exceptions from the principle can be made by inserting a clause to that effect in the articles of association. Thus, it can be concluded that the majority shareholders have some ability to reduce the power of the minority by altering the articles of association, e.g. by reducing the voting power connected to a minority's shares. However, if such alteration is meant to affect shares already issued, the decision must be made with such a high supermajority that it in practice is impossible to make without the consent of the minority shareholders.[165] In publicly held companies such a decision is hardly ever possible to make at all.

F. The Purpose of the Company's Business and the Interest of the Company

An important rule in this context is the one on the purpose of a company's business, which *in dubio* is to make a profit for the shareholders.[166] This rule applies to all company organs, which must always act in a way that is not contrary to the company's purpose. This means that the company organs must at all time consider the economic interests of the shareholders. Another thing is that an action that is profitable in the long run can be expensive from a more short-term point of view, and *vice versa*.[167] An action can also be profitable on a more non-tangible level, for example, when a company donates money to charity or protects the environment in a way that is more efficient, but also more expensive, than required by law. Therefore, the rule about the company's business purpose in reality gives the board of directors a broad spectrum of actions, that can all be claimed to fall within the framework of the company's business purpose. The purpose of a company's business can be reached in basically three ways. First, the company can earn money and pay dividends to the shareholders. Secondly, the company can earn money and not pay dividends to the shareholders, which makes the company rich and causes the price of the shares to rise.[168] Thirdly, the company can carry out its business in a way that creates no profit at all to the company, but lets the shareholders use the company's assets at a low price.[169] As long as all the shareholders agree, the Act has nothing to say about the choice between the three methods mentioned.

162 Cf. chapter 3, s. 1, para. 1.
163 Ibid., chapter 8, s. 13, para. 1 and chapter 9, s. 16.
164 See further, e.g. S. Johansson, *op. cit.*, note 108, pp. 118 et seq.
165 Such a decision require a majority of 100 per cent of the shareholders at the general meeting, representing at least 90 per cent of the shares in the company (see chapter 9, s. 15, para. 1, item 3 of the Companies Act).
166 Chapter 12, s. 1, para. 2 of the Companies Act *e contrario*.
167 See further, e.g. S. Johansson, *op. cit.*, note 108, pp. 114 et seq., with further references.
168 This second way of making a profit for the shareholders was, for tax reasons, very popular in Sweden some years ago.
169 Cf. the situation in *NJA* 1947 p. 647. The third method is, of course, hardly ever possible to use in publicly held companies.

The Supreme Court has stated that the interests of the company are nothing more or less than the joint interests of the company's shareholders.[170] The view, that the law recognize a separate interest for the company as such, must therefore be regarded as rejected as far as present Swedish law is concerned.

G. The Relation Between the Shareholders and the Board in Practice

To a certain extent, boards of directors in Swedish companies collect proxies from the shareholders,[171] but there has only been a few real proxy contests in Sweden. Instead, the shares in several publicly held companies are owned by a few large shareholders, who appear at the general meetings. The strong position of the Swedish shareholders, naturally, has the effect that the owners and the controllers of Swedish companies are the same persons. However, the use of shares with different voting power can give shareholders with a relatively small proportion of the shares in a company a controlling position. The 25 companies with highest market capitalization on the Stockholm Stock Exchange in January 1992 were controlled by the following owners: investment companies controlled nine companies, non-financial companies controlled four companies, foundations controlled two companies, the Swedish State controlled one company, four companies had no controlling owner, due to cross-ownership, and five companies had no controlling owner, due to restriction on the right to vote.[172]

The Companies Act is based on the presumption that the shareholders' power is exercised at the general meeting of shareholders. In reality, there are rarely any real conflicts or discussions at general meetings. Instead, the board is informed of the majority shareholders' views in a more informal way.[173] This, however, does not diminish the importance of the rules that regulate the shareholders' power, for these provide the stick that enable the shareholders to speak softly to the board. The rules can also be used by minority shareholders to protect their interests.

H. The Board

The primary tasks of the board are to appoint the managing director in companies that must have one,[174] and to supervise the work of the managing director. Also, the board often passes resolutions on important matters, that are not decided by the general meeting. Actually, the Companies Act is based on the assumption that the board decides in more important matters.[175] Finally, the board is, in relation to the managing director, the superior company organ. The board has the power to do anything that the managing director can do, except reduce the managing director to a mere supernumerary. This rule is based on the same arguments as those that are put forward to motivate that the general meeting is not allowed to take the place of the

170 *NJA* 1981 p. 1117. See S. Johansson & L. Pehrson, Styrelsejäv, *Juridisk Tidskrift* 1992-93, p. 426, Hj. Karlgren, *Studier över privaträttens juridiska personer* (Gothenburg, 1929), p. 236 and K. Rodhe, *op. cit.*, note 125, p. 267.

171 See, for one practical example of a board collecting proxies, S. Johansson, *op. cit.*, note 108, pp. 244 f.

172 See M. Isaksson & R. Skog, *op. cit.*, note 20, p. 292 (Table 2).

173 See, e.g. H. Nial & S. Johansson, *op. cit.*, note 88, p. 121.

174 See chapter 8, s. 3, para. 1 of the Companies Act.

175 Ibid., chapter 8, s. 6, para. 1.

board.[176] The right of the board is, in this context, a power to decide in all matters concerning the company that are not reserved exclusively for the general meeting, as long as the general meeting has not decided otherwise. The nature of the assignment of the director of a board is somewhat unclear. Some legal scholars are of the opinion that being a director is a kind of assignment that often is not to be paid, unless otherwise decided by the general meeting.[177] However, it seems more likely that a director *in dubio* has the right to a fee on the same grounds as any other agent.[178]

I. The Managing Director

The managing director has the power to decide in all matters concerning the company that are not referred to the exclusive power of the general meeting or the board of directors, as long as the general meeting or the board has not decided otherwise. The basic content of the managing director's power is to decide and act in matters concerning day-to-day business. In his work, the managing director must obey the board's instructions.[179] Unlike a director of the board, the managing director is almost always employed by the company. However, the legal position of managing director follows the appointment of the board of directors, and the board can remove the managing director instantly, even though he is still employed by the company and still has the right to salary and other benefits according to the employment contract.

J. Fiduciary Duties of the Directors

In the nineteenth century, it was argued that the directors should be considered as agents for the shareholders.[180] This view was, however, abandoned before the turn of the century, and today the directors of a Swedish company are regarded as agents of the company. The basic rule about directors' liability to the company is found in chapter 15, section 1, item 1 of the Companies Act, which states that a director has to pay for any damage that he has caused the company by wilful or negligent actions. This is basically the same rule that applies to any agent.

In principle, the directors' fiduciary duties are derived from the provision in chapter 15, section 1, item 1 of the Companies Act. Basically, the fiduciary duties have the same meaning in Sweden as in most countries. The directors have a duty of loyalty and a duty of care.[181] The directors' fiduciary duty has practically no limits, besides the fact that it only demands loyalty and care and is sanctioned by a *culpa*-rule. The broad scope of the fiduciary duties in Swedish law can be explained mainly by two circumstances. First, the assignment of a director of a board is looked upon as an assignment of trust,[182] and the law protects that trust by giving a broad scope to the fiduciary duties of a director. Secondly, the board of directors is a mandatory company organ, that shall manage the company's business and affairs

176 See supra at IV.C.

177 See, e.g. G. Kedner & C. M. Roos, *op. cit.*, note 98, 9:5.05. It is, of course, very common that the general meeting decides about fees to the directors.

178 Cf. chapter 18, s. 5 of the Trade Code. See S. Johansson, *op. cit.*, note 108, p. 336.

179 Chapter 8, s. 6, para. 1 of the Companies Act.

180 See J. Hagströmer, *Om aktiebolag enligt svensk rätt* diss. (Upsala, 1872), p. 240.

181 See further R. Dotevall, supra note 134, pp. 278 et seq.

182 See, e.g. H. Nial & S. Johansson, *op. cit.*, note 88, p. 194.

and *in dubio* has the power to make decisions about the company as well as possesses the power to bind the company in relation to third parties. Therefore, the company is quite exposed to the actions of the directors, and needs the protection of a broad scope of their fiduciary duties.

K. Conflicts of Interest of Directors

The situations where the Swedish rules on conflicts of interest apply, have been significantly reduced during the years.[183] Especially the rule on conflicts of interest of shareholders[184] has became very limited. The situations involving actual conflicts of interest are instead supposed to be regulated by more flexible rules, for example, the general clauses that have been mentioned above under Section IV.E.[185] The basic rule on directors' conflicts of interest in the Swedish Companies Act states that a director may not deal with a contract or a court action between him and the company.[186] A director is also prohibited from dealing with a contract or a legal process between the company and a third party, if the director has a substantial interest in the issue, and that interest can be contrary to that of the company.

The Swedish legislature has found that when a director dealing directly with the company involves such a typical conflict of interest, the directors should always be prohibited from dealing with the matter. In this situation, the Act leaves no room for any discretionary judgment; no matter how much the company will gain from a proposed contract with a director, the director may not deal with the matter. However, the purpose of the rule of directors' conflicts of interest is to protect the company from a director using his position to gain benefits at the expense of the company.[187] As stated above, the interests of a company are the same as the joint interests of the company's shareholders. Consequently, the Supreme Court has found that the rule on conflicts of interest of directors does not apply when a sole director owns all shares in the company.[188]

Applied to a contract proposed to be entered into between the company and a third party, for example, another company partially owned by a director, the rule on conflicts of interest is based on the assumption that such a contract is not *per se* harmful for the first-mentioned company.[189] A director is, therefore, allowed to deal with the contract as long as he does not have a substantial interest in the matter that is contrary to the interest of the company. It is not possible to state generally what kind of interests are substantial interests in the legal sense, and this question must be answered on a case-by-case basis. However, it seems obvious that if a director has a personal economic interest of any significance in the business of the other party of the contract, that interest should be considered as a substantial interest.

One consequence of the present Swedish rule on conflicts of interest, is that the law does not prevent a person who is a director in two companies from dealing with

[183] Cf. S. Johansson & L. Pehrson, supra note 170, pp. 418 et seq.
[184] See supra at III.E.
[185] Chapter 8, s. 13, para. 1 and chapter 9, s. 16 of the Companies Act.
[186] Ibid., chapter 8, s. 10.
[187] See K. Rodhe, *op. cit.*, note 125, pp. 242.
[188] *NJA* 1981 p. 1117.
[189] See *prop.* 1975:103 pp. 391 et seq.

a contract between the two companies.[190] The problems that occur when the same person is director of the board in two companies that are parties to a negotiation of a contract, are considered in the preparatory works of the Companies Act of 1944.[191] The Swedish Act contains (with some exceptions that are irrelevant in this context) no special provisions regulating groups of companies. The legislative history states that there can be loyal and legitimate reasons for a parent company wanting to appoint its own directors as directors of the board of subsidiaries, and that too strict a rule on conflicts of interest could result in a difficulty in procuring a sufficient number of persons to fill the boards in all companies belonging to the same group of companies. The same arguments are still made,[192] but their weight in today's business world has been questioned.[193] In its latest proposal, the Company Law Committee suggests that the rule on conflict of interests be extended to cover also the situation discussed here.[194]

Today's absence, in the rules on conflicts of interest, of a prohibition on serving as a director in two companies that deal, or compete, with each other, has in practice made judgments concerning the directors' fiduciary duties more difficult. A director owes his company both loyalty and care at all times. This means that if a person is director of both company A and company B, he must protect the interests of both companies. In a certain situation a director could, for example, be obliged to take care of company A's interests by revealing some information, and at the same time be obliged to be loyal to company B by keeping the information secret. The situation can easily become precarious.

Even if the conflicts of interest rule is not applicable to a certain situation, a director may appropriately abstain from dealing with a special matter. Normally, a director can recuse himself in a certain matter, but sometimes his fiduciary duties can oblige him to participate in the work of the board, if the Act does not explicitly prevent it.[195]

L. Sanctions

The board of directors may, on behalf of the company, bring a tort claim against a director of the board. Since the directors are unlikely to bring a claim against themselves, such a claim will in practice be brought only after the replacement of the directors. A minority of the shareholders can also bring a tort claim on behalf of the company. Such a minority must consist of owners of at least 10 per cent of the shares in the company.[196] Any damages imposed because of such a claim are paid to the company, but the shareholders are entitled to recover their trial costs from the company, to the extent these are covered by the damages paid.

A claim of damages by the company or the minority shareholders on its behalf against the directors requires that the general meeting passes a resolution stating either that the directors are denied discharge from liability or that a tort claim is to be

[190] See, e.g. C. Hemström, "Något om jäv i aktiebolags och myndigheters styrelser", *Perspektiv på arbetsrätten. Vänbok till Axel Adlercreutz* (Lund, 1983), p. 181.
[191] See *SOU* 1941:9 pp. 333 f.
[192] See, e.g. G. Kedner & C. M. Roos, supra note 98, 8:10.04.
[193] See S. Johansson & L. Pehrson, supra note 170, pp. 434 et seq.
[194] See *SOU* 1995:44 pp. 208 and 280.
[195] See S. Johansson & L. Pehrson, supra note 170, p. 422 with further references.
[196] Chapter 15, s. 5, para. 2 of the Companies Act.

brought.[197] It is mandatory for the annual general meeting to decide on the issue of discharge from liability for the directors.[198] The Swedish regulation on the resolution on discharge from liability for the directors is, from an international point of view, peculiar, but will not be further discussed here.[199] However, if the general meeting grants the directors discharge from liability, and it is later shown that the directors by negligence have caused damage to the company, a tort claim can still be brought, if the resolution was passed without knowledge of the directors' action. Therefore, it is not possible for the directors to avoid liability merely by keeping their mistakes or misdeeds secret until discharge has been granted.

The possibility of bringing a tort claim against the directors suffers from the same shortcomings in Sweden as in many other countries. The directors are often appointed by, and connected to, the majority shareholders in a way that in practice excludes a tort claim by the company itself.[200] When minority shareholders investigate the possibilities of claiming damages, they will find that the burden of proof is placed on the plaintiff,[201] and this burden can be hard to carry, since the directors are the ones who have access to the books and records of the company. Furthermore, if the shareholders lose the trial, they have to pay, not only their own, but also the directors' trial costs.[202] In practice, directors are rarely sued for damages in Sweden.

The Companies Act supposedly allows no possibilities to attack the validity of a resolution by the board,[203] but the Act provides that the validity of general meeting resolutions can be challenged at the court by any shareholder, the board, any director of the board, or the managing director.[204] A challenge of a resolution by a general meeting can be successful if the resolution has not been passed in the correct form or violates the Companies Act (e.g. one of the general clauses mentioned above) or the articles of association. In theory, the possibility of challenging resolutions passed at general meetings constitutes a powerful tool in the hands of the shareholders. In reality, this ability is limited by the same obstacles as mentioned above in connection with tort claims. The plaintiff, i.e. the challenging party, carries the burden of proof, while the directors of the defendant have access to the books and records of the company. If a challenge fails, the challenging shareholder must pay his own and the company's trial costs. In practice, challenges of resolutions passed at general meetings seldom lead to court verdicts.

Instead of having resolutions at general meetings altered or annulled, the ability to challenge resolutions is sometimes used to get a court to impose a temporary order that a resolution may not be executed.[205] If the challenging shareholders

197 Ibid., para. 1.

198 Ibid., chapter 9, s. 5, para. 2, item 3.

199 See further, e.g. N. Sjögren, *Ansvarsfrihet för styrelsen i aktiebolag* (Stockholm, 1993).

200 There are, of course, some exceptional situations in practical business life, e.g. in bankruptcy cases, when a company claims damages from its previous directors. See, e.g. the verdict of the District Court of Stockholm on 22 March 1991, Dt nr 47.

201 See, e.g. R. Dotevall, supra note 134, pp. 102 et seq.

202 Chapter 18, s. 1 of the Code on Procedure.

203 See, e.g. H. Nial & S. Johansson, *op. cit.*, note 88, p. 197. In some special situations a court might – according to chapter 13, s. 2 of the Code on Procedure – establish that a board resolution is invalid. This possibility is left aside here.

204 Chapter 9, s. 17 of the Companies Act.

205 A temporary order may be imposed according to chapter 15, s. 3 of the Code of Procedure. See, e.g. the decisions by the District Court of Sollentuna (case number T 221/83), the District Court of Stockholm (case number T-6-236-88) and Svea Court of Appeal (case number Ö 1849/88).

successfully obtain such an order, the company often finds itself in a position where a negotiated settlement is the only economically acceptable solution. On the other hand, a shareholder who fails to obtain a temporary order normally gives up the challenge, because a verdict delivered after the execution of the resolution will be of little or no use.[206]

Challenges of resolutions passed at general meetings are most common in smaller companies. As to publicly held companies, a much stronger factor makes them adhere to the rules, namely the press in general and the financial press in particular. Publicly held companies are constantly watched and examined by journalists, and any breach of the rules always involves the risk of having the mistake announced all over the country. Such negative press can certainly influence the market price of the shares of the company in question, a factor that at least the shareholders – and accordingly the directors of the board – are very sensitive to. As Swedish rules on freedom of the press are regarded to protect journalists' right to publish price-affecting articles according to their own discretionary judgment,[207] public relations issues often come much higher on the agenda when a certain action is planned, than questions about the potential judicial sanctions.

V. THE INFLUENCE OF EXTERNAL CONSTITUENTS

A. General

Everyone concerned must, in one way or another, observe the shareholders extensive power in Swedish companies. The directors of the board, the managing director and all officers of the company have to obey and execute a resolution passed at a general meeting, unless, of course, the resolution is null and void.[208] Third parties, such as the company's creditors, must accept that the shareholders at a general meeting have the power to pass binding resolutions on how the company's affairs are to be run, unless such a resolution violates any legal provision intended to protect third parties.

B. Creditors and Future Shareholders

The shareholders' power is limited by the provisions of the Companies Act that aim to protect those other than the present shareholders, i.e. in reality the creditors of companies and potential future shareholders. Such provisions can be found in various parts of the Act, which also contains some rules that can be regarded as protecting the players on the stock market. For example, chapter 12 in the Companies Act contains rules that, generally speaking, provide that a company may pay dividends to the shareholders only with funds that exceed the company's restricted equity,[209] that the Act contain a provision about compulsory winding up because of loss of capital,[210]

[206] Cf. the situation in case number T 348/94 at the District Court of Umeå.

[207] See *SOU* 1994:68, pp. 71 et seq.

[208] Chapter 8, s. 13, para. 2 of the Companies Act.

[209] See further, e.g. S. Lindskog, *JF-kommentaren, Aktiebolagslagen. 12:e och 13:e kap.* (2nd ed., Stockholm, 1995), 12:2.

[210] Chapter 13, s. 2 of the Companies Act. See from the Supreme Court *NJA* 1927 p. 154, 1942 p. 696, 1988 p. 620 and 1993 p. 484.

and that the Act demands that a prospectus shall be produced and published by the board when a large company or a shareholder in such a company, is to issue or sell shares in an amount of at least SEK 1 million, and the offer to buy the shares is made to the public.[211]

Rules in the Companies Act aimed to protect third parties are often sanctioned by a tort liability for the directors. However, this tort liability goes only so far as to a liability to pay damages for negligent or wilful violations of the Act or the articles of association.[212] The liability against those other than the company is thus not as extensive as the liability that rests on an ordinary agent.

C. Acts Other Than the Companies Act

Substantial limitations of the shareholder's power can also be found in relation to parties other than the management. Naturally, the shareholders cannot use their power to protect their interests in violation of acts other than the Companies Act, for example, the Penal Code, labour laws or the rules governing the stock market. That the directors of the board are agents of the company, whose interests are the joint interests of the shareholders, does not prevent the directors from having responsibilities against others than the company. A company is, of course, like any other physical or legal person, obliged to follow the compulsory rules of the society within which the company acts.[213]

D. The Work of the Board

When it comes to the work of the board of directors, Swedish law (as for example in Germany) recognizes that constituents other than the shareholders, primarily the employees, have an interest in how a company's business is run. Therefore, the trade unions have the power to appoint two, and in parent companies three, directors of the board in larger companies.[214] However, directors appointed by the trade unions are directors of the board of the company, with the same duties and responsibilities as any other director. In reality, the employees' interests in how the companies are managed, are to a much higher extent safeguarded by the Act (1976:580) on Co-Determination at Work. This Act requires an employer to initiate negotiations with the trade unions before making any major changes in the business,[215] and gives the trade unions the right to demand negotiations about anything that concerns the relations between the employer and a present or former member of the union. The obligations of an employer are the same, whether the employer is a company or not, and does not change depending on the company organ that makes the relevant decision. The practical effect of, primarily, the Act on Co-Determination at Work is, presumably, that the trade unions are taking part in the decision-making process at a very early stage, which probably is a great advantage for the Swedish industry. Further-

[211] Chapter 4, ss. 18-26 of the Companies Act. See also the Financial Supervisory Authority's Regulations on Prospectus.

[212] Chapter 15, s. 1, item 2 of the Companies Act.

[213] See, e.g. S. Johansson, *Minoritetsrätt på bolagsstämma* (Stockholm, 1990), p. 7.

[214] See the Act on Board Representation for Employees in the Private Sector.

[215] The Swedish labour court has stated that the appointment of a managing director, which is required by the Companies Act, is such a major change that it imposes an obligation to initiate negotiations on the employer. See AD 1980 nr 72 and 1981 nr 8.

more, the trade unions have a right to inspect the books of employers,[216] a rule that applies also when a company is the employer.

The Companies Act and the acts regulating the financial market do not give the companies' creditors any influence on how the companies are run. Such influence can be obtained on a contractual base, and the creditors ultimate protection is – besides those creditor protection rules in the Companies Act that have been mentioned above – found in bankruptcy law.

E. Other External Influences on Corporate Governance

A powerful device for enforcement of the stock market rules is the surveillance carried out by the Stockholm Stock Exchange. For most companies with quoted shares, the listing is of great value, for example, to raise capital, and the companies therefore have a strong incentive to act in compliance with the Exchange's requirements. To many shareholders – even if not to all – a deregistration of the company's shares from the Exchange would be disastrous. Also, the surveillance work of the Stockholm Stock Exchange is often surrounded by much publicity.

On a general level, it is almost impossible to discuss the factors that influence the exercise of corporate governance. Factors such as the charisma of the directors of the board, the investment policy of major shareholders (and their shareholders) and the liquidity of the company's shares, have a great influence on the exercise of corporate governance, but these also differ from company to company. On a case-by-case basis, pressure from the government or the trade unions can also affect how shareholders decide to act. However, some general remarks can be made. One important factor influencing the exercise of corporate governance is the financial press. Because of the importance of good public relations, media coverage can induce shareholders both to act and to refrain from acting. Another influencing factor is the reactions by the players on the market. Of course, the exercise or non-exercise of corporate governance influence the market values of the company's shares, and this is sometimes, but not always, an important factor when a shareholder decides on a course of action.

VI. FUTURE DEVELOPMENT OF SWEDISH COMPANY LAW

A. Background

Swedish law provides a fairly beneficial framework, within which shareholders can manage their companies, either by replacing directors that do not act in the way the shareholders want, or by passing binding resolutions in managerial matters at general meetings. The Swedish system must, from a general point of view, be considered to function quite well within the Swedish society and to be well-adapted to its purpose. The system, which has worked for nearly 150 years, does not require that the shareholders exercise their potential power, but the power is there for the shareholders if they want it. The rules are very flexible, and can be used to the extent that is motivated in each particular case. Furthermore, the point in giving the shareholders the ultimate power over managerial questions is not to make them pass resolu-

[216] Section 19 of the Act on Co-Determination at Work.

tions on details concerning the day-to-day business of the company. Frequent resolutions of that kind would be a counterproductive way to use the shareholders' power, and the common shareholder can probably not be expected to act counterproductively. The advantage of a system that gives the shareholders such power over managerial questions is instead that there hardly ever has to be any problems with the drawing of borderlines.

Today, Sweden has two kinds of companies with limited personal liability. The vehicle of the public company is intended for big business and that of the private company for smaller firms, which is why one might have expected that the Swedish legislature would have followed the examples from other countries and reduced the formal power of the shareholders in public companies. However, as has been pointed out above, the contractual approach has worked quite well in Sweden, and there is no passage in the preparatory works where such an idea is even discussed. The recent changes in the Companies Act were made to bring the Swedish Act into conformity with the EC rules, and since the EC rules do not prevent Sweden from keeping the present system, it is not possible to draw too far-reaching conclusions from the absence of a discussion about reducing the shareholders power in public companies during the preparation of the new legislation.

In spite of the theoretical power that rests in the hands of the Swedish shareholders, the big institutional shareholders traditionally have not used this power. Instead, the normal way of acting has been to sell the shares in companies in which business has not been conducted in a satisfactory way. However, in the spring of 1996 some of the big institutional shareholders on the Swedish market have adopted – and announced – corporate governance policies, to clarify the way the institutions are going to act as shareholders. These policies state – with minor differences – that there shall be cooperation between larger shareholders, that calls for general meetings shall be formulated in an informative way, that the directors of the board shall be nominated by a special committee, and that the boards of directors shall be constructed in an efficient way. It remains to be seen how important these policies will be in practice.

B. The Company Law Committee

In Sweden, the term corporate governance is normally used when discussing how companies are governed, from a shareholder point of view. The Swedish Company Law Committee regards the shareholders' monitoring function as very important, and the suggestions in the Committee's latest proposals[217] aim to strengthen the position and power of Swedish shareholders. The Committee's work has not yet concluded. So far the Committee, in this context, has proposed, for example, rules about clearer calls to general meetings, limitations on the possibilities to give someone other than the shareholders the right to appoint directors in public companies, a broader scope of possibilities to raise capital and rules that would make it a bit easier for the shareholders to claim damages from directors of the board. The Committee has also rejected the idea that the Act should regulate the personal qualifications of directors further than is the case today.

When the work of the Swedish Company Law Committee is completed – and the parliament has had its say – Sweden will have quite a modern legislation on com-

[217] *SOU* 1995:44 and 1997:22.

panies, exchanges and the stock market. Almost all relevant acts will have been exposed to legislative measures during the 1990s. Therefore, it is unlikely that the Swedish legislation will be changed drastically within the foreseeable future. Furthermore, if such changes are to occur, it seems likely that they will deal with more lenient rules for private companies, exploding the possibilities opened by the division of the Swedish companies in public and private companies. Swedish company law has always developed under the heavy influence from the laws of other countries, especially from Germany, and – especially since Sweden now is a member of the European Union – it is safe to presume that the future development of the law will be inspired by corresponding developments in other European countries.

C. The Future

In general, Sweden is becoming more and more internationalized. Therefore, it appears likely that the future development of the law will facilitate international ownership and trading, for example, by allowing the use of the English language at general meetings and when communicating with the Registration Office, by demanding annual reports be written in both English and Swedish or by encouraging appointments of foreign directors (e.g. by special tax laws). As to stock market companies, it seems likely that requirements will be raised as a result of the development process. The Companies Act may for example be amended to require more extensive disclosure or better guarantees for the equal treatment of shareholders in public companies. Another area where Swedish Company Law is facing an interesting challenge, is regarding the responsibility for false statements in prospectuses.

It appears, on the other hand, very unlikely that the concept that company law to a larger extent should recognize the demand for influence from external constituents, would gain any support in Sweden. The traditional Swedish approach is that company law regulates the relationship between shareholders and the limitations hereon that is motivated by consideration for the companies' creditors. Other constituents' demands for influence over how businesses are run, are taken care of by external legislation that has to be obeyed by everyone concerned, whether a company or not. At least within the prevailing climate in the Swedish society, this approach works well, and will therefore probably be used during the foreseeable future. In fact, any development in this field is likely to go in the opposite direction. As mentioned above, the Company Law Committee is aiming to strengthen the position of shareholders in Swedish companies, and this effort is almost certainly going to diminish the possibilities, within company law, for external constituents to exercise influence over how the companies' businesses are run. This development will probably result in fewer company law rules obliging the company organs to act in the interest of external parties.

7

Switzerland

*Peter Böckli**

I. INTRODUCTION

Switzerland is the "land of corporations":[1] 45 per cent of all registered companies have chosen this legal form.[2] That is a sharp contrast to other European countries, Germany especially. In Germany, only about 2,500 (less than 1 per cent) of all registered business firms are corporations.[3] While in France their share is somewhat higher, it is limited to approximately 8 per cent.[4]

What are the reasons for this pre-eminence of corporations in the Swiss business world? First, of course, the corporation itself offers obvious advantages such as limited liability, independence of the business from its owners, a clear and well-structured organization, simple ways for raising capital, and easy transfer to subsequent generations. Secondly, unlike Germany or France whose legislators followed the idea of the corporation as a public company, Swiss law has consistently maintained a flexible framework for corporations, thus allowing a broad range of business firms to use this vehicle. Swiss corporation law today is a law of core rules with differentiations for small and large companies.[5] All of the corporations, from dwarf to giant, whether public or closed, are based on common rules. There are relatively few additional provisions for public corporations (such as financial reporting and share transfer restrictions). Swiss corporation law is adaptable: one can find midget corporations having a share capital of 100,000 Swiss Francs with just one employee (normally the owner and only member of the Board) and behemoths like Novartis Ltd with 117,000 employees and a 1.4 billion Swiss Francs share capital.[6]

* Professor of Law – Universitat Basel. Reviewed version of the paper presented at a Leadership Session of the St. Gallen University's "International Management Symposium", 20 May 1996. The author is most grateful to Mr. David Mann for his advice as to both the content and the language of this chapter. See at the end the wording of the main parts of the Cadbury Report, London 1992.

1 Peter Böckli, *Schweizer Aktienrecht, Darstellung für den Pratiker* (2nd revised and enlarged edition, Zurich,1996), p. 25.

2 *Statistic Yearbook of Switzerland* (1997), p. 166.

3 *Statistisches Jahrbuch für die BRD* (1996), p. 167.

4 *Annuaire statistique de la France* (1993), p. 385.

5 Peter Böckli, supra note 1, p. 5.

6 *Novartis AG*, Annual Report (1996).

© Kluwer Law International 1998

Actually, there is another legal form which has been thought to be suitable for closed corporations: the GmbH (limited liability company) which has been derived from the German concept, like the French or Italian SARL, but this form never enjoyed the same popularity in Switzerland. Only since 1991, when the minimum share capital for corporations was raised to 100,000 Swiss Francs, has the GmbH been growing in number (from 2,756 to more than 16,000).[7]

Another reason for the overwhelming popularity of the corporation in Switzerland is to be found in the field of taxation. For many years, a large number of holding companies have been created in the form of corporations, first of all by domestic business, under the relatively favourable cantonal tax regimes for such entities. But also many foreign individuals or groups of companies formed Swiss corporations as holding companies for the coordination of their international business entities (Pirelli, Michelin, Metro, Richemont, de Beers Centenary etc. to name but a few).

All in all, the Swiss concept of corporation law has always remained closer to the English and the American "Board" system, steering clear of the German "double-tier" structure of *Aufsichtsrat/Vorstand.* But even in Switzerland some hold that Swiss law primarily had the public corporation in view.[8] In reality, less than 250 Swiss corporations are listed on the Stock Exchange or regularly traded over-the-counter.

An entirely different point, however, is the **economic importance** of these public corporations: The group of approximately 100, mostly public, corporations[9] with a nominal capital of more than 100 millions Swiss Francs represents one-third of the stated capital of all Swiss corporations.[10] At the end of January 1997, the total capitalization of Swiss corporations in the Stock Exchange was close to 600 billion Swiss Francs,[11] Swiss total Stock Exchange capitalization thus counting among the top five in Europe, and the top ten in the world.[12]

Like in most other countries, **institutional investors** (pension funds and mutual funds, banks, insurance companies) hold an ever-increasing percentage of all shares. In 1994, the Swiss National Bank already estimated their share to be above 30 per cent. From 1988 to 1993 holdings belonging to this group of investors increased by almost 250 per cent. Simultaneously, the importance of foreign investors in Swiss corporations is also steadily growing: in 1993, their share reached 35.7 per cent with an increase of 141 per cent. During the same period of time, Swiss domestic holdings grew only by 99 per cent.[13]

The reasons for this development, especially the ever-increasing weight of foreign shareholders, cannot be attributed to legal developments alone, but the new Swiss corporation law, enacted in 1991 and introduced in 1992, has played a positive role. Rules for financial reporting have been improved and are approaching international standards. Nowadays most of the important Swiss public corporations adhere to the International Accounting Standards (IAS), based upon an authorization contained in Article 663g of the new corporate law. The restrictions by which a public

[7] *Statistic Yearbook of Switzerland* (1997), p. 166, as for 1995.

[8] Swiss Federal Council, Bill of 23 February 1983 on the Revision of the Corporation Law, Federal Register 1983 II 747.

[9] Peter Böckli, supra note 1, p. 5.

[10] Federal Office of Statistics, *Corporations in Switzerland*, 1988, p. 12.

[11] Swiss National Bank, Monthly Report, February 1997, p. 71.

[12] Banque Pictet & Cie, *The Swiss stock market*, (monthly report), Geneva, 1996.

[13] *Neue Zürcher Zeitung*, No. 236, 11 October 1995, Grossaktionäre steigern den Firmenwert.

corporation could prevent a foreigner from becoming a voting shareholder have practically disappeared and shareholders' rights have been enhanced in many ways. Last but not least, the duties, the function and the responsibilities of the Board of Directors have been defined in a more effective and transparent way: **Corporate Governance** has indeed been a main subject matter of the 1991 corporate law reform.

II. CORPORATE GOVERNANCE: THE "CADBURY REPORT" AND THE SWISS BOARD CONCEPT OF 1991

In the revision of Corporation Law, which entered into force and effect on 1 July 1992, the Board of Directors was attributed new powers and obligations of self-regulation and core duties. In late 1992, the "Cadbury Report" was published in London which established precise rules for Corporate Governance applicable to British listed companies. A comparison shows an astonishing concurrence in the principal problems and ways to solve them.

The discussion of "Corporate Governance" had its origin in the United States and Britain, but spread to continental Europe and suddenly became a topic in Switzerland in the Nineties. Today, it is not without interest to compare the British approach, as laid down in the "Cadbury Report" of 1992, with the Swiss Concept of the three Articles 716, 716a and 716b in the Corporation Law as revised in 1991.

It is a fact that those to whom corporate law really addresses its messages (businessmen) are likely to experience Law and Regulation as a strait-jacket at the worst, and as a nuisance in the best case. Still, in the area of corporate governance company law definitely is playing a positive role of guidance and even, to some extent, of innovation.

A few premises:

(i) This chapter addresses *Swiss public or larger private companies*. This is justified through the fact that a considerable number of the more important European companies today are operating under Swiss corporation law. Smaller corporations do have their own corporate governance problems but they differ in a number of respects.

(ii) Not only is the term corporate governance *Anglo-American*, but also the phenomenon as such. Corporate governance has been perceived as a problem and dealt with both in theory and practice in America first, and then in Britain, as a corollary of another new phenomenon, the growing importance of *institutional shareholders*.[14] In Switzerland it has been taken up as a problem of proper functioning of managerial and monitoring powers at the top of business corporations in the law revision process between 1983 and 1991.

[14] Where institutional investors today own the majority of all outstanding shares (pension funds, mutual funds and other institutional investors combined), Russell Reynolds Associates, *Redefining Corporate Governance, 1995 U.S. Survey of Institutional Investors* (1995), p. 3; Davis/Lowry, "Institutional shareholders to take a newly active role in enforcing good governance", *Journal of British Business Law* (1994), p. 58.

(iii) *Corporate governance* is, as a technical term, hard to define and, therefore, hard to translate into French or German. One should see in this term,[15] whose vagueness adds to its popularity, reference to the *art of structuring the top levels of a business corporation so as to ensure a balanced and efficient functioning of leadership and control.* Although "corporate governance" and "shareholder value" are topics often discussed in common, the notions are different; "governance" has an organizational importance beyond the question of economical and sociological priorities attributed to the main objective of a business company.

(iv) The *Cadbury Code of Best Practice* is largely about "NEDs"; to those who are not familiar with the latest Anglo-Saxon acronyms it may help to learn that a "NED" is a "non-executive director" in the British variety of the English language, more or less equivalent to an "outside director" in Americanese.[16]

The discussion on Corporate Governance has reached a certain stage of maturity also internationally through the publication in England of the *Cadbury Code of Best Practice* for Boards of Directors in late 1992. In the process of juxtaposition of Cadbury with the revised responsibilities of the Board of Directors in the Swiss Corporation Law one should keep in mind the antipode of Anglo-American and also Swiss ideas on Corporate Governance: the German "two-tier" system *of Aufsichtsrat/Vorstand*, established by 1870, in a remarkably early anticipation of modern ideas about separation of leadership and control. Swiss lawmakers have steadfastly refused to adopt it ever since. In fact, the Swiss law's concept of corporate governance probably is the closest of all in continental Europe to Anglo-Saxon ideas.

Following a glance at the British initiative of 1992 and the Swiss Board concept which entered into force and effect the same year, both will be compared with the two-tier German system. It will be shown that self-regulation of governance is a striking characteristic of Swiss Corporation Law. Finally, the chapter will touch on the current introduction of Board Committees in Switzerland and deal with a significant unresolved problem (effective provision of information for NEDs or outside directors) and look at latest trends.

III. THE CADBURY REPORT OF 1992

A. Cadbury's Main Messages

It is hard to imagine today how any discussion of Corporate Governance could by-pass the *Cadbury Report* and the corresponding *Code of Best Practice* which both came out

[15] *Cadbury Report* (1992) para. 2.5: "Corporate Governance is the system by which companies are run", an apogee of the English art of definition; more specifically: "Corporate Governance is the system or matrix of responsibilities of directors and shareholders by which companies are governed and controlled".

[16] As regards the discussions in Switzerland, see Marie-France Berset, "L'administrateur non-directeur de la societé anonyme en droit suisse et americain", thèse Neuchatel (1988), p. 133; Peter Forstmoser, "Organisation und Organisationsreglement nach neuen Aktienrecht", *Schriften zum neuen Aktienrecht* no. 2 (Zurich, 1992), p. 31, Peter Nobel, "Corporate Governance – Moglichkeiten und Schranken gesellschaftsrechtlicher Gestaltung", Der Schweizer Treuhander (1995), p. 1057, Peter Böckli, supra note 1, p. 826 and Rita Trigo Trindade, *Le conseil d'administration de la societe anonyme* (thèse Geneve), (Bale et Francfort-sur-le-Main, 1996), p. 62.

in London as a draft in May 1992. A committee headed by Sir Adrian Cadbury had been set up a year before by a coalition of the London Stock Exchange, the British accountancy profession and other influential bodies of the Island set in Silver Sea, to address, precisely defined, the "financial aspects" of corporate governance. The committee, clearly created on the background of a general feeling of discontent, was to show ways to raise the standards of corporate governance in the United Kingdom.

The influence of the *self-regulatory set of rules* that came out of the effort of Sir Adrian and his colleagues today is by no means limited to Britain where an annual report on compliance with Cadbury has become a listing requirement. In continental Europe, too, it has unfrozen the debate which, for years, was focused on the German *Aufsichtsrat/Vorstand*[17] and provoked either enthusiastic adherence or stiff-necked opposition to the two-tier system.

While the substance of the Cadbury Report and the Code of Best Practices cannot be reduced to a few words, its *salient points* carry, in reality, five fundamental messages:

(1) It maintains *Unitary Board,* but assigns special roles to NEDs (non-executive or outside directors) by entrusting them with *specific monitoring functions.*

(2) It *structures the Board* by formalizing the NEDs' selection, insisting on their independence, stressing the need for NEDs with calibre and giving NEDs the right to independent professional advice (at the company's expense, and outside of the legal department of the company, to be sure). An abandoned controversial part of the draft version even went to the heretic point of calling for an *appointed leader* of those NEDs whenever the chairman is also the chief executive. Sir Adrian retreated on this point, and in the final version of Cadbury, this obvious San Andreas fault in the legal board landscape was deftly plastered over by the request merely for the NEDs to form a "strong and independent element on the Board, with a recognized senior member".[18]

(3) Cadbury in essence calls for *three special Board Committees* composed of NEDs, namely (i) an *audit committee* to form an opinion on the quality of auditing, (ii) a *nomination committee* to carry out the selection of outside directors,[19] composed of a majority of NEDs,[20] and (iii) a *remuneration committee* to review compensation of all sorts at the top level of the company. Their respective Chairs (the "recognized senior members of calibre", to stay within the terminological world of Sir Adrian) stand in the annual shareholders meeting to directly answer questions from shareholders (such a thing, incidently, would be quite unthinkable in Swiss corporate practice).

(4) Cadbury calls for a *schedule of matters specifically reserved* for decision by the full Board.[21]

(5) Cadbury finally calls for certain *formal disclosures* by NEDs: First, on the basis on which they assess performance of the chairman, and, secondly, a report on the effectiveness of internal financial control.

[17] The 5th European Directive on Company Law (Proposal) was – and still is – deadlocked for decades because of the German insistence on "Mitbestimmung" at Board level.

[18] *The Code of Best Practice* (1992), final version, para. 1.2 (2nd sentence).

[19] What has been rejected is a more formal and direct role of shareholders in the appointment of directors.

[20] *The Code of Best Practice* (1992) Note 7.

[21] Ibid., Note 2.

B. Appreciation of Cadbury

The Cadbury approach is characteristic of present corporate law development inasmuch as it is largely based on *self-regulation* and *soft law.* No democratically elected body or emanation thereof was involved in the shaping of the Code, and no such body is involved in its enforcement. Some hand-picked elite personalities of the British establishment drew up the Code, and enforcement goes through the powers of the London Stock Exchange towards listed companies.[22] Quite characteristically for such a self-regulatory approach, Cadbury also carries added recommendations, which are not compulsory but may not be lightheartedly disregarded, such as:

(i) the insistence on interim reports with balance sheet information to be given to the shareholders (something the Swiss corporate world has to live with, too, due to the 1996 Listing Regulations);
(ii) the issuance of a "Statement of directors' responsibilities" in the field of accounting and finance, a concept extremely close to the Swiss law's Article 716a, numbered paragraph 3; and
(iii) the rotation of persons responsible for the company's external audit (something completely unknown so far in Corporatio Helvetica).

Still, viewed from the concepts of Swiss Company Law, Cadbury also has obvious *weak spots.*

(i) Cadbury does not sufficiently stress *internal auditing,* which is an indispensable part of the entire auditing process and without which monitoring is not possible, and which should also be a source of information for the Audit Committee.
(ii) A clear statement to the effect that NEDs should remain *non-executive* is missing, too. While Cadbury appears to recognize the importance of an unhindered area of initiative and free decision for the chief executive management, it lacks a clear-cut caveat against a more and more "managerial role" of NEDs or outside directors.[23] What has been said by a CEO on the relationship between staff and executive management should be applied to outside directors: "Ideally you should have a minimum of staff to disturb the operating people and prevent them from doing their more important jobs"[24] – one should in fact see to it that non-executive directors are not preventing executives from doing their jobs.
(iii) Moreover, within the mechanism proposed by Cadbury, there is a *distinct potential for malfunctioning.* The tasks of assessing key persons and company auditors, nominating candidates and appraising compensation are spread out between three sub-bodies within the main body, each one chaired by a different outside personality "of sufficient weight and calibre". With so many Chiefs among the Indians, a question arises: *Who will monitor these monitors?* The Chairman will have to apply considerable time and effort to inform and rein in his "Sub-Chair men" if he does not want to loose coordination and guidance within the board.

[22] The listing rules impose a continuing obligation on companies to state in their annual return and accounts whether or not they have complied with the Code. Listing Rule 12.43 (j).

[23] The danger is that the Cadbury Code "... will impose a 'strait-jacket' uniformity on companies' structures, a move resisted by the United Kingdom in response to community initiatives over many years", Janet Dine, "The Governance of Governance", *The Company Lawyer*, vol. 15 (1994), p. 75.

[24] Percy Barnevik in *Fortune,* 29 June 1992, p. 25.

A sceptical view questions the basic idea behind the new role to be played by NEDs and has it that "non-executive directors are part of the problem rather than the solution ... it is hard to believe that the relationship between the two animals will be other than cozy".[25] A similar view is shared by many observers in Great Britain who suspect that if it is the role of NEDs to check and monitor top management, the latter must have a natural tendency to promote candidates to these Boards "who can be trusted not to rock the boat".[26] Cadbury has by no means squelched bitter criticism of the Board as a working institution.[27]

C. Proposals Rejected

It may be of interest to have a quick glance at proposals which were rejected in the recent discussion in the UK and the US.[28] These include a requirement for shareholders' vote on the remuneration of the Board of Directors,[29] the prohibition of combining the functions of Chairman and Chief Executive, the rule of compensating Board members *exclusively in shares,* and disclosure of detailed information to shareholders about the decision-making process and decisions taken by the Board.[30] It is obvious that such a transparency requirement for Board decisions would be a prerequirement for a new legal instrument, often discussed and always rejected in Switzerland – the right of shareholders to directly challenge Board resolutions in Court.[31]

IV. THE SWISS BOARD CONCEPT IN COMPARISON WITH CADBURY

A. The Basic Content of the Swiss Provision on Corporate Governance

The revised Swiss Corporation Law which entered into force and effect on 1 July 1992 was essentially drafted in the distant years 1980 and 1981[32] by a Government-appointed Work Group. At that time, in a small drafting team, long before anybody

25 *Financial Times, 28* May 1992, p. 14.

26 John Cadman, "Non-executive Directors: Are They Truly Independent?", *Solicitors Journal* (1995), p. 347.

27 "There are strong tendencies for Boards to evolve culture and social norms that reflect optimal behaviour under prosperity, and these norms make it extremely difficult for the Board to respond early to failure in its top management team." See Michael C. Jensen, "The Modern Industrial Revolution, Exit, and the Failure of International Control Systems", Harvard Business School, *The Journal of Finance*, vol. 48 (1993), p. 867.

28 As regards better involvement of *shareholders,* many more ideas have been canvassed: "Forms to be attached to Annual Reports on which shareholders could send in *written questions* in advance of Annual Shareholders Meetings so that prepared answers can be given and, secondly, for a brief summary of points raised at the AGM to be sent to all shareholders after the event.", Vanessa Finch, "Board Performance and Cadbury on Corporate Governance", JBC (1992), p. 586.

29 *Financial Times,* 28 May 1992, p. 14.

30 Russell Reynolds, supra note 14, p. 13.

31 There is a legal possibility to challenge the Board decision in court in the rare cases of *null and void acts* of the Board, Arts. 706b and 714.

32 *Swiss Federal Council,* Bill of 23 February 1983 on the Revision of the Corporation Law, Federal Register 1983 II 745.

in Switzerland was aware of the term "corporate governance", a double conclusion was reached:

> "First, Swiss law should *not adopt the German system,* with its rigid separation in a mandatory two-tier system of control and nomination, on the one hand, and leadership, on the other hand. Secondly, the Board should either be eliminated as an institution, or then the law *should create a set-up of mandatory functions* to be fulfilled by the Board, and specifically mandate each Board *to self-regulate* its structure and functioning within the new legal framework."

The law, which in the end was enacted practically unchanged by Parliament ten years later, embodies this concept of a Board with a distinct field of competences. It is, strikingly enough, close to "Cadbury" in its main points, but it is not confined to financial aspects. The Board, without a possibility of a subsequent approval of the shareholders' meeting,[33]

(1) has the ultimate responsibility for the *strategy* (*Oberleitüng* in the German version)[34] of the company; [35]
(2) is responsible for the *basic organization* of the company, it must decide on the shaping of the company's *accounting system, financial control* and financial planning;[36]
(3) has to see to *monitoring the executive function;*[37]
(4) elects and dismisses the *top executives* of the company;[38]
(5) is to draw up *by-laws* by which it structures the executive branch and determines its functions; and
(6) it regulates *reporting*.[39]

B. Problems of Acceptance in Switzerland

There is no doubt that the significance of this concept of the 1991 Swiss corporation law had not been grasped by everybody in the earlier phases of debate. And even after its entering into force and effect there was quite some resistance against a more clearly defined function of the Board as an intermediate corporate body, placed between shareholders and day-to-day management. The law now calls for a distinct "shaping and structuring work" to be performed on behalf of the Board and to be adopted by it in its ultimate responsibility. The Board, of course, is a decision-making body responding to the needs of the moment, but it is also called upon to have the final say in the shaping of strategy, financial organization and hiring of the top executives. While in the Swiss view, it is not the Board which necessarily does the actual legwork and fine-tunes the alternatives for the ultimate decision, it is the

33 See Section III.B hereinafter.
34 Article 716a(1)(1.).
35 *The Code of Best Practice* (1992), para. 1.4 and Note 2.
36 Article 716a (1)(2. and 3.).
37 Article 716a (1) (5.).
38 Article 716a (1) (4.).
39 Article 716b (2).

Board that has to order it, discuss it, choose a coherent set of rules, and see to it that these are followed. Articles 716a and 716b are clearly based on the concept of *Board self-regulation* in this core area of Corporate Governance. Indeed, they do call for "persons on the Board who are" – as the Cadbury Report puts it "non-executive directors of sufficient calibre and number for their views to carry significant weight in the Board's decisions."[40]

Yet resistance against the concept of restricted but final powers for the Board (i.e. in the core areas of strategy, financial organization, and hiring of the top executives) has also been voiced by a legal scholar.[41] Rejecting both the wording of the Government Commentary to the 1983 Bill which had explained the specific function of Article 716a excluding interference of the Shareholders' Meeting in the core domain of the Board,[42] and disregarding the precise term *unentziehbar,* which was added by Parliament, he considers a charter-based requirement for shareholders' approval in the core area of Article 716a to be possible and legally effective. The fact that the term *unentziehbar* cannot be adequately rendered in the French language and, therefore, in the French version of the Swiss law must be noted but does not suffice, of course, to explain the theory which will not fail to shed quite some confusion and uncertainty in this area.[43]

C. A Comparison of the Swiss Approach with Cadbury

The Swiss Board rules which entered into effect on 1 July 1992 have a conceptual, although by no means complete, affinity to the Cadbury concepts. Article 716a specifically provides, in its second paragraph, for *Board Committees,* and probably the most striking parallel is in the Swiss law requirement of financial control[44] and monitoring of executive activities.[45]

Otherwise, the weights are placed somewhat differently, inasmuch as Swiss law insists on a full area of *decisions reserved to the Board,* a subject which in the Anglo-Saxon discussions is being addressed, but is less dominant.[46] Swiss law also stresses the final responsibility of the Board for the *basic organization* of the company, something which is not really to be found in Cadbury.

Cadbury, for its part, is following the classical Anglo-Saxon approach in its heavier insistence on *disclosure* (explanatory statements and special reports) and in its formal requirement of three Committees – the Audit Committee, Remuneration Committee and Nomination Committee. Cadbury, moreover, only indirectly

40 *Cadbury Code of Best Practice* (1992), para. 1.3.

41 Alain Hirsch, at the Zurich Seminar of 13 June 1996 ("Aktienrechts-Forum").

42 *Federal Monitor* 1983 II, Nr. 215.3.

43 Rita Trigo Trindade, supra note 16, p. 172, takes a position against that of Alain Hirsch (see note 41 supra).

44 Swiss Corporation Law 1991, Art. 716a(1)(No. 3).

45 Ibid., Art. 716a(1)(No. 5).

46 The necessity for decisions reserved to the Board has been stressed e.g. by Vanessa Finch, supra note 28, p. 589. It is striking, too, that the UK Code of Best Practice has no reference to one point on which the American practice, Russell Reynolds, supra note 14, p. 18, and Swiss corporation law (Peter Böckli, supra note 1, p. 822) converge: The necessity for specific approval by the Board of significant transactions decided by management outside the normal course of business.

addresses internal financial control[47] by obliging the Board to report on its effectiveness to the shareholders. The Swiss concept makes financial control a central element of the Board's shaping and structuring responsibilities. It goes beyond Cadbury by requiring the Board to establish coherent "organizational by-laws" or regulations for the top layers of executive functions.

V. A COMPARISON OF "CADBURY" WITH THE GERMAN TWO-TIER SYSTEM

A. Mutual Exclusivity between Aufsichtsrat and Vorstand

The British were the first to note that the Cadbury proposals (at least in their first draft published in May 1992 calling for "an appointed leader" of the NEDs)[48] went pretty close to splitting up the top body of the corporation in two parts.[49] Indeed, the Cadbury approach was said to lead to a fragmentation of the concept of the Unitary Board,[50] and even to be a Trojan Horse for the introduction of a two-tier Board.[51]

Still, the *German system* of *Aufsichtsrat/Vorstand* (which was introduced, on an optional basis, into the French corporation law, among others, 30 years ago)[52] is profoundly different from the Unitary Board,[53] whether it be organized along Cadbury or along Swiss law lines. The striking difference to the one-tier system is the far-reaching absence under German law of any self-regulatory leeway in this area; there is rigidity and mutual exclusivity of the Supervisory Board, on the one hand, and the Management Board, on the other.[54] In a Unitary Board of the American, British or Swiss variety, as structured as it may be, the executive directors are also directly participating in the final debate of the main Board, even if they are in the minority. They have a word in the election of top executives, too, in Board decisions, monitoring, and also in nominating new candidates for Board membership. In the two-tier

47 It is difficult to see why Vanessa Finch has formed the following opinion: "The internal audit is not seen as a useful and continuing source of information for the Audit Committee.", Vanessa Finch, supra note 28, p. 588.

48 *Cadbury Draft Report,* issued for public comment on 27 May 1992, The *Code of Best Practice,* Draft para. 1.2 (second sentence).

49 "If the members of the Cadbury Committee believe in a Unitary Board ... this is nonsense. If they seek this kind of Segregation, they should have the courage of their convictions and advocate a two-tier Board structure", O. Green, "Why Cadbury leaves a bitter taste", *Financial Times,* 9 June 1992, quoted by Vanessa Finch, supra note 28, p. 593.

50 Gerard M.D. Bean, "Corporate Governance and Corporate Opportunities", *The Company Lawyer,* vol. 15 (1994), p. 266.

51 Ernst & Young, *Response to the Cadbury Proposals, A Critique of the Draft report* (London, 1992), p. 10.

52 *Loi sur les sociétés commerciales* (1966) art. 96 et seq.

53 As regards a comparison of the unitary and the two-tier systems, see Peter Böckli, *Verwaltungsrat oder Aufsichtsrat? Konvergenz der Systeme in der Spitzenverfassung der Aktiengesellschaft, Festschrift für Walter Reist,* Verlag Neue Zürcher Zeitung (Zurich, 1992) and supra note 1, p. 925.

54 Cf. Knut Bleicher, *Der Aufsichtsrat im Wandel,* Gütersloh (1987); Münchener Handbuch des Gesellschaftsrechts, Bd. 4, Aktiengesellschaft, München 1988, 250; Michael Hoffmann-Becking, "Rechtliche Moglichkeiten und Grenzen einer Verbesserung der Arneit des Aufsichtsrates", in: *Festschrift für Hans Havermann* (Düsseldorf, 1996), p. 230.

system, all this is strictly excluded – top managers are legally disqualified from playing a role in these functions which are exclusively assigned to the *Aufsichtsrat*. Conversely, under the Unitary Board system, the outside directors are participating in the ultimate shaping and decision on the company's business strategy, while under the two-tier system this again is as a principle excluded.[55]

B. The Supervisory Board as a Landing Area for the German Mitbestimmung

While, upon a closer look, the unitary and the two-tier Board systems remain distinct in spite of many points of convergence, there remains one overwhelming fact which is often and wrongfully excluded from the discussion: the *Aufsichtsrat* is, in public companies, playing the main role of "landing area" for the *Mitbestimmung* of employees.[56] As things now are, *Aufsichtsrat* in the German reality of today means, to a considerable extent, *Mitbestimmungsrat*. It functions, in this context, as a place for practical compromises in social politics which in essence have nothing to do with either monitoring or nominating functions.

If apart from this aspect there is one definite benefit to the two-tier system, it is its clear insistence on a reserved decision area for the top executive management, as, by its legal concept, the German *Aufsichtsrat* cannot prevent the operating people from doing their more important jobs.

VI. SELF-REGULATION AT BOARD LEVEL UNDER SWISS LAW

A. The Areas of Autonomous Action

The Swiss Board concept of 1991[57] can be said to comprise four areas of *self-regulation* in which the Board is called upon to elicit a *coherent set of rules*, within a certain legal framework but without a duty to follow any given details. Always in a comparison with Cadbury, they are the following:

(i) *Oberleitung* or strategy (Cadbury: "issues of strategy", "full and effective control over the company", and "direction of the company firmly in its hands");
(ii) Basic organization (not mentioned in Cadbury);
(iii) Financial control (Cadbury: "Directors' report on the effectiveness of the company's system of internal control");
(v) Monitoring management (Cadbury: "The Board should ... monitor the executive management").

The Swiss Boards, as mentioned before, are also called upon to establish *rules for reporting*.[58]

[55] Jonathan Charkham, *Keeping Good Company, A Study of Corporate Governance in Five Countries* (Oxford/New York, 1995), p. 347; Peter Böckli, supra note 1, p. 922.
[56] Michael Hoffmann-Becking, supra note 54, p. 240.
[57] Article 716a/716b.
[58] Article 716a (2) and Art. 716b (2).

Viewed from this angle, the Swiss Board concept of 1991 is largely compatible with the latest Anglo-Saxon tendencies.[59] While Swiss company law, in clear distinction from Cadbury, does not go so far as to specifically decree audit, compensation and nomination committees, it is hard to see how a Board of a Swiss public company could live up to all its self-regulating duties without a formation of an audit committee and a combined compensation/nomination committee. Such a Committee can, and should, be small i.e. two to three persons; in a medium-size company a single Board member can take on the specific assignment and prepare the respective proposals for the Board.

B. The Problem of Mutual Interference

An important problem of self-regulation is, however, left untouched by both the Cadbury Report and the Swiss Board Provisions of 1991.

This is the *paramount factual importance of the leader of the company.* While Cadbury insists that "no one individual has unfettered powers of decision",[60] it remains that the leader of a company – be he called CEO or Managing Director, or whatever else – has an absolutely pre-eminent role in leading and inspiring the organization.[61] While it is true that his powers should not be "unfettered", they must be unchallenged in their core area. The more the Board is split up between inside and outside members, divided into committees and sub-committees who end up reporting directly to the shareholders, and the more "their views carry significant weight",[62] the more we should be aware of the fact that a leader, who is in a strait-jacket constantly jumping procedural booby-traps and has to spend his time following meandering committee work, will hardly be able to lead a company to success.[63]

C. Hidden Conflict Potential in the Role of NEDs

There is a problem on the side of the NEDs, too. NEDs are to fulfill demanding roles assigned to them both by Cadbury and Swiss company law: Without interfering with genuine leadership to be deployed by the company head, they should heed the trap of coziness,[64] they should remain independent enough to resist certain stubborn ideas of their chairman, but at the same time be cooperative enough to participate in confident teamwork. Those gifted tight-rope walkers will be hard to find.

59 See e.g. "Self-Regulation at Board Level", in Davis/Lowry, supra note 14, p. 58. (1994) 58.
60 *Cadbury Report* (1992) para. 4.6 and Code para. 1.2 (first sentence).
61 Cf. Russel Reynolds, supra note 14, p. 6.
62 *Cadbury Code of Best Practice* (1992) para. 1.3.
63 For most investors, Corporate Governance becomes an issue only when triggered by the circumstances of poor financial performance, *Russell Reynolds* (1995) 5.
64 *Financial Times,* 28 May 1992, p. 14.

VII. BOARD COMMITTEES

At this point, it is appropriate to add some brief remarks to the most visible outgrowth of Cadbury, and, of course, of American corporate life in the last 25 years: the *board committees.*[65]

A. The Audit Committee

The audit committee, which has made its way to the larger Swiss public companies in the last few years, is a *valuable institution* in general. Indeed it fills an empty space, fulfilling a task which cannot be taken on completely by either the chairman or the main board:

(i) following the work of both outside and inside auditors;
(ii) viewing the quality of their cooperation;
(iii) reviewing their work products;
(iv) drawing conclusions for follow-up by management, auditors and themselves;[66] and
(v) assisting the board in selecting new auditors, when necessary.

Such a committee is valuable as long as the list of its core duties is focused on obtaining a fair view of the audit functions. Of course, the Audit Committee certainly will blow the whistle and alert the Chief Executive whenever it comes across a really serious impropriety or functional disorder. Yet its assignment will become an impossible task as soon as it is called to proceed to audit steps by itself, as its slightly misleading name indicates, or to independently ascertain compliance with auditing standards by its own means.[67] Such a tendency, to be noted especially in the publications emanating from the accountancy profession, as well as the trend to engage Audit Committees in specific investigating activities[68] and to extend their scope of activities to legal compliance – which is a function proper to executive management and monitoring – are bound to confuse responsibilities and will be counter-productive in the end. The audit committee does not audit – this is one of the most basic rules for its functioning.[69] The audit committee, in any way, is treading a

[65] As regards developments in Switzerland, see Peter Böckli, "Die unentziehbaren Kernkompetenzen des Verwaltungsrates", *Schriften zum neuen Aktienrecht*, no. 7 (Zurich, 1994), p. 44 and supra note 1, pp. 826, 932.

[66] The proper attributions of an Audit Committee have been described as follows by Vanessa Finch, supra note 28, p. 593: "The committee should have authority to investigate and seek external professional advice _ its duties should include making recommendations to the Board on auditor appointments, dismissals and fees, reviewing half-yearly financial statements, conducting discussions with auditors on the nature of the audit, *reviewing internal audit programmes* and *reviewing the auditors' management letter* and the company's *statement on internal control systems.*" (Emphasis added).

[67] "The Audit Committee should have explicit authority to *investigate* any matters within its terms of reference, the resources which it needs to do so, and full access to information. The committee should be able to obtain outside professional advice and if necessary to invite outsiders with relevant experience to attend meetings", Cadbury Code, Audit Committees, para. 6 (e). (Emphasis added.)

[68] Cadbury Code (1992), Audit Committee, para. 6 (e). Of course, the Audit Committee should have "explicit authority to *investigate* any matters", but this should be an exception under exceptional circumstances.

[69] It would be even more disastrous for Audit Committees in practice if certain initiatives should be followed which call for the Audit Committees to be *"beefed up to take on greater responsibility for*

difficult path between the auditing bodies, executive management and the main Board:[70] It should never act as a barrier,[71] but as a synapsis. It should not "stifle entrepreneurial skills"; instead of weakening the main Board's awareness of auditing matters, it is to strengthen it.

B. The Remuneration Committee

The *Remuneration Committee*[72] also has a valuable function as long as the scope of its activity is strictly defined. It should shape its opinion not only on the remuneration of the Board's executive and non-executive members,[73] but should also have a distinct role in determining the total compensation, basic pay, performance-related stock options and pensions of top executives who are not members of the Board. Cadbury specifically assigns it the role of determining the basis on which the performance of the chief executive is assessed – something unheard of in corporate Switzerland during these last years of the millennium. The Remuneration Committee is instrumental in avoiding outgrowths of conflicts of interest, thereby supporting the public credibility of the Board as a corporate institution.

C. The Nomination Committee

The *Nomination Committee* (which often is combined with the Remuneration Committee) is not yet a standing institution of Swiss corporate practice.[74] Traditionally, all the functions which "Cadbury" assigns to the Audit, Remuneration and Nomination Committees were matters for the so-called *Ausschuss* or inner circle of the Board (formed by the chairman, the vice-chairman and two or three senior board members) – if these functions were at all taken care of in a distinct manner. In view of the responsibility of the Swiss Board regarding the appointment of top management it is, however, almost mandatory today that the functions of a Nomination Committee – whether or not combined with the Remuneration Committee – be taken seriously. The cases where the Board was asked to elect "names" – people it never saw – to top executive posts were frequent, but by now definitely should be historic reminiscences.

In all areas of Committee work, the main Board holds on to its ultimate power of decision. The Committee's work product, as important as it may be in practice, legally is a structured proposal to the Board. The Committee members are appointed by the main Board, operate in a transparent way, and annually report on their work and results in writing – even if such statements may be brief. Rumours that in some Swiss companies the Chairmen used to discreetly hand-pick some Board members and convene them in the dark, keeping both their proceedings and their results secret, could refer to myths and legends of the past.

cont.

monitoring aspects of management performance on behalf of shareholders", Financial Times, 10 December 1994.

70 *Cadbury Report* (1992), Audit Committee, para. 5.

71 Ibid.

72 *Cadbury Code of Best Practices* (1992) para. 3.3 and Note 9.

73 *"Greenbury Report"* on Directors' Remuneration (1995), Section A.

74 *Cadbury* only refers to it in an indirect way, see para. 2.4 and Note 7.

VIII. AN UNRESOLVED QUESTION: EFFECTIVE PROVISION OF INFORMATION FOR OUTSIDE DIRECTORS

At this point, an *unresolved problem* must be mentioned: although Swiss Company Law has greatly improved the access of each board member to company information,[75] in this area shortcomings abound. While in a corporation where the chairman is himself also fulfilling the functions of the chief executive officer, outside board members are called to monitor and control this central function, it is again this one person at the centre and nobody else who decides on the time, scope and depth of information given NEDs to exercise their monitoring and control.[76] But also in other configurations, the combination of legal monitoring duties with a lack of any independent source of information is a conceptual fault of the present corporate governance system. This is true, by the way, whether we look at the Cadbury or the Swiss legal system. It has been warned that non-executive directors, through this functional weakness of the system "can be expected to be unable to perform the policing role effectively".[77]

The basic information problem for NEDs has in fact been recognized and briefly addressed by the Cadbury Report.[78] But, significantly enough, the 1992 Code of Best Practice itself does not provide any help in this respect.[79] The right for NEDs to resort to independent professional advice at the company's expense aims more at the intellectual processing of information and its legal appraisal than at the proactive sourcing of new information. Apart from the unique "right to advice" there is no assistance to NEDs in getting at information potentially detrimental to the inside directors and, more precisely, damaging to the power of the top executive and his inner circle. Lately, there have been a considerable number of publications also in Switzerland on this subject,[80] but the information problem remains to a large extent what it was ten years ago – unresolved.

IX. PRESENT AND FUTURE TRENDS IN CORPORATE GOVERNANCE

Having taken a view on present corporate governance developments mostly in the UK and Switzerland, and, to some extent, in Germany, it is now the time to look at the latest trends:

75 Swiss Corporation Law 1991, Art. 715a.

76 "CEOs have the power to control the Board... the CEO almost always determines ... the information given to the Board. This limitation on information severely hinders the ability of even highly talented Board members ...", Michael C. Jensen, supra note 27, pp. 863-864.

77 John Cadman, supra note 26 , p. 347; Gerard M.D. Bean, supra note 50, p. 270.

78 *Cadbury Report* (1992) para. 4.5.

79 "As to the information made available to 'NEDs', this has often been sighted as a weakness of the outside director", Vanessa Finch, supra note 28, p. 591.

80 Marcel Dietrich, *Der Verwaltungsrat und seine Information*, Diss. (oec.) (Fribourg, 1990); Jean Nicolas Druey, "Das Informationsrecht des einzelnen Verwaltungsratmitglieds", *Schweizerische Zeitschrift fur Wirtschaftsrecht*, vol. 65 (1993), p. 49; Peter V. Kunz, "Die Auskunfts- und Einsichtsrechte des Verwaltungsratsmitglieds", *Aktuelle Juristische Praxis* 3 (1994), p. 572; Muller/Lipp, *Der Verwaltungsrat, Ein Handbuch für die Praxis* (Zurich, 1994); Martin Wernli, *Kommentar zum schweizerischen Privatrecht*, Honsell/Vogt/Watter (Hrsg.), (Basel/Frankfurt am Main, 1994); Peter Böckli, supra note 1, p. 60 (1994) and p. 779 (1996).

(i) The pressure of institutional shareholders for a more professional corporate governance will continue to be felt. This is a fact, but, on the other hand, the very persons exerting such power as speakers for anonymous investment institutions will *themselves* undergo more serious scrutiny as regards their legitimacy, procedural propriety, and control.[81] Eventually, there must be "institutional governance" rules as well.

(ii) The Swiss Board Concept and Corporate Governance Rules of 1991 generally are in conformity with the Cadbury approach. They call, although some companies and public opinion have not yet fully grasped this fact, for substantial self-regulatory functions of each Board in the core domains of basic organization, financial control, monitoring, auditing review and *nomination.* The next few years will bring about clearer structures in Swiss Boards in all these areas, and five years from now a Swiss public company Board without an Audit Committee and a Compensation/Nomination Committee – however the respective committees will be actually called – will be quite unthinkable.

(iii) The dispute on splitting up the functions of the Chair and the Chief Executive is unresolved. The "Chairman and CEO" remains frequent in practice. Recent tendencies, however, both in the Anglo-American world and in Switzerland, favour separation of the two functions.[82] Yet separation, as nice as it looks from a theoretical point of view, may bring about terrible practical problems as soon as the two corporate heads become rivals and start politicking against each other.

(iv) There must be a strong commitment to maintain an autonomous area of executive responsibility. Top executive prerogatives must remain unhampered by board interference, if the company is not to lose speed. Tendencies to create an entangled series of board sub-bodies, of certain board members responding directly to shareholder questions in the Annual Shareholders' Meeting, and, generally speaking, board paperwork, must be resisted if all these wonderful corporate governance ideas are not to end up in corporate indigestion.

Today there is only one tendency for the quality of candidates for non-executive positions on Swiss Boards: up. The trend goes *to smaller Boards,* of 5 to 12, or at the *most* in big companies and under special circumstances, 15, with a median size of 7 to 11. The trend goes for the recruiting of new Board members through a formal selection process, and on the basis of clearly defined criteria.[83] Boards will have to be composed of people who in fact qualify for the judgment and work which, from the day they are elected, will be specifically assigned to them in the three areas of monitoring, audit review, and nomination. A Board member who does not understand the basic concepts of the company's financial statements and cannot draw concrete conclusions from its flow of funds will become a rarity.

[81] See *Neue Zürcher Zeitung* No. 137 of 15/16 June 1996, p. 21.

[82] The Cadbury Committee did not go as far as to edict a recommendation in this respect. Favoring separation of the functions is a majority view among US institutional investors according to Russell Reynolds, supra note 14, p. 5, in the same sense also Vanessa Finch, supra note 28, p. 593 who says that in the Unitary System the roles of Chairman and Chief Executive offices are often "incompatible." "Therefore, for the Board to be effective, it is important to separate the CEO and Chairman's position.", Michael C. Jensen, supra note 22, p. 866.

[83] As regards the developments in Germany see Michael Hoffmann-Becking, supra note 54, p. 231 et seq.; in Switzerland see Rita Trigo Trindade, supra note 16, p. 114.

Still, there remains an unresolved problem on which corporate lawyers and business executives will have to work intensively: the provision of information to non-executive Board members, and the final question, as the Roman jurists already knew: *QUIS CUSTODIAT CUSTODES* – who will monitor the monitors? The answer is clear: the shareholders. Their job will be more effectively done in a system of good corporate governance.

X. APPENDIX

"CADBURY REPORT" – EXCERPTS RELEVANT FOR SWISS COMPANIES

The Cadbury Code

i The Code of Best Practice

1 The Board of Directors

1.1 The board should meet regularly, retain full and effective control over the company and monitor the executive management.

1.2 There should be a clearly accepted division of responsibilities at the head of a company, which will ensure a balance of power and authority, such that no one individual has unfettered powers of decision. Where the chairman is also the chief executive, it is essential that there should be a strong and independent element on the board, with a recognized senior member.

1.3 The board should include non-executive directors of sufficient calibre and number for their view to carry significant weight in the board's decisions. (Note 1)

1.4 The board should have a formal schedule of matters specifically reserved to it for decision to ensure that the direction and control of the company is firmly in its hands. (Note 2)

1.5 There should be an agreed procedure for directors in the furtherance of their duties to take independent professional advice if necessary, at the company's expense. (Note 3)

1.6 All directors should have access to the advice and services of the company secretary, who is responsible to the board for ensuring that board procedures are followed and that applicable rules and regulations are complied with. Any question of the removal of the company secretary should be a matter for the board as a whole.

2 Non-Executive Directors

2.1 Non-executive directors should bring an independent judgement to bear on issues of strategy, performance, resources, including key appointments, and standards of conduct.

2.2 The majority should be independent of management and free from any business or other relationship which could materially interfere with the exercise of their independent judgement, apart from their fees and shareholdings. Their fees should reflect the time which they commit to the company. (Notes 4 and 5)

2.3 Non-executive directors should be appointed for specified terms and reappointment should not be automatic. (Note 6)

2.4 Non-executive directors should be selected through a formal process and both this process and their appointment should be a matter for the board as a whole. (Note 7)

3 Executive Directors

3.1 Directors' service contracts should not exceed three years without shareholders' approval. (Note 8)

3.2 There should be full and clear disclosure of directors' total emoluments and those of the chairman and highest-paid UK director, including pension contributions and stock options. Separate figures should be given for salary and performance-related elements and the basis on which performance is measured should be explained.

3.3 Executive directors' pay should be subject to the recommendations of a remuneration committee made up wholly or mainly of non-executive directors. (Note 9)

4 Reporting and Controls

4.1 It is the board's duty to present a balanced and understandable assessment of the company's position. (Note 10)

4.2 The board should ensure that an objective and professional relationship is maintained with the auditors.

4.3 The board should establish an audit committee of at least 3 non-executive directors with written terms of reference which deal clearly with its authority and duties. (Note 11)

4.4 The directors should explain their responsibility for preparing the accounts next to a statement by the auditors about their reporting responsibilities. (Note 12)

4.5 The directors should report on the effectiveness of the company's system of internal control. (Note 13)

4.6 The directors should report that the business is a going concern, with supporting assumptions or qualifications as necessary. (Note 13)

Notes

These notes include further recommendations on good practice. They do not form part of the Code.

1 To meet the Committee's recommendations on the composition of sub-committees of the board, boards will require a minimum of three non-executive directors, one of whom may be the chairman of the company provided he or she is not also executive head. Additionally, two of the three non-executive directors should be independent in the terms set out in paragraph 2.2 of the Code.

2 A schedule of matters specifically reserved for decision by the full board should be given to directors on appointment and should be kept up to date. The Committee envisages that the schedule would at least include:

(a) acquisition and disposal of assets of the company or its subsidiaries that are material to the company;
(b) investments, capital projects, authority levels, treasury policies and risk management policies.

The board should lay down rules to determine materiality for any transaction, and should establish clearly which transactions require multiple board signatures. The board should also agree the procedures to be followed when, exceptionally, decisions are required between board meetings.

3 The agreed procedure should be laid down formally, for example in a Board Resolution, in the Articles, or in the Letter of Appointment.

4 It is for the board to decide in particular cases whether this definition of independence is met. Information about the relevant interests of directors should be disclosed in the Directors' Report.

5 The Committee regards it as good practice for non-executive directors not to participate in share option schemes and for their service as non-executive directors not to be pensionable by the company, in order to safeguard their independent position.

6 The Letter of Appointment for non-executive directors should set out their duties, term of office, remuneration, and its review.

7 The Committee regards it as good practice for a nomination committee to carry out the selection process and to make proposals to the board. A nomination committee should have a majority of non-executive directors on it and be chaired either by the chairman or a non-executive director.

8 The Committee does not intend that this provision should apply to existing contracts before they become due for renewal.

9 Membership of the remuneration committee should be set out in the Directors' Report and its chairman should be available to answer questions on remuneration principles and practice at the Annual General Meeting. Best practice is set out in PRO NED's Remuneration Committee guidelines, published in 1992.

10 The report and accounts should contain a coherent narrative, supported by the figures, of the company's performance and prospects. Balance requires that setbacks should be dealt with as well as successes. The need for the report to be readily understood emphasizes that words are as important as figures.

11 The Committee's recommendations on audit committees are as follows:

(a) They should be formally constituted as sub-committees of the main board to whom they are answerable and to whom they should report regularly; they should be given written terms of reference which deal adequately with their membership, authority and duties; and they should normally meet at least twice a year.
(b) There should be a minimum of three members. Membership should be confined to the non-executive directors of the company and a majority of the non-executives serving on the committee should be independent of the company, as defined in paragraph 2.2 of the Code.
(c) The external auditor and, where an internal audit function exists, the head of internal audit should normally attend committee meetings, as should the finance director. Other members should also have the right to attend.
(d) The audit committee should have a discussion with the auditors at least once a year, without executive board members present, to ensure that there are no unresolved issues of concern.
(e) The audit committee should have explicit authority to investigate any matters within its terms of reference, the resources which it needs to do so, and full access to information. The committee should be able to obtain outside professional advice and if necessary to invite outsiders with relevant experience to attend meetings.
(f) Membership of the committee should be disclosed in the annual report and the chairman of the committee should be available to answer questions about its work at the Annual General Meeting.

Specimen terms of reference for an audit committee, including a list of the most commonly performed duties, are set out in the Committee's full report.

12 The statement of directors' responsibilities should cover the following points:

- The legal requirement for directors to prepare financial statements for each financial year which give a true and fair view of the state of affairs of the company (or group) as at the end of the financial year and the profit and loss for that period;
- the responsibility of the directors for maintaining adequate accounting records, for safeguarding the assets of the company (or group), and for preventing and detecting fraud and other irregularities;
- confirmation that suitable accounting policies, consistently applied and supported by reasonable and prudent judgements and estimates, have been used in the preparation of the financial statements;
- confirmation that applicable accounting standards have been followed, subject to any material departures disclosed and explained in the notes to the accounts. (This does not obviate the need for a formal statement in the notes to the

accounts disclosing whether the accounts have been prepared in accordance with applicable accounting standards.)

- The statement should be placed immediately before the auditors' report which in future will include a separate statement (currently being developed by the Auditing Practices Board) on the responsibility of the auditors for expressing an opinion on the accounts.

13 The Committee notes that companies will not be able to comply with paragraphs 4.5 and 4.6 of the Code until the necessary guidance for companies has been developed as recommended in the Committee's report.

14 The company's statement of compliance should be reviewed by the auditors in so far as it relates to paragraphs 1.4, 1.5, 2.3, 2.4, 3.1 to 3.3, and 4.3 to 4.6 of the Code.

ii Audit Committees

1 In the main body of the report the Committee recommends that all listed companies which have not already done so should establish an audit committee, and places great emphasis on the importance of properly constituted audit committees in raising standards of corporate governance.

2 Many UK companies already have an audit committee, and a recent research study ("Audit Committees in the United Kingdom", published by the ICAEW, April 1992) has found a steady growth in their number. Audit Committees are now established in 53% of the top 250 industrial firms in the Times 1000, and the figures rises to 66% if unlisted companies and foreign subsidiaries are excluded from the calculation. Most major UK listed financial institutions have also formed an audit committee.

3 Audit Committees are well established in the United States, where they have been a listing requirement of the New York Stock Exchange since 1978. A 1989 study revealed that 97% of major corporations had them. In Canada, they are a legal requirement.

4 If they operate effectively, audit committees can bring significant benefits. In particular, they have the potential to:

(a) improve the quality of financial reporting, by reviewing the financial statements on behalf of the Board;
(b) create a climate of discipline and control which will reduce the opportunity for fraud;
(c) enable the non-executive directors to contribute an independent judgement and play a positive role;
(d) help the finance director, by providing a forum in which he can raise issues of concern, and which he can use to get things done which might otherwise be difficult;

(e) strengthen the position of the external auditor, by providing a channel of communication and forum for issues of concern;
(f) provide a framework within which the external auditor can assert his independence in the event of a dispute with management;
(g) strengthen the position of the internal audit function, by providing a greater degree of independence from management;
(h) increase public confidence in the credibility and objectivity of financial statements.

5 The effectiveness of audit committees will be reduced, however, if they act as a barrier between the auditors and the executive directors on the main board, or if they encourage the main board to abdicate its responsibilities in the audit area, so weakening the board's collective responsibility for reviewing and approving the financial statements. They will also fall short of their potential if they lack the understanding to deal adequately with the auditing or accounting matters that they are likely to face, if they remain under the influence of any dominant personality on the main board, or if they simply get in the way and obstruct executive management, and stifle entrepreneurial skills.

6 Audit committees will be as good as the people on them: effectiveness depends crucially on a strong, independent chairman who has the confidence of the board and of the auditors, and on the quality of the non-executive directors. Structure is also important, however, and adherence to the following recommendations, repeated here from the main part of the report, will ensure that audit committees are soundly based.

(a) Audit committees should be formally constituted as sub-committees of the main board to whom they are answerable and to whom they should report regularly; they should be given written terms of reference which deal adequately with their membership, authority and duties; and they should normally meet at least twice a year.
(b) There should be a minimum of three members. Membership should be confined to be non-executive directors of the company and a majority of the non-executives serving on the committee should be independent of the company. This means that apart from their directors' fees and shareholdings, they should be independent of management and free from any business or other relationship which could materially interfere with the exercise of their independent judgement as a committee member. It is for the board to decide in individual cases whether this definition is met.
(c) The external auditor and, where an internal audit function exists, the head of internal audit should normally attend audit committee meetings, as should the finance director. Other board members should also have the right to attend.
(d) The committee should have a discussion with the auditors, at least once a year, without executive board members present, to ensure that there are no unresolved issues of concern.
(e) The audit committee should have explicit authority to investigate any matters within its terms of reference, the resources which it needs to do so, and full access to information. The committee should be able to obtain outside profes-

sional advice and if necessary to invite outsiders with relevant experience to attend meetings.

(f) Membership of the committee should be disclosed in the annual report and the chairman of the committee should be available to answer questions about its work at the Annual General Meeting.

7 Specimen terms of reference for an audit committee, compiled from the many examples that are available, are annexed. They are intended simply as a guide for companies who will wish to adapt and build on them to suit their own circumstances. They will particularly need tailoring for group rather than single company audit committees. The list of duties in the annex reflects the most commonly performed duties in the UK and the US but no single set of duties has emerged as standard practice.

8 (...)

8

United Kingdom

*Sheldon Leader and Janet Dine**

Corporate governance has gradually moved into a central place in public debate in the UK. Because of concerns as diverse as worries about international competitiveness on the one hand, and the impact of corporate policy on employment on the other, there is an unusual degree of convergence on the need for change in the management of corporate affairs. Proposals are coming from sources as diverse as the Institute of Directors on the one hand, and groups close to the trade union movement on the other. Naturally, proposals being made differ among themselves in several important respects, as shall be seen. First, however, the issues will be placed in their institutional context; some relevant features of company law will then be looked at in detail, after which the debate about reform will be considered.

I. INSTITUTIONAL BACKGROUND

A. Economic Significance of the Publicly Held Corporation in the UK

As at March 1995, there were 981,800 registered companies in the UK, of which about 1.2 per cent are public companies. Given that many of these are members of groups of companies, it is also important to note that about 30 per cent of the registered companies are independent companies and groups.[1] The category of "public company" can be a misleading one to use when trying to assess the importance of different sorts of corporate entity in the economy. Although the major difference between public and private companies is the ability of public companies to offer their shares "to the public" many do not do so. A significant number are wholly owned subsidiaries of other public companies. Some may be holding companies, formed to manage a group and thus be involved in no significant economic activity at all. The real distinction is between companies whose shares are traded on the London Stock Exchange and those that are not.

* Professors of Law, University of Essex. The authors wish to acknowledge the invaluable and well-informed assistance of Mr. Massimo Giordano.

1 Department of Trade and Industry: *Companies in 1994-5* (London: HMSO, 1995).

© Kluwer Law International 1998

There are about 2,000 UK-registered companies listed on the London Stock Exchange, and the equity capital of these companies has a total market value of £1,011.7 billion.[2] Few of them will have total capitalization of less than £700,000. Listed companies represent about 0.26 per cent of all domestic registered companies.[3]

B. The Creation of a Publicly Held Corporation

There is no special procedure to be followed, different from that for private companies, in order to create a public company in the UK. The law does impose more stringent requirements for the operation of the company, as opposed to its creation, covering such matters as the appointment of directors; accounting; and shareholders voting rights. But the only requirements for the creation of the public company, which the creators of a private company do not face, is that the former must have a minimum capital of £50,000; must have a memorandum that follows a particular form and contains certain basic information; and must have at least two directors. Apart from that, the public company is formed in exactly the same way as is a private company – by lodging the relevant documents with the Registrar of Companies. It is extremely easy as a procedure.

It is, however, much more difficult for a company to surmount the hurdle of becoming a company with securities listed on the Stock Exchange. This point will be treated more fully below.

C. Sources of Law Affecting Corporate Governance

As one would expect from a common law country, the system of corporate governance in the UK is underpinned by a mixture of statute and case law. In the case of the "regulated" sectors such as insurance and financial services there is also an elaborate system of "self-regulation". Of course, much of the statute law has been put in place in order to comply with EC obligations. The most significant statute is the Companies Act 1985 which was a consolidation of a number of previous statutes. Two particular features of the Companies Act are important. The first is that an enormous amount of discretion is left to individual companies as to the detailed management of affairs. In this sense it may be seen as a "minimum standards" Act. The second is that it covers both public and private companies. There is no separate "close corporations Act".

The first characteristic is most clearly illustrated by the fact that the Act does not contain any indication concerning board structures or employee participation. The whole detail of the way in which meetings should be held, votes counted etc. appear not in the legislation but in subordinate legislation (statutory instruments).[4] Furthermore it must be noted that the regulations that are there set out are *advisory* only. They are intended as model rules. So long as a company complies with the minimum requirements in the statute (number of directors, secretary, financial reporting etc.) the exact mechanisms it adopts are a matter for that company alone. There is nothing in the statute to prevent a UK company from adopting a two-tier structure with

[2] *Key Facts about the Main Market* (London: Stock Exchange, 1997).

[3] Mayson, et al, *Company Law* (London: Blackstone, 1996), p. 184.

[4] Companies (Table A-F) Regulations 1985 (SI 1985/805).

employee participation at board level, provided the rights of shareholders enshrined in the statute are preserved. These include section 313 of the Companies Act which provides that a majority vote of shareholders must be effective to dismiss a director. The detailed regulations in the statutory instrument apply only in the event that no contrary provisions appear in the articles of the company in question.

The use of a statutory instrument was intended to permit quick and easy amendment to be made to the detailed regulations as the full Parliamentary process does not apply to them. However, it should be noted that a change in regulation will not affect an individual company unless it so chooses. If a company has any of the regulations embodied in its constitution they will remain as they were even if the statutory instrument is amended. Thus there are very many companies still using the model rules found in the 1948 Act and some using even earlier versions. Some companies have wholly excluded the regulations altogether, others have partially excluded them.

There is a separate statute and rules for insolvency issues.[5] The Financial Services Act 1986 puts in place a whole structure of "self-regulation" for the Financial Services Industry,[6] and issues such as Disqualification of Directors and Insider Trading[7] are dealt with by other pieces of legislation. It will be evident that the sources of statute law alone are prolific. Added to that is the interpretation of the law by the courts. In some cases such as the issue of director's duties the law is entirely found in the cases. There is no statutory description of the general duty of the director of an ordinary commercial company to be found in statute law.

D. Quasi-legal Regulation

Having looked at the traditional legal sources, we must add the rules of various organizations. If the company is listed, the "Yellow Book" which contains both the Listing Rules of the Stock Exchange and a listed company's ongoing obligations will be important. This is increasingly the case as the listing rules have been used as a way of implementing the recommendations of two recent investigations into corporate governance: the Cadbury Report on the Financial Aspects of Corporate Governance, and the "Greenbury Report on Directors Pay". In the former case, listed companies must now provide a statement of compliance with the Code which was appended to the Cadbury Report and represents behaviour which the committee considered to be "best practice" or provide reasons for non-compliance. In the latter case implementation in the same way is imminent. In the case of a takeover the rules of the City Panel on Takeovers and Mergers will have an effect, setting out, for example the duties of the directors of the predator and target companies. This Code is said to be voluntary but non-compliance can be punished by the Stock Exchange or (where the company is in a regulated sector) by its regulator.

Outside the company structure itself the Press clearly has some influence on governance. However, its effect is debatable. One interesting issue which has been the subject of recent heated debate is that of directors' pay (especially where utility industries have recently been privatized). Despite the negative publicity that high remuneration has received, anecdotal evidence seems to indicate that greater atten-

[5] Insolvency Act 1986, Insolvency Rules 1986, SI 1986/1925 (subject to many amendments),

[6] With specialist statutes for Building Societies and Friendly Societies.

[7] Company Directors Disqualification Act 1986, and Criminal Justice Act 1993.

tion given to the pay of directors merely enables good executives to negotiate higher wages because each company is anxious to be seen as able to attract the "best" person at the top of the company.

E. The Financial System and the Structure of Share Ownership

The financial system of the UK is clearly structured so that provision of finance is by loan or by purchase of securities. The corporate governance role of those who provide loan capital is very limited, if we take corporate governance to be concerned with the internal workings of a company. However, the external influence on the company by those providing loans is in fact extremely extensive. While it is unusual for a provider of loan finance to have a representative within the decision-making machinery of the company, the structuring of financial provision may mean that pleasing the bank may be a powerful motivation behind decisions made at board level. This is because loans will be secured either by a fixed charge (mortgage) over the assets of the company or by a floating charge which will crystallize into a fixed charge should there be a default in payment of instalments of capital or interest due. In the event of such a default the lender will have the power to appoint a receiver who acts to recover assets for the company, but with the primary aim of ensuring that the loan is fully repaid. In these circumstances it is uncommon for significant assets to be available to shareholders after the lenders have been satisfied. The power of lenders has been reflected in the debate as to whether banks could properly be considered to be "shadow directors" under section 741 of the Companies Act 1985. A shadow director is someone in accordance with whose directions and instructions the directors of a company are accustomed to act. The courts have accepted that a bank *could* be in such a position although it would require unusual circumstances.

The power of lenders is further emphasized by the fact that the courts accept that the less solvent the company is, the more nearly the "interests of the company" correspond o the interests of creditors as opposed to those of shareholders.[8]

Institutional shareholding has been greatly increased in recent years at the expense of individual shareholders. This has fuelled a debate as to the corporate governance role of institutional investors. Some feel that the maximization of the value of their investment should be the sole concern of an institutional fundholder. This view tends to the conclusion that in the event of poor management a fundholder should "vote with his feet" and reinvest in a better run company. Others have taken the view that they ought to have a concern to see companies in which they invest properly run. In those cases a role in corporate governance may be undertaken. Intervention by institutional investors was encouraged by the Report of the Cadbury Committee.[9] However, such a role is only unusually enacted in the formal shareholder arena, via for example general meetings. It is much more likely that the power of institutional shareholders will be wielded behind closed doors or on a golf

[8] *Lonhro v Shell Petroleum* Co. (no. 2) [1980] 1 WLR 627; *Standard Chartered Bank v Walker* [1992] BCLC 603 and see Dine "Shareholders Denied Voting Rights" 7 *Insolvency Law and Practice* No. 5 (1992), p. 150.

[9] Report of the Committee on the Financial Aspects of Corporate Governance, London 1992. The report to some degree reflected the work of the Institutional Shareholders Committee (see *Responsibilities of Institutional Shareholders in the UK*, London 1991).

course. The extent of this power is therefore extremely difficult to assess. However, it is argued that the quiet use of such power is sensible since if institutional investors were observably at odds with management the share price would be disastrously affected.

The change in the pattern of share ownership was reported by Davies and Stapleton[10] showing that institutional shareholdings in listed companies rose from 20 per cent in 1963 to 60.4 per cent in 1992.[11] However, the authors also make the point that the institutions have normally built up a wide portfolio of shares in a range of companies. This dilutes the possibility of effective intervention in any one company.

The figures leave some 40 per cent of shareholdings in the hands of individual investors. Of these some will be held by management and thus be ineffective as a control mechanism. Other individual shareholders are mostly ineffective because of lack of information, diffusion and apathy. The archetypal individual shareholder in the UK is "Aunt Agatha" who is unaware of and cares little about corporate decision-making and is thus in need of protection by regulators such as the Stock Exchange and the Financial Services regulators.

F. The Place and Structure of Pension Funds

Many pension funds are set up by employers to hold and invest the contributions which are due from employers and employees in accordance with contracts of employment. The fund is held by trustees who will usually appoint a fund manager who will have the responsibility of actually carrying out the investment policy which is, in theory, determined by the trustees. Unless the trust deed confers on the employees a right to have a say in the management of the trust (which it usually will not), they will have no influence over the persons managing the trust or the investment policy.

Other pensions are offered by insurance companies which will suffer from the normal lack of shareholder control but are externally regulated by the Department of Trade and Industry. A small part of the pensions industry is operated by Friendly Societies which are mutual organizations owned by their members. In theory these are very democratic institutions whose rules require the consent of members at every turn. The reality is very different, with many ballots receiving a member response of less than 10 per cent. The running of these wealthy institutions is often left to a small group of persons and passed down from father to son. As with insurance companies, they have external regulators, in this case the Friendly Societies Commission. In theory the Commission must ensure that the interests of members are a paramount concern, but this is an empty power when institutions are aware that if members are consulted only a few (usually those motivated by management) will respond.

G. The Public Securities Market

A full listing by a company may be obtained on the London Stock Exchange if the market value of the shares being listed is at least 700,000 pounds; at least 25 per cent

[10] In Isaksson and Skog, *Aspects of Corporate Governance* (Stockholm: Jurist for laget, 1994), p. 55.

[11] The Stock Exchange estimates that 77 per cent of the shares in listed companies are held by insurance companies, pension funds, investment and unit trusts. (Mayson et al, *Company Law* 1997, p. 184.)

of the shares are held by persons not associated with directors or major shareholders and the company; and the company has a three-year trading record. The Unlisted Securities market requires a two-year trading record and a minimum capitalization of £500,000, as does the new Alternative Investment Market, which will eventually take over the role of the unlisted securities market.[12]

Two tiers of regulation generally affect the securities market,

(i) the Stock Exchange listing rules backed by the Financial Services Act regulations, equivalent requirements for public offers of non-listed securities under the Prospectus Offers Regulations 1995; and
(ii) the authorization requirements under the Financial Services Act 1986, which prohibit the sale of shares by anyone who is not authorised under the Act.

The latter provision is aimed at investor protection rather than corporate governance, whereas the former has recently addressed the matter of corporate governance.

This use of the listing rules for corporate governance issues is relatively recent and follows the publication of a Code of Practice issued by the Cadbury Committee on the Financial Aspects of Corporate Governance. This Code will be considered below, but here it is important to notice that the listing rules now provide that before a listing can be continued, non-compliance with the recommendations of the Code of good practice on corporate governance requires an explanation. Further consideration of corporate governance issues is being carried out by a successor to the Cadbury Committee, the Hampel Committee, which issued its preliminary report in August 1997. Some of its recommendations will also be mentioned below.

Apart from that, the listing rules have long contained the requirement that directors must have appropriate expertise and experience and be free from conflicts of interests.[13] The rules also require a company to be able to make decisions independently of any controlling shareholder.[14] Companies are also required to take steps to prevent insider dealing by taking all proper and reasonable steps to secure compliance with the Model Code on dealing.

It should also be noted that the City Code on Takeovers and Mergers contains rules about management behaviour which the City Panel will expect management to abide by in the event of a takeover.

H. Government Presence in Market Regulation

There is continuing debate in the United Kingdom surrounding the regulation of the securities and investment services markets. In 1986 there came into force a huge bureaucracy to govern the investment services industry. It is known as "self-regulation" and is supposedly non-governmental. Many involved in the debate are sceptical of these claims. The ultimate responsibility for the system lies with the UK Treasury department which has delegated control to the Bank of England which in turn has set up a regulatory authority "The Securities and Investment Board" (SIB). This Board authorizes "self-regulating organizations" (SRO) and "recognized professional bodies" (RPB). Anyone who carries out investment business in the United

[12] The Stock Exchange Official Year Book 1993-4.
[13] Rules 3.8, 3.9.
[14] Rule 3.13.

Kingdom must be authorized by the Board (not encouraged) or by an SRO or RPB. All the securities regulators are thus one or more steps removed from governmental control. However, most of the rules of the SIB, SROs and RPBs were drafted by civil service lawyers and, despite attempts to simplify the system, it remains an immensely complex set of rules, calling for further reliance on lawyers and compliance officers by the end user.

One curious feature of this system is that the SROs have a dual role. They exist both to regulate and to encourage a sector of the market. Further, they must raise their money from the client base whom they are simultaneously policing. This dual role has caused some difficulties. The new UK Government has announced draft plans to reform the system. It will take all regulatory roles away from the Bank of England and allocate them to the SIB. It is also intended to abolish the SROs and require SIB to exercise their current regulatory powers in their place.

So far as the market in securities is concerned this attracts two other sets of regulations as well as the investment services structures. The listing rules have been mentioned above but also deserving of mention is the City Panel on Takeover and Mergers. This Panel issues the City Code on Takeovers and Mergers and is an interesting feature of commercial life in the UK as it has no statutory basis. Compliance with its findings are voluntary although non-compliance may be considered a disciplinary offence by a relevant SRO or cause the Stock Exchange to consider de-listing a company. The City Panel was instrumental in drafting the first draft EC 13th Directive on Takeovers with a view to regulating takeovers in the EC, in particular in ensuring fair treatment of all shareholders, not just those in the majority. However, assistance turned to opposition when the Commission insisted that the body set up to oversee the workings of the directive should have a statutory base. Despite the apparently more flexible approach to the most recent draft on this point, there is still UK opposition.

To the extent that these regulatory measures and statutes forbidding money laundering and insider trading "clean-up" the market they may be said to encourage public ownership. That was certainly the intention of the previous government which was wedded to the idea of large-scale public ownership of shares.

However, it is not clear that the market has in fact been rendered "clean", nor has the drive to wide share ownership been a significant sucess, although a wide number of shares are purchased by the public when significant privatization of industries occurs, these are generally held for a short time and fall back into the hands of the most significant UK investors which are the big institutions, especially pension funds.

I. An Overview of Corporate Monitoring Devices

It is generally accepted that despite the wide range of monitoring devices that influence management decisions, there is little real control over corporate executives.[15] There are voices which regard this as a proper position, but there has been considerable debate over recent years seeking to identify a control mechanism which is effective and yet not so burdensome as to prevent effective response to market pressures.

[15] For an analysis of reasons for this see "Corporate Governance and Conflicts of Interest", below, p. 238 et seq.

Monitoring devices include formal internal controls such as division of powers, legal sanctions available to insiders, formal external controls e.g. regulatory structures and the general legal framework, informal internal controls, for example pressure which may be brought to bear by employees other than through formal representation or consultation, institutional investor pressure, informal external controls, for example press coverage seeking to mobilize public opinion.

The inadequacy of the formal internal controls has been the factor which has fuelled the current corporate governance debates which are discussed below. The division of powers between management and the shareholder's general meeting leaves management virtually free from shareholder interference save in very extreme cases, shareholder apathy is rife among individuals and the growing sector of institutional shareholders are uncertain about exercising a corporate governance role rather than an investment role. Actions for breach of directors duties are difficult and expensive to mount. This position may explain the plethora of formal external controls which have proliferated in recent years. These include the "self-regulating" structures which regulate the Financial Services and Insurance market, increased Stock Exchange regulation, some of it following the Cadbury and Greenbury reports,[16] as well as increased use of the power to disqualify directors. None of these controls are seen as effective in putting pressure on managers, and debate has centred around how corporate governance can be revised in order to encourage management to take a long term view and to prevent the payment of excessive remuneration to executives by the company. It may well be that the perceived ineffectiveness of controls on the executives has encouraged the press to mount campaigns on particular issues. As explained above, a favourite concern has been the amount of pay executives receive but other company specific issues arise from time to time and a press campaign is occasionally effective in rousing shareholders to question and, even more occasionally, block executive actions.

II. THE PRESENT CORPORATE STRUCTURE IN THE UK

The formal model of the creation of a company in the UK places the shareholders, as members, at the centre of a contractual arrangement. The members form the company, and its memorandum and articles are said to "bind the company and its members to the same extent as if they respectively had been signed and sealed by each member...".[17]

The members in turn appoint directors, who form a single-tier board. Members have the power, provided by statute, to alter the articles of the company by three-quarters majority of those voting.[18] They also have a statutory power to remove a director by a resolution supported by a simple majority.[19] The earlier structure of the company gave a stronger place to the director. Prior to 1948 he or she could not be removed by the shareholders, unless they had a specific power to do so given by the company's articles or they were able to alter the articles themselves. It was in 1948 that a general power of removal by ordinary resolution appeared in the law. This has

[16] *Report On the Financial Aspects of Corporate Governance* (1992) and *Directors' Remuneration: Report of a Study Group chaired by Sir Richard Greenbury* (1995).

[17] Section 14 of the Companies Act, 1985.

[18] Ibid., s. 4.

[19] Ibid., s. 303.

formed part of a succession of measures which gives shareholders greater constitutional powers, including now their ability to alter the corporate objects, which were previously reated as immutable once established.[20]

However, this does not mean that shareholders occupy a dominant role in the day-to-day affairs of the company. Their role as potential overseers of the decisions of management is controlled by company articles. In the majority of companies this will be contained as a provision in the model rules offered for adoption by the Companies Acts, 1948 and 1985. These give a large measure of autonomy to directors. The 1985 formulation reads: "subject to the provisions of the Act, the memorandum and the articles and to any directions given by special resolution, the business of the company shall be managed by the directors who may exercise all the powers of the company".[21] Some authors are of the opinion that while it is clear that this has the effect of removing the power of shareholders to give directions as to the running of the business by ordinary resolution, they do still have the power to do so by way of three-quarters of those voting. However, there are others who take the view that even that amount of shareholder support for a resolution would be ineffective to contradict the day-to-day judgment of management, and that it does no more than reiterate the power of shareholders to alter the articles or to remove management if they are unhappy with the way things are being run. This latter interpretation would split the power of shareholders: it remains in sovereign control over directors in one way, by the drastic power of removal from office; but not in another, having to cede to the judgment of directors on particular issues if they are not willing to remove them.

Those taking the latter position have often done so out of concern for the protection of groups with interests in the company apart from the majority of current shareholders: minority shareholders; employees; and creditors. They feel that management should be assigned the role of keeping a balance between such interested parties in the company, and that this is not a balance that should be upset even by particularly large majority of shareholders.[22]

The clearest recent declaration of this view has come from a surprising source: a group of businessmen and women who run some of the largest firms in the UK. They make it clear that, in their view, a director could actually be in breach of her fiduciary duty to the company if she listened too closely to the majority of shareholders.

> "[T]he directors' duties are owed to their company, not to any specific third-party group. They must, as fiduciaries, have regard to the interests of shareholders, but that obligation is not related to the holders of shares at one particular time – it is related to the general body of shareholders from time to time."[23]

Case law could be cited to complement this view. In the early part of this century, the judiciary was saying that,

[20] Ibid., s. 4.

[21] Article 70, Table A of the Companies Act 1985.

[22] See on this issue Leader, "Private Property and Corporate Governance: Part I: Defining the Interests"; and Dine, "Private Property and Corporate Governance Part II: Content of Directors' Duties and Remedies", *Perspectives on Company Law:1* (ed. F. Patfield) 1995.

[23] See *Tomorrow's Company* (Royal Society for the Arts, Manufacture and Commerce, June 1995), p.12.

> "The directors are not servants to obey directions given by the shareholders as individuals .... They are persons who may by the regulations be entrusted with the control of the business, and if so entrusted they can be dispossessed from that control only by the statutory majority which can alter the articles."[24]

As is well recognized in various countries, the danger is that declarations such as these in favour of a relatively autonomous management – free from dominance by a particular majority of shareholders – can usher in an even less accountable oligarchy. Responsibility to everyone being in practice responsibility to no-one, it might be thought that at least responsibility to shareholders serves to provide some check on power, if not an ideal one. But even this notional reliance on shareholders does not hold the promise it might. Most shareholders' meetings of public companies are poorly attended. The previous UK government's policy of encouraging small shareholdings (in, for example, privatized industries) would seem likely to exacerbate this problem, as the difficulty and expense of attending a meeting when the shareholder has only a small sum at stake will not be undertaken. In large public companies, the management is sometimes in effective control of enough of the shareholders that they are not effectively accountable to the remainder. This perception may have fuelled one aspect of the ongoing debate about the virtues of a two-tier structure of management, with a supervisory board of directors overseeing the directors involved in day-to-day business decisions.[25] For this form of supervision would provide not only a different channel of control to the general meeting of shareholders, it is also likely to widen the constituencies represented to including representatives of employees. There has been a thorough review in the UK of corporate structure by the Cadbury Committee, referred to above. This produced a Code of Practice, which rejected supervisory boards, and instead relies heavily on the appointment of non-executive directors to single-tier boards as impartial contributors to decision-making. All companies whose shares are listed on the Stock Exchange must either comply with the Code or make an annual statement to say why it does not comply.

While the single-tier board seems set to stay, since the Hampel Committee has already made it clear that it opposes moving away from it, the issue of whose interests the director must serve in the process of discharging his duty to the company in a single tier board, remains an open one. On the face of it, that would not seem to be so, since Hampel has said quite firmly that in its view, "the single overriding objective shared by all listed companies ... is the preservation and the greatest possible enhancement over time of their shareholders' investment."[26] It says that "directors are responsible for relations with stakeholders, but they are accountable to the shareholders."[27] It then, however, joins the earlier law in making it clear that this is a duty owed to the shareholders "collectively, both present and future, not the shareholders at a given point in time."[28]

We shall argue in the following pages that these statements, taken together, force us to separate two questions: how should a company's performance be evaluated?,

[24] *Gramophone and Typewriter Ltd v Stanley* [1908] 2 KB 89 per Buckley.

[25] Such a system is an option that a company could adopt under the EC proposals for a Fifth Directive and for a European Company Statute.

[26] Para 1.15, *Preliminary Report.*

[27] Ibid.

[28] Ibid., para 3.2.

and who should be the constituencies to whom the directors are answerable? It is often thought that if you answer the first question by saying that the company must enhance shareholder investment over time, then this automatically provides an answer to the second question, to the effect that shareholders are the sovereign group, as compared with employees and others. However, in our view, there is no good reason for such a link between the answers to the two questions: the need to enhance investments over time may well require spreading accountability among a wider set of constituencies than the shareholders. This point becomes clearer if one works out the concrete meaning and implications of the distinction that the law draws between the will of the majority of shareholders in their individual capacities at a point in time, to which directors should not necessarily defer, and the interests of "shareholders as a whole" which is a body changing through time, whose interests they are meant to serve. How exactly the interests of the latter group are meant to be given concrete content, and how these relate to other stakeholders in the company, is one of the central questions in the corporate governance debate. It requires the position of the shareholder in UK law and practice today be looked at more closely.

III. PARTICULAR FEATURES OF CORPORATE GOVERNANCE IN THE UK

A. Shareholders' Powers: to What Extent Does the System Allow Shareholders to Protect their own Interests?[29]

Here, several ways can be distinguished in which shareholders can protect their own interests: via their ability to complain of unfair or otherwise oppressive behaviour by directors; via their ability to complain of the same thing from other shareholders; and via their exercise of their power to vote.

1. Unfair Prejudice

The Companies Act 1985 provides a remedy for a member when "the company's affairs are being or have been conducted in a manner which is unfairly prejudicial to the interests of its members generally or of some part of its members".[30] A member of a company will be able to bring himself within the section if he can show that the value of his shareholding in the company has been seriously diminished or at least seriously jeopardized by reason of a course of conduct on the part of those persons who do have de facto control of the company, which was unfair to the member concerned.[31] The courts suggest that the test should be an objective one: would the reasonable bystander observing the consequences of their conduct regard it as having unfairly prejudiced the petitioner's interest?

[29] The UK Law Commission is currently looking at a portion of this issue, to do with minority rights, and a final report has been published, entitled *Shareholder Remedies* (Cm 3769) (London: HMSO, 1997).

[30] Section 459.

[31] *Re Bovey Hotel Ventures* (1981) unreported, quoted in *Re R. A. Noble & Son (Clothing) Ltd* [1983] BCLC 273.

2. *The Right to Vote*

While this topic will be dealt with in more detail in a moment, here it is useful to indicate its overall place in the law of corporate governance. It is important to distinguish the use of right to vote as an instrument to protect a shareholder's personal interests, and as an instrument of participation in determining the company's overall interest. The former relates to the shareholder's interest in voting on those policies that will affect her level of dividend; on her relative position of strength as a proportion of the whole of issued shares; on the value of her share in the open market, etc. The latter relates to the same shareholder's interest in the successful functioning of the company, which, for some judges, may point to solutions that are different from those that produce good personal results for any particular shareholder.

These two different understandings of the vote are based on two different approaches to the share: the one as an object of property in itself; and the other as sign of property rights in the company.[32] The difference in perspective is reflected in different emphasis given by different judges to the notion that the shareholder is obliged to cast his vote "bona fide in the interests of the company". Judges who see the right to vote as a shareholder's property right in the company will take seriously the constraint that the vote be exercised bona fide in the company's interest, and will disqualify a vote that they think is biased.[33] Other judges, who treat the right to vote as an incident of the property right to the share, rather than the company, think that it is unrealistic to require the shareholder to vote for anything other than his own interests.[34]

B. The Extent to Which Shareholders' Powers can be Changed or Altered Through the Majority

Any given shareholder has a right not to be subject to victimization, as an attack on his personal interests, by the majority. Thus, if he can show bad faith in an alteration that has the effect of expropriating or otherwise weakening his position in relation to other shareholders, he can resist it.[35] What if no such special reasons for invalidating the vote can be shown, and the minority nevertheless objects that it has been expropriated or otherwise weakened even though they were not themselves harming the company? Here again there are two views among the judges: there have been those who argue that the majority of shareholders are entitled simply to consider their own self-interest and do not have in addition to show that the presence of the minority is harming the company.[36] This is probably the dominant view. A minority view, however, insists that any given shareholder could find his position worsened by the majority only if they could indeed show that in so disadvantaging the minority they were acting for the good of the company.[37] This view places the judiciary in a position both to judge whether or not this was the shareholders' motive *and* whether or

[32] See Leader, supra note 22, pp. 95 et seq. and J. Dine, supra note 22, pp. 118 et seq.
[33] *Sidebottom v Kershaw, Leese & Co.* [1920] 1 Ch 154.
[34] *Shuttleworth v Cox Bros & Co. (Maidenenhead) Ltd* [1927] 2 KB 9 at 26. On this issue, see Leader and Dine, supra note 22.
[35] *Clemens v Clemens* [1976] 2 All ER 268.
[36] *Peter's American Delicacy Co. Ltd v Heath* (1939) 61 CLR 457.
[37] *Dafen Tinplate Co. Ltd v Llanelly Steel Co* (1907) Ltd [1920] 2 Ch 124.

not what they did was in fact in the interests of the company. As it was put in *Dafen Tinplate*, the court must not simply abide by the shareholder's estimate of what is in the company's interests, but also ask whether in fact the alteration is genuinely necessary and for the benefit of the company.[38]

C. Voting Rights

1. Underlying Theory

As already indicated, the courts seem to subscribe to two different and conflicting theories about the right to vote. One places emphasis on the shareholder's property in her share. This has the result of allowing the votes to count even if they do not plausibly advance the interests of the company, since the right to vote is seen as a right of private property which can be deployed in the self-interest of the owner. The alternative theory sees the right to vote as reflecting the shareholder's property in the company, and as such demands that the vote be bona fide for the benefit of the company as a whole.

2. Topics on Which it is Permissible to Vote

Shareholders have a statutory right inter alia to vote for alteration of the articles; for the removal of directors; to authorize changes in the share capital. They also have the power to ratify conflicts of interest and some other breaches of fiduciary duties by management. We have already indicated that managerial freedom from shareholder control over their decisions holds at least for votes cast by way of ordinary resolution, and it may also extend to limit the reach of votes by special resolution.[39]

There are special cases, however, in which the available topics for vote widen, and the shareholder does have the right to override management decisions. These are where one can generally suspect a self-interested decision by management, even if it does not go so far as to break a director's obligation not to allow his duty and interest conflict. In such situations, even though directors have not broken any other requirement, the law nevertheless sometimes allows shareholders to override management. The cases in which this has happened have primarily focused on management attempts to prevent the arrival of a new, controlling group of shareholders, usually by way of a takeover. In these situations the courts have declared that the shareholder has a constitutional right not to see his position weakened by management's defensive tactics.[40]

3. Collateral Rights of Expression

In order to provide some counter-balance to the ability of directors to make their views known on company policy, the law provides that a proportion of members can require the company to circulate a statement not exceeding 1,000 words relating to the business of a meeting.[41] The demand must be made by not lesss than 5 per cent

38 Ibid.
39 This incapacity is a common law presumption, though the articles can provide otherwise.
40 *Howard Smith Ltd v Ampol Petroleum Ltd* [1974] 1 AER 1126.
41 Section 376(1)(b)of the Companies Act 1985.

of the total voting rights, or not less than 100 members who have shares on which at least £100 is paid up per member on average.[42] It is not yet decided whether or not the critics are entitled to have their expenses reimbursed if they are successful in having their recommendation adopted.[43]

D. To What Extent Can Voting Rights Be Legally Differentiated Between Classes and Within Classes?

It is possible to vary voting rights between and within classes. While ordinary shares usually carry one vote per share, it is possible to have non-voting ordinary shares, but this is not common and is not approved of by the Stock Exchange, even though this does not stand in the way of listing. The words non-voting must appear in the description of the share.[44]

At the other end of the spectrum, it is also possible to allocate more than one vote per ordinary share, or indeed to increase the voting power of certain shares on the happening of certain specified events. For example, in one case a company's articles provided that if any given director faced the prospect of a shareholders' resolution proposing his removal, each of his shares carried the rights to three votes on a poll in respect of any such resolution. This provision was upheld, despite the fact that in the circumstances of this case, it effectively sabotaged the provision in the Companies Act which states that a company may by ordinary resolution remove a director notwithstanding anything in its articles. The House of Lords reasoned that "the practice of giving special voting rights or special lack of voting rights to a particular class of shares is old and is recognised in art 2 of Table A in Sch 1 to the 1948 Act. ... we must take the law as we find it."[45] Usually, voting rights of preference shares are restricted to meetings considering a variation of their rights. The Stock Exchange would not permit such a clause in the articles of a listed company.

It should be noted that the law will not usually act to protect the relative voting strength in any given share, as a proportion of the whole. This relative strength can diminish, with the accompanying loss of impact for any single vote, and yet this will not amount to a "variation" of the class right. In general there will be a "variation" if the alteration directly affects the way the rights are described, but not if the value of the shareholding has been altered in some other way, for example, by varying the rights of another class of shares.[46] In *Greenhalgh v Arderne Cinemas Ltd*[47] the company, by resolution, subdivided some ten shilling ordinary shares into five two shilling ordinary shares. The votes created by this were used to pass a resolution for increasing the capital of the company. The effect of this was explained by Greene MR as follows:

> "As a result of those two resolutions, if they are valid, the voting power of the appellant, which previousdly gave him a satisfactory measure of voting control, is liable to be completely swamped by the votes of the other ordinary shareholders."

[42] Ibid., s. 376(2).
[43] On this point see *Farrar's Company Law*, 3rd ed., p. 327.
[44] Admission of Securities to Listing 9.04, and Farrar, ibid., p. 225.
[45] *Bushell v Faith* [1970] AC 1099.
[46] *White v Bristol Airplane Co. Ltd* [1953] Ch 65 at 74.

Despite this, the resolution was held not to have varied the rights of the appellant:

> "As a matter of law, I am quite unable to hold that, as a result of the transaction, the rights are varied; they remain what they always were – a right to have one vote per share *pari passu* with the ordinary shares for the time being issued which include the new two shilling ordinary shares resulting from the subdivision."

In *Re Old Silkstone Collieries*[48] it was held that a reduction of capital by repayment of preference shareholders so that they would lose their right to compensation due to them under a government scheme did constitute a variation. However, where a class of shareholders is eliminated and a proper price paid this will not normally constitute a variation. Where a true "variation" occurs there are special protections for each class of shareholders and voting is by class not in general meeting.[49] Where particular rights are granted to an individual shareholder they would not be alterable without the consent of that shareholder: in those circumstances the individual concerned would constitute a class of one. It might in some cases be possible to say that the right had not been granted to the individual "in his capacity as shareholder" but in some other capacity. If that is not so, provisions very common in the articles of private companies will become, for all practicable purposes, unalterable. For the time being it is clear that "class rights" is to be widely defined.

E. The Extent to Which Voting Rights can be Separated from Ownership Interests

As indicated above, it is possible to issue non-voting shares. This is quite a common practice for family controlled companies when they want to raise capital from outside investors. It is also possible that an outside body, such as the Broadcasting Authority, can effectively impose non-voting shares, since legislation can require that the relevant authority consent to any transfer of a voting share.

The legislation provides that in the case of a company originally having a share capital, every member has one vote in respect of each share or each £10 of stock held by him; and in any other case every member has one vote.[50] This provision is, however, subject to the memorandum or articles which may provide for as complicated a structure of voting rights as may be desired.

The use of the non-voting share provides another method of maintaining control by the existing directors, and is not as yet regulated in any way. They are the simplest and most straightforward method whereby directors can render themselves irremovable without their own consent, notwithstanding that they only own or control a fraction of the equity. It is only of recent years that this has become a major issue, though the idea of non-voting shares has been attacked from time to time as incompatible with basic principles of company law.[51]

47 [1946] 1All ER 512.

48 [1954] Ch 169.

49 See s. 125 of the CA 1985.

50 Ibid., s. 370(6.)

51 "In our opinion the growth of non-voting and restricted voting shares strikes at the basic principle on which our Company Law is based". Note of Dissent to the Jenkins Committee report, by Mr L. Brown, Sir George Erskine and Professor L. C. B. Gower

F. Transferability Rights

Every company must keep a register of its members giving details of the name addresses and holdings of its shareholders.[52] This acts as a restriction preventing the creation of bearer shares. A company is free to limit the transferability of shares by provision in the articles of association and the law also provides mandatory pre-emption rights, which are, however, the subject of extensive exceptions.[53] Share transferability may thus be restricted by the constitutional arrangements in the articles of association. In many of the industries recently privatized in the United Kingdom, the Government retained a "golden share" which enabled it to veto certain decisions by a company including a decision to transfer ownership to a foreign buyer.

In the typical company constitution, the directors will be empowered to refuse to register transfers and frequently this will be accompanied by provisions affording the other members or the company rights of pre-emption, first refusal or even compulsory acquisition. Such provisions face the courts with difficult questions of interpretation. But in line with the usual approach to interpretation the extent of the restriction is solely a matter of construction of the articles of association. However, shareholders have a prima facie right to transfer to whomsoever they please. Consequently their rights cannot be removed by uncertain language.[54] In the event of uncertainty a narrow construction will be adopted.

However, courts will, where possible, adopt a purposive construction. In *Lyle & Scott Ltd v Scott's Trustees*[55] the articles conferred a right of pre-emption on the other shareholders when any shareholder was "desirous of transferring his ordinary shares". Certain shareholders sold their shares to a takeover bidder, received the purchase price and gave him irrevocable proxies to vote on their behalf, but, agreed that in order to avoid the pre-emption rights given by the articles, the transfers were not to be lodged for registration. The House of Lords held that in the context "transferring" meant assigning the beneficial interest and not the technical process of having a transfer registered. The shareholders had clearly manifested an intention to sell their shares and could not continue with the sale without giving the other shareholders a right to exercise their option under the articles. But this decision was distinguished in *Safeguard v NatWest Bank* [1981] 1 WLR 286 where a very similar question arose but the relevant transfer was a transfer of the beneficial interest to executors on a death. The Court of Appeal refused to extend the pre-emption provisions to this situation.

As with other discretions exercisable by directors, the decision to accept or refuse transfers is a power held in a fiduciary capacity.[56] The power must be exercised in what the directors consider – not what the court considers – to be in the interest of the company, and not for any collateral purpose. But the court will presume that they have acted bona fide, and the onus of proof of the contrary is on those alleging it and is not easily discharged. However, the court will intervene if the directors are shown to have exercised their powers on grounds other than those prescribed in the art-

52 Section 352 of the Companies Act 1985.
53 Ibid., ss. 89, 90, 95 and 738.
54 Per Greene MR in *Re Smith & Fawcett Ltd* [1942] Ch 304.
55 [1959] AC 763.
56 See note 54 supra.

icles.[57] The articles often provide that the directors shall not be bound to state their reasons.[58] But if the directors do state their reasons the court will investigate them and will overrule their decision if they have acted on considerations which should not have weighed with them.[59]

IV. DISCLOSURE REQUIREMENTS AS PART OF CORPORATE GOVERNANCE

A. The Basic Requirements

Requirements for disclosure are mostly to be found in the Companies Act 1985. By far the most extensive requirements relate to disclosure of financial information and the Act follows the provisions of the 4th and 7th EC directives in this respect, requiring disclosure of a "full and fair view" of the financial state of the company or group to be given in the annual accounts. The accounting information is in the public domain via the Companies Registry. Other requirements have been imposed from time to time, notably in respect of directors' contracts of employment, salaries and payments made as compensation for loss of office as well as requirements to disclose interests in contracts. Many of these requirements are to be found in Part X of the Companies Act 1985 which is currently being reviewed by the Department of Industry and Employment because its long and complex provisions are extremely difficult to follow.

The governmental requirement for disclosure is strengthened so far as listed companies are concerned by the listing rules issued by the London Stock Exchange. These mirror the provisions of the EC Listing Particulars Directives (EC 79/279 and EC 80/390) so far as initial listings are concerned and they also impose continuing requirements for disclosure in accordance with EC Directive 82/121.

The expectations of disclosure of first the Cadbury and recently the Greenbury Committee would be higher so far as disclosure of information relating to directors' contracts of service are concerned. Compliance with the Cadbury Code has generally been reasonable (see Compliance with the Code of Best Practice 24 May 1995). Although the length of directors' contracts appeared to have changed very little, there was a very significant increase in the disclosure of separate remuneration Committees. This latter was one of the key Cadbury recommendations. It is too early to tell what affect the Greenbury report will have on executive pay. Both these bodies were non-governmental, Cadbury was set up by the Stock Exchange and Greenbury by the Confederation of British Industry. To that extent these can be seen as responses by Industry to public concern over corporate governance.

B. Failure to Disclose

So far as Part X of the Companies Act 1985 is concerned, failure to disclose should be sanctioned by a mixture of civil and criminal penalties. So far as criminal penalties are concerned, no proceedings have ever been brought under these sections and

[57] *Re Bede Steam Shipping Co* [1917] 1 Ch 123 (CA).

[58] *Berry & Stewart v Tottenham Hotspur Football Co* [1935] Ch 718.

[59] See note 54 supra.

there is currently a policy not to use the criminal sanctions. Civil proceedings are also rare and these sections are often only invoked as a bolster to action under section 459 or a derivative action where more substantial breaches of director's duties are at issue.[60]

Turning to the listing particulars requirements, the Stock Exchange may refuse to list or suspend listing or trading for failure to comply. It is now a requirement of continuing listing obligations that companies should issue a statement of compliance with the Cadbury Code or an explanation of why non-compliance still exists within a particular company.

C. Failure to Comply with Accounts Requirements

Following reforms in 1989 it was decided that the overall objective should be to ensure that good accounting information is ultimately produced, rather than the punishment of transgressors. Accordingly, there was a repeal of the criminal offence of laying non-complying accounts before the general meeting or registrar and now the only criminal liability is for knowingly not complying with the Act.

Created were new civil procedures: including the opportunity voluntarily to prepare revised accounts or a directors report once it is clear that they are non-complying. At a second stage the Secretary of State can require explanation or require revision; at a third stage a court order can be obtained by the Secretary of State to revise accounts, and he can authorize other bodies to do so, such as the Financial Reporting Review Panel. The Financial Reporting Review Panel will concentrate on public and large private companies, and the Department of Trade and Industry will concentrate on small- or medium-sized companies.

Professional accounting requirements now affect the content of company accounts. There is a Financial Reporting Council, below which is the Accounting Standards Committee, which issues Statements of Standard Accounting Practice. An Accounting Review Panel examines material departures from accounting standards by public or large private companies, involving issues of principle, or which might involve accounts not giving a true and fair view. The accountancy profession has a disciplinary role and may prevent individual accountants from continuing in practice.

The information that is disclosed to existing shareholders is normally recycled and packaged for the investment market and creditors particularly where good news is available. This is often achieved by extraction of some snippets of news from the Chairman's statement at the annual general meeting. The accounts will be used for tax purposes, they are public in any event.

D. Information to Employees

This is primarily at the moment via collective bargaining obligations. There is no obligation per se to provide the annual report to them, though there was under the Industrial Relations Act 1971, section 57 for companies of more than 350 people. Seventy-seven per cent of companies nevertheless do so voluntarily. As explained above there are information and consultation requirements on collective redundancy and transfer of undertakings.

[60] See *Guinness v Saunders* [1990] 2 AC 663.

E. Information to Government

The Government has no specific right to any more information than is made public in accordance with the general requirements already discussed. As indicated, these appear in legislation, especially the Companies Act 1985, which reflects in part the impact of 4th and 7th Directives on harmonization of legislation on company and group accounts in the EU.

F. Accountants' Liability

A company's auditor is a "watchdog but not a bloodhound".[61] Auditors are liable to the company for negligence in carrying out their duties. The standard of care is that of an ordinary reasonable auditor.[62] Increasingly it is argued that auditors should take on a more active role. If a company becomes insolvent and profits had been overstated, resulting in wrongful payment of tax or dividends, then the liquidator can enforce the company's right of action against the auditors. Section 310 of the CA 1985 prevents auditors from limiting or excluding their liability.

However, while auditors owe a duty of care to the company, the case of *Caparo v Dickmen*[63] decides that a duty is not normally owed to its shareholders or to members of the public who may rely on the accounts in deciding whether or not to invest, unless there are special facts showing that auditor knew that information would be communicated to an investor or a class in relation to a particular transaction. Vulnerability to takeovers and reliance by bidders is not enough.

G. Information about Quality of Employment

A company with over 250 employees must report on the employment of disabled persons, what action is taken to promote employee involvement including information and consultation on matters likely to affect their interests, share schemes, and similar measures.[64]

V. CORPORATE GOVERNANCE AND CONFLICTS OF INTEREST: DIRECTORS AND SHAREHOLDERS

A. Directors

There are statutory rules preventing conflicts of interest which arise in for example, self dealing contracts,[65] and it is also the case that a director who finds herself in a position where interest and duty conflict will be in breach of her fiduciary duty to the company. The decision made in these circumstances may be challenged by a shareholder bringing a derivative action (see below) or possibly an action for "unfair prejudice" under section 459 of the Companies Act 1985. As explained below these

61 *Re Kingston Cotton Mill No 2* 1896 2 CH 279 at 288 per Lopes LJ.
62 *Re London and General Bank (No. 2)* (1895) 2 Ch 673 at 682-683.
63 *Caparo Industries plc v Dickmen* [1970] 2 AC 605.
64 Schedule 7, Part V of the CA 1985.
65 Ibid., Part X.

are not significant controls, nor is the theoretical possibility that the shareholders may dismiss directors by a simple majority vote.[66] Three factors militate against shareholder control and in favour of management. These are (i) the apathy of shareholders generally and the continued reluctance of large institutional shareholders to be involved in corporate governance issues in the companies in which they invest (ii) the system of proxy voting which is heavily weighted in favour of management to the extent that proxies may be solicited by management at the company's expense (iii) the absolute control of information in the hands of management. Apart from financial information required by the accounting provisions, very little information needs to be given to shareholders and none to employees.

There is a technical debate surrounding the interplay of statute and common law with respect to the self-dealing prohibition. It is clear from the cases that self-dealing is regarded as a breach of fiduciary duty. However, the courts have also accepted that the articles of association of companies can define in advance circumstances in which self-dealing is permissible.[67] This is despite a statutory provision[68] preventing a company from exempting a director from or indemnifying them against breaches of fiduciary duty. The courts are caught between the conception of directors as trustees and fiduciaries with an absolute duty to the company and the more realistic conception of them as commercial agents. The ambit of the law on this issue is therefore not clear.

The control exercised over management by this route is significantly lessened by the willingness of the courts to accept ratification of a director's breach of duty by a majority of shareholders even when those voting in the majority have an interest in the outcome (see below).

The theoretical position is that it is a breach of duty to engage in operations where interest and duty conflict (subject to the debate mentioned above), and that the duty may be breached even after resignation. Thus, use of information or opportunity which comes to the director because of her position in the company will be very likely to be a breach of her duty to the company even if she tries to dissociate herself from the company by saying that she is acting in a private capacity or by resigning in order to exploit the opportunity. Unfortunately the reality of enforcement does not match the strictness of the duty.

B. Directors in Corporate Groups

Interlocking directorships, particularly between a financial institution and a trading company, have always been a feature of the corporate scene. From the point of view of empirical research into corporate control they are significant as an indicator of intercorporate cohesion and interdependence. Certain institutions may be found to be central to a number of relationships and therefore occupy an important position in the constellation of interests. From a company law point of view, the principal question is whether this gives rise to a conflict of interest. The older authorities saw nothing wrong in the holding of competing directorships. In *London and Mashonaland Exploration Co Ltd v New Mashonaland Exploration Co Ltd*[69] it was held that a

[66] Ibid., s. 303.
[67] *Movitex v Bulfield* [1988] BCLC 104.
[68] CA 1985, s. 310.
[69] (1891) WN 16.5

director would not be restrained from acting as a director of a rival company except where there is a prohibition in the articles or where the director is about to disclose confidential information or can be restrained because there is a clause in his contract prohibiting him from so acting.

Later cases have undermined the multiple director's apparently secure position. In the Canadian case of *Abbey Glen Property Corpn v Stumborg*,[70] McDonald J thought that the *Mashonaland* dicta were too widely expressed, and that "there might well be cases in which a director breaches his fiduciary duty to Company A merely by acting as a director of Company B, even where there is no question of passing on confidential information". In New Zealand, the matter was considered by Mahon J in *Berlei Hestia (NZ) Ltd v Fernyhough*.[71] The learned judge thought there was a wide distinction between asking a director to account for a profit made out of his fiduciary relationship, and asking a director not to join the board of a competing organization in case he should, at some future time, decide to act in breach of his fiduciary duty". Only the former was regulated. However Mahon J appears to overlook the point that the making of a profit is only one facet of the conflict of interest rule. It exists to prevent decisions being made which have as a motive either a personal interest or another professional interest such as the position of another company within the group and can therefore apply to render a director in breach of his fiduciary duty even where he makes no profit.

The cases thus take a surprisingly lax approach which some would argue is justified from the point of view of commercial convenience. However, in certain circumstances interlocking directorships may give rise to an action for breach of confidence or to a petition under section 459.

The situation was considered in the context of a predecessor to section 459 under which "oppression" of shareholders needed to be established. In *Scottish Co-Operative v Meyer*[72] It was made plain that consideration of the interests of a parent group while making decisions for the board of a subsidiary was a breach of fiduciary duties. The sole consideration for directors should be the interest of the company on whose board they are sitting at any one time and considerations of the interest of the group or parent company are not proper considerations. This harsh rule which would operate to make directors breach their fiduciary duty regardless of any profit made by them is much honoured in the breach. Directors do, of course, take note of the interests of related companies. However, the theory is that they must justify this by saying that to take account of those interests is itself in the best interests of the company whose immediate affairs they are conducting.

Interlocking relations between companies in closely related industries tend to forestall the development of competition which otherwise would occur in the normal expansion and diversification of each of the respective companies. Common directors between companies that are in a supplier-purchaser position to each other may result in preferential treatment in periods of short supply to the impairment of competition generally throughout the affected industry. Similarly, preferential treatment may occur in access to market outlets. An interlock between a manufacturing corporation and banks and insurance companies or other sources of financial services may estab-

70 (1978) DLR (3d) 35.
71 (1980) 2 NZLR 150.
72 [1959] AC 324.

lish a community of interest that would tend to assure adequate credit to a favoured company and a withholding of credit and capital from disfavoured competitors.

C. The Sanction of Disqualification of Directors

The increased use of the Company Director Disqualification procedure in recent years raises a number of fundamental questions about corporate governance. Judges have found profound difficulty in determining the nature and purpose of these provisions and the contradictions and complications of the ensuing cases are notorious. In a number of cases the purpose of the legislation is said to be "protection of the public". This may mean that no immediate victim of the director's behaviour can be identified so that the protection of the general public is the aim of the disqualification provisions. If this were the case, the "liberty-limiting" principle[73] would be the same as if a single victim or multiple victims could be pointed to. The liberty limiting principle is a principle that can be used to support a penal approach to particular behaviour. The limitation of liberty inherent in penalizing the behaviour would be justified on the basis that harm will be caused to others by allowing the directors to continue in their negligent or unfit behaviour.

If, however, such is not the case, penalizing the behaviour may rest only on the principle that it is contrary to general commercial morality. This invites the question: is there any such thing as general commercial morality? It is clear that there is at least a judicial perception of a standard of commercial morality. A form of commercial morality is evident even in the early refusal of judges to interfere in "hard bargain" cases.[74] The morality adhered to was that of self-reliance and made no attempt to tip the scales in favour of those who might be in a weaker bargaining power.

This defence of morality may explain why a government's credibility is so nearly tied up with these sanctions, the element of public protection rather than commercial regulation making it imperative that a party in power must be seen to condemn such behaviour.

If the measure under consideration is in place to protect commercial morality, there is a real question as to whether this is a proper use of criminal or quasi-criminal law. There are different implicit answers to this question from the judiciary, resulting from different fundamental standpoints about the role of directors and their companies. There is, on the one hand a view with which reformers of corporate governance often have sympathy: that the right to form and to direct a company is grounded on the social value and responsibility that corporations have. The rival view sees companies as valuable in themselves, so that a directorship becomes an employment right and not a potentially abused privilege subject to control.[75] If the former stance is taken it is arguable that on the approaches of both Mill and Devlin, harm done to companies could be regarded as an attack on a valuable institution within society, protection of which is a legitimate aim of the criminal law.[76]

[73] A categorization used by Joel Feinberg, *Harmless Wrongdoing* (OUP, 1988).

[74] See Paul Finn, *Commerce, The Common Law and Morality* (1990).

[75] Vanessa Finch, "Disqualifying Directors: Issues of Rights, Privileges and Employment" 1993 *Industrial Law Journal*, p. 35.

[76] See J.S. Mill, *On Liberty* (Everyman Edition), p. 138 and commentary on the argument in H.L.A. Hart, *Law Liberty and Morality* (OUP, 1963), pp. 42-43; Devlin, *The Enforcement of Morals* (OUP, 1965); Leader in *Tradition and Progress in Modern Legal Cultures*, Jorgensen et al ed., (Steiner/ARSP, Stuttgart 1985).

So far, the dominant judicial rules that have been developed can be seen as protecting public morality or protecting a company as a socially valuable institution. The disqualification rules have a role as punishment for directors and as a mode of ensuring a higher standard of behaviour for directors. Both these roles would have a direct impact on decision making and are an example of rules from outside the company seeking to influence managers. Its increased recent use to attempt to achieve these purposes may reflect the partial vacuum of control which internal mechanisms are displaying.

D. Shareholders and Conflicts of Interest

1. Conflicts Between Shareholders

Can the shareholders vote or sell their shares according to their own self-interest? Here, it is necessary to distinguish voting from the sale of the share.

(a) Voting

Regarding voting, the orthodox principle is that the shareholder is not obliged to exercise his vote in a way that is bona fide and for the benefit of the company as a whole. Exceptionally as explained above, when votes are cast for the alteration of articles, the general rule is that an alteration is valid only if it respects that constraint. Even in these circumstances the case law reveals considerable reluctance by the courts to intervene in favour of an aggrieved minority. When they do intervene, it is either because they detect bad faith, as when the alteration of the articles is a subterfuge, hiding personal hostility to a shareholder or because they apply what is in other contexts called a proportionality principle. This requires that the company show that the alteration was a necessary means to achieve the objective at which it had declared it wanted. For example, the courts have disallowed alterations that were said to be aimed to helping raise fresh capital, but which actually had no such demonstrable link.[77] Even if there is such a link, the court may require that the voted alteration be no wider than is strictly necessary. It will be wary of alterations that confer too much power on a majority, as with clauses empowering them to compulsorily purchase the shares of any member who requests to transfer them.[78]

However, there are other cases in which the courts have backed away from such a proportionality principle, preferring to defer to the majority of shareholders own estimate of where the interest of the company lies, and only intervening in those most extreme cases when no reasonable man could believe that the alteration could be good for the company. The only other requirement here is that the majority be of good faith as they cast their votes. As one judge of this persuasion put it,

> "[to] suppose that in voting each shareholder is to assume an inhuman altruism and consider only the intangible notion of the benefit of the vague abstraction . . of the company as an institution".[79]

77 *Brown v British Abrasive Wheel* [1919] 1 Ch 290.

78 *Dafen Tinplate Co. Ltd. v Llanelly Steel Co.* (1907) Ltd [1920] 2 Ch 124.

79 *Peter's American Delicacy Co. LTD v Heath* (1939) 61 CLR 457 (High Court of Australia) per Dixon J.

These two approaches to majority voting powers reflect the impact of the two different theories of the shareholder's right, discussed above, that underlie the cases. The former approach focuses on the shareholders' property right in the the company, while the latter focuses on their personal rights in their own shares. The former aproach is therefore willing to highlight the interest of the company as a whole, and demands that voting be in that interest, such that any harm done to a minority stands in need of justification as a step taken that was necessary to protect the company. The latter approach, sees the shareholders' use of their voting rights as like the use of any other item of private property: something which can be legitimately deployed on the owners' estimate of what their self-interest requires.

(b) Sale

Apart from the restrictions on transfers that might appear in company articles, the law does not impose a similar restriction on the shareholder's ability to sell, as opposed to vote. The shareholder is entitled to sell for any reason, and indeed there are some special situations – such as the takeover – in which she is entitled to resist measures taken that would dilute the value of her shares, as when new shares are issued so making the existing ones less attractive to a bidder who wanted them because they formed a large percentage of the total.[80]

2. *Conflicts of Interest Between the Shareholder and the Corporation*

Are there any rules that restrict shareholders' rights when they have a conflict of interest with the corporation? The basic rule is that the shareholder, unlike the director, is not subject to the principle that he must avoid a conflict between his interest and his duty. For example, in one case a director who was also an important shareholder cast his votes in favour of the purchase by the company of a large item of his own property, so validly ratifying a sale that would, apart from that, have been challenged as an abuse of the director's duty to avoid a conflict of interest.[81]

However, there are points at which the law will make an exception to this principle. Thus, the majority of shareholders cannot prevent litigation on behalf of the company, when it is clear that in doing so they have a special interest to protect. Furthermore, statute imposes two restrictions on self-interested voting: when counting votes in favour of a special resolution of a private company to make a payment out of capital to redeem shares, votes attaching to the shares to be redeemed must be ignored (CA 1985, 174(2)). Also, when counting votes in favour of a special resolution to confer, vary, revoke or renew authority to make an off-market purchase of its own shares, or to make a contingent purchase contract for its own shares, votes attaching to the shares to be purchased must be ignored.[82]

Judicially, this is by use of section 459 of the Companies Act 1985 which is available to a single shareholder who shows that the company is being run in a way that is "unfairly prejudicial" to her. This remedy is available only to shareholders and is said to be effective both in actions which reach court and, probably more importantly, as a threat to gain a fair price for shares. The most usual result of a successful

[80] *Howard Smith Ltd v Ampol Petroleum Ltd* [1974] 1 AER 1126.
[81] *North-West Transportation Co. Ltd v Beatty* (1887) 12 App Cas 589.
[82] CA 1985, ss. 164(5), 165(2); Mayson, *Company Law*, p. 377 (5th ed., 1994).

action is that the plaintiff shareholder is bought out at a fair price (although the court has an almost unfettered discretion as to the remedy it may grant). It is thus most used against private companies and would not usually be brought by a shareholder in a listed company as the "fair price" would be available on the market.

The other action to enforce fiduciary duties is a derivative action which may be brought by a single shareholder or a class of shareholders. It is cumbersome and expensive. It may only be brought by shareholders despite the fact that one of the duties laid on directors by statute is to take account of the interests of employees.[83] Employees have no enforcement mechanism available. To be successful a shareholder must show that there has been a "fraud on the minority" or, more properly a "fraud on the company". To accomplish this she must show that there has been a breach of directors' fiduciary duties and that the company has wrongfully failed to take action against that director. This latter hurdle is difficult to surmount since there may be many good reasons for failing to bring actions and, one of the pieces of evidence that the action was in the company's interest is a vote by a majority of shareholders not to bring an action. Judges tend to give such evidence great credence. If this has occurred, even if the interested parties have voted, then it is only in extreme cases that the court will permit an action to proceed. The two-stage nature of the action together with the fact that judgment in a successful action will be given for the company, not the complaining shareholder, makes the action a great risk with no great gain to the complainant and actions are rare. It is most doubtful whether this antiquated procedure is an effective enforcement mechanism for directors' duties, particularly given the monopoly of information which directors retain.

In the very unlikely event of shareholders discovering in advance that directors intend to act outside the constitutional powers of the company, shareholders will be able to obtain an injunction to restrain them.[84] The myth of shareholder democracy in the UK is founded on section 303 of the CA 1985 which purports to safeguard the right of shareholders to rid themselves of directors by a simple majority vote. As previously mentioned the effectiveness of this is undermined by shareholder apathy, management control of information and proxy voting mechanisms.

Extra-judicial mechanisms of control include the scrutiny of non-executive directors. This is not thought to be very effective because directors are drawn from a small community and their power is small compared with the executive directors. Again the control of information flow is an issue here. Large institutional shareholders are in a position to exercise some control but have traditionally been reluctant to become involved in corporate governance issues of the companies in which they invest. Finally, press coverage of some issues, seen recently in relation to larger pay awards taken by some directors is a way of exerting pressure in respect of a limited range of concerns. None of these mechanisms is manifestly successful as may be seen from the continuing number of scandals, including the Guinness and Maxwell affairs.

There is no doubt that in the United Kingdom management exercises shareholder power. Management will often have a significant shareholding held both personally and in the hands of nominees. They will also have significantly proxy voting power. Perhaps most importantly, the stranglehold on information which management have

[83] CA 1985, s. 309.
[84] Ibid., s. 35.

prevents an intelligent use by shareholders of their theoretical powers both in voting and in acting as plaintiffs in available enforcement mechanisms.

VI. DEBATES

A. A Framework

Concerns about the proper regulation of corporate power cover formal, legal methods as well as informal means, such as the mobilizing of public opinion, the exercise of personal influence by non-executive over executive directors, etc. The former fixes a framework within which the latter operates, though of course informal pressures also follow channels that the law has little role in defining.

The proposals for institutional changes that are currently being aired in the UK can best be analyzed if concerns about corporate governance are divided into three broad elements.

- One element fixes a *link of information* between those who hold and those who are subjected to corporate power: it consists, for example, of obligations on directors to provide information in various forms about the company's performance; or to make known any conflict of interest they may have; or to inform and consult with employees before certain major corporate decisions. This category can be sub-divided into:
  (a) rules of strict accountability, requiring management to report to their ultimate controllers, be they the shareholders, or a mixed set of constituencies; and
  (b) rules encouraging the flow of information towards those who are not in a position of ultimate control in the corporation, such as works councils. The objective here is to aid better informed decisions by management and better informed responses by those subjected to those decisions: here we could, for example, locate the information and consultation requirements for transfers of undertakings and collective redundancies.
- A second element consists of rules that *allocate competence* among various parties. It is here that can be located what is generally known as a concern for the balance of power within the corporation. Directors, for example, are assigned a certain domain in which they can make decisions free from shareholder interference, and shareholders have another domain in which they have the last word; employees can be assigned a role in management via their representatives; possibly a more direct role in shaping corporate policy via the franchise similar to that exercised in the general meeting of shareholders; and finally boards of directors can be assigned competence within themselves between executive/non-executive – all with the object of regulating corporate power.
- A third element fixes certain *limits on the use and abuse of power*. The concern is not so much to fix the correct structures that balance power, but rather to regulate particular cases of the misuse of power that has been allocated via the second element. Here can be located items such as the protection of minority shareholder rights against abuses by the majority; the protection of any given

shareholder, in her personal capacity, from unfair or oppressive action by the directors; the protection of employees from wrongful or unfair dismissal, either on procedural or substantive grounds; and finally the control, via the laws of tort and crime, of damage that corporate activity can do to third parties.

We then face, as the last part of a framework for analysis, the issue of legitimacy. In seeing which configuration of these elements in the regulation of corporate power is justified, there is the question that is put in many jurisdictions, "in whose interests does and should the corporation function?" In the UK, as elsewhere, the answers vary between those given by the Institute of Directors and Confederation of British Industry, endorsed as we have seen by successive committees on corporate governance, claiming that the company exists primarily to serve the interests of shareholder[85] through to the proposals that continue to come from various quarters that a wider set of constituents could be enfranchised.[86] We shall argue in a moment that this part of the debate poses the wrong issue, and that the problem of legitimacy should be differently addressed.

B. Two Positions

As we pointed out at the beginning of this chapter, there is a surprising degree of unanimity, coming from many sides in the business community, that changes are needed in the regulation of corporate affairs. But both the diagnoses and the prescriptions that emerge are quite varied. There is, in one group of proposals coming from conferences organized by the Institute of Directors, the belief that companies are not serving the interests of shareholders well enough within their present structure: they are doing their business less well – by their own traditional standards of evaluation – than they could do. Here, we find those who claim that the problem comes from the short-term outlook that managers are forced to take arising from the short-term outlook of investors.[87]

Others, including some major advisors to the new Labour Government, doubt that the shortage of long-term investment is as great a difficulty as has been made out.[88] They prefer to locate the problem not in the strategy of investors but rather in the strategy of corporate managers, who often see mergers and acquisitions as central to their activity, but in fields that often bear little relation to the core experience of their companies.

> "The senior executive [is] a meta-fund manager, juggling a portfolio of businesses as an investor juggles a portfolio of shares. ... and these preoccupations persist despite analysis which suggests that the contribution of corporate ownership to performance is almost negligible and that competitive advantages are to be found in operating businesses rather than in buying and selling them."[89]

[85] e.g. *Enterprise and Governance* (London, Institute of Directors: October 1995) passim.

[86] e.g. Kay and Silberston, infra note 82.

[87] See the contribution by Allen Sykes, Chairman, Economic Insurance Co. to *Enterprise and Governance* (London, Institute of Directors: October 1995), pp. 17 et seq.

[88] J. Kay and A. Silberston "Corporate Governance" *National Institute Economic Review* August 1995, pp. 84, 92.

[89] Ibid., p. 89.

On this view, the solution is that companies re-focus on a sustained path of development and not diversify over too broad and incoherent a range of objectives. As a further implication of this view, it is argued UK companies should begin to function more like communities and in less of an adversarial way. It looks to a conception of the company as "a community in itself and an organisation in turn embedded in a community". It believes in "corporate growth sought for its ability to utilise and enrich human resources .... workers identify their interests with those of the company which, as a consequence, is regarded as a sort of community."[90]

Finally, alongside these two groups of opinion are those who object to particular features of corporate practice and do not take on the larger issues: they focus on features which we have grouped under the category of objections to abuses of power and demands for better flows of information, covering items such as better reporting about executive remuneration; more adequate information and consultation with employees about investment and location plans; strengthening the rights of minority shareholders against abuse by directors able to manipulate dominant shareholdings; strengthening employee rights against abuse of power via unfair dismissals; etc.

Turning from diagnosis to the major proposals that are offered for solving the problems identified, we can again see important differences among them. According to the view that focuses on the need for a better quality of finance made available to the company, the solution sought is a more central role to those institutions and other investors prepared to take a long term position. This aims to change what we have called the allocation of competence by drawing the long-term investor into closer control over executive strategies via their nominees. Mr. Allen Sykes, for example, has made a recent, influential suggestion that 60 major investment institutions and the 100 largest companies be brought together. Each major company would have four to five of these institutions as long term investors, holding between them between 10 and 20 per cent of the shares. These institutions would appoint certain non-executive members of the board who, given their status as nominees of the institutions, would hopefully be free from undue influence exercised by the rest of the board. At the same time, Sykes proposes that these individuals not be drawn from the ranks of fund managers or from the institutions themselves, but instead be experienced businessmen from outside from outside those circles.[91]

There is no question, in this camp, of enfranchising employees so that their representatives can sit on the boards as well, nor is there an inclination to involve any other portions of the wider community in management issues. It is here, on the allocation of competence, that there is fundamental debate brewing. For the "stakeholder" proposals all point to a wider set of inputs into management than those simply provided by investors. Though there have been no detailed suggestions yet, the published work of those taking this can be read as favouring employee representatives sitting on either a single-tier or a two-tier board. While this would not be an imposed, uniform solution for all companies, inducements would be sought to

[90] For a similar view that the company should be seen as a community, see the influential document *Tomorrow's Company* (Royal Society for the Arts, Manufacture and Commerce, June 1995), p. 12. The Royal Society does not propose widening representation on boards of directors to include other constituents along with shareholders.

[91] *Enterprise and Governance* (London, Institute of Directors: October 1995), pp. 22-23.

encourage it among the larger entities.[92] This is in many ways a repeat of the same debate that occurred 20 years ago, when worker representation on corporate boards was last suggested in 1976, as a result of a report by Lord Bullock. At that point, the unions rejected the offer as a recipe for diluting the role of a trade union representative, calling on him to do two incompatible things at once: act as a fiduciary for the company and as a representative of a particular constituency, the employees.[93] It is too early to say how the unions will react this time.

This debate over allocation of competence is paralleled by a debate over the flow of information. While all sides seem to favour as much information as possible going to shareholders, they diverge over the proper information made available to employees. This difference emerges most concretely in the reactions to the new European Works Councils. This directive imposes requirements of information and consultation on companies on various important matters of policy, and parallels the requirements already in place that do bind the UK for transfers of undertakings and collective redundancies. The investor-focused school wishes to minimise the growth of this sort of constraint on management, while the stakeholder school wishes to increase it.[94]

These diverging views tie in with other fundamental and ongoing debates about the place of the company in modern society. One concerns the place of the profit motive and the priority of shareholder interests. The first, investor led school, of which the participants in the Institute of Directors are typical, sees no need to alter the basic understanding of the importance of profitability and the centrality of shareholder interests in any corporate culture. On the contrary, their proposals are aimed to increase that profitability. The second set of positions also does not question the need for a profit motive as central but argues that it is less likely to be a sustainable objective unless there is a change in the tendency to measure success by returns from the diffuse, short-term buying and selling of companies. They argue for more of a focus on sustained development of a business with a clear and single identity. This, it is argued, will come about if we move away from shareholder dominance and towards a larger group of constituents who would be given the ultimate power to control the managerial board. They could impose their own sense of the core identity of the company, and resist acquisitions or other activity that strays too far from that core. In a two-tier structure, this could require management to obtain the consent of the supervisory board before any important decisions were taken concerning the company's assets and/or its employees.[95]

92 Will Hutton, "All Together Now" *Guardian*, 14 November 1995; Will Hutton, "Raising the Stakes" *Guardian* 17 January, 1996, p. 22; and Kay and Silberston, supra note 82.

93 For aspects of this issue, see Davies & Wedderburn, "The Land of Industrial Democracy" 1977, 6 *Industrial Law Journal*, p. 197.

94 There is a position that occasionally appears in the debates, but which is not embraced by any of the major parties at the moment, that does question the centrality of the profit motive in corporate activity, and claims that the social responsibility of the larger companies requires an alteration of their commitment to profit in favour of a more mixed set of objectives, ploughing more of their resources into the needs of employees and of the wider community in a way that clearly and permanently draws the company away from more profitable uses of its resources. See J.E. Parkinson, *Corporate Power and Responsiblity* (OUP, 1995), Ch 10. cf. "Company Law and Legal Theory", *The Law of the Business Enterprise*, ed. Sally Wheeler (OUP, 1994), p. 109.

95 This could be true when a company proposes to invest in new technology, so prejudicing some employees and the dividends going to some shareholders.

C. Assessment

It is clear that the two broad positions sketched above will call for some clear policy choices. Basically, they seem to revolve around the question of whose interests the company should serve; and who should be in positions of control over company strategy and tactics. It is also clear that both positions are broadly results oriented. That is, they want the company to perform better according to the standards for such performance they set, and then search for a set of structures that will best produce that result.

However, this results-led orientation dictated by policy-makers can fail to capture the variety of situations that face the wide variety of companies. Thus, for some companies a short-term strategy may be best, and this may well include pursuing a diverse set of acquisitions; whereas for another it may be the very worst solution. The important thing is that the best strategy should emerge from a representative body of people within the company: a decision that emerges from a balanced set of inputs to such a strategy from all relevant and concerned groups.

In searching for this balance, there are two basic questions to consider: one about the interests that should count in formulating daily company policy; and the other about the interests that should count in controlling who it is that sits in the position of management.

1. Whose Interests is it the Duty of the Company to Serve?

This question has dominated UK debate, but we submit that, as formulated, it poses a false dilemma. It asks for a choice between classes of individual: the alternatives said to be shareholders or some wider set of constituents. However, the difference between interests which are properly dominant on the corporate agenda and those which are secondary is not a difference connected to *people*, but arises out of the quality of the interests themselves.[96] We can already see in corporate law that human interests and corporate performance are linked in two ways: derivitavely and personally. When shareholders can deploy a derivative action, they speak for the company and complain of a wrong done to it. They have an interest in the outcome, for damage is done to them, but it is understood in the law as damage arising via the damage done to the company itself. Alongside this, but quite different from it, are the personal interests of those same people, who can be abused *by* the company in one way or another. This is reflected in their ability to bring personal actions for unfair and oppressive acts done to them by the directors, in their capacity as directors. In the second case the tables are turned: rather than interests being identified with the company, deriving their satisfaction from its successful pursuit of its objective, they demand compensation or some other remedy *from* the company for abuse of its power.

If we then ask, which interests does the company exist to serve?, the answer would seem to be that it exists, by definition, in order to *satisfy* a shareholder's derivative, not personal interests. As a side-constraint, it must also not *abuse* (without due compensation) those personal interests, but that is not its very reason for existence. While at the moment in the UK these two distinct sorts of interest are rec-

[96] For an earlier and fuller version of the argument to follow, see Leader and Dine supra note 22.

ognized in the UK for shareholders, the mix of interests characteristic of shareholders is also duplicated elsewhere in the enterprise, for employees and creditors. Indeed, the success of the company depends on satisfying a varying mix of wants among these groups at any given moment, when satisfying that particular mix is the best way in which it can pursue its objectives. The people who should benefit from this commitment cannot be limited to shareholders. It is not that they should not be so limited; they cannot be if the present principles of company law are to be respected – and this is true even if one accepts the view that the reason a company exists is to enhance the value of shareholder investments in it over time.

In other words, a notional circle must be drawn that places outside the company's interest certain personal interests, but not certain types of person. You cannot exclude any one of them in advance, with their right to insist that their derivative interests be satisfied, without running the risk of impeding the company's function. While the company exists in order to satisfy some, not all interests, these must be at the same time a subset of the interests of all, not some of the relevant people able to contribute to the company's successful function. Shareholders themselves do not drop out of the picture, of course, but become one of the constituencies, as indeed do sub-groups of shareholders. It becomes possible to work out balances of interests between majorities and minorities as well, but in a context in which some of the shareholders may have alliances of interest with employees and creditors while others are in conflict with them.[97] The people who should benefit from this commitment cannot be limited to shareholders.

Consider, by way of an example, the competing interests of employees and shareholders in a hypothetical land company, which earns a revenue from rents and employs workers on the upkeep of the land. Were we to consider their respective claims on the revenue of the company as a strict matter of what is fair and just in the light of the personal needs of each, we might get a particular answer, A (which we can allow the reader to fill in the light of her general political convictions). However, if it is clear that more cash has to be injected into the business by way of a further issue of shares so as to carry on with the upkeep of the land, that would properly cut across, and as far as the *company* was concerned take priority over, the just and fair distribution, A, looked at simply from the point of view of the respective personal needs of shareholders and workers. We can call this distribution B. B may actually yield more for the employee or shareholder than A, though it may well yield less, depending on how vital upkeep of the land is, how scarce labour for it is, and how crucial injection of fresh capital is, etc. In any event, the company's interest is in distribution B, not A. The employee's and shareholder's interest is in both distribution A and in B, and these may come into conflict with one another. Here, however, we can see that the interests of the company are identified in part by the purpose for which it exists, and as such are independent from some, but not all, of the interests of those affected by it. The difference is reflected in these two possible distributions of its revenue: the one fixed by reference to the personal needs of the parties affected, the other fixed by the purpose the enterprise is there to accomplish. This would be as true, it should be noticed, if the enterprise in question were a worker controlled cooperative.

97 There is a third possibility, which is that we define the interest of the company by building A into B, such that a background fair wage goes into the distribution B, if the company can afford it. At this point, he is claiming that it is against the company's interest to pay him less than the fair wage.

For any given worker or shareholder, Jones, these two sets of interests may complement one another, or they may conflict. When a worker in our land company has to take less of a wage in order that more money be raised by a share issue to be invested on upkeep of the property, his personal interest in a fair distribution of the revenue is in conflict with his shared interest with shareholders in seeing the company successfully manage its land. If he knows that the company will, for example, go broke if it cannot raise further capital, he will often allow his personal interest to take second place, preferring distribution B over A. On the other hand, if the company is prospering, and its directors want to expand operations by raising more capital while holding down wages, then the interest of the company and his own in a fair distribution of its revenue may well diverge, and he may give priority to the latter by way of pushing for a successful round of collective bargaining.

That is precisely why the interests of the company should not be all that dominates in the working world or the community at large, even as members of the latter do count in making up that corporate interest in the first place. The company's interest may well overlap with, but may not be not identical with the interests of wider society, such that the latter can only plausibly claim to control the former in the name of what is "really" in that company's interest. This is what is misleading in those theories which tell us that since the corporate form is a creation of the state, the state is entitled to intervene in the name of making sure that social utility and corporate interest coincide.[98] There will be many instances where they do not, and cannot, and we should be clear about that when we allow the former to dominate the latter. For example, we can see social interests conflict with and take priority over the company's interest in that section of the Companies Act 1985 which says that a company may make provision for the benefit of employees in connection with (inter alia) the transfer of an undertaking, even if such a provision is not in the best interests of the company.[99]

It follows, in our view, that the conception of the company as a set of constituencies is partly right: no single group can be allowed to dominate the allocation of the company's resources if it is to function successfully. On the other hand, it is wrong to see the company as the "community" we have seen described in at least one influential stakeholder theory. That view fails to appreciate how there will inevitably be tensions – and often necessary tensions in a democracy – between personal and derivative interests within the enterprise. It is a tension which will sometimes pit workers against management in collective bargaining, even as there are other points at which both will come together on the best corporate strategy to follow. Contrary to the views of the trade union movement mentioned earlier, it seems wrong to be deterred by a fear of split allegiance here. There is already an equivalent split for many nominee directors, who feel constrained to make one decision for the benefit of a company even though it is not in the optimal interests of the institutional investor, or holding company, which has nominated them to the board.[100]

[98] M. Lipton and S. Rosenblum, "A New System of Corporate Governance" 58 U. Chi. L. Rev. 187 [1991] at 188.

[99] CA 1985, s. 719.

[100] *Kuwait Asia Bank v EC v National Mutual Life Nominees Ltd* [1991] 1 AC 187.

2. *Who Should Control Corporate Power?*

We have seen two broad reasons for advocating new allocations of competence in corporate governance, the one focused on the poor quality of available investment and the other focused on the poor quality of corporate strategy. The former widens control to the extent that greater influence is given to long-term investors; the latter wants to widen control to a wider set of constituents, and would be sympathetic to two-tier boards with employee representatives included on the top tier.

In our view, the latter is the more convincing position. However, for the reasons explored this is not in order to obtain a fixed result dictated from the outside, such as a more stable set of corporate objectives. That must be an internal decision from all relevant parties. However, the relevant parties are all of the individuals with derivative interests at stake: they should all have their represenatives participating in a supervisory capacity over management. The alternative is to enfranchise only one such body with derivative interests: the shareholders. The latter solution allows the personal interests of shareholders inevitably to mix in when they vote: often dominating when they should not – and often reflected in a greater concern for the exchange value of their shares than for other relevant features of the well-being of the company.

A further point, however, is that this proposal is not made out of a concern to achieve greater social equity across groups within the enterprise: imposing that duty on management would be a recipe for impasse and an invitation to persistent wars of attrition from interest groups. Issues of social justice and social policy generally must remain on the agenda, but as separate domains of law: employment, environmental, and constitutional.

VII. CONCLUSION

The general election in the UK was the occasion for fundamental debates about the nature and quality of democracy in the country. It has congealed around the merits and demerits of a stakeholder model of democracy. The wider implications of accepting or rejecting this model are not obvious, but within the realm of corporate governance the options are becoming clearer. It is both an economic and political set of concerns, in which – whatever the formal position that emerges – the UK may already be moving closer to some of the corporate structures to be found on the continent, and discussed elsewhere in this book.

9

The United States

*Arthur R. Pinto**

I. INTRODUCTION

Although various constituencies are affected by how the publicly traded corporations are governed, the primary relationship which has shaped corporate law is between the managers and the owners.[1] The issue of the allocation of power within the corporation and the need to control management's power without harming the operation of the business has long been the focus of corporate law.[2]

Under traditional corporate structure, control of a corporation is vested in the board of directors elected by the shareholders and these directors chose the managers to run the business. In 1933, Professors Berle and Means published their study of publicly held corporations and concluded that ownership had become widely dispersed in many such corporations with the result that control had become separated from ownership in these companies.[3] The Berle and Means study found a large number of public companies in which no single shareholder owned a large amount of stock. The dispersion of ownership of shares effectively transfers control of the corporation to its managers because the managers have control of the corporate assets and of the proxy voting mechanisms. In practice, shareholder dispersion and the resulting passivity allows managers to act freely with little recourse. This separation of ownership and control can be beneficial when the managers are operating the business well. But if managers are acting for their own interests or poorly manage, the owners may suffer losses.

This chapter will focus on the different legal and market monitoring devices available to protect shareholders from losses due to this separation of control. This chapter will also discuss changes in the ownership of shares by large institutions

* Professor of Law and Co-Director Brooklyn Law School Center for the Study of International Business Law. This chapter is adapted from Arthur R. Pinto, "Corporate Governance: Monitoring The Board of Directors in American Corporations", 46 Am.J.Comp.L., p. 317 (Suppl 1998).

[1] The term managers generally includes the board of directors but more significantly the officers and inside directors who in reality control and run the corporation. For a broader view see Margaret M. Blair, *Ownership and Control* (1995).

[2] In closely held corporations, there is often a group of shareholders who control the corporation by virtue of their ownership and ability to elect the directors. In that context the issue of governance involves the protection of the minority shareholders from oppression by the control group.

[3] *The Modern Corporation and Private Property* (1933).

© Kluwer Law International 1998

such as pension funds and mutual funds, and the implications of these changes to American corporate law.

II. BACKGROUND

American corporate law must be understood in the context of the American federal system. Federal law is enacted by the United States Congress while state law is enacted by individual state legislatures. Each state has its own judiciary and legal system, separate from the federal system that encompasses all states. Generally, it is state law that provides for incorporation and for the rules of corporate governance. Therefore, in order to incorporate, a certificate of incorporation must be filed in a specific state. It is that state's law which usually provides the rules and regulations governing the relationship between the shareholders and the managers.[4]

Incorporating in the United States is a fairly simple and inexpensive procedure, usually requiring the filing of a certificate of incorporation in the state in which one chooses to incorporate. There are generally no minimum capital requirements in establishing a corporation. A company can issue shares at any price since shares need not be issued at a certain par or minimum amount.[5] The stock does not need to be offered to everyone at the same price so long as there is full disclosure. The simplicity of corporate formation encourages the use of the corporate form for business.

Every state has its own corporate law statute that provides the corporate rules. These statutes generally do not differ significantly among the states. The statutes indicate how to incorporate, deal with financing and legal capital rules, establish the basic structure of the board of directors, deal with shareholder power and rights, and address a variety of other issues. Every state also has its own body of judicially created law, or common law. Common law has a deep tradition in the United States, as in England, and American judges generally have significant discretion in interpretation of the law. A significant example, which will be discussed later, is the concept of fiduciary duty. While fiduciary duty is often defined by statute,[6] it is courts which in reality make the law through their decisions when applying the statute to a particular set of facts.

Corporations are permitted complete freedom in selecting the state of incorporation and often do not choose the state in which they have either their main office or assets. A large number of publicly held corporations have chosen to incorporate in the state of Delaware. Fifty-six per cent of the largest companies in America, known as the "Fortune 500", are incorporated in Delaware. Forty-five per cent of the companies that are traded on the New York Stock Exchange are incorporated in Delaware.[7] Although, most of these companies have at most a small presence in the

[4] One conflict of law principle provides that the internal affairs of a corporation shall generally be governed by the state of incorporation. Restatement (Second) of the Conflict of Laws, § 302 (1971). The states generally accept the idea that the state of incorporation should govern internal affairs. This does not mean that the law of the state of incorporation governs other corporate dealings such as commercial transactions, contracts or tort law.

[5] No par shares are permitted by most states, e.g. Revised Model Bus. Code Ann. § 6.21 [hereinafter RMBCA].

[6] See text at note 74 infra.

[7] "Delaware Says, 'Raider, Shoo!'", *Time*, 15 Feb. 1988, p. 85 (there were 180,000 companies incorporated in Delaware, including 45 per cent of those listed on the NYSE). In 1986, Delaware received 16

state, these statistics are significant because Delaware law is applied to the internal affairs of these companies.[8] Thus, Delaware statutory and case law is significant to an understanding of the regulation of publicly held corporations.[9]

The prevalence of state law dealing with corporate governance does not mean that there is not also a federal presence. Federal securities law deals with some issues involving corporate governance.[10] The Securities Act of 1933[11] ("the 1933 Act") generally deals with the regulation of the offering of securities to the public and the Securities and Exchange Act of 1934[12] ("the 1934 Act") focuses on the trading of securities. While the 1933 Act provides for full disclosure about the securities of companies that are to be sold to the public,[13] the 1934 Act regulates the trading of those securities. Thus, the 1934 Act provides for continuous disclosure of informa-

cont.
per cent of all its revenues from corporate fees. Delaware has a direct economic interest in encouraging incorporation within its borders. See Barrett, "Delaware Moves Closer to Adopting Law to Deter Hostile Takeovers", Wall St. J., 9 Dec. 1987, p. 41.

8 There are several reasons why states tend to honor the internal affairs doctrine. A provision in the United States Constitution, called the "full faith and credit clause", directs that states should respect the laws of the Constitution of other states. There are also arguments that the commerce clause could require such a deference. However, the application of one state's corporate law is a more a principle of conflict of laws than constitutional law. See Arthur Pinto, "The Constitution and the Market for Corporate Control: State Takeover Statutes After CTS Corp.", 29 Wm. & Mary L. Rev., p. 699, (1988) (hereinafter "State Takeover Statutes").

9 Legal scholars have long debated whether state corporate law protects investors and whether there is a need for federal incorporation. Those on both sides of the debate recognize that states compete for incorporation, creating a market for corporate charters but disagree about whether the market protects shareholders. Compare William H. Cary, "Federalism and Corporate Law: Reflections upon Delaware", 83 Yale L. J., p. 663 (1974), (argues for minimum federal standards) with Ralph Winter, *Government and the Corporation* (1978) (argues for the continued use of state corporate law). See generally Roberta Romano, "Law as a Product: Some Pieces of the Incorporation Puzzle", 1 J. of Law, Eco, & Org., p. 225 (1985). Regardless of the outcome of this debate, Delaware continues to dominate corporate law in the United States. One of the major advantages resulting from the presence of so many corporations in Delaware, is that an excellent corporate bar has evolved as well as a judiciary who understand the complexities of corporate law. The significant amount of state case law means that in Delaware judges will understand complex corporate cases and extensive case law facilitates legal advice.

10 In order to appreciate federal securities law, one must understand its historical context. The first federal securities laws were passed by Congress during President Franklin Delano Roosevelt's first term in office and the New Deal. Some believed that the economic depression in the nation was precipitated by a stock market crash which took place in 1929. It was contended that the crash was caused in part by the actions of some securities dealers who had defrauded the public through the sale of securities without full disclosure and by market manipulations. To prevent a recurrence, Congress studied the stock market crash and provided a system of full disclosure. In addition the study by Professors Berle and Means also influenced the legislation.

11 The Securities Act of 1933, 15 U.S.C. §77a-77aa [hereinafter 1933 Act].

12 The Securities Exchange Act of 1934, 15 U.S.C. §§78a-78kk (1988) [hereinafter 1934 Exchange Act].

13 The issuance of securities is regulated by the 1933 Act which requires the use of a full disclosure statement with all material information about the investment when selling securities in a public offering. A full disclosure document, called a registration statement, is filed with the SEC and securities are usually sold through a document called a prospectus which is part of the registration statement. The basis for the regulation is the theory that full disclosure allows investors, not the government, to decide if the security is a good investment. There is no federal "merit" regulation where the government must first approve the sale of the security in terms of the quality of the investment. There may also be some state regulation called "Blue Sky laws" which were designed to curb promoters who sell securities with no more value than "so many feet of blue sky". *Hall v Geiger-Jones Co.*, 242 U.S. 539, 550 (1917).

tion to the market, the regulation of brokers, dealers, stock exchanges and the over-the-counter markets, and includes anti-fraud and anti-manipulation rules which may directly or indirectly affect corporate governance.[14] There are also provisions of the 1934 Act which enhance shareholder rights.[15]

The 1934 Act also established the Securities and Exchange Commission (the "SEC") which is a government agency empowered to enforce and to interpret federal securities law. Enforcement takes place through issuing rules that interpret the law, and using a variety of powers to punish those who violate the securities laws. In addition, investors can sometimes initiate private litigation under the securities laws to seek a variety of remedies that protect their interests and enforce the law.

Federal securities law deals primarily with disclosure while state law deals with how the company is managed and controlled. That dichotomy does not seem to create a conflict, but the line between disclosure and behaviour is often unclear. If a company is required to make certain kinds of disclosures this may influence how the company behaves and in fact regulate the activity.

Federal and state corporate law co-exist so long as federal law allows it. If Congress wanted to establish a single body of federal corporate law it has constitutional authority to do so. Although there have been calls in Congress to mandate federal incorporation for large companies, the passage of such legislation has never been a serious possibility because of concerns for federalism and views that the current system works well.

III. THE PUBLICLY HELD CORPORATE PHENOMENON

The United States has the largest number of publicly traded corporations in the world where the ownership of many large corporations are owned by the public and the shares traded in the stock markets. In addition to a public market for shares there is also a public market for corporate debt so that banks do not dominate the lending to corporations. The fact that in the United States there is a market-oriented system where there are numerous sources of capital for a corporation facilitates the diffusion of ownership without any dominating shareholder and influences the monitoring systems that have developed.

While the vast majority of business entities in the United States are either sole proprietorships, partnerships or closely held corporations,[16] the publicly held corporation remains a significant economic actor in the United States economy. In 1994 there were approximately 9,600 publicly held corporations trading in various markets, generating a market capitalization of over $5 trillion.[17] Stock market capital-

[14] For example the 1934 Act deals with insider trading which restricts managers ability to use non-public information for their own personal benefit. Insider trading implicate issues of fiduciary duty and the integrity of the market. See *Dirks v Securities and Exchange Commission*, 463 S.Ct. 3255 (1983).

[15] See discussion of disclosure rules at Section VI.B infra.; right to communicate at VI.D infra and challenges to management at VI.E infra.

[16] In 1988 there were over 3.5 million corporations doing business in the United States. See *Statistical Abstract of the United States Table 827* (1992).

[17] Greg Steinmetz, "Mergers and Acquisitions Ran at Record Pace in Third Quarter", Wall St. J., 30 Sept. 1994, at C1.

ization of United States corporations represents approximately 95 per cent of Gross Domestic Product.[18]

These corporations are not only major employers and taxpayers with a significant impact on the United States economy but also are important to the savings of its citizens. As of 1992 over 51 million Americans own shares in public corporations or in stock mutual funds.[19] Even though a majority of the American public do not directly own shares, there is a strong interest in how well the public companies perform because of other indirect investments. For example pension funds that represent the retirement funds for many citizens, held $1.8 trillion in corporate equities as of 1995.[20] Thus, the publicly held corporation not only provides employment but constitutes a substantial amount of the nations savings.

There are numerous reasons that publicly traded corporations developed in America. It can be viewed as a natural result of growth fuelled by technology that required access to large amounts of capital and specialization provided by professional managers.[21] Companies can go public to provide the original investors and entrepreneurs who establish a company with the ability to gain a return on their investment. In addition, if a company grows and employees are given stock as an incentive, it may need to sell their shares to the public in order to create a trading market that will allow them to trade their shares. With the liquidity of a market, employees and other investors can sell their stock and gain a return on their investment.

The sale of securities to the public also provides companies with significant amounts of capital for expansion. For example in 1996, approximately $1.2 trillion was raised in public security offerings and of that $691 million involved equity with $185.5 billion raised by companies going public for the first time.[22] The public markets also have advantages for corporations because the cost of selling equity and debt to the public is generally lower then private sales. The cost is generally lower because the trading markets provide investors with liquidity. If one cannot easily sell the security the buyer will need to be compensated for the greater risk by seeking a greater rate of return and thus resulting in higher costs to the company.

A. Trading Markets

Given the number of publicly held companies and shareholders, there is an extensive market for the trading of stock. For example in 1996 there were over 2,900 corporations listed on the New York Stock Exchange, the largest and most significant auction market. A total of over 100 billion shares were traded annually with a daily volume of approximately $16 billion.[23] There are also over-the-counter markets

18 Michael Sesit Easdaq, "Europe's Version of Nasdaq, To Open Monday, Faces growing Pains", Wall St. J., 23 Sept. 1996, C1.

19 New York Stock Exchange, *Fact Book 1995*, p. 53.

20 Ibid., at p. 57. More than one adult in three owns stock directly or indirectly. Ibid., at p. 53.

21 Mark J. Roe, *Strong Managers Weak Owners*, pp. 3-8 (1994). Professor Roe has argued that political considerations are a major factor in the need to raise capital from the markets as opposed to large institutions such as banks and insurance companies. Ibid. Analysis of the history of American corporations also uncovers other reasons for the creation of public markets. See Michael C. Jensen, "Eclipse of the Public Corporation", 67 Harv. Bus. Rev., p. 61 (1989).

22 United States Securities and Exchange Commission, *1996 Annual Report*, p. 77.

23 New York Stock Exchange, *Factbook 1996 Data*, pp. 5-6 (1997).

where trading is done between dealers acting for customers or for their own accounts.[24]

All these markets are important even though they are secondary markets because the initial sale of stock to the public is through direct sales by the corporation using underwriters to sell to investors. The trading of stock in turn in these secondary markets provides liquidity for investors which in turn encourages them to purchase securities which facilitates the raising of capital.

Thus the regulation of the markets is designed to protect investors and encourage public ownership and is an important aspect of the protection of shareholders. The markets themselves provide some corporate governance rules designed to protect the shareholders.[25]

The stock markets are also significant because the active trading of shares provide a market mechanism to monitor the running of the business. An economic theory on which a stock market functions as a monitoring mechanism is based upon the Efficient Capital Market Hypothesis ("ECMH"). As a result of studies of the stock markets, particularly the New York Stock Exchange where most large companies trade, the ECMH contends that the numerous active traders react quickly and efficiently to information. Thus whenever new information is available about a company it is immediately reflected in the price of the stock. Efficiency means that all relevant information is gathered in the price. According to the ECMH, the only factor that will change the value of a company's stock is new information.[26] The ECMH has had a significant impact on several corporate law issues[27] and monitoring mechanisms.[28]

IV. THE CORPORATE STRUCTURE

The governing structure of a corporation is composed of the shareholders as the owners of the company and the board of directors who manage the company. For example, § 141 of Delaware Corporation Law provides that "the business of a corporation shall be managed by, or under the direction of, the board of directors".[29] The board of directors are usually elected by the shareholders each year at the

[24] The NASDAQ is the over-the-counter market and has over 5,500 listed companies. NASDAQ advertisement, *New York Times*, 11 Nov. 1997, D5.

[25] See e.g. text at notes 96-97 infra.

[26] See James H. Lorie, Peter Dodd and Mary Kempton, *The Stock Market: Theories and Evidence*, pp. 55-87 (2d ed. 1985). See also Christopher Paul Saari, "The Efficient Capital Market Hypothesis, Economic Theory and the Regulation of the Securities Industry", 29 Stan. L. Rev., p. 1031 (1977).

[27] For example, an efficient market where information is quickly assimilated into the price of stock also suggests that investors are unable to beat the market on a consistent basis. Thus shareholders should buy a portfolio of stocks to diversify and maximize their return. If owning a portfolio is the norm, some would argue that this reality should be recognized and considered in making corporate rules and may be fashioned to look to maximizing the value of the portfolio and overall corporate interests as opposed to shareholder interests in a specific corporation. See generally Easterbrook & Fischel, "Proper Role of Target's Management in Responding To a Tender Offer", 94 Harv. L. Rev., pp. 1161,1165-1174(1981) (argues that directors should not defend a target from a takeover so long as there is a premium offered since shareholders owning a portfolio of stock will benefit because of increased takeovers).

[28] See e.g. text at note 113 infra.

[29] Delaware General Corporation Law § 141 [hereinafter Del. GCL].

annual meeting. In a publicly held company, the board of directors sets policy and selects the officers who in reality manage the business with the board monitoring them.

A. Shareholders

The common shareholders, as owners of the corporation, are viewed as the residual claimants because their claim comes after creditors and preferred stock which usually has a fixed claim to corporate assets. All amounts above those fixed claims inure to the benefit of the common stock, so as the value of a firm increases so does the value of the common.

A significant issue for corporate law is how power is allocated between the shareholders and the directors and officers. Although the common shareholders are owners who select the directors, the relationship between them is not legally an agency-principal relationship because the principal (the shareholders) does not control the decisions of the agent (the directors).[30] Once elected the directors must act on behalf of the corporation and all of the shareholders not for the group that elected them.[31]

The primary source for the allocation of the power within a corporation is state law which provides the overall framework.[32]

The right of shareholders to vote is a fundamental power provided by statute. The usual voting required for shareholder action is a majority vote although some states use a supermajority vote for certain actions and corporate charters can require a supermajority vote. Generally there must be a least one class of stock with voting rights. The norm for most publicly traded corporations is to have one class of common stock with each share having one vote.[33] The certificate of corporation can

[30] Economists describe the relationship in terms of agency. See text at notes 53-54 infra.

[31] See Robert Charles Clark, *Corporate Law*, pp. 93-104 (1986). See Section VII infra where there is a shareholder control group.

[32] The state corporate law statutes have many different rules. Some are mandatory which cannot be altered; others are enabling which permits the corporation to select a rule if they chose; while other rules are suppletory or default rules which are used but can be altered. See Melvin Eisenberg,"The Structure of Corporation Law", 89 Col.L.R., pp. 1461, 1480-1485 (1989).

[33] One of the most controversial defensive tactics developed to avert hostile takeovers was the attempt by target managers to change the one share one vote rule by reclassifying shares into two classes. The reclassification created reallocated voting rights by placing significant voting power in only one of the resulting classes of shares largely owned by the managers. The result was that a successful hostile tender offer was impossible. This tactic was controversial because the change in voting rights was implemented when the company's one class of common stock was already widely held by public shareholders. Many felt it was a disenfranchisement of the public shareholders and the process of change raised questions of fairness. Jeffrey N. Gordon, "Ties that Bind: Dual Class Common Stock and the Problem of Shareholder Choice", 76 Calif. L. Rev., pp. 3, 40-41 (1988). The tactic requires a shareholder vote and arguably may even encourage the managers with the voting power to increase shareholder value. Ronald J. Gilson, "Evaluating Dual Class Common Stock: The Relevance of Substitutes", 73 Va. L. Rev., pp. 807, 811-23 (1987). The S.E.C. reacted to the New York Stock Exchange's attempt to change their requirement of one share one vote in order to continue to list companies after a dual-class recapitalization. The S.E.C. enacted 1934 Act rule 19c-4 which barred all regulated markets from listing companies that adversely changed existing voting rights. Ultimately the courts found that the S.E.C. did not have the authority to promulgate this rule, and that voting rights are traditionally matters of state corporate law. *Business Roundtable v SEC*, 905 F.2d. 406 (D.C.Cir.1990).

provide for more than one class of stock with voting rights and those rights can vary between classes.[34]

In terms of the allocation of power between the shareholders and the board of directors, the statutes are explicit on certain issues. The general scheme is for ordinary business decisions to be made by the board while certain structural and governance decisions are for the shareholders and sometimes with the board. Shareholders generally can vote on the election of directors, amendments to the by-laws and certificates and certain major structural issues such as mergers and sale of substantially all of the assets.

The right to vote for directors is the most significant right that shareholders of publicly traded corporations have when there is no large shareholder group. There is the idea of shareholder democracy which is often cited when voting rights are interfered with.[35] Managers need the votes of these shareholders to be re-elected and remain in power. They cannot vote shares held by either the corporation or its subsidiary. One would assume that given the need to get shareholder votes, managers would be concerned with their re-election and retention. But managers have control over corporate information and the corporation's proxy materials which are produced at corporate expense. In addition, shareholders in publicly traded corporations are viewed as passive with a preference to exit by selling rather than using their voice to challenge management.

The passivity of shareholders and failure to exercise their voting rights has been described as involving a "collective action" problem. First, there is an issue of whether or not the cost of activity is greater than the benefits. For example, if one owns shares in a company, and the managers of the company are stealing $10, yet it will cost $15 to enforce shareholder rights, then the shareholder will do nothing because the costs of recovery exceed the benefit. A rational profit maximizer will not spend the money. Even if it were to cost $5 to avoid losing $10, choosing not to act may still be justified by a shareholder's "rational apathy". Although the benefits exceed the cost, a rational profit maximizer would rather let someone else, particularly a larger shareholder, enforce rights on their behalf and thus "free-ride". If one shareholder waits and allows the large shareholders to act, then the small shareholder gets a free ride on another's work which raises an issue of fairness.[36]

In addition to the power to vote, shareholders are granted the right to receive some information under both federal securities laws and state law. [37]

B. Board of Directors

The board of directors must serve a dual function of allowing managers the flexibility they need to run the business while monitoring the managers to limit self-dealing

[34] By creating different classes it may allow different shareholder groups to have representation on the board of directors which may be important in a closely held corporation or a publicly held where a family or large shareholder group are involved.

[35] State courts have generally scrutinized closely actions taken by the board that affects voting rights that entrench managers. see e.g. *Blasius Industries, Inc. v Atlas Corp.*, 564 A.2d 651 (Del. Ch. 1988) (burden on the directors to show a compelling justification when directors acted to increase the number of directors to thwart an attempt by shareholders to elect directors that would have transferred power).

[36] Clark, supra note 31 at pp. 390-396.

[37] e.g. Sections VI.B and C infra.

and poor management. There has been a significant amount of commentary over how the board should act and its composition. Most of the legal monitoring devices are aimed at trying to get the board with outside directors to monitor without too much interference.

The unitary board of directors is the statutory norm for American corporations. The number of directors are usually set in the by-laws or certificate and elected by the shareholders at their annual meeting for a one-year term.[38] The board acts for the corporation and as a group and traditionally takes actions at meetings usually by a majority vote. Individual directors who are not officers have no authority to act except through the board.

Statutes generally permit boards to establish committees which are given particular tasks and can act for the board.[39] For example, many publicly traded corporations have executive, finance, nominating, audit and compensation committees. These and other committees serve a useful function allowing for fewer directors to focus on important issues.[40]

The actual role of the board will depend on many factors, including its make-up. There are generally no legal requirements that establish any particular norm for either board make-up or functioning. Those issues are more the result of other influences.[41] In general the larger public companies tend to have a certain number of independent directors that are not directly affiliated with the corporation and have committees of the board with independent members. This can be partially explained by corporate governance rules which the markets themselves have developed. For example, corporations listed on the New York Stock Exchange are required to have at least two independent directors and to have a separate audit committee made up of all independent directors.[42]

Given that directors are not legally the agents of the shareholders means that they can act within their power to run the corporation even if the majority of the shareholders disapprove.[43] If the shareholders seek change they can elect different directors at the next annual meeting or try to remove the directors by calling a special meeting prior to the annual meeting.[44] But once elected directors as fiduciaries to the corporation they must look out for all shareholders and the corporation.[45]

38 Shareholders can opt to stagger the election of the board so that directors have terms longer than a year. Such an arrangement may make it more difficult for someone wanting to challenge a board to gain immediate control.

39 e.g. RMBCA §8.25.

40 Whether most committees should consist of independent directors is a recent issue of corporate governance. See Section VIII.B infra.

41 See note 146 infra.

42 New York Stock Exchange, *Listed Company Manual*, §303. The over-the-counter market also requires listed companies to have a minimum of two independent directors and an audit committee comprised of independent directors. NASDAQ, *By-Laws*, Schedule D.

43 e.g. *People Ex Rel. Manice v Powell*, 201 N.Y. 194, 200-01 (1911).

44 The statutes generally allow for removal of directors for cause. They also may provide for removal by the shareholders without cause. RMBCA § 8.08. Prior to the statutory enactments courts found an inherent right to remove directors for cause by shareholders because shareholders as owners had the right to protect the corporation. See *Campbell v Loew's, inc.*, 36 Del. Ch. 563, 134 A.2d 852 (1957).

45 But the fact that the shareholders cannot force the directors to act does not mean that they cannot influence them. See discussion at Section VI.D infra.

C. Officers

The daily operations of the business are usually delegated to the officers who are elected by the board of directors. The election may be for a term but officers can be removed by the directors even if there is no cause.[46] The designation of officers is usually done by the corporation through the board or by designation in the bylaws.[47] Often one finds a president, one or more vice-presidents, a treasurer and a secretary. The statutes usually say very little about the actual power an officer has but it originates from the board and is delegated although some powers cannot be delegated.[48] Officers have a fiduciary duty to the corporation since they are corporate agents. Some of the officers also serve as inside directors.

While the legal model described allows flexibility in board structure and officer power, the usual management structure of publicly traded corporations centralizes power in the chief executive officer and senior officers. While there are concerns expressed over this power and the need to strengthen the outside directors' monitoring,[49] this structure will remain the norm given the business necessity of insiders managing the company.

V. WHAT CONSTITUTES CORPORATE GOVERNANCE?

Issues of corporate governance generally have revolved around shareholder rights and the power of managers. The system of regulation to prevent managers from using their power to the disadvantage of the shareholders while allowing them the flexibility to manage is a major focus of corporate law. In addition, the extent to which other constituencies such as labour and creditors should have a role in the corporate governance structure has also been an issue but with less significance.

A. Models of Governance

Legal scholars have studied the implications of the separation of ownership from control and debated whether such separation is harmful and how the law should deal with it. This debate has produced different theories of the firm and corporate law models.

The traditional approach to the perceived problem of managers taking advantage of the widely dispersed shareholders was a regulatory approach which would include calls for stronger state law protection of shareholders and an increased federal presence through expanding the reach of federal securities law[50] or federal incorporation of large publicly traded corporations.[51] The strengthening of shareholders rights and role in monitoring is the primary focus of this approach. This

46 e.g. RMBCA §8.08(a).

47 Ibid., §8.40.

48 For example, the board under state statutes initially approves of mergers and other fundamental transactions which cannot be delegated to officers.

49 See Section VIII.B infra.

50 See Joel Seligman, "The New Corporate Law", 59 Brook.L.Rev., p. 1 (1993).

51 See Ralph Nader et al., *Constitutionalizing the Corporation: The Case for the Federal Chartering of Giant Corporations* (1976).

approach requires that certain corporate rules must be mandatory with minimal standards to protect shareholders.

There is a pro-management approach that favours laws giving managers tremendous latitude in their activities. This model is premised on the idea that managers will protect the interests of shareholders because they have a mutual interest in protecting the corporation. Although managers do not own a large amount of shares, their livelihood depends upon a successful company. Thus, the shareholders and managers share similar goals of corporate advancement. In addition managers are arguably better able to look out for the entire corporation and its other constituencies since they are in the best position to consider different demands on the corporation. Yet these managers may also seek expansion and enlargement of the firm which supports their increased compensation without a corollary benefit for shareholders.[52]

The dominant theory of the firm that is debated is the law and economics approach or contractual model. An economic view of the corporation would describe the relationship between shareholders and managers as an agency relationship.[53] In any such relationship, the agent (managers) will not always act in the best interests of the principal (shareholders) thus there will be certain costs (i.e. agency costs) associated with the relationship. The principal will attempt to limit that from happening and incur monitoring expenditures. The agent will attempt to assure the principal that it will not happen by incurring bonding expenditures. In any case even with such expenses there will inevitably be some losses to the principal and that cost is referred to as a residual loss. From this analysis, it is generally beneficial to have a system that will reduce all of these agency costs. The law and economics approach views a market-oriented approach as the optimal way of looking at the firm and lowering agency costs rather than government regulation.[54]

Some law and economics theorists argue that a corporation can be seen as a nexus of contracts through which various claimants such as creditors, workers, shareholders, and consumers enter into agreements. Under a contractual approach, corporate law should provide the basic terms of the contract between shareholders and managers, but the parties should be allowed to change any terms at any time.[55] Such changes are seen as beneficial in providing a flexible, optimal and mutually agreeable system. Private contracting arguably allows different corporations to design different systems which is a more efficient means to lower agency costs.[56] Critics of this theory argue that some protection and regulation are needed, and these rules should not be changed so easily.[57]

52 The empire building of managers could justify higher compensation even where the larger enterprise did not produce gains for shareholders. See William A. Klein & John C. Coffee, Jr., *Business Organization and Finance*, pp. 172-173 (6th ed., 1996).

53 Michael C. Jensen and William H. Meckling, "Theory of the Firm: Managerial Behavior, Agency Costs and Ownership Structure," 3 J. Fin. Econ., pp. 305, 308 (1976). The legal relationship is not viewed as an agency relationship. See text at notes 30-31 supra.

54 See text at notes 71-72 infra.

55 Many state corporate statutory provisions do provide for changes in the rules when approved by a majority vote. For example, the norm for shareholder voting is a majority vote but a greater vote can be required if approved by the shareholders by amending the certificate of incorporation. E.g. RMBCA §10.21.

56 See Frank H. Easterbrook & Daniel R. Fischel, *The Economic Structure of Corporate Law* (1991).

57 One of the most convincing arguments against the contract theory is that a public company with thousands of shareholders cannot be involved in any real bargaining over the terms of the contract. The management of the company presents to the shareholders a proposal and they vote without negotia-

B. The Role of Constituencies

Corporate governance could also deal with the expansion of the obligation of directors to constituent groups or stakeholders other than the shareholders. This raises the issue of whether a corporation should be managed to not only benefit the shareholders but other constituencies such as labour, consumers, creditors[58] or the community. This responsibility is particularly important in the publicly held corporation because of its size, wealth and impact on society.

The advocates of shareholder gain as the sole motive for corporations believe that they are formed to run a business and other social activities should not be within their focus. Allowing managers to pick and chose which philanthropy or socially beneficial activity to undertake means that they are using shareholder money for their preferences and acting like unelected civil servants. In addition, profit is an easy yardstick to measure the success of a business whereas other socially beneficial activities are more difficult to gauge and thus the monitoring of managers becomes more difficult. Ultimately what is viewed as socially responsible is to maximize profits.[59]

Others view the corporation as being composed of other stakeholders than shareholders. Recognizing that the large publicly traded corporations have considerable power and play a significant role in the economy, that power should be exercised with a broader view of its responsibility. Thus fiduciary duty of managers should be to the enterprise not just to shareholders and should be viewed in a larger context.[60]

It is generally recognized that the main objectives of corporations is corporate profit and shareholder gain.[61] Imposing this duty is seen as necessary because unlike other constituencies which can be protected by bargaining and regulation, shareholders who are spread out and rationally apathetic need the protection of directors who are elected by the shareholders. While courts have expressed the primary purpose of the corporation as being profit-making,[62] there is considerable discretion in decision-making by the managers. Many publicly traded corporations play an active role in socially responsible activities and do look out for other interests.[63]

cont.

tion. Shareholders are often passive and rationally apathetic and do not possess perfect information about the corporation. Thus certain rules such as fiduciary duty should never be changed by contract. See Robert C. Clark, "Agency Costs Verses Fiduciary Duties", in *Principles and Agents: The Structure of Business* (John W. Pratt & Richard J. Zeckhauser eds., 1985).

58 When a corporation is insolvent and the equity has no value, the fiduciary duty shifts to the creditors because creditors become the owners. The Delaware courts have recognized that there may be some obligation to creditors prior to actual insolvency but when a corporation is close to it. *Credit Lyonnais Bank Nederland, N.V. v Pathe Communications Corp.*, 1991 WL 277613 (Del.Ch. 1991).

59 See generally Milton Friedman, *Capitalism and Freedom* (1962).

60 See Lawrence Mitchell, "A Theoretical and Practical Framework for Enforcing Corporate Constituency Statutes", 70 Tex. L. Rev., p. 579 (1992).

61 The A.L.I. Principles §2.01. Notwithstanding this objective a corporation may take ethical considerations into account and devote reasonable amounts to public welfare, humanitarian, educational, and philanthropic purposes. American Law Institute, *Principles of Corporate Governance* (1994) [hereinafter A.L.I. Prin. Corp. Gov.].

62 See, e.g. *Dodge v Ford Motor Co.* 170 NW 668 (Mich. 1919).

63 The broader view of social responsibility is often expressed as in the long-term interests of the corporation and shareholders which courts do not like to second-guess under the business judgment rule. See, e.g. *Shlensky v Wrigley* 237 NE 2d 776 (1968).

Over the years there have been attempts to change the board of directors to include representatives of particular groups or the public but it has rarely occurred.[64] Attempts to change or modify corporate activities have been more successful through publicity and pressure. One tactic has been the use of shareholders proposals on social issues through the federal proxy rules.[65] But even in that context a proposal needs to relate to the business activities of the corporation.[66]

In the 1980s threats of hostile takeovers were prevalent and target company managers argued that in considering the takeover there should be consideration of the shareholders and other constituencies such as creditors and employees. The Delaware Supreme Court had recognized "concern for various corporate constituencies is proper when addressing a takeover threat, that principle is limited by the requirement that there be some rationally related benefit accruing to the shareholders."[67] But many states went further and enacted statutes which attempt to broaden the fiduciary duty of directors to consider other constituencies in exercising their power.[68] The impact of these statutes remains uncertain because it is unclear whether they will be broadly or narrowly interpreted and used.[69]

VI. MONITORING MECHANISMS

The rights given to shareholders in the corporate governance structure in publicly traded corporations are limited to allow managers the freedom to run the business. While most corporations are well run and protect shareholders, the separation of ownership from control has the potential for those in control to be unaccountable and either poorly manage the business or take advantage of their power through self-dealing. Monitoring concerns the ways in which the system attempts to allow managers to operate the business effectively while limiting their ability to take advantage of their power and harm the shareholders.

While the primary focus of this chapter is on legal mechanisms, there are other significant monitoring devices. Publicity and politics can have a significant impact on attitude and rules.[70]

64 Two rare examples are Chrysler had a labour representative on its board as a result of its precarious financial situation in the 1970s when labour was asked to modify its benefits. Exxon put an environmentalist on its board after the Exxon Valdez oil spill in the 1980s.

65 See Section VI.D infra.

66 See *Medical Committee for Human Rights v SEC*, 432 F.2d 659 (1970).

67 *Revlon Inc v MacAndrews & Forbes Holdings, Inc*, 506 A.2d. 173,176 (Del. 1985).

68 See Roberta Karmel, "Implications of the Stakeholder Model", 61 Geo. Wash L. Rev., p. 1156 (1993). These statutes can be viewed more as attempting to protect the directors of the corporation from the takeover than protecting constituencies.

69 Compare e.g. NYBCL §717(b) (expands fiduciary duty when there is a change of control) with 15 Pa. Cons. Stat. Ann. §715 (Purdon) (general expansion of the duty).

70 For example, in 1992 President Bush visited Japan to pressure the Japanese to open their markets and was accompanied by some corporate executives. The result of the visit was embarrassing for Mr. Bush because it was revealed that these American executives who were complaining about the Japanese, received compensation that was extremely high in comparison to their Japanese counterparts. American chief executive officers were paid 150 times more than the average American worker whereas Japanese executives were paid 17 times more than the ordinary Japanese worker. See Byrne, "How CEO Paychecks Got So Unreal", Bus. Wk., 18 Nov. 1991, p. 20 The public outrage about the high compensation influenced the SEC to submit a proposal to require companies to disclose more information about executive compensation. The SEC also changed its position and now allows share-

There are important markets that serve to protect shareholders. The market for a company's products provides the most significant impact. If the company is run poorly and its products do not compete successfully in the market for products, the company could fail and the managers would lose their positions. The stock market provides a significant mechanism to monitor managers. Assuming the ECMH and the pricing of shares reflects information about the company, then if a company is poorly managed it would be reflected in the price of that company's stock and could also raise the cost of its debt. This raises its cost of capital which hurts it in competition with other businesses.[71] Therefore, management will attempt to manage efficiently to keep the stock price high and capital costs low. There is also a market for managers which encourages managers to do an efficient job because it enhances their ability to move to another position.[72]

A. Fiduciary Duty

An important monitoring device is the imposition of fiduciary duty obligations on directors and managers. Directors as fiduciaries, must act with due care and loyalty to the corporation by protecting corporate interests over their own. Directors and managers are made fiduciaries because shareholders who invest their capital need such protection.[73]

The directors' fiduciary duty is often described as consisting of the duty of care and the duty of loyalty. While the duties have primarily developed through case law, the duty of care is generally described in state corporate statutes. For example, the Revised Model Business Corporation Act, § 8.30 indicates that directors must dis-

cont.

holders to make recommendations about compensation to the board of directors under the federal proxy rules. See Regulation of Communications Among Security holders, Exchange Act Release No. 34-30849 (24 June 1992) (Revision of proposed rules on proxy proposals concerning executive compensation). High executive compensation also became a campaign issue and President Clinton proposed and Congress enacted changes in the tax law that tied compensation to performance. I.R.C. § 161(m) (1995).

71 For example, a low-stock price requires the company to sell a greater number of shares to raise the same amount of capital as a competing business with a higher stock price.

72 In light of the monitoring of the markets, the law and economics model argues that law should only facilitate market mechanisms or provide rules when markets fail. See generally, Daniel R. Fischel, "The "Race to the Bottom" Revisited: Reflections on Recent Developments in Delaware's Corporation Law", 76 Nw. U. L. Rev., p. 913 (1982). There is also the market for corporate control which although a market mechanism its existence and effectiveness is heavily influenced by law. See Section VI.E infra.

73 Those who approach corporate law from the law and economics perspective see fiduciary duty rules as representing the terms of a contract between investors and managers. While investors could contract for this obligation, the law imposes this responsibility because it would be expensive and time-consuming to negotiate detailed contracts delineating managers' obligations and the law eliminates the need to actually enter a contract. Thus the law provides standardized rules which lowers transaction costs and avoids free riding, where the small shareholders avoid costs by relying on the monitoring activities of larger shareholders. Given the need for managerial flexibility these rules are rarely detailed. See Easterborook & Fischel, supra note 56. Whether these rules should be modifiable to allow shareholders to contract with the managers for different rules, see text at notes 55-57 supra. There is also a strong moral basis for imposition of fiduciary responsibility and some cases reflect this attitude. A line in the New Testament is often quoted: "No servant can serve two masters: for either he will hate the one and love the other; or else he will hold to the one, and despise the other." Luke 16:12 (King James).

charge their duties in good faith; with the care an ordinarily prudent person in like position would exercise under similar circumstances; and in a manner he reasonably believes to be in the best interests of the corporation.[74] It is the courts that will determine, in a given case, liability and the parameters of fiduciary duty. Generally, the directors acting in the corporation's interest must not be negligent in their duties.[75] The courts in determining liability will distinguish between directors who are insiders and outsiders, holding insiders to higher standards of care.[76] In addition, if certain directors are placed on the board for their particular skills, their performance may be tested by a different standard measured by their expertise.[77]

Plaintiffs bringing duty of care cases are rarely successful.[78] When decisions are made there is a judicial principle called the business judgment rule which limits judicial inquiry into business decisions and protects directors who are not negligent in the decision-making process.[79] Under the rule, the courts will not review a director's decision itself, even if it is a wrong or poor decision. The rule provides a presumption that directors, when they make decisions, will not be second-guessed by the courts. The courts believe it is not their role to make business decisions. Directors should make business decisions without fear of liability because shareholders select directors to take risks even though mistakes lose money. The idea of a court second-guessing business decisions and then creating liability for directors could make directors overly cautious with reduced economic gain.[80] The rule protects mis-

[74] The fiduciary duty imposed upon managers is not the same duty imposed upon other fiduciaries such as trustees. The law recognizes that a fiduciary duty can differ based upon the nature and circumstances of the relationship. For example, it is recognized that when money is placed into a trust, trustees have strict duties on how they can invest that money. These duties are measured under a "prudent man" standard, which requires extreme care when investing. The same rule is inapplicable in the corporate context since, unlike trustees, directors are hired to take risks because greater profits require risk and profit is what shareholders seek in buying stock. The courts recognize the responsibilities of fiduciaries in different contexts and necessarily impose different rules. *Joy v North,* 692 F.2d 880, 885-6. (2d Cir. 1982), cert. denied, *Cititrust v Joy*, 460 U.S. 1051, 103 S.Ct. 1498 (1983).

[75] (76) The standard in Delaware is gross negligence. See *Smith v Van Gorkom*, 488 A.2d 858, 872-73 (Del. 1985).

[76] (77) See *Bates v Dressler*, 251 U.S. 524, 40 S. Ct. 247, 64 L. Ed. 388 (1920).

[77] James Cox, et. al., *Corporations*, p. 188 (1997) (hereinafter "Cox").

[78] Many states have provisions which permit corporations to amend their certificates to eliminate monetary damages in duty of care cases. See, e.g., Del. Stat. 102(b)(7). See Hanks, "States Move To Adopt Statutory Limitations On Director Liability", *Legal Times*, 12 Oct. 1987, p. 19. See also Douglas M. Branson, "Assault On Another Citadel: Attempts To Curtail The Fiduciary Standard Of Loyalty Applicable To Corporate Directors", 57 Fordham L. Rev., pp. 375, 376 (1988). Most publicly traded corporations have such provisions.

The impetus was the case of *Smith v Van Gorkom*, 488 A.2d 858 (Del. 1985) where the Delaware Supreme Court found directors liable for gross negligence in deciding to sell the corporation in a two-hour board meeting without complete information. The case was controversial because the sale was arm's length, shareholders received almost a 50 per cent over the market price and half the directors were outside directors. In response states concerned over director liability and rising costs of insurance enacted various statutory provisions.

[79] Directors can also be liable for their failure to monitor and their inaction can create liability. But generally its needs to be established that the directors had actual knowledge of wrongdoing or that there was a sustained or systematic failure of board oversight causing harm. In *Re Caremark International Inc. Derivative Litigation* (Del. Ch. 1996).

[80] Joy, 692 F. 2d 880, 885-886. In addition, the business judgment rule is inapplicable where the directors make a decision that has no business purpose; the decision is irrational; the directors have a conflict of interest; there is fraud, bad faith or illegality; the decision creates a no win situation; or there is a prolonged failure to exercise. Ibid. at 886.

takes in the decision but does not protect negligence in the decision-making process.[81]

The duty of loyalty is different from the duty of care because directors are accused of a conflict of interest for receiving a personal benefit from a business decision. The self-dealing context, while sometimes beneficial to the corporation, raises the spectre of corruption and personal profit at the expense of shareholders and may be difficult to detect.[82] Thus the fiduciary duty rules on duty of loyalty are stricter.

In duty of care cases, the plaintiff usually has to prove that the directors were negligent in the process of making a decision and the courts rarely scrutinize the decision. In duty of loyalty cases, the courts usually change the litigating process by shifting the burden of proof to the directors and the transaction is scrutinized and tested against a fairness standard.[83] Thus in duty of loyalty cases there is more judicial involvement.[84] The difference is justified because in a duty of care case the courts want to protect the business decisions that are intended to enhance corporate gain while a decision with self-interest may not be motivated to help the business.

Fiduciary duty serves to restrain managers by setting some rules and allowing courts the ability to scrutinize some transactions for their effects. The flexibility of those rules are advantageous because courts can adapt to different contexts but the disadvantage is that its enforcement is based upon litigation with costs.[85] Duty of care cases are difficult and rare which means duty of loyalty cases are the more litigated cases. But even in loyalty cases the tendency is to make litigation more difficult when independent directors are involved in the decision-making process.[86] In addition there are some areas, such as issues involving control transactions, which do not neatly fit within the categories of either duty of care or loyalty and which require a different kind of analysis.[87]

[81] Even if there is negligence in the decision-making process, the plaintiff may have to prove causation between the negligence and the harm which can be difficult. In cases involving a failure to monitor or nonfeasance, it is particularly difficult to connect the failure to act with the damage. It may be necessary to establish not only that the directors committed a wrong, but that what they did or should have done was a substantial factor in the damage. *Barnes v Andrews,* 298 Fed. 614 (S.D.N.Y. 1924). But see *Cede & Co. v Technicolor, Inc.*, 634 A.2d 345 (Del. 1993). (The court held that if a plaintiff establishes a breach of the duty of care then there is a prima facie case of liability without showing causation.)

[82] See Alison Anderson, "Conflicts of Interest: Efficiency, Fairness and Corporate Structure", 25 U.C.L.A.L.Rev., p. 737 (1975).

[83] The involvement of independent directors or the vote of the shareholders on a particular transaction can affect the extent of the judicial scrutiny. For example, the use of independent directors to negotiate for the minority shareholders in a freeze-out transaction may shift the burden of proof from the controlling shareholder to the minority shareholder. See *Kahn v Lynch Communication Systems*, 638 A.2d. 1110, (Sup. Del. 1994). In Delaware disinterested shareholder approval with full disclosure can cure a duty of care breach and shift the burden of proof in loyalty cases. Depending on the particular circumstances involved in the loyalty claim, the court in shifting the burden can invoke the business judgment rule or keep fairness as an issue. See *In Re Wheelabrator Technologies Shareholders Litigation*, 663 A.2d 1194 (Del. Ch 1995) (court retains fairness in control transactions and business judgment in interested directors transactions).

[84] Ahmed Bulbulia & Arthur R. Pinto, "Statutory Responses to Interested Directors' Transactions: A Watering Down of Fiduciary Standards?", 53 Notre Dame L.Rev., p. 201 (1977).

[85] See Section VI.F infra.

[86] e.g., A.L.I. Prin. Corp. Gov. §5.02(2)(B).

[87] See text at notes 117-121 infra.

B. Disclosure

An important monitoring device that protects shareholders is the requirement of full disclosure to the shareholders on issues of significance. Disclosure is mandated by both fiduciary duty and federal securities law.[88] Justice Brandeis wrote that "Sunlight is said to be the best of disinfectants; electric lights the most efficient policeman".[89] Disclosure informs potential investors and existing shareholders about their investment and can inform the shareholders that the managers are acting adversely to shareholder interests. The theory behind mandating disclosure is that it informs investors and also affects the way persons behave.

As discussed, federal securities law provides many disclosure rules. The 1933 Act regulates the sale of securities to investors and requires that whenever securities are sold to the public a full disclosure document is filed with the SEC and made available to investors. This document is intended to provide investors with the opportunity to decide if the investment is worthwhile. If one invests when there is a lack of full disclosure, the investor can recover against the company. The directors, officers, underwriters and experts can also be liable if, in the preparation of disclosure documents, they did not act with due diligence. Due diligence requires a certain amount of investigation and holding these people liable forces them to take an active role in disclosure.[90]

Under the 1934 Act, there are several disclosure requirements for public companies.[91] These companies are required to make continuous disclosure to the markets through public filings with the SEC. For example, every year an annual report must be filed with audited financial statements. Shareholders usually receive an annual proxy statement that not only discusses the issues to be voted on at a shareholders meeting but includes an annual report to the shareholders. Any special meetings to vote on major decisions, such as a merger or amendments to the certificate of incorporation, also require a proxy statement with full disclosure to inform the shareholders and the market.[92]

[88] It is unclear whether federal law can be used when the primary harm is due to a breach of fiduciary under state law. See *Santa Fe Industries, Inc. v Green*, 430 U.S. 462 (1977). If as a result of the failure to fully disclose shareholders lose some remedy under state law such as the right to seek appraisal or equity then federal law securities law could be implicated. See e.g. *Goldberg v Meridor*, 567 F2d. 209 (2d. Cir. 1977).

[89] Louis D. Brandeis, *Other People's Money and How the Brokers Use It*, p. 92 (1932).

[90] Section 11 of the 1933 Act does create civil liability for the underwriters, directors and certain officers of a corporations who fail to exercise their due diligence in ensuring that the registration statement used in issuing securities is not misleading. It is interesting to note that the federal standard of care is the person who is reasonably prudent in their own affairs which is a higher standard than the state law norm for directors of the reasonably prudent person in similar circumstances. 1933 Act, supra note 12, at 15 U.S.C. §§ 77(k)(1988). In addition there is a general requirement of periodic management discussion and analysis of the financial condition of the company. See Management Analysis and Discussion of Financial Condition, Sec. Act Rel. No.33-6835 (SEC 18 May 1989).

[91] section 12 of 1934 Exchange Act, 15 U.S.C. 781(g)(1). Companies that are listed on a national exchange or has 500 shareholders and $10 million in assets are reporting companies required to comply with various regulations under the 1934 Act.

[92] The scope of full disclosure depends upon the transaction involved. The SEC has explicit requirements of what must disclosed yet companies also have no obligation under federal securities law to ensure that disclosure documents contain all available material information. The test for materiality is the substantial likelihood that a reasonable shareholder would consider the information important in making the particular decision. *TSC industries v Northway Inc.*, 426 U.S. 438, 449 (1976).

An important aspect of disclosure is the financial accounting conducted by the corporation. Significant information is disclosed through financial statements prepared by accountants. Public companies under federal securities law are required to conduct audits of their financial statements by independent accountants, who have no financial interest in the company.[93] This is a significant part of the process of disclosure because statements prepared and audited by independent accountants are designed to limit manipulation and fraud. Although they are hired by the company, independent accountants have some obligation to creditors and investors.[94]

The SEC also participates in corporate financial accounting. While it has the power to impose rules on how financial statements should be prepared and presented, the SEC does not usually take an active role in spelling out these rules. Instead it allows the accountants and their professional organizations to establish and promulgate these rules known as generally accepted accounting principles.[95]

The markets also have a role in disclosure. Inadequate disclosure is a grounds for delisting a security from trading. The rules of some markets such as NYSE encourage companies listed to make prompt disclosure of material information.[96] In addition, NYSE-listed companies are required to have an audit committee consisting of independent directors who choose the auditors and review their reports.[97]

Finally, state law has a role in encouraging disclosure. A fiduciary under state law has an obligation in certain contexts to fully disclose material information on specific corporate issues.[98] In some instances the lack of disclosure is enough to violate the fiduciary duty even without regard to the underlying transaction.[99]

C. Right to Information

Under state law, shareholders' are granted rights and access to corporate information. Shareholders may sometimes inspect the books and records of the company they have invested in, or the list of the other shareholders.[100] This list of sharehold-

[93] The Foreign Corrupt Practices Act of 1977, 15 U.S.C. §78dd-2, added §13(b)(2) to the 1934 Act requiring reporting companies to keep accurate and detailed books and records and have internal accounting controls.

[94] If the accountant preparing the statements finds something that appears inconsistent or fraudulent, ignoring it could be negligent and lead to liability. Imposing this obligation helps to ensure the accountability of the company to its investors. It is not a perfect system because the information used to prepare it is supplied by the company. See generally, Joel Seligman, "Accounting and the New Corporate Law", 50 Wash.&Lee L.Rev., p. 943 (1993).

[95] The SEC has delegated to the Financial Accounting Standards Board, an independent private body consisting of both private and public representatives, the responsibility for proposing accounting principles. The SEC has influenced the formation of these principles which at times can be controversial. The recent controversy over how companies should report their derivative activities indicates that these principles can be controversial. Roger Lowenstein, "Corporate America Bullies FASB Part II", Wall St. J., 11 Sept. 1997 at c1.

[96] N.Y. Stock Exch., Listed Company Manual Para. 202. While investors are not able to enforce these requirements directly, the markets can take action against the company.

[97] See generally, Joel Seligman, *Corporations Cases and Materials*, p. 373 (1995).

[98] e.g., *Rosenblatt v Getty Oil Co.*, 493 A.3d 929 (Del. 1985) (The court adopted use of the Northway Test, supra note 92).

[99] See e.g. ALI Prin. Corp. Gov. §5.02(a) (failure to disclose an interested directors transaction violates the duty of loyalty).

[100] There is both a common law and statutory right of inspection. In order for a shareholder to get the shareholders' list or to inspect the books and records, states require the shareholder to have a proper purpose. This requirement seeks to prevent shareholders from using this valuable information to

ers enables communication between shareholders about how the company is managed or whether to take over the company.

D. Right to Communicate

There is a right of shareholders to express some opinions about their companies. A significant New York case allowed shareholders to vote on a resolution at a share holders meeting on whether or not they approved of the performance of the former president of the company. Managers argued that shareholders should have no right to express their opinion about the officer since shareholders did not have the right to select officers. The court ruled that even though shareholders have no right to elect the officer, they have a right to express their opinion.[101] This case was influential in expressing shareholder voice and democracy in voting.

This right to express an opinion is a major issue under the federal proxy rules. SEC Rule 14a-8 allows shareholders of publicly traded corporations the right to place in management's proxy statement certain proposals concerning the company so long as state law permits the subject. The rule permits exclusion of matters that are unrelated to the corporation or in the ordinary course of business.[102] The line between what relates to the corporation and what is not ordinary or significant is not always clear. The rule has been used for a variety of purposes.[103] More recently institutional investors have been more active using both the shareholder proposal rule and using their own proxy materials to try to influence management on corporate governance issues.[104]

E. Challenges to Management Control

When there is separation of ownership from control, no shareholder group controls and the market for corporate control is available as a monitoring device. Through this market, challengers to management seek to replace them if they are not acting for the shareholders. There are two ways to replace management in this market: the proxy fight and the hostile tender offer. In either case these are extraordinary rem-

cont.
harass management or for personal benefits. It is a proper purpose to want to change the management or generally communicate to shareholders on financial matters. It is generally easier to get the shareholder list with the burden on the corporation to show improper purpose. See *Compaq Computer Corp. v Horton*, 631 A.2d 1 (1993).

101 *Auer v Dressel*, 118 N.E.2d. 590 (N.Y. 1954).

102 1934 Exchange Act, 15 U.S.C. §§78n(a)(8)(C)(5)-(7).

103 For instance, during the Vietnam war, a number of companies that produced weapons faced proposals to be voted on at the annual meeting suggesting they not make weapons. While it is unacceptable for stockholders to tell directors what to manufacture these proposals were deemed acceptable because they gave the shareholders the right to express themselves on a significant issue which did have an impact for the company given public concerns about the war could affect corporate operations. See *Medical Committee for Human Rights v SEC*, 432 F.2d 659, 681 (1970). Whether a shareholder proposal relating to ordinary business is significant appears to depend upon the political and economic climate. For example, the SEC now allows proposals concerning the compensation of executives. The SEC's previous position was to reject such proposals because compensation was an ordinary business decision. Due to public attention focused on high executive compensation, the SEC has changed its position and now permits shareholders to place their proposals in the proxy materials dealing with compensation. See note 70 supra.

104 See text at note 145 infra.

edies. While not always successful the threat of a takeover can influence the managers in running the company.

1. Proxy Fight

The proxy fight usually involves a shareholder group nominating their own group of directors to replace the current management by seeking the votes of the shareholders. There can also be a proxy fight over a specific issue such as recommendations about splitting the corporation up or changing corporate governance rules. When engaging in a proxy fight, the challengers must prepare their own proxy statement in advance of the annual meeting since the large number of shareholders means that voting occurs prior to the annual meeting through the solicitation of proxies.

State law deals primarily with the mechanics of the voting process. It determines voting rights, dates and notice of the meetings and the use of proxies.[105] Proxy fights are also significantly influenced by federal law through the proxy rules issued under the 1934 Act. Under the rules, the shareholders must be provided with a proxy statement which requires full disclosure concerning the vote. In addition to the specific requirements of the SEC rules, there is also a general rule against fraud and misleading statements in a proxy contest.[106] Failure to comply with the rules may result in an action by the SEC or a private cause of action by shareholder.[107]

Proxy fights for control of the company are rarely successful although proxy fights over specific issues can produce positive results by influencing board decisions.[108] Parties desiring to engage in a proxy fight face the rational apathy problem of shareholders[109] and the reluctance of large institutions to vote against the managers.[110] The incumbents have the advantage of control of corporate information and use of corporate assets including reimbursement for the costs of the battle. Insurgents have to convince the shareholders to change directors with the uncertainty of their management and must usually bear the costs of their fight.[111]

2. Hostile Tender Offers

Another method of changing the company directors is through a hostile tender offer. A hostile tender offer is an offer to buy control of a company by purchasing shares directly from the shareholders with the disapproval of corporate management. The purchase of shares through a tender offer does not require board approval like a merger or sale of assets. Thus, the tender offer is the only hostile acquisition tech-

105 But even when the law gives management discretion on the mechanics, fiduciary duty limits the ability of managers to manipulate the rules to their advantage. See note 35 supra.

106 Exchange Act of 1934, 15 U.S.C. § 78n(a)(9).

107 See note 125 infra.

108 There are times when large shareholders use their own resources not to elect directors but to challenge management on an issue by preparing their own proxy materials. For example, a large shareholder tried to convince United States Steel to split the steel operations from the oil business in order to increase the market value of the stock. The shareholder lost the vote but management eventually agreed to the proposal.

109 See text at note 36 supra.

110 See generally Bernard Black, "Shareholder Passivity Reexamined", 89 Mich. L.Rev., p. 520 (1990).

111 Unsuccessful insurgents are not entitled to reimbursement for their proxy expenses which can be expensive although there are times when such expenses will be paid. See Clark, supra note 31 pp. 394-400.

nique. While a proxy fight can give one control of the board, it does not provide ownership control unless one wins the proxy fight and proposes a friendly merger or purchase of the assets. The tender offer, if successful, transfers control quickly without board approval. Shareholders are offered a premium over the current market price to encourage them to tender their shares. If enough shares are tendered one can gain control of the corporation.[112]

The use of a tender offer as a monitoring device remains controversial. Those who favour tender offers view it as beneficial because shareholders benefit by being offered a premium over the market price, shareholders generally benefit because the threat of a takeover encourages managers to run the business more efficiently to avoid a takeover and the economy benefits because the acquired business should be run more efficiently.[113] Critics see the hostile tender offer as hurting the corporation and its other stakeholders and discouraging long-term investment.[114]

Both state and federal law regulate tender offers and takeovers. The Williams Act, which is part of the 1934 Act, governs tender offers. The law does not take a position on the merits of tender offers but provides rules to protect the shareholders of the target company. There are anti-fraud and disclosure rules. The offeror must make full disclosure to the target shareholders about their background, financing and plans for the business. Target management is also required to disclose its position on the tender offer. There are also procedural rules that deal with timing issues and other rights.[115] There is also an anti-fraud rule applied to tender offers.[116]

112 See Arthur R. Pinto, "Corporate Takeovers Through the Public Markets in the United States", 42 Am.J.Comp.L., pp. 339, 350-366 (1994).

113 Many who believe that takeovers are beneficial approach the issue from a law and economics perspective and see the hostile tender offer as a market mechanism to monitor managers. Their argument uses the ECMH and argues that the market price of a stock accurately reflects the value of the issuing company. Thus, a stock trading at a low price means that the company is not well managed. If an outside investor believes that the company could run more efficiently by replacing the managers, the value of the stock would increase. That investor would be willing to offer the shareholders more than the present market value to take control. See generally, Easterbrook & Fischel, "Proper Role of Target's Management in Responding To a Tender Offer", 94 Harv. L. Rev., pp. 1161, 1173-1174 (1981). A takeover may also prevent managers from directing excess cash flow to marginally profitable ventures. Jensen, "The Agency of Free Cash Flow, Corporate Finance and Takeovers", 76 Am. Econ. Rev., p. 323 (1986).

114 See generally Martin Lipton & Steven A. Rosenblum, "A New System of Corporate Governance: The Quinquennial Election of Directors", 58 U.Chi.L.Rev., p. 187. Critics have attacked the efficient capital market hypothesis theory which underlies the arguments in favour of hostile tender offers by questioning its efficiency. See e.g., Jeffrey N. Gordon & Lewis A. Kornhauser, "Efficient Markets, Costly Information, and Securities Research", 60 N. Y. U. L. Rev., p. 761 (1985); William Wang, "Some Arguments that the Stock Market is Not Efficient", 19 U.C. Davis L. Rev., p. 341 (1986). Economic literature has not only questioned the accuracy of the underlying tests for market efficiency but suggests that "noise" which are influences unrelated to rational expectations about assets may play a greater role in market pricing. Donald C. Langevoort, "Theories, Assumptions, and Securities Regulation: Market Efficiency Revisited", 140 U. Pa. L. Rev. 851, pp. 853-854 (1992). Some critics claim that the market price does not accurately reflect the value of the company as a whole. E.g., Louis Lowenstein, "Pruning Deadwood in Hostile Takeovers: A Proposal for Legislation", 83 Colum. L. Rev., pp. 249, 274-276 (1983).

115 See Pinto, *Corporate Takeovers*, supra note 112, pp. 350-354. For example, the Williams Act provides that all target shareholders have the right to be included in the tender offer and receive the same price. Thus, if an acquiror announces a willingness to buy 50 per cent of the company for $40 a share, then the offeror must acquire 50 per cent of all those shares tendered on a pro rata basis. The offeror need only offer to buy the number of shares it wants and is not required to buy all the shares.

116 See ibid., pp. 353-354.

Fiduciary duty under state law is a significant aspect of tender offer regulation. These duties arise because target managers who oppose a hostile takeover may not be looking out for corporate or shareholder interests. In response they may implement various defensive tactics which make a takeover difficult.[117] Delaware case law on the fiduciary duty of directors implementing defensive tactics against takeovers is significant because of the large number of publicly traded companies incorporated there. An important question that its courts had to decide was whether the use of defensive tactics was a duty of care case involving a business decision or a duty of loyalty case involving a conflict of interest.[118] The courts recognized that tender offers are different from the typical duty of care or loyalty cases because directors must protect the interests of the company yet they face some conflict of interest in protecting their management of the company. Due to the special nature of tender offers, Delaware created a "modified business judgment rule". Under the rule, directors must prove that their actions and decisions were made in good faith and were reasonable. The burden is on the directors to show that they reasonably believed there was a threat to the corporation. Even though the burden of proof is shifted on this issue to the directors, unlike loyalty cases they do not have to show it is fair. Directors must only prove that they reasonably believed there was a threat to the corporation and then that the defensive mechanisms used were reasonably related to the threat to the company.[119] This allows the courts to scrutinize the process and the transaction without applying a fairness test. If independent directors are involved, the courts will shift the burden of proof to the plaintiff.[120] But if in response to a takeover, the directors put the company up for sale or enter into a transaction where there is a change of control then the directors may no longer claim that resisting sale is in the corporations best interest and may be responsible to act as an auctioneer to find the best price for the shareholders.[121]

[117] One way to avoid a hostile takeover is for management to buy out the public shareholders in a management buyout which can be financed through borrowing and called a leveraged buyout. These buyouts were controversial and raise similar issues of freeze-outs by controlling shareholders. *see* text at note 138 infra. Given the fact a management buyout could result in a competing bid from outsiders they may be treated differently from freeze-outs with controlling shareholders who already have the necessary votes proposes a buyout. See *Field v Allyn*, 457 A2d 1089 (1983).

[118] The decision on whether to implement defensive tactics can be viewed as an ordinary business decision protected by the business judgment rule. Lipton, "Takeover Bids in the Target's Boardroom", 35 Bus. Law., pp. 101, 109-110 (1979). Some commentators argue for director passivity allowing any offer above the market to be given to the shareholders for fear that defensive actions by the directors will deter not only the specific tender offer but tender offers in general by raising the costs for bidders. Any actions which limit the advantages of the market for corporate control should be restricted. Easterbrook & Fischel, supra note 27. Others argue that directors should be allowed to facilitate an auction for the target to seek the highest bid for the shareholders. Bebchuck, "The Case for Facilitating Competing Tender Offers", 95 Harv.L. Rev., p. 1028 (1982); Gilson, "A Structural Approach to Corporations: The Case Against Defensive Tactics in Tender Offers", 33 Stan. L. Rev., p. 819 (1981).

[119] The independent directors are given a lot of discretion in defending their strategy as being beneficial to its shareholders. In *Paramount Communications, Inc. v Time Inc.*, 571 A.2d.1140(Del. 1989) the Delaware Supreme Court put into the hands of the directors the decision on the "selection of a time frame for achievement of corporate goals." Ibid., at p. 1154. The court was unwilling to enter the debate between the short-term value of Paramount's bid with the alleged long-term value of Time's strategy. The court stated that "the question of 'long-term' versus 'short-term' values is largely irrelevant because directors, generally, are obliged to charter a course for a corporation which is in its best interests without regard to a fixed investment horizon." Ibid., at p. 1150.

[120] See *Unocal Corp. v Mesa Petroleum Co.*, 93 A.2d 946,954-5 (Del. 1985).

[121] *Paramount Communications, Inc. v QVC Network*, 637 A.2d 34 (1994); see also Pinto, *Corporate Takeovers*, pp. 357-362, supra note 112.

In addition to case law, many states have enacted statutes designed to deal with takeovers. These statutes generally assist management's attempt to defend the company by making takeovers in the state more difficult. Some states attempt to protect local interests because of concerns that if a company is taken over, it may move its headquarters and facilities elsewhere. There are many types of state statutes and they are often effective.[122]

Hostile tender offers have been made more difficult as a result of case law that is usually supportive of defensive tactics, state takeover statutes and economic conditions, they do remain available as a potential monitoring device.[123]

F. Shareholder Suits

In enforcing a federal securities law claim[124] or fiduciary duty claim under state law, there are generally two kinds of harm that may need a remedy through litigation by shareholders. There may be a direct cause of action (or class action, if brought by the shareholders as a group) where the manager harms the interests of the shareholder directly as an owner of the shares. There may be a derivative suit where the corporation, rather than the shareholders, is primarily harmed by the action.[125] While harm to the corporation is not a shareholder cause of action because it is indirect, courts recognize that when directors injure the corporation they will not usually sue themselves. Therefore, courts used the power of equity to recognize that shareholders have the right to sue in a derivative action in the name of the corporation for an injury to it.

These lawsuits are controversial. Both derivative suits and class actions serve as monitoring devices that keep managers in check because of fear of liability.[126] This

122 These statutes have been attacked on constitutional grounds as an unreasonable interference with interstate commerce. They have generally been upheld because states have the right to govern the internal affairs of corporations incorporated in the state. Pinto, *State Takeover Statutes*, supra note 8, at pp. 718-723.

123 While the costs of a hostile takeover are higher because of these developments, they have usually not made them impossible. For example, the poison pill which is a tactic which makes the target corporation difficult to acquire, usually allows the directors the to redeem it so long as the offeror has not reached a threshold purchase. One tactic used to cause the redemption has been the offeror buying enough shares to avoid the threshold and threatening a proxy fight to replace the board with friendlier directors. See *Moran v Household Int'l, Inc.*, 500 A.2d 1346, 1355 (Del. 1985).

124 The SEC is empowered to bring actions under Federal securities law including in some cases recommending to the Justice Department to bring criminal actions. But the SEC has limited resources so private litigation is available to some investors. In order to bring an action for violations shareholders must either be granted an express remedy under the statute or the courts have to imply a private cause of action. Most of the liability provisions that deal with corporate governance such as the proxy and tender offer rules do not provide for an express private remedy. As a result, the courts have frequently been faced with the issue of allowing one for the shareholders. Whether or not there is such a cause of action is ultimately a question of Congressional intent. See *J.I. Case v Borak*, 377 U.S. 426 (1964). The Supreme Court has also stated that under the proxy rules not only can a shareholder bring a cause of action, but the attorneys if they win can recover fees. See *Mills v Electric Auto-Lite Co.*, 396 U.S. 375 (1970).

125 See A.L.I. Prin. Corp. Gov. §7.01.

126 Often directors can be reimbursed and indemnified from the corporation by direct payment or through insurance. While they are generally entitled to such payments if successful, payments when there is liability depends on the statutory provisions applicable and the coverage of the insurance. Cox, supra note 77 at §15.19.

provides both relief from injury and deters harmful conduct. The law established by such litigation also establishes legal rules affecting future conduct. But some maintain that the litigation is driven by attorneys seeking fees and raises the costs of doing business without significant benefit. Plaintiffs in civil litigation pay their own legal fees regardless of outcome. In class actions, attorneys fees can come from the class if there is a judgment or settlement. In a derivative suit the corporation is nominally the plaintiff and will often pay the fees if liability is found or there is a settlement. Since the legal system allows attorneys to be paid on a contingency basis plaintiffs can bring an action without paying fees if the attorney is willing to bet on a recovery. There are attorneys who specialize in such suits willing to fund the litigation and have been accused of bringing "strike suits" only for the fees. They are accused of controlling the litigation forcing settlements with small recoveries and large fees from the corporation who wants to avoid the burdens and costs of litigation with extensive discovery.[127] But the attorneys willingness to fund the litigation helps solve the collective action problem by putting the initial costs of monitoring on them.

Given the problems of the litigation, there are often rules that try to deal with them.[128] Most states require that a plaintiff bringing a derivative suit must demand approval of the board of directors before bringing the suit.[129] This gives the board the first opportunity to act and possibly correct the problem. If a majority of the directors are independent and not involved in the wrongdoing, then the board's decision that maintaining the litigation is not beneficial is usually upheld under the business judgment rule and ends the litigation. To avoid demand the shareholder must claim that demand would be futile and thus excused because a majority of the board was involved in the wrongdoing.[130] In a case of demand futility, the litigation is allowed to proceed.[131]

127 See Jonathan Macey & Geoffrey Miller, "The Plaintiff's Attorneys' Role in Class Actions and Derivative Litigation: Economic Analysis and Recommendations for Reform", 58 U.Chi.L.Rev., p. 1 (1991).

128 For example, courts have to the power to approve all settlements to avoid collusion of strike suits and harm to the corporation. There are also special rules that apply to derivative suits. For instance, in order to bring a derivative suit, the plaintiff must have been a shareholder in the corporation at the time of the harm and continue to own the shares throughout the litigation. In some states the plaintiff may have to post a bond (called security for expenses) to defray the cost if the derivative suit is unsuccessful. e.g., NYBCL §620.

129 In some cases, before a derivative action is brought, the shareholder must ask the other shareholders whether or not to bring the action. However, many states dispense with the requirement because the costs of such communication make it impracticable in a large public company. Cox, supra note 77 at §15.4.

130 See generally, *Marx v Akers*, 88 N.Y.2d 189 (1996) (discusses different approaches to demand futility).

131 In some states, the board cannot stop the litigation as a whole but they may appoint a smaller committee composed of independent directors to review the litigation and decide if it is in the corporation's best interests to pursue. A decision by this committee not to pursue the litigation is subject to review. Some courts will only look at the process and independence of the committee while others will also look at the decision not to allow the suit to see if it was proper. *Compare Zapata Corp. v Maldonado*, 430 A.2d 779 (Del. 1981); *Auerbach v Bennett,* 393 N.E.2d 994 (N.Y. 1979) (once the committee is found to be independent New York will use the business judgment rule while Delaware will review the decision itself).

While the courts today are stricter in finding such causes of action and there have been legislative attempts to limit shareholder litigation,[132] litigation remains as a monitoring device.

G. Appraisal

Many state statutes provide that shareholders may have the right to seek an appraisal of their shares in certain fundamental transactions such as a merger. In the nineteenth century when corporations were small and formed for limited purposes mergers required a unanimous shareholder vote. As corporations grew that requirement was viewed as restrictive and was changed to a lower vote but the legislatures provided for an appraisal remedy. With appraisal, shareholders can seek a court valuation of their shares based upon fair value and be paid in cash. This right of exit can serve as a monitoring device because arguably directors would seek the highest price in such a transaction to avoid many shareholders seeking this remedy. But appraisal has limitations because it used to employ conservative methods of valuation, it was time consuming, did not require any payments until the appraisal proceeding was completed, attorneys and experts fees were expensive and interest was not assured.

VII. CONTROLLING SHAREHOLDERS

While much of the corporate governance debate concerns corporations where there is a separation of ownership from control, there are many publicly traded corporations where there is a control group.[133] The control group may be a family or managerial group or a parent corporation owning control of a subsidiary. With such a control group one would expect that the directors selected by the group would generally represent those interests. Problems arise when the control group's interests differ from the public shareholders and particularly in conflicts of interest.[134] In this context, many of the monitoring devices described such as takeovers and proxy fights are not prevalent. Instead disclosure and fiduciary duty remain the most significant monitoring devices.

Generally, a shareholder can vote and sell shares at will[135] and is not in a fiduciary relationship with other shareholders. But shareholders who control a corporation may have a fiduciary duty to the company or to other shareholders even when

132 In 1995 Congress enacted the Private Securities Litigation Reform Act which had several provisions to reform class actions under federal securities laws. See Joel Seligman, "The Private Securities Litigation Reform Act of 1995", 38 Ariz.L.Rev., p. 717 (1996).

133 Control usually involves ownership of more than 50 per cent of the voting shares of a corporation. In publicly traded corporations where ownership is wide spread and diffused, control often represents ownership of less than 50 per cent.

134 The problems of the minority shareholders are similar to those shareholders in a closely held corporation except there is the liquidity of the market and the right to exit. In addition federal securities law involving disclosure will apply.

135 An issue which has generated debate is whether controlling shareholders have an obligation, when selling their shares at a premium over the market price, to provide all the shareholders with an equal opportunity. American law embraces the idea that people have the right to sell their property and use it freely, including shares. Sale of control could also be beneficial by bringing in new management creating value for all shareholders. Thus, a controlling shareholder can generally sell their shares to

acting as a shareholder. Under state law, when a controlling shareholder unfairly uses their control of the board of directors to benefit themselves, not only are the directors liable but the controlling shareholder is also liable under the theory that the directors are agents of the shareholder.[136] This implicates the duty of loyalty because the controlling shareholders and directors are not acting for all the shareholders equally. Thus the controlling shareholders are treated as interested directors because they have assumed that role.[137]

A controversial transaction by controlling shareholders involves the freeze-out of minority shareholders. For example, a freeze-out can occur when the control group uses its control to eliminate the minority shareholders in a cash out merger. If the transactions are arm's-length transactions between independent companies, the board of directors would normally negotiate a fair deal for their shareholders, but when transactions involve control groups acquiring the corporation the duty of loyalty comes into play. Freeze-outs became an important issue in the 1970s and 1980s and raised the issue of whether appraisal was the exclusive remedy for the minority shareholders. Because of appraisal's limitations they would prefer an action in equity with the possibility of greater damages. The Delaware courts require freeze-outs to be entirely fair i.e. fair dealing and fair price. This means full disclosure and an attempt to structure the deal as an arm's-length bargain. Fair price is a new form of appraisal which allows a court to be more flexible and use modern valuation techniques used by financial markets such as the discounted cash-flow analysis. The court usually places the burden on the interested directors to prove that they dealt with the company fairly and that the price was fair.[138] Other courts additionally require a business purpose for the freeze-out and allow equity to review the case.[139]

VIII. REFORMS

Corporate governance is a major issue with the current focus on corporate performance with a number of different suggested reforms. The focus of recent reforms has been to provide effective monitoring by enhancing and enlarging the role of large investors in monitoring or strengthening the role of the independent directors in their monitoring.

cont.

someone at a higher price than is being offered to the other shareholders, i.e. a control premium. If the sale results in damage to the corporation because the buyer loots the corporation or steals a corporate opportunity then the result may be different. Cox, supra note 77, at §11.10.

136 (137) *Zahn v Transamerica Corp.*, 162 F.2d 36 (3rd Cir. 1947).

137 In the parent-subsidiary context where there are some minority shareholders this issue is raised because many of the transactions take place between the subsidiary and the controlling parent. However, courts may approach this context differently and place a heavier burden on the complaining shareholder since there is an expectation of self-dealing in this context. See *Sinclair Oil Corp. v Levien,* 280 A.2d 717 (Del. 1971).

138 See *Weinberger v UOP*, Inc.,457 A 2d. 701 (Del. 1983).

139 See generally, Arthur R. Pinto, "Takeovers of Public Corporations in the United States", 34 Am.J.Comp.L., p. 271 (1988). Minority shareholders had also sought relief in federal court and argued for a federal remedy claiming an unfair freeze-out without a business purpose was a fraud and covered by federal securities anti-fraud rules. The Supreme Court ruled that since there was full disclosure there was no federal remedy and that fiduciary duty claims belong in state court. See note 88 supra. Under federal securities law, SEC Rule 13e-3 requires extensive disclosure in a freeze-out including a discussion of its fairness. 17 C.F.R. §240.13e-3 (1996).

A. Institutional Investing

For most of this century the ownership of stock of publicly traded corporations was primarily in the hands of private individuals and corporate law was influenced by and recognized this primacy. In the last several decades the ownership of stock has shifted to large institutions comprised of private and public pension funds, insurance companies, bank trust companies and mutual funds.[140] This trend continues and is very significant for the future of corporate governance.

In the past, shareholders disappointed with their investment would follow the "Wall Street rule" and chose to sell their shares rather than try to influence corporate behaviour. With the concentration of ownership, certain large institutional investors (particularly public pension funds) have become more active in the corporations whose shares they own.[141] Large investors may find that quick sales may be difficult and more active influence may be profitable.[142] This development has already had an impact on many of the issues discussed and will continue to influence the development of corporate law.[143]

There has been some discussion of relational investing which recognizes the possibility of a long-term relationship between a corporation and large shareholders. But the growth of institutional ownership does not mean that any one institution is likely to dominate the ownership of a corporation. There are a large number of these institutions many of which are not interested in increased activity or ownership which have costs that must produce benefits.[144]

Some large institutional investors have begun to try to influence corporate decisions through voting, meetings with managers and exerting pressure for change on independent directors. Shareholder proposals supported by institutional investors have been directed at suggestions that the directors modify or drop anti-takeover devices or strengthen corporate governance mechanisms.[145]

140 (141) In 1950 91 per cent of equity was held by households. The figure now is approximately 48 per cent. Pension funds hold 22 per cent of all equities. New York Stock Exchange, *Factbook 1996 Data*, p. 59 (1977).

141 See Bernard S. Black, "Agents Watching Agents: The Promise of Institutional Investor Voice", 39 U.C.L.A.L.Rev., p. 811 (1992). The control of institutions also raises issues of agency costs and who monitors the monitors. Ibid. pp. 850-852.

142 While increased monitoring may lower agency costs, there are costs to both the shareholders and the corporation associated with the exercise of influence. For example, management fears that too much shareholder involvement will adversely affect their freedom and thus the business. There is also a concern that if institutions become too involved in the management of the company, they could be liable for either violating insider trading rules or as a control person under federal securities laws. Ibid.

143 (144) For example, in 1992 the SEC modified the proxy rules to facilitate communications between institutional investors. See Thomas W. Briggs, "Shareholder Activism and Insurgency Under the Proxy Rules", 50 Bus. Law., p. 99 (1994). The Private Securities Litigation Act of 1995 provided for a lead plaintiff provision with the idea that institutions with large shareholdings should exercise control over class action. See generally, Jill E. Fisch, "Class Action Reform: Lessons from Securities Litigation", 39 Ariz.L.Rev., p. 533 (1997).

144 See generally, Ian Ayres & Peter Crampton, "Relational Investing and Agency Theory", 15 Cardozo L.Rev., p. 1033 (1994).

145 See John C. Coffee, Jr., "The Bylaw Battlefield: Can Institutions Change the Outcome of Corporate Control Contests?", 51 U.Miami L.Rev., p. 605 (1997) (discussion of whether institutional investors can mandate action on issues involving corporate control contests).

B. Directors

Many of the recent corporate governance proposals have centred around proposals to strengthen the board of directors. While many publicly traded corporations have some independent directors,[146] they are not required by law.[147] The hope is that a truly independent and strengthened board of directors will function to monitor managers.[148] There have been many examples in the last few years of independent directors acting to make major changes including the replacement of the president or chief executive officer and creation of standards of conduct for the board.[149]

The problems with reliance on an independent board to monitor are that independent directors are often selected by the inside directors; there may be personal or professional relationships between inside and independent directors that do not create a legal conflict of interest but can create bias; the insiders control information; they may not have sufficient economic incentives to act for the corporation; and part-time status may not provide sufficient time to truly monitor. Recent reform proposals have focused on more involvement by independent directors by use of a lead independent director or separation of the position of the chief executive office from the chairman of the board who should be an independent director. Other reforms have sought independent directors on all key board committees, increased stock ownership and compensation for both independent directors and managers hoping to align their interests with the shareholders.[150]

IX. CONCLUSION

The United States has a market-oriented economy with extensive use of public markets to provide capital for corporations. Thus corporate governance and the legal and market monitoring mechanisms must be understood in this context. The separation of ownership from control in publicly traded corporations provides for beneficial specialization yet potential for abuse. Corporate governance, influenced by both the role of markets and law, tries to balance the needs of managers with the protection of

146 There are several explanations for this phenomena. First, various stock market rules require some independent directors. See e.g., note 42 supra. Secondly, investors may prefer corporations with some independent directors and corporations may use these directors to attract investors (i.e. a bonding cost under agency theory). Thirdly, the law encourages it because independent directors may change the legal standard used when courts apply standards of fiduciary duty. See e.g. notes 83 and 119 supra.

147 The initial proposals of the A.L.I. Principles of Corporate Governance called for a majority of independent directors for many publicly traded corporations. This was changed to a recommendation after opposition developed. The opposition preferred optional rules which could recognize different structures for different corporations. C.f., Easterbrook & Fischel, supra note 56, at pp. 14-15.

148 See Ira M. Millstein, "The Professional Board", 50 Bus. Law., p. 1427 (1995); See James M. Tobin, "The Squeeze on Directors — Inside is Out", 49 Bus.Law., p. 1707 (1994).

149 In the 1990s heads of several major corporations were replaced by the directors including General Motors, Kodak, American Express, Sears, Westinghouse and IBM. This unusual development involved pressures from institutional investors. Mark J. Roe, *Strong Managers Weak Owners: The Political Roots of American Corporate Finance*, vii-ix (1994).

150 See generally, Warren F. Grienenberger, "Institutional Investors and Corporate Governance", PLI/Corp, p. 970 (1997); It is not clear whether the use of independent directors have in fact been effective. See Laura Lin, "The Effectiveness of Outside Directors as a Corporate Governance Mechanism: Theories and Evidence", 90 Nw.U.L.Rev., p. 898 (1996).

shareholders. Corporate governance is a dynamic concept which continues to evolve through legal rules and business practices influenced by many factors including economics and politics. The increasing role of ownership of publicly held corporations by institutional investors will continue to greatly influence future developments in corporate governance.

Appendix

General Outline

The purpose of this book is to compare and contrast different corporate law systems on the governance of publicly held corporations and is designed to help understand how differences in economic systems affect corporate law systems and how in turn the corporate law system affects the economy. By looking at the operations of the different systems and how and why those systems developed, it is the intention that the book will not only improve our understanding of each country's law but explore the actual and potential influence among the systems.

Here the term "*publicly held corporation*" stands for any corporation whose shares are held by the public and are publicly traded in the market, even though there might be one or more main or controlling shareholder.

Publicly held corporations,[1] rather than other types of corporations such as closely held, are focused on because of their size and impact on the world economy and trade. As business becomes more international in scope, a growing need for capital could expand the use of publicly held corporations tapping both domestic and foreign markets for funds. They will compete for capital and thus different corporate systems may also find themselves competing. Thus an understanding of how and why different systems operate and whether they facilitate capital formation is important.

Corporate governance in the publicly held corporation deals with how different systems regulate the problems of separation of shareholder ownership from managerial control of the business. The chapters focus on monitoring mechanisms and their effectiveness in protecting shareholders and other constituencies, and allowing for efficient corporate operations.

The legal systems described are the following:

- France: Prof. James A. Fanto (Brooklyn Law School, New York).
- Germany: Prof. Rolf Birk (Universität Trier Quint).
- Japan: Prof. Hideki Kanda (University of Tokyo).
- Italy: Prof. Gustavo Visentini and Dr. Eugenio Ruggiero (LUISS Guido Carli University, Rome).

[1] It should be kept in mind that, under the common heading "corporation", there are entities that are quite different in the way they operate and in the problems they raise. The main distinction is between publicly held and closely held corporations, according to the share-ownership structure. A third category includes what may be called "publicly held but privately controlled corporations", where there is a dominant shareholder while the rest of the shares are widely spread among the public. In most European systems, another distinctive element is the presence of corporations whose main shareholder is the State.

© Kluwer Law International 1998

- Netherlands: Prof. Martin van Empel (Europa Instituut – University of Amsterdam).
- Sweden: Prof. Svante Johansson (Stockholms Universitet).
- Switzerland: Prof. Peter Böckli (Universität Basel).
- U.K.: Prof. Sheldon Leader and Prof. Janet Dine (University of Essex, Colchester).
- U.S.A.: Prof. Arthur R. Pinto (Brooklyn Law School, New York).

The following outline is the result of the discussion at the preparatory meeting held at LUISS University on 29 March 1993, which served to review and clarify the outlines previously prepared by each participant and to set the definitive focus of the symposium,[2] and from the comments and suggestions that were given on a previous draft outline.

The final purpose of the project was to collect, into a formal publication, the writings all the professors who had prepared a paper on the subject in view of the common framework singled out by the meeting itself.

It was decided that each paper should focus on legislative and judicial developments in each country concerning **the philosophy underlying corporate law in the context of corporate governance**. The papers are not designed to be a description of each country's law, but an explanation of how and why different rules and regulations have developed. The basic principles should be set out and then the rules deriving from the principle discussed. Each paper, therefore is required to analyze, where relevant, historical, economic, cultural and other non-specifically legal factors which contributed to this development. The reasons why a particular rule has proven to be effective (or not) in the context of the country's legal system should be discussed in each chapter.

It was decided that the following points should be addressed in each chapter:

I. DESCRIPTION OF THE PUBLICLY HELD CORPORATE PHENOMENON

A. How relevant is the publicly held corporation phenomenon to economic activity? This point requires quite basic information as to the number of publicly held corporations, compared to the total number of corporations and business entities in the economy. Also, it is important to know the "qualitative" impact of publicly held corporations on the national economy as a whole, in terms of market share, production, number of employees, etc.[3]

B. Is it easy or difficult to be a publicly held corporation?[4]

[2] Participants to the meeting were Prof. Pinto, Prof. Leader, Prof. Köhler, Prof. van Empel, Prof. Nuzzo, Prof. Visentini, and Dr. Ruggiero.

[3] In Italy, for instance, this is quite a limited phenomenon: formally it only involved the companies whose shares were traded on the stock exchange, but in reality the phenomenon is even more restricted to fewer companies whose weight on the economy is not as relevant. In Germany there is a very similar situation, in that though there are few public companies, there is a very high number of closely held companies which also have a different legal treatment. In the U.S. on the other hand, the phenomenon might seem limited if the sheer numbers of publicly held corporations are looked at, compared to closely held corporations and sole proprietorships, but their impact on the economy is a very strong one since they account for most of the national wealth.

[4] Is there a legally relevant process through which corporations become publicly held? Which authorities are involved in the process, and to what purpose? For example, in Italy a company wanting to go public

C. Can the transferability of publicly traded shares be restricted?
D. Is there a significant public securities market: discuss how developed the market is, why it developed the way it did (or it did not) and its significance to economic activities and sources of capital?
E. The securities market: discuss the structure of the market (how they work and how they are regulated) as relevant to the ownership structure and to the internal relationships in the company.
F. Is there a major government presence in the regulation of the markets and does it hinder or facilitate public ownership?

II. THE CORPORATE STRUCTURE

A. Brief description of the corporate structure (that is, the distribution of powers within the corporation and how that power is exercised): how the various constituencies interact with each other within the corporation.
B. How and why the system developed, and works.
C. Discussion of basic shareholders' rights, directors' rights, or other management structures (i.e. supervisory board, board of internal auditors, independent directors, or similar structures, etc.).
D. Distribution of power between these structures.[5]

   1. Is the board of directors a mere agent of the shareholders, or does it have a separate responsibility to other structures (e.g. the corporation, the shareholders, creditors, labour, etc.)?

E. Discuss briefly the nature and the scope of the fiduciary duty obligation (duty of care, duty of loyalty) and its rationale.
F. Discuss the reason why the scope of the duty is either limited or broad.

III. WHAT CONSTITUTES CORPORATE GOVERNANCE?

A. To what extent are the corporate governance rules applicable to different constituencies?
B. What are the constituencies to which corporate governance rules apply, other than shareholders, including management, labour, creditors, government, the public at large?
C. Why, if so, are these groups considered part of the constituencies?

cont.
raising capital for an amount greater than 10 billion lire would have to seek authorization from the Treasury, which can refuse it on grounds of jeopardy to the financial and monetary stability of the system; also there are several disclosure requirements administered by *Consob* (the securities market supervisor) for the protection of investors. In Germany, particular rules only apply to public offers of securities to be listed on a stock exchange (the selling of the shares must go through a bank which signs the prospectus and assumes the liability arising therefrom: there is no public authority involved). At the EEC level there is no material piece of legislation on the subject. In the U.S., once a corporation becomes publicly held, the stringent regulations arising from the Securities Act and the Securities and Exchange Act apply.

[5] One of the questions is whether the corporate system is oriented towards a total centralization of managerial power in the governing body, or whether this power can, or must be shared (and to what extent) with the body of shareholders or other bodies.

IV. SHAREHOLDERS' POWERS

A. The extent to which the system allows shareholders to protect their interests.

B. Discuss to what extent shareholders' powers can be changed or altered through the majority.

C. Voting rights.

1. Is there an underlying theory in respect to voting rights?
2. Topics on which shareholders can vote.
3. To what extent can shareholders express their views beyond what is explicitly permitted by the statute?[6]
4. To what extent can voting rights be legally differentiated between classes and within classes?
5. The extent to which voting rights can be separated from ownership interests and why such arrangements are common.[7]
6. Do voting rights, in practice and/or in law, differ according to who the shareholder is (e.g. institutional investors, banks, the state, etc.)?[8]

D. Transferability rights.

1. Can the transferability of shares be restricted after the shares are issued?

E. Disclosure.

1. Given that disclosure is generally recognized as a universal right, one needs to briefly discuss the following topics:

(a) where do the disclosure obligations come from: government mandated, market mandated, privately mandated, or else, and why?

(b) how is the failure to disclose enforced, and is it effective (liability for financial statements, accountants' liability: is there case law showing the enforcement of the liability).

(c) is disclosure designed to reach other constituencies, other than the shareholders, such as investors, market, labour, creditors, tax authorities, etc.

V. CONFLICTS OF INTEREST

A. Discuss how and why the rules dealing with conflicts of interest restrict the ability of the control group to exercise their control for their own benefit.

1. Conflicts of interest of directors.

(a) Protection of minority shareholders against the use of the corporate structure by the control group[9]

[6] For example, in the United States shareholders may offer their views on matters not directly related to their voting (e.g. a resolution about officers' status may be permissible, even though they have no power to appoint or remove them; that power is, in fact, in the board of directors).

[7] E.g. proxy rules, selling of voting right, splitting the voting right from the ownership interest.

[8] In Italy, for instance, there is a debate on whether mutual funds should exercise their vote on the shares they hold.

[9] E.g. intercompany transactions in parent-subsidiary situations where at least the subsidiary has public shareholders, freeze-outs, elimination of ownership interests, dilution of ownership interests, anti-takeover tactics.

(b) Discuss any rules established with respect to corporate groups.

2. Conflicts of interest of shareholders.

(a) conflicts of interest between shareholders: can you vote or sell your shares according to your own self-interest (e.g. sale of control).

(b) conflicts of interest between the shareholder and the corporation: discuss any rules that restrict shareholders' rights when they have a conflict of interest with the corporation (e.g. are there restrictions on shareholders voting on certain transactions).

B. Discuss the legal devices provided for the enforcement of the breach of fiduciary duty: judicial and extra-judicial remedies.[10]

1. What kind of action – who can bring the action – are there other actors, besides the shareholders, who can bring the action – how effective are these mechanisms?
2. Where relevant, discuss how effective market mechanisms can be in enforcing fiduciary duties (e.g. is there a market for corporate control?): discuss how and why these markets developed.[11]

VI. FINAL REMARKS: THE PUBLICLY HELD CORPORATION IN THE PRESENT CONTEXT AND IN PERSPECTIVE: SOCIAL, ECONOMIC, POLITICAL, LEGAL ASPECTS

A. Discuss what factors influence the markets that could serve to restrain the actions by the actors in the corporate governance structure.

B. Who exercises, as a matter of fact, the power of the shareholders?[12]

C. On a comparative basis, do you think there are any universal principles concerning corporate governance that emerge from the study of each other's system (or, should there be any)?

D. Discuss what external forces are influencing the future development of the country's corporate law system. For instance, EEC proposals and directives (e.g. Bangemann Report); cross-trading of securities (e.g. listing in more than one country); internationalization of ownership; other economic or market driven forces affecting how the corporations may behave in the future.

E. Discuss the extent to which the rules as established will affect international ownership and trading.

[10] For instance, direct actions, class actions (e.g. protection of minority shareholders' interests) and derivative actions: in what terms and limits can these different actions be brought.

[11] One would need to briefly discuss who owns the companies, what is the ownership structure of large economic units, and why did this structure develop as such (e.g. bank ownership, institutional ownership, individual ownership, state ownership, etc.)? Is it relevant, and to what extent, to corporate governance?

[12] For example, does the proxy system encourage or discourage shareholders' voting? In the U.S. the proxy regulations favour the exercise of the voting power by the management on behalf of shareholders, while in Italy these regulations favour shareholders' apathy whose vote is hardly ever actually exercised.

Select Bibliography

Adams, *Restructuring the French Economy: Government and the Rise of Market Competition Since World War II* (1989).

Albert, *Capitalisme contre capitalisme* (1991).

Alcouffe & Alcouffe, "Control and Executive Compensation in Large French Companies", 24 J. L. & Soc'y 85, Mar. 1997.

Anderson & Anthony, *Corporate Directors, Insights for Board Members and Executives*, New York (1986).

Anderson, "Conflicts of Interest: Efficiency, Fairness and Corporate Structure", 25 U.C.L.A.L.Rev. 737 (1975).

Aoki & Dore (eds.), *The Japanese Firm* (1994).

Aoki, "The Japanese Firm As a System of Attributes: A Survey and Research Agenda", in Aoki & Dore (eds.), *The Japanese Firm* (1994).

Aoki, "Toward an Economic Model of the Japanese Firm", 28 *Journal of Economic Literature* 1 (1990).

Assmann & Schutze, *Handbuch des Kapitalanlagerechts* (1990).

Assmann, in: *Großkommentar zum Aktienrecht* (1992).

Ayres & Crampton, "Relational Investing and Agency Theory", 15 Cardozo L.Rev. 1033 (1994).

Bacon & Brown, *Corporate Directorship Practices: Role, Selection and Legal Status of the Board*, The Conference Board (New York, 1975).

Bacon, *Corporate Boards and Corporate Governance*, Report Number 1036, The Conference Board (New York, 1993).

Baums, Buxbaum & Hopt (eds.), I*nstitutional Investors and Corporate Governance* (1994).

Baums, et al., *Institutional Investors and Corporate Governance* (1994).

Bean, "Corporate Governance and Corporate Opportunities", 15 *The Company Lawyer* 266 (1994).

Bebchuk, "The Case for Facilitating Competing Tender Offers", 95 Harv.L. Rev. 1028 (1982).

Bebchuk & Jolls, *Managerial Value Diversion and Shareholder Wealth* (Harvard Law School John M. Olin Center for Law, Economics, and Business Discussion Paper No. 179, 1996).

Berglof & Perotti, "The Governance Structure of the Japanese Financial Keiretsu", 36 *Journal of Financial Economics* 259 (1994).

Berle & Means, *The Modern Corporation and Private Property*, 1932 (Transaction Publishers, Murray L. Weidenbaum & Mark Jensen, int., reprinted 1991).

Berset, *L'administrateur non-directeur de la société anonyme en droit suisse et américain*, thèse Neuchâtel (1988).

Biland, *Die Rolle des Verwaltungsrates im Prozess der strategischen Unternehmensführung* (Diss. St. Gallen, 1989).

Bisconti & Monaco, *Italy*, in F. Schwank & F.R. Ryder (eds.), *Banks abroad* (1986).

Black, "Agents Watching Agents: The Promise of Institutional Investor Voice", 39 U.C.L.A.L.Rev. 811 (1992).

Black, "Shareholder Passivity Reexamined", 89 Mich. L.Rev. 520 (1990).

Blair, *Ownership and Control: Rethinking Corporate Governance for the Twenty-First Century* (1995).

Bledstein, Burton J., *The Culture of Professionalism: The Middle Class and the Development of Higher Education in America* (1978).

Bleicher, *Der Aufsichtsrat im Wandel* (Gütersloh, 1987).

Bleicher, Leberl & Paul, *Unternehmungsverfassung und Spitzenorganisation* (Wiesbaden, 1989).

Böckli, *Verwaltungsrat oder Aufsichtsrat? Konvergenz der Systeme in der Spitzenverfassung der Aktiengesellschaft*, Festschrift für Walter Reist, Verlag Neue Zürcher Zeitung (Zürich, 1992).

Boot, *Naar een dynamischer structuur-regime*, Maandblad NV 73 (1995).

Bouloc, "Le droit pénal des sociétés", in *La Modernisation du Droit des Sociétés: Premières réflexions sur le Rapport Marini* 69 (Jean-Jacques Daigre, éd. 1996).

Brandeis, *Other People's Money and How the Brokers Use It* (1932).

Branson, "Assault On Another Citadel: Attempts To Curtail The Fiduciary Standard Of Loyalty Applicable To Corporate Directors", 57 Fordham L. Rev. 375 (1988).

Brealey & Myers, *Principles of Corporate Finance* (4th ed., 1991).

Briggs, "Shareholder Activism and Insurgency Under the Proxy Rules", 50 Bus. Law. 99 (1994).

Brown, *Putting the Corporate Board to Work* (New York/London, 1976).

Brudney & Bratton, *Cases and Materials on Corporate Finance* (4th ed., 1993).

Bulbulia & Pinto, "Statutory Responses to Interested Directors' Transactions: A Watering Down of Fiduciary Standards?", 53 Notre Dame L.Rev. 201 (1977).

Burnham, *The Managerial Revolution. What is happening in the world?* (New York, 1941).

Buxbaum, *Comparative Aspects of Institutional Investment and Corporate Governance*, in: Baums, Buxbaum & Hopt (Publ.), *Institutional Investors on Corporate Governance* (Berlin/New York, 1994).

Cadbury, *The Company Chairman* (Cambridge, 1990).

Cadman, "Non-executive Directors: Are They Truly Independent?", in *Solicitors Journal* 1995, 346.

Cary, "Federalism and Corporate Law: Reflections upon Delaware", 83 Yale L. J. 663 (1974).

Chandler, Jr. & Daems, *Introduction*, in *Managerial Hierarchies: Comparative Perspectives on the rise of the Modern Industrial Enterprise* 1 (Alfred D. Chandler, Jr. & Herman Daems, eds.), 1980.

Chandler, *The Visible Hand: The Managerial Revolution in American Business* (1977).

Charkham, *Keeping Good Company, A Study of Corporate Governance in Five Countries* (Oxford/New York, 1995).

Charreaux, éd., *Le Gouvernement des Entreprises: Corporate Governance Théories et Faits* (1997).

Chernoff, "Shareholder power grows: France's first proxy solicitations are big step forward", Pens. & Inv., 19 (10 June 1996).

Clark, *Agency Costs Verses Fiduciary Duties*, in *Principles and Agents: The Structure of Business* (John W. Pratt & Richard J. Zeckhauser eds.), 1985.

Clark, *Corporate Law* (1986).

Coffee, Jr., "Liquidity versus Control: The Institutional Investor as Corporate Monitor", 91 Colum. L. Rev. 1277 (1991).

Coffee, Jr., "The Bylaw Battlefield: Can Institutions Change the Outcome of Corporate Control Contests?" 51 U.Miami L.Rev. 605 (1997).

Conard, *Corporations in Perspective* (1976).

Couret, *Chronique: Le gouvernement d'entreprise: la corporate governance*, 22 *Recueil Dalloz Sirey* 163 (1995).

Cox, et. al., *Corporations* (1997).

Cozian & Viandier, *Droit des Sociétés* (9ème éd., 1996).

Dadomo & Farran, *The French Legal System* (2d ed., 1996).

Daigre & Sentilles-Dupont, *Pactes d'actionnaires* (1995).

Davies & Wedderburn , "The Land of Industrial Democracy", 6 *Industrial Law Journal* (1977).

Davis & Lowry, "Corporate Governance and Cadbury: Selfregulation and Alternatives", *Journal of British Business Law* 1994, 51.

De Gennaro – Musolino – Torchia, *Struttura proprietaria e modelli di controllo con riferimento alle società italiane quotate: alcune considerazioni alla luce di una verifica empirica*, forthcoming publication (1998).

De Vauplane & Bornet, *Droit de la Bourse* (1994).

Demb & Neubauer, *The Corporate Board, Confronting the Paradoxes* (New York/Oxford, 1992).

Den Broeder, *Governance of stakeholder relationships, The German and Dutch experience*, Centraal Planbureau, Research Memorandum No. 127 (1996).

Devlin, *The Enforcement of Morals* (1965).

Dezalay, *Marchands de Droit: La Restructuration de l'Ordre Juridique International par les Multinationales du Droit* (1992).

Dietrich, *Der Verwaltungsrat und seine Information*, Diss. (oec.) (Fribourg, 1990).

Dine, "Shareholders Denied Voting Rights", 7 *Insolvency Law and Practice* No. 5 (1992).

Dine, "The Governance of Governance", in *The Company Lawyer*, 15 (1994).

Dion, *Corporate governance et sociétés françaises*, Édit. du Juris-Classeur, Dr. des Sociétés 8 (juillet-août 1995).

Dompe & Dorison, *Entretiens de la COB*, Novembre 1994: Les Pouvoirs dans l'Entreprise (1994).

Dompe, *Offres publiques: Réglementation et contestation*, Petites Affiches 27, (7-12 juin 1994).

Dorresteijn, "De ondernemingskamer en de ondernemingsraad", in *25 jaar Ondernemingskamer* (1996).

Dotevall, *Skadeståndsansvar för styrelseledamot och verkställande direktör*, diss., Stockholm (1989).

Druey, "Das Informationsrecht des einzelnen Verwaltungsratmitglieds", in *Schweizerische Zeitschrift für Wirtschaftsrecht* (1993).

Ducouloux-Favard, *Délits financiers et boursiers*, in *Dictionnaire Permanent Epargne et Produits Financiers*, feuillets 53 (15 mars 1995).
Ducouloux-Favard, "L'histoire des grandes sociétés en Allemagne, en France et en Italie", 44 R. I. D. C. 847 (1992).
Ducouloux-Favard, *Société Anonyme, Aktien Gesellschaft, Società Per Azioni* (1992).
Easterbrook & Fischel, "Proper Role of Target's Management in Responding To a Tender Offer", 94 Harv. L. Rev. 1161 (1981).
Easterbrook & Fischel, *The Economic Structure of Corporate Law* (1991).
Eck, *Histoire de l'Économie Française Depuis 1945* (1994).
Eisenberg, "The Structure of Corporation Law", 89 Col.L.R. 1461 (1989).
Elson, "Shareholding Directors Create Better Corporate Performance", 11 *Issue Alert* 3 (May 1996).
Emmerich & Sonnenschein, *Konzernrecht* (4th ed., 1992).
Enterprise and Governance (London, Institute of Directors: October 1995).
Ernst & Young, *Response to the Cadbury Proposals, A critique of the Draft Report* (London, 1992).
Estrin & Perotin, "Does ownership always matter?", 9 Int'l J. Indus. Org. 55 (1991).
Fanto, *Corporate Governance in American and French Law* (1997).
Fanto, "The Absence of Cross-Cultural Communication: SEC Mandatory Disclosure and Foreign Corporate Governance", 17 NW. J. Int'l L. & Bus. 119 (1996).
Fanto, *The Role of Corporate Law in the Adaptation of French Enterprises* (unpublished manuscript, 1997, prepared for the Columbia Law School Sloan Project on Corporate Governance, Cross-Border Views of Corporate Governance, March 17-18, 1997).
Fanto, "The Transformation of French Corporate Governance and United States Institutional Investors", 21 Brook. J. Int'l L. 1 (1995).
Farrar's, *Company Law*, Third Ed..
Feddersen, Hommekhoff & Schneider (eds.), *Corporate Governance – Optimierung der Unternehmensführung und der Unternehmenskontrolle im deutschen und amerikanischen Aktienrecht* (1996).
Feinberg, *Harmless Wrongdoing* (1988).
Finch, "Board Performance and Cadbury on Corporate Governance", in JBC 1992, 581.
Fisch, "Class Action Reform: Lessons from Securities Litigation", 39 Ariz.L.Rev. 533 (1997).
Fisch, "Relationship Investing: Will It Happen? Will It Work?", 55 Ohio St. L. J. 1009 (1994).
Fischel, "The 'Race to the Bottom' Revisited: Reflections on Recent Developments in Delaware's Corporation Law", 76 Nw. U. L. Rev. 913 (1982).
Fleischer, Harzard & Klipper, *Board Games: The Changing Shape of Corporate Power* (Boston, 1988).
Forstmoser, *Organisation und Organisationsreglement nach neuem Aktienrecht*, Schriften zum neuen Aktienrecht Nr. 2 (Zürich, 1992).
Friedman, *Capitalism and Freedom* (1962).
Fukao, *Financial Integration, Corporate Governance, and the Performance of Multinational Companies* (Brookings Institute, 1995).
Nord, " 'Corporate governance' på svenska", in *Juridisk Tidskrift* 1989-90.

Germain, "Les sociétés qui font appel public à l'épargne", in *La Modernisation du Droit des Sociétés: Premières réflexions sur le Rapport Marini* (Jean-Jacques Daigre, éd.), (1996).

Gibirila, *Le Dirigeant de Société: Statut Juridique, Social et Fiscal* (1995).

Gilson & Kraakman, "Reinventing the Outside Director: An Agenda for Institutional Shareholders", 43 Stan. L. Rev. 863 (1991).

Gilson & Kraakman, "The Mechanisms of Market Efficiency", 70 Va. L. Rev. 549 (1984).

Gilson & Roe, "Understanding the Japanese Keiretsu: Overlaps Between Corporate Governance and Industrial Organization", 102 *Yale Law Journal* 871 (1993).

Gilson, "A Structural Approach to Corporations: The Case Against Defensive Tactics in Tender Offers", 33 Stan. L. Rev. 819 (1981).

Gilson, "Corporate Governance and Economic Efficiency", in Isaksson & Skog (eds.), *Aspects of Corporate Governance* (Juristförlaget, 1994).

Gilson, "Corporate Governance and Economic Efficiency: When do Institutions Matter?", 74 Wash. U. L. Q. 327 (1996).

Gilson, "Evaluating Dual Class Common Stock: The Relevance of Substitutes", 73 Va. L. Rev. 807 (1987).

Glaus, *Corporate Audit Committee*, in: Festschrift André Zünd (Zürich, 1988).

Goetzmann & Jorion, *A Century of Global Stock Markets* (unpublished paper, Dec. 1996 draft).

Goldman, "The Modernisation of the French Securities Markets: Making the EEC Connection", 60 Fordham L. Rev. S227 (1992).

Goldstein, "Privatizations and Corporate Governance in France", in BNL Q. Rev. 455 (No. 199, Dec. 1996).

Gordon & Kornhauser, "Efficient Markets, Costly Information, and Securities Research", 60 N. Y. U. L. Rev. 761 (1985).

Gordon, "Ties that Bind: Dual Class Common Stock and the Problem of Shareholder Choie", 76 Calif. L. Rev. 3 (1988).

Grienenberger, *Institutional Investors and Corporate Governance*, 970 PLI/Corp 371 (1997).

Großkommentar zum Aktiengesetz (various authors) (4th ed., 1992).

Hagstromer, *Om aktiebolag enligt svensk rätt diss.* (Upsala 1872).

Hart, *Law Liberty and Morality* (1963).

Hemstrom, *Corporations and Partnerships, Sweden*, in *International Encyclopaedia of Law*, Suppl. 12 (The Hague, London and Boston, 1995).

Hoffmann-Becking, *Rechtliche Möglichkeiten und Grenzen einer Verbesserung der Arbeit des Aufsichtsrates*, in: *Festschrift für Hans Havermann* (Düsseldorf, 1996), 230.

Hopt & Teubner (Publ.), *Corporate Governance and Directors' Liabilities* (Berlin/New York, 1985).

Houston & Lewis, *The Independent Director: Handbook and Guide to Corporate Governance* (Oxford, 1992).

Hurstel & Bieder, "Est-il urgent et indispensable de réformer le droit des sociétés au nom de la 'corporate governance'?", in Rev. Soc. 633 (oct.-déc. 1995).

Institute of Directors (Publ.), *Guidelines for Directors* (London, 1991).

Isaksson & Skog, *Corporate Governance in Swedish Listed Companies, Institutional Investors and Corporate Governance* (editors: Baums, Buxbaum & Hopt) (Berlin and New York, 1994).

Jansson, *Regelbildning på värdepappersmarknaden* (Stockholm, 1995).
Jeantin, *Droit des Sociétés* (2ème éd.), 1992.
Jennings, et al., *Securities Regulation: Cases and Materials* (1992).
Jensen & Meckling, "Theory of the Firm: Managerial Behavior, Agency Costs and Ownership Structure", 3 J. Fin. Econ. 305 (1976).
Jensen, "Eclipse of the Public Corporation", 67 Harv. Bus. Rev. 61 (1989).
Jensen, "The Agency of Free Cash Flow, Corporate Finance and Takeovers", 76 Am. Econ. Rev. 323 (1986).
Jensen, "The Modern Industrial Revolution, Exit, and the Failure of Internal Control Systems", 68 J. Fin. 830 (1993).
Jensen, *The Takeover Controversy: Analysis and Evidence*, reprinted in Chew, Jr., Ed., *The New Corporate Finance: Where Theory Meets Practice* (1993).
Johansson & Pehrson, *Styrelsejäv*, in *Juridisk Tidskrift* (1992-93).
Johansson, *Bolagsstämma*, diss. (Stockholm, 1990).
Johansson, *Minoritetsrätt på bolagsstämma* (Stockholm, 1990).
Johansson, *The Allocation of Power Between the Management and the General Meeting of Shareholders*, Scandinavian Studies in Law (1992).
Kanda, "Politics, Formalism, and the Elusive Goal of Investor Protection: Regulation of Structured Investment Funds in Japan", 12 *University of Pennsylvania Journal of International Business Law* 569 (1991).
Kaplan & Minton, "Appointments of Outsiders to Japanese Boards: Determinants and Implications for Managers", 36 *Journal of Financial Economics* 225 (1994).
Kaplan, "Top Executive Rewards and Firm Performance: A Comparison of Japan and the U.S.", in *Journal of Political Economy* 102 (1994).
Karlgren, *Studier över privaträttens juridiska personer* (Gothenburg, 1929).
Karmel, "Implications of the Stakeholder Model", 61 Geo. Wash.L.Rev. 1156 (1993).
Kay & Silbertson, *Corporate Governance*, in *National Institute Economic Review* (August 1995).
Kedner & Roos, *Aktiebolagslagen* part I, 5th ed. in co-operation with R. Skog (Stockholm, 1995).
Keller, "Regulation of Large Enterprise: The United States Experience in Comparative Perspective", in *Managerial Hierarchies: Comparative Perspectives on the Rise of the Modern Industrial Enterprise* 161 (Chandler & Daems, eds. 1980).
Kerninon, *Les Cadres Juridiques de l'Économie Mixte* (1992).
Klein & Coffee, Jr., *Business Organization and Finance: Legal and Economic Principles* (1996).
Kojima, *Corporate Governance: An International Comparison* (A Discussion Paper, May 1995).
Kölner Kommentar zum Aktiengesetz (various authors) (4th vol., 1985).
Kristiansson, *Aktiemarknadsnämndens praxis under tio år* (Stockholm, 1996).
Kubler, *Gesellschaftsrecht* (4th ed., 1994).
Kunz, "Die Auskunfts- und Einsichtsrechte des Verwaltungsratsmitglieds", in *Aktuelle Juristische Praxis* 3 (1994) 572.
Kusano, "Corporate Law of Japan", in Hiag Ochigian (ed.), *The Law of Commerce in Japan*, 1993.
Langevoort, "Theories, Assumptions, and Securities Regulation: Market Efficiency Revisited", 140 U. Pa. L. Rev. 851 (1992).

Le Cannu, "Légitimité du pouvoir et efficacité du contrôle dans les sociétés par actions", in *Bulletin Joly* 637 (juillet 1995).

Leader, "Private Property and Corporate Governance", in *Perspectives on Company Law* (ed. Patfield), 1995.

Levy-Leboyer, "The Large Corporation in Modern France", in *Managerial Hierarchies: Comparative Perspectives on the rise of the Modern Industrial Enterprise* 117 (Chandler Jr., & Daems, eds.) (1980).

Liden, *Makten över företaget* (Stockholm, 1973).

Lin, "The Effectiveness of Outside Directors as a Corporate Governance Mechanism: Theories and Evidence", 90 NW. U. L. Rev. 898 (1996).

Lindskog, *Aktiebolagslagen* (2nd ed., Stockholm, 1995).

Lipton & Rosenblum, "A New System of Corporate Governance: The Quinquennial Election of Directors", 58 U.Chi.L.Rev. 187.

Lipton & Rosenblum, "A New System of Corporate Governance", 58 U. Chi. L. Rev. 187 (1991).

Lipton, "Takeover Bids in the Target's Boardroom", 35 Bus. Law. 101 (1979).

Lorie, Dodd and Kempton, *The Stock Market: Theories and Evidence* (2d ed., 1985).

Lorsch & Mciver, *Pawns and Potentates: The Reality of America's Corporate Boards* (1989).

Lowenstein, "Financial Transparent and Corporate Governance: You Manage What You Measure", 96 Colum. L. Rev. 1335 (1996).

Lowenstein, "Pruning Deadwood in Hostile Takeovers: A Proposal for Legislation", 83 Colum. L. Rev. 249 (1983).

Lutter, "Das neue 'Gesetz für kleine Aktiengesellschaften und zur Deregulierung des Aktienrechts', in *Die Aktiengesellschaft*, 1994, 429.

Macey & Miller, "Corporate Governance and Commercial Banking: A Comparative Examination of Germany, Japan, and the United States", 48 Stan. L. Rev. 73 (1996).

Macey & Miller, "The Plaintiff's Attorneys' Role in Class Actions and Derivative Litigation: Economic Analysis and Recommendations for Reform", 58 U.Chi.L.Rev. 1 (1991).

MacKenzie, *The Shareholder Action Handbook, Using Shares to Make Companies more Accountable* (Newcastle-upon-Tyne, 1993).

Maeijer, *Vertegenwoordiging en Rechtspersoon, De Naamloze en de Besloten Vennootschap* (1994).

Matter & Ball, *Handbook for Corporate Directors* (New York, 1985).

Mayson, et al, *Company Law* (London, 1996).

Merle, "Les contrôles internes", in *La Modernisation du Droit des Sociétés: Premières réflexions sur le Rapport Marini* (Jean-Jacques Daigre, éd.), 1996.

Milhaupt, "Managing the Market: The Ministry of Finance and Securities Regulation in Japan", 30 *Stanford Journal of International Law* 423 (1994).

Mill, *On Liberty.*

Millstein, "The Professional Board", 50 Bus. Law. 1427 (1995).

Mitchell, "A Theoretical and Practical Framework for enforcing Corporate Constituency Statutes", 70 Tex. L. Rev. 579 (1992).

Mohr, "De rol van de Ondernemingskamer in het kader van de problematiek rond beschermingsconstructies en betwiste overnames", in *25 jaar Ondernemingskamer* (1996).

Morin & Dupuy, *Le Coeur Financier Européen* (1993).

Morin, *Le règle capitaliste entre laxisme et détournement*, in *Rapport Moral sur l'Argent dans le Monde*, 207 (1996).
Morin, "Privatisation et dévolution des pouvoirs: Le modèle français du gouvernement d'entreprise", in Rév. Écon. 1253, (No. 6, novembre 1996).
Muller & Lipp, *Der Verwaltungsrat, Ein Handbuch für die Praxis* (Zürich, 1994).
Nader et al., *Constitutionalizing the Corporation: The Case for the Federal Chartering of Giant Corporations* (1976).
Nial & Johansson, *Bolag, föreningar och stoftelser, Norstedts Juridiska Handbok* (15th ed., Stockholm, 1994).
Nial & Johansson, *Svensk associationsrätt i huvuddrag* (6th ed., Stockholm, 1995).
Nobel, Corporate Governance – Möglichkeiten und Schranken gesellschaftsrechtlicher Gestaltung, in Der Schweizer Treuhänder, 1995, 1057.
North, "Economic Performance Through Time", 84 Am. Econ. Rev. 359 (1994).
Nuzzo – Casadei – Ruggiero, *Testo unico delle disposizioni in materia di intermediazione finanziaria. Osservazioni e commenti in relazione al progetto di disciplina delle società quotate* (CERADI-LUISS research paper, 1997).
Obst & Hintner, *Geld-, Bank- und Börsenwesen* (38th ed., 1988).
Okazaki, *The Japanese Firm under the Wartime Planned Economy*, in Aoki & Dore (eds.), *The Japanese Firm* (1994).
Oudemans, *Dutch Defences in Legal Danger*, in *Issues of European Integration* (1991).
Pagano, et al., *Why Do Companies Go Public? An Empirical Analysis* (Centre for Economic Policy Research Discussion Paper No. 1332, 1996).
Palisi & Ricci, *L'obbligo di offerta pubblica di acquisto in borsa* (Roma, 1993).
Parkinson, *Corporate Power and Responsibility* (1995).
Pastre, "Le gouvernement d'entreprise: questions de méthodes et enjeux théoriques", 31 R. Écon. Fin. 15 (1994).
Pastre, *Les dix commandments du gouvernement d'entreprise*, in *Rapport Moral sur L'Argent dans le Monde*, 201 (1996).
Pastre, *Les Nouveaux Piliers de la Finance* (1992).
Patfield (ed), *Perspectives on Company Law* (London, 1995).
Pezard, *À propos du Rapport Viénot sur le gouvernement d'entreprise*, in *Rapport Moral sur L'Argent dans le Monde*, 197 (1996).
Pezard, "The Golden Share of Privatized Companies", 21 Brook. J. Int'l L. 85 (1995).
Pinto, "Corporate Takeovers Through the Public Markets in the United States", 42 Am.J.Comp.L. 339 (1994).
Pinto, "Takeovers of Public Corporations in the United States", 34 Am.J.Comp.L. 271 (1988).
Pinto, "The Constitution and the Market for Corporate Control: State Takeover Statutes After CTS Corp.", 29 Wm. & Mary L. Rev. 699 (1988).
Planck, "Kleine AG als Rechtsform – Alternative zur GmbH", in: *GmbH Rundschau* 1994, 501.
Pound, "The Rise of the Political Model of Corporate Governance and Corporate Control", 68 N.Y.U. L. Rev. 1003 (1993).
Price Waterhouse (Publ.), *Improving Audit Committee Performance: What Works Best*, Altamonte Springs (Florida, 1993).
Raiser, *Recht der Kapitalgesellschaften* (2d ed., 1994).
Rajan & Zingales, "What Do We Know about Capital Structure? Some Evidence from International Data", 50 J. Fin. 1421 (1995).

Ramseyer, "Columbian Cartel Launches Bid for Japanese Firms", 102 Yale L. J. 2005 (1993).
Ramseyer, *Explicit Reasons for Implicit Contracts: The Legal Logic to the Japanese Main Bank System*, in Aoki & Patrick (eds.), *The Japanese Main Bank System*, 1994.
Ramseyer, "Takeovers in Japan: Opportunism, Ideology and Corporate Control", 35 *UCLA Law Review* 1 (1987).
Ricci, *L'obbligo di offerta pubblica di acquisto tra tutela degli azionisti e tutela del mercato* (Roma, 1996).
Robert, "The Internationalization of the Markets and the Experience of the French COB with Mergers and Acquisitions", in *European Takeovers: law and practice* (Hopt & Wymeersch, eds.), 1992.
Rock, "America's Shifting Fascination with Comparative Corporate Governance", 74 Wash. U.L. Q. 367 (1996).
Rock, "Controlling the Dark Side of Relational Investing", 15 Cardozo L. Rev. 987 (1994).
Roe, "Chaos and Evolution in Law and Economics", 109 Harv. L. Rev. 641 (1996).
Roe, "Some Differences in Corporate Structure in Germany, Japan, and the United States", 102 *Yale Law Journal* 1927 (1993).
Roe, *Strong Managers, Weak Owners: The Political Roots of American Corporate Finance* (1994).
Romano, "Corporate Law and Corporate Governance", 5 Indus. & Corp. Change 277 (1996).
Romano, "Law as a Product: Some Pieces of the Incorporation Puzzle", 1 J. of Law, Eco, & Org. 225 (1985).
Roos, *Avtal och rösträtt diss.* (Uppsala, 1969).
Roos, "Comparative Notes on Shareholders' Voting Agreements", in *Scandinavian Studies in Law*, 1971.
Russell Reynolds Associates, *Redefining Corporate Governance*, 1995 U.S. Survey of Institutional Investors (1995).
Rydqvist, *The Pricing of Shares with Different Voting Power and the Theory of Oceanic Games diss.* (Stockholm, 1986).
Saari, "The Efficient Capital Market Hypothesis, Economic Theory and the Regulation of the Securities Industry", 29 Stan. L. Rev. 1031 (1977).
Sarfatti Larson, *The Rise of Professionalism: A Sociologic Analysis*, 1977.
Schmitz, *Gesellschaftsrecht* (2d ed., 1991).
Schmitz, *How can the Supervisory Board's Monitory Function be made more efficient?* Conference of the Dräger Foundation: Corporate Governance, Heidelberg, 1995 (not in print).
Schoen, *The French Stock Exchange: A Practical Guide for Investors and Advisors* (1995).
Schwark, *Börsengesetz* (2d ed., 1994).
Seligman, "Accounting and the New Corporate Law", 50 Wash.&Lee L.Rev. 943 (1993).
Seligman, *Corporations Cases and Materials* (1995).
Seligman, "The New Corporate Law", 59 Brook.L.Rev. 1 (1993).
Seligman, "The Private Securities Litigation Reform Act of 1995", 38 Ariz.L.Rev. 717 (1996).
Sheard, "The Main Bank System and Corporate Monitoring and Control in Japan", 11 *Journal of Economic Behavior and Organization* 399 (1989).

Shleifer & Vishny, *A Survey of Corporate Governance* (National Bureau of Economic Research Working Paper No. 5554) (1996).

Sjogren, *Ansvarsfrihet för styrelsen i aktiebolag* (Stockholm, 1993).

Skog, "Adapting the Swedish Companies Act to the requirements of the European Union", 8 *International Company and Commercial Law Review* 286 (1994).

Skog, *Does Sweden Need a Mandatory Bid Rule? A Critical Analysis* (Stockholm, 1995).

Sprungli, *Die neue Rolle des Verwaltungsrates*, Diss. (St. Gallen, 1990).

Svensson, *Juridisk Handbok. Bolagsrätt I* (Stockholm, 1993).

Teubner, *Corporate Fiduciary Duties and their Beneficiaries: A Functional Approach to the Legal Institutionalization of Corporate Responsibility*, in: Hopt & Teubner (eds.), *Corporate Governance and Directors Liabilities* (1985).

Thiel & Konig, *Die Ausgestaltung des Rechnungswesens, der Finanzkontrolle und der Finanzplanung als unübertragbare Aufgabe des Verwaltungsrates,* in: *Jahrbuch zum Finanz- und Rechnungswesen*, (Hans Siegwart, ed.) (Zürich, 1994).

Thiveaud, "De la gouvernance des grandes sociétés: un incessant différand dans l'espace et le temps", 31 R. Écon. Fin. 243 (1994).

Tobin, "The Squeeze on Directors — Inside is out", 49 Bus.Law. 1707 (1994).

Trigo Trindade, *Le conseil d'administration de la société anonyme*, Bâle et Francfort-sur-le-Main (1996).

Tunc, *Les Prises de contrôle par l'intermédiare du marché*, in *Corporate Takeovers Through the Public Markets* (P.J. Kozyris, ed.) (1996).

Valuet, "Fonds de pension américains: incidences de leur politique d'actionnariat sur les sociétés françaises", in *Bourse et Produits Financiers* (janvier-février 1996).

Visentini, "Compatibility and competition between European and American corporate governance. Which model of capitalism?", in *Brooklyn Journal of International Law*, 1998, 1.

Visentinti, *L'evoluzione del sistema finanziario italiano. I problemi attuali* (Milano, 1995).

Visentini, *Osservazioni sulla recente disciplina delle società azionarie e del mercato mobiliare (spunti di riflessione sulla sensibilità democratica nella formulazione delle scelte politiche)*, in *Riv. soc.*, 1998, 172.

Wang, "Some Arguments that the Stock Market is Not Efficient", 19 U.C. Davis L. *Rev.* 341 (1986).

Wernli, *Kommentar zum schweizerischen Privatrecht*, Honsell, Vogt & Watter (Hrsg.), Basel/Frankfurt am Main 1994, Art. 715a.

West, "The Pricing of Shareholder Derivative Actions in Japan and the United States", 88 *Northwestern University Law Review* 1436 (1994).

Wiedemann, *Gesellschaftsrecht*, vol. I, 1980.

Williamson, *The Economic Institutions of Capitalism* (1985).

Winter, *Government and the Corporation* (1978).

Wunderer, *Der Verwaltungsrats-Präsident*, Diss. (oec.) (Zürich, 1995).

Wymeersch, *Problems of the Regulation of Takeover Bids in Western Europe: A Comparative Survey*, in *European Takeovers: Law and Practice* (Hopt & Wymeersch , eds.), 1992.

Wymeersch, *The Mandatory Bid: A Critical View*, in *European Takeovers: Law and Practice* (Hopt & Wymeersch, eds.), 1992.

Index